Jack the Ripper and the Case for Scotland Yard's Prime Suspect

Jack the Ripper and the Case for Scotland Yard's Prime Suspect

ROBERT HOUSE

WILEY

John Wiley & Sons, Inc.

Published by John Wiley & Sons, Inc., Hoboken, New Jersey
Published simultaneously in Canada

Photo credits begin on page 341 and constitute an extension of the copyright page.

For general information about our other products and services, please contact our Customer Care Department within the United States at (800) 762-2974, outside the United States at (317) 572-3993 or fax (317) 572-4002.

Wiley also publishes its books in a variety of electronic formats. Some content that appears in print may not be available in electronic books. For more information about Wiley products, visit our web site at www.wiley.com.

ISBN 978-1-63026-122-1

Printed in the United States of America

10 9 8 7 6 5 4 3 2 1

Contents

Photo gallery begins on page 169

PART THREE   AARON KOZMINSKI

Photo gallery begins on page 248

PART FOUR   A MODERN PERSPECTIVE

Foreword

by Roy Hazelwood

Jack the Ripper. The name itself speaks of serial murder, mutilation, and fear. Even though his identity remains shrouded in mystery, he is, without question, the most infamous serial killer in the history of the world. It has always been interesting to me that Jack's fame persists in spite of the fact that by today's violent crime standards, he would not rate more than a passing interest by the media. After all, there were only five or six or seven victims.

I first became intimately familiar with the case in 1988 when John Douglas and I were invited to prepare a profile of the unidentified serial killer known as Jack the Ripper. We were asked to present our findings on a television special, before a live audience, marking the one hundredth anniversary of the Ripper's crimes. This program was on a major network and was hosted by the noted actor Peter Ustinov. We were provided with police and autopsy reports, background information on each of five Ripper victims, maps depicting the crime locations, and articles and book chapters written about the killings.

We prepared the profile and traveled to Hollywood to rehearse for the show. We met with the other guests who were to appear on the program: a noted forensic pathologist, the curator of Scotland Yard's Black Museum, and a female jurist from London. John and I shocked our new colleagues when we quickly told them that it was our opinion that Jack the Ripper was a paranoid schizophrenic and that his criminal successes could be attributed more to luck than to skill and intelligence.

We were surprised to learn that the program's producers had identified five suspects from the 1888 case. Included in the group was a schoolteacher who had committed suicide, a surgeon for the royal family, a prince, and a mentally disturbed person named Aaron Kozminski. John and I studied what was known about the suspects, compared our profile to the group of suspects, and determined that Kozminski most closely matched our profile. We then informed our colleagues that if Kozminski wasn't the Ripper, then it was someone just like him.

Over the intervening years, I have been made aware of a number of other men who were forcefully put forth as the Ripper. I have not, however, been convinced that any of those men were as likely to be responsible for the murders as Kozminski was.

Over those same years, I have often longed for more information on Kozminski, and periodically I have attempted to delve into his background. Because of a lack of time and patience, however, I was largely unsuccessful. But finally, thanks to Robert House, I am able to satisfy my curiosity. Does Mr. House resolve the identity of Jack the Ripper? Probably not, but no one else has either, and besides, that isn't his purpose. He simply wants to provide his readers with the most complete history of a most likely suspect, and he has done a masterful job.

Aaron Kozminski was a Polish Jew who spent the first fifteen years of his life in Russia. Mr. House begins his book by providing us with an overview of Jewish life in nineteenth-century Russia. He then transitions the Kozminski family to the East End, or Whitechapel section, of London (where the murders eventually occurred) and situates them geographically, economically, and socially for us. In doing so, he sets the stage for the murders that follow.

Mr. House takes us into the corridors of Jack's murders through a number of different doors. He provides detailed information on each of the Ripper's victims, interspersing the murder accounts with informative and interesting material about the police investigation, other main suspects, and even the infamous letter allegedly written by Jack.

As I mentioned earlier, John Douglas and I felt that Jack the Ripper was a paranoid schizophrenic, and Mr. House documents Kozminski's mental deterioration. What will be new information for many readers (as it was for me) is Mr. House's description of witness and informant accounts that led to the identification of Kozminski as a viable suspect.

Mr. House then brings the reader into the modern era of the serial killer phenomenon. He discusses the FBI study conducted by John Douglas and Bob Ressler, both of whom served in the Behavioral Science Unit at the FBI Academy in Quantico, Virginia. Mr. House also describes the application of a relatively new law enforcement tool, geographic profiling, to the Ripper case. This process has been effectively used by investigators across the western world and is a most valuable tool in such crimes. The reader will find the procedure and its findings in this case to be illuminating and very interesting.

As an FBI agent, I was fortunate to have served in the Behavioral Science Unit with Bob and John and to have consulted on serial murder cases across the United States, Canada, and Europe. I have also conducted face-to-face interviews with killers, rapists, sexual sadists, and child molesters and their wives and girlfriends, and I can unequivocally state that no case has ever captured the attention of criminologists or the imagination of the public like Jack the Ripper—not the Atlanta Child Murders, Ted Bundy, the notorious Night Stalker of Los Angeles, or even the infamous Citizen X case involving the murders of more than one hundred children in Russia.

Jack the Ripper is unsolved and from all indications will remain so. Mr. House, however, has done for all who are fascinated by this case a great favor by writing an extremely well-researched book that sheds light on the individual who is, in my opinion, the most viable of all suspects in this, the most studied serial murder case in all of history. Jack the Ripper still stands apart from all other serial killers, and it is my belief that he will continue to do so far into the future.

Read, learn, and enjoy!

Robert R. "Roy" Hazelwood is a retired FBI agent with the Academy Group Inc. (AGI) and author of *The Evil That Men Do* and *Dark Dreams*.

Acknowledgments

Thanks to Chris Scott, R. J. Palmer, Robert Linford, Phillip Hutchinson, Debra Arif, John Bennett, Rob Clack, Neal and Jennifer Shelden, Neil Bell, Andrew Firth, Scott Nelson, Paul Begg, Stewart Evans, Keith Skinner, Jonathan Menges, Richard Jones, Dick Bonier, Lauren Post, Roy Hazelwood, D. Kim Rossmo, Colin Roberts, *Ripperologist* magazine, Eduardo Zinna, Chris George, Adam Wood, Martin Fido, the Polish National Archives at Poznan, the London Metropolitan Archives, Don Axcell and the Christian Police Association, Chris Hogger, David Wright, Andy Aliffe, Alan McCormick, Norma Buddle, Jeff Leahy, Howard Brown, Stephen Ryder, Katarzyna Grycza, Iana Ulianova, Anya Razumnaya, Peter Higginbotham, Tomek Wisniewski, Adam Weglowski, Chris Reynolds, Joy Azmitia, Tim Seldes, Stephen Power, and Ellen Wright.

Special thanks to John Malcolm for his feedback and encouragement and the many hours we spent discussing the case over beers at the Burren, and to Laura Malcolm, who graciously translated countless Polish documents for me. My deepest thanks also to the descendants of Woolf Abrahams, Isaac Abrahams, and Matilda and Morris Lubnowski Cohen, and Nevill Swanson and the descendants of Donald S. Swanson.

Finally, none of this would have been possible without the research and insights of Chris Phillips, a tireless investigator whose contributions as my partner in this endeavor I could not possibly overstate.

Note: Polish vital records from the nineteenth century used the dual dating format, showing both the Gregorian and the Julian calendar dates (for example, "It happened in the town of Kłodawa on 2nd, 14th May 1851"). For the sake of clarity, I will simplify these and show only the modern Gregorian date.

Introduction

> This is an obscure and fantastic case, a contemporary case,
> something that could only happen in our day, when the
> heart of man has grown troubled, when people quote sayings
> about blood "refreshing," when the whole of life is dedicated
> to comfort . . . there is resolution evident here, for the first
> step, but resolution of a special kind—a resolve like that of
> a man falling from a precipice or flinging himself off a tower;
> this is the work of a man carried along into crime, as it were,
> by some outside force.
>
> —*Fyodor Dostoyevsky*, Crime and Punishment, 1866

In the summer of 1888, a brutal killer emerged like a plague in the very epicenter of what was at the time one of the worst slums in the world. To the residents of London's crime-ridden East End, the monster seemed to be lurking in every alley, just beyond the edge of every shadow. By the end of the summer, three local prostitutes had been brutally murdered, and a frenzied panic had taken hold of the heart of the British Empire. To both the baffled police force and a morbidly fascinated public, it was clear that these were no ordinary

1

crimes. This was a new and largely misunderstood type of horror, like something out of a nightmare. It was the modern world's introduction to the phenomenon of the serial killer.

Then, in late September, the police received a taunting letter from someone claiming to be the killer; it was signed "Jack the Ripper." The murders quickly became an international sensation, and detailed accounts of the murders were reported in newspapers across the globe. As a bloody summer gave way to an even bloodier autumn, there were more murders, each more gruesome than the last. The victims were often disemboweled or mutilated beyond recognition. The police were at a dead end, completely defeated, and the Home Office began to worry that the murders might give rise to social upheaval among the lower classes. And then, after butchering five (or six) prostitutes in the span of only a few short months, the phantom suddenly vanished.

The Jack the Ripper crimes were never solved, and largely because of this the murderer attained an almost mythic notoriety. He was a real-life exemplar of the bogeyman; mothers would scare their children into avoiding mischief with the warning, "You better watch out, or Jack the Ripper will come and get you." The archetype of the preternatural supervillain, Jack the Ripper eventually earned his place alongside more traditional figures from the Western canon of monster mythology like Dracula and werewolves. In a sense, the crimes served as a harbinger of the twentieth century and of the rapid and unnerving changes being ushered in by both the industrial revolution and modernization in general. As author Paul Begg has noted, the Ripper was "the embodiment of the public's fears of the East-End slums—poverty, disease, upheaval . . . fear of what lurked in shadows."[1] The Ripper was then, and yet remains, a manifestation of our darkest fears and anxieties, still haunting the remote gaslit corners of the collective subconscious, invariably wearing a cape, a top hat, and a dark overcoat.

Jack the Ripper is now widely considered to be the most famous serial killer of all time, and the case ranks as one of the world's most notable unsolved mysteries. The allure of the case has proved irresistible to scholars (commonly referred to as Ripperologists) who, over the course of the last century, investigated every imaginable facet of the story. Yet despite a veritable mountain of documentation in the form of police files, inquest testimony, newspaper reports, and memoirs, there are still huge gaps in our knowledge. Many of the original police files were lost, stolen, or simply discarded, while the memories of those who actually investigated the murders gradually faded. What has survived is a complex jigsaw puzzle of fragments, vague statements, and documents that are often contradictory and difficult to interpret. The inevitable result for those who try to solve the case is frustration, and the general consensus now among most Ripperologists is that the killer's identity will remain a mystery forever.

Such is the basic gist of the Jack the Ripper story. Contrary to the general public knowledge, however, there was one man who repeatedly stated that the London police in fact knew the identity of Jack the Ripper. The killer was an insane Polish Jew, he claimed, "whose utterly unmentionable vices reduced him to a lower level than that of the brute." Intriguingly, the man who made this provocative statement was not a mere crank or an armchair theorist, but instead was none other than Sir Robert Anderson, the assistant commissioner of the London Metropolitan Police Force and the head of Scotland Yard's Criminal Investigation Department (CID) during the Ripper murders. In his 1910 autobiography, Anderson bluntly stated that the Ripper's identity was a "definitely ascertained fact," and that a witness had in fact identified the killer but then refused to testify to his identification in court. Anderson noted that he was "almost tempted" to disclose the name of Jack the Ripper, if "the publishers would accept all responsibility in view of a possible libel action."[2] Yet in the end, he never revealed the name of the suspect in question, and his cryptic statements on the matter were soon forgotten.

Then in 1959 a document emerged from the fray of research that seemed to back up Anderson's claim. The document in question was an internal London Metropolitan Police memorandum that had been written in 1894, in which the former assistant chief constable Melville Macnaghten listed three "strong suspects" in the case. One of these was "Kosminski," a man described as "a Polish Jew, & resident in Whitechapel." According to Macnaghten, Kosminski "had a great hatred of women, specially of the prostitute class, & had strong homicidal tendencies," and was "removed to a lunatic asylum about March 1889."[3] Unfortunately, despite the obvious similarities with Anderson's unnamed suspect, nobody seemed to make a connection between the two, and it was generally assumed that Anderson and Macnaghten were talking about two different people.

In 1987 there was another important discovery—this time simply a few handwritten notes that had been penciled into a copy of Anderson's autobiography by one of his subordinates at the Yard—a man named Donald Swanson. In the book, Swanson jotted down a few brief notes about Anderson's suspect, then turned to a blank page at the end of the volume and wrote an additional paragraph about some of the details of the inquiry. At the bottom of the page, Swanson added, "Kosminski was the suspect."[4]

The discovery of the "Swanson marginalia" was immediately recognized as an important break in the case, so to speak. To Ripper scholars, it was as if someone had suddenly turned on a light in a dark room. For not only did the marginalia put a name to the man Anderson insisted was Jack the Ripper, but this handwritten note also made it manifestly clear that Anderson's "Polish Jew" was the same suspect referred to as Kosminski in the Macnaghten memorandum. Yet the marginalia was even more compelling because of who Swanson was—for in 1888, Chief Inspector Donald Sutherland Swanson had been the man in overall charge of the Ripper case.

Around the time that the Swanson marginalia came to light, a Ripperologist named Martin Fido conducted a search of Victorian London asylum records in an effort to discover the full name of Kosminski, the suspect Macnaghten claimed was admitted to an asylum in March 1889. He found only one Kosminski who seemed to fit the bill—specifically, Aaron Kozminski, an immigrant Polish Jew who had been admitted to Colney Hatch Lunatic Asylum in February 1891, apparently suffering from schizophrenia. This discovery, published on the heels of the Swanson marginalia, led several newspapers in 1987 to announce that the case was apparently solved after all and that Jack the Ripper was a destitute and insane hairdresser named Aaron Kozminski.

Unfortunately, a number of well-known Ripper scholars (including Fido himself) dismissed Kozminski as a suspect almost immediately. For starters, they pointed out, almost nothing was known about Aaron Kozminski. In addition, several aspects of the Swanson marginalia and the Macnaghten memorandum were apparently inconsistent with

Kozminski's asylum record, a fact that led some researchers to wonder if Aaron was the right Kosminski. Yet an even more serious problem, ultimately, was that Aaron Kozminski simply did not seem to fit the profile of Jack the Ripper. The asylum record plainly stated that Kozminski was not dangerous to others and that he ate food out of the gutter. It just didn't seem to add up.

As a result, Ripper authorities declared that the case was not in fact closed. As the years went by and no new information emerged, Aaron Kozminski drifted back into the relative obscurity from whence he came, until eventually he came to be regarded as just another name on a long list of Ripper suspects. Somewhere along the line, Anderson's "definitely ascertained fact" about the Ripper's identity had gone by the wayside, and his statements had come to be regarded as little more than a curious and perplexing footnote in the case. Few Ripperologists now seem to consider the possibility that Anderson may have been right. Most assume that he was wrong and focus their efforts on trying to figure out why he made such an audacious claim in the first place. It has been routinely suggested, for example, that Anderson either lied outright or became clouded and confused in his memory of events.

Is this dismissal of Scotland Yard's top man justified? Or is it possible that Anderson was right, and that Jack the Ripper has been right under our noses for the last hundred years? To answer this question, we must take a long hard look at Anderson's suspect, the insane hairdresser Aaron Kozminski. Of course, it would have been much easier to research a member of the British Royal family or a well-known celebrity suspect such as the artist Walter Sickert, about whom there exists a vast amount of biographical documentation. Kozminski, by contrast, was a member of the lowest class of London's citizenry, living on the very fringes of society. Historically speaking, he remains an elusive figure, and the surviving documentation on him is sparse and riddled with apparent contradictions.

Although a more substantial account of Kozminski's background must have once existed in a police dossier, such a file no longer exists. In short, comparatively little is known about Kozminski, and I have been forced to make several assumptions or guesses about his life. To fill in the gaps, I will present Kozminski's life story in its historical context, against the backdrop of those Jews who fled persecution in Russia in the 1880s and immigrated to a depressed London slum already suffering from extreme poverty and high competition for jobs. I will talk about Kozminski's family and the tailoring trade in which they were employed. I will analyze several contemporary newspaper accounts and the memoirs of police detectives and others, which seem to implicate Kozminski in connection with the Whitechapel murders. Finally, I will use a modern theoretical approach to see whether Kozminski fits the generic profile of a serial killer as defined by the FBI and other sources.

To begin with, we must attempt to understand the fractured and oppressive cauldron from which Aaron Kozminski emerged—in other words, nineteenth-century Poland. And perhaps fittingly, at the time of Kozminski's birth in 1865, Poland did not even technically exist.

PART ONE

Coming to London

I

"Fear God and the King"

For at least two hundred years after Jews first settled in Poland in the eleventh century, the region was a sort of haven, comparatively speaking. The Polish aristocracy regarded the Jewish population as a valuable part of the country's economy and culture and actively protected the Jews from persecution by the Roman Catholic Church. But in the fourteenth century, the Jews were falsely blamed for causing the Black Death pandemic, and they fell victim to widespread persecution across Europe. Gradually, the tolerant atmosphere in Poland began to deteriorate. The political and economic instability of Poland only worsened matters, and by the eighteenth century, the Polish-Lithuanian Commonwealth was crumbling from within, plagued by corruption and an outmoded economy. The country was weak and vulnerable, and as a result, it became a pawn, subject to the manipulation of its powerful, vulturelike neighbors, Russia, Prussia, and Austria. In 1732, these countries signed a secret pact called Löwenwolde's Treaty (also known as the Alliance of the Three Black Eagles), the goal of which was to undermine the stability of Poland and influence the succession to the Polish throne. The treaty was essentially nullified a few years later, but the writing was on the wall—the "Black Eagles" (especially Russia) intended to keep Poland weak. Russia's ultimate goal in fact, was to liquidate Poland completely.

It took only about fifty years to dismantle Poland entirely. In 1764, the Russian empress Catherine II installed her former lover on the Polish throne. Three years later she forced a constitution on Poland, weakening the state further and increasing its dependency on Russia. Poland made a brief attempt to reassert its national autonomy in the War of the Confederation of Bar, when a group of Polish nobles assembled armies to expel Russian troops from its territory. Yet within a few short years Russia had squashed the uprising, and as punishment, Catherine took direct control of the Polish government through a council made up of her envoys and ambassadors. In 1772, she further applied the rod by enacting the first of three partitions of Poland, seizing a third of Poland's territory. A final partition twenty-three years later wiped Poland off the map completely—Russia absorbed a vast geographical area in the east; Prussia took the west, including Poland's foreign trading ports; and Austria took a smaller region in the southwest. As a result of the partitions, the majority of Poland's Jews fell into the hands of the Russian Empire.

In Russia, distrust and a lack of tolerance for Jews had existed since the Middle Ages, and there was a deep-rooted anti-Semitism among the aristocracy, based largely on the idea that Jews had been responsible for the execution of the Christian messiah. Moreover, ever since the French Revolution, Russia's czars and ruling aristocracy had been terrified that a populist uprising might take place, and the keepers of the old order perceived themselves to be under attack by a variety of radical "modern" theories, including democracy, nihilism, and socialism. Assuming that many of the rabble-rousers behind such theories were Jewish, the government increasingly resorted to treating the Jews as scapegoats for a wide variety of social and economic problems and encouraging anti-Semitic nationalism among the peasants, who likewise perceived the Jews to be interlopers, with a strange and exclusive culture. The peasants openly accused the Jews of exploitation, especially in the trade of alcohol, which they claimed was "sucking their vital juices." As historian Shlomo Lambroza noted, "The official view was that Jews were a parasitic element in the Russian Empire who lived off the hard earned wages of the narod [people]."[1]

Thus, when close to a million Polish Jews suddenly became absorbed into the Russian Empire, the government immediately recognized what it termed "the Jewish problem." In "defense" of her Christian subjects, Catherine created the Pale of Settlement, a vast geographical area in western Russia where the Jews were forced to live, and the shtetls in the region soon became dangerously overcrowded with what John Doyle Klier described as "a huge, pauperized mass of unskilled or semi-skilled Jewish laborers, whose economic condition steadily worsened." On the legal front, the Russian Empire addressed the Jewish problem by imposing severe restrictions on the Jews in the Pale of Settlement and Congress Poland. What followed was "a century-long program of social engineering" and repression.[2]

The reign of Czar Nicholas I from 1825 to 1855 was a particularly bleak era for Russia's Jews. Nicholas had nailed his colors to the mast in 1816, when he wrote in his diary, "The ruin of the peasants of these provinces are the Zhyds. . . . They are everything here: merchants, contractors, saloon-keepers, mill-owners, ferry-holders, artisans. They are regular leeches, and suck these unfortunate governments to the point of exhaustion."[3] Nicholas I was a ruthless autocrat and a Slavic nationalist, who believed in the idea of one people, one language, and one religion. During his twenty-nine years as emperor, Nicholas passed a number of laws designed to assimilate Jews into Russian culture and, if possible, convert them to Christianity.

Foremost among these laws was the dreaded Ustav Rekrutskoi Povinnosti (Statute on Conscription Duty) of 1827—essentially a draft law, by which Jewish youths and young men were forced to enlist in the Russian army for a period of twenty-five years. As noted by historian William Fishman, this was, practically speaking, a death sentence for those who received it, and "it was common for the ritual kaddish (prayer for the dead) to be pronounced on the young conscript." The recruits often fled into the woods or to neighboring towns to avoid the service, and those who were captured were shipped to far-off army bases in eastern parts of the empire. Many doggedly refused to eat the nonkosher meals that were forced on them, and they died on the long journey from exposure to cold, epidemics, exhaustion, and starvation. As Fishman noted, "The roads to Siberia were littered with the corpses of young Jews."[4] Those who survived the trek were subjected to beatings, forced baptism, and various methods of torture designed to encourage apostasy.

As the *Jewish Chronicle* put it, "The Russian army was a veritable Moloch for Jewish children."[5]

In 1835, Nicholas formally passed many of the government's already existing anti-Semitic policies into law. The Jews in the Pale were henceforth barred from agriculture and, as a result, turned to earning a living as petty traders, middlemen, shopkeepers, peddlers, and artisans. They were also forbidden to employ Christian domestic servants or to build synagogues near churches and were prohibited from traveling into the Russian interior, except on temporary furlough, and only then if they wore Russian dress. Furthermore, all official documents were to be written either in Russian or in the local dialect, but "under no circumstances the Hebrew language."[6] Even as early as 1840, however, the government began to realize that it had failed to "correct" the Jews. Nicholas tried various other assimilation techniques, but all of them came to the same result. In the Kingdom of Poland, in the far western part of the empire, it was argued that Jews were multiplying so rapidly that the entire region might soon become a "Jewish country" and "the laughing-stock of the whole of Europe."[7] The prescribed remedy was to treat the Jewish population as you would the "carriers of disease," and to segregate them in ghettos.

By the end of the 1850s, the general feeling in government was that Russia needed to evolve into a modern industrial nation on par with those in Western Europe. Russia had been bankrupted by its loss in the Crimean War, and its economy still depended almost entirely on agriculture and the backward system of fiefdoms, in which serfs were literally property attached to the estates of nobles. All of this changed abruptly in 1861, when the new czar Alexander II signed a law emancipating the serfs, a move that was mirrored by the spirit of abolitionism and the onset of the Civil War over slavery in the United States. The emancipation marked the beginning of a major tectonic shift in Russia's economy and social structure, which led to progressive reforms in all branches of government. As London's *Jewish Chronicle* noted, it was "a piece of philanthropy never equaled in the history of man, since no single man has ever had absolute command over such a number of men."[8] Millions of former serfs moved to the cities to find work in factories. It was to be a new Russia, one founded on Western principles of freedom and justice.

The "Czar Liberator" likewise enacted several progressive reforms related to the "Jewish question." Alexander lifted some of the oppressive restrictions on Jews in the Pale, and certain Jews (doctors, merchants, possessors of higher education, skilled artisans) were even allowed to settle outside the Pale. The improved conditions did not last long, though. In 1863–1864, the January Uprising in favor of Polish independence led to more than 150 battles across Congress Poland. Yet the revolt, which had considerable support from the Jewish community, was quickly suppressed, and in retaliation the Russian army mercilessly wreaked havoc on the conquered areas with such extreme violence that its actions were condemned across Europe.[9] Tens of thousands of Polish men and women were exiled to Siberia, and more than one hundred rebels were hanged for their "crimes" against Russia. Many of the Jews who had participated in the uprising escaped to London. The uprising forced the Russian government to reconsider the benefits of progressive reform and turn back to stricter ways.

By the 1870s, anti-Semitism was again on the rise. In 1871, tensions erupted when major anti-Jewish riots broke out during religious festivities in Odessa, and "for three days a horde of Greeks and Russians, undisturbed by police or troops, roamed the city burning, looting and beating up Jews."[10] According to Russian newspaper reports, the riots were caused by "religious antipathy" and Jewish exploitation of the Russian people. As the *Saint Petersburg News* put it, "Where the Jews have the mass of the population in their hands, they are able to build a many-sided instrument for their exploitation and the people there every minute feel themselves under an unbearable yoke, with which the serfdom of the past cannot even compare."[11] The riots resulted in two deaths and more than a thousand Jewish homes and businesses being damaged and/or looted.

Equally troubling was the reappearance of the "blood libel" myth, which is essentially a form of anti-Jewish propaganda that held that Jews murdered Christian children as part of their rituals. Variations of the myth started to crop up as early the fifth century. One notable example was the story of Simon of Trent, a two-year-old child who was said to have been murdered by Jews during Passover week in 1475 in Trent, Italy. According to legend, the child was kidnapped and then brutally slaughtered by several Jews. While one strangled the child with a handkerchief, the others cut flesh from the boy's neck and collected his blood in a bowl. The conspirators then cut pieces of flesh from the boy's arms and legs, punctured him with needles, and threw his body into the river. A number of Jewish men were arrested for the crime and ultimately confessed after "a series of interrogations that involved liberal use of judicial torture."[12] It is now impossible to know what really happened or who killed the boy, but the myth took on a life of its own and was used to spread anti-Semitic propaganda for centuries afterward.

Although Alexander I had outlawed the blood libel myth in Russia in 1817, the law was never fully enforced. Accusations reemerged during the reign of Nicholas I, who declared, "Among the Jews there probably exist fanatics who consider Christian blood necessary for their rites."[13] In 1878, when Aaron Kozminski was twelve or thirteen years old, references to the blood libel myth began to resurface in anti-Semitic Russian newspapers such as *Novoye Vremya*.

By the 1880s, high competition for jobs, exacerbated by crop failures in 1880 and 1881, had led to widespread famine and unemployment in the southwestern regions of Russia, and large numbers of peasants were roaming from town to town looking for work.[14] The government was becoming increasingly worried about rising unrest among the peasants, capitalism and industry loomed as threats to the traditional social structure, and many of the educated sons of the landed aristocracy turned to dangerous revolutionary theories such as socialism and nihilism that were being espoused by leftist intellectuals. As usual, the government blamed the Jews for the unrest in the land. In a memorandum to the czar, General Nicholas Ignatiev, later the minister of the interior and a member of the anti-Semitic Sacred League, wrote, "Every honest voice is silenced by the shouts of Jews and Poles who insist that one must listen only to the 'intelligent' class, and that Russian demands must be rejected as backward and unenlightened."[15]

This volatile mixture was about to explode—all that was needed was a spark.

2

1881: The Storm Breaks

I am glad in my heart when they beat the Jews, but it cannot
be permitted.

—*Czar Alexander III, 1881*

On March 1, 1881, Alexander II was assassinated by members
of the Narodnaya Volya (the People's Will), a revolutionary
group intent on overthrowing the Russian autocracy and
replacing it with a democratic-socialist republic. The attack took place
midafternoon on a Sunday, as the czar was returning to the Winter
Palace after reviewing a parade of Imperial Guards in an equestrian
training hall called the Manezh. Alexander was riding through the
snowy St. Petersburg streets in a closed carriage with six Cossack body-
guards, followed by two open sleighs carrying the chief of police and
the chief of guards with a number of additional policemen. When the
cavalcade reached a bridge over the Catherine Canal, a young revolutionary named Nikolai Rysakov stepped forward and threw a package
containing an explosive device under the carriage wheels. The bomb
caused a massive explosion that hurled the assassin across the street
into a fence. Several people were wounded in the blast, but the czar

was unscathed because his carriage was iron-plated and bulletproof to guard against just such an attack. Rysakov, in a rather weak attempt to divert attention from himself, shouted, "There he goes! Get him!" but the ruse failed, and he was captured almost immediately. The police tackled him and discovered a pistol and a knife hidden under his coat.

Ignoring the frantic protests of his guards, the czar emerged from his carriage to survey the damage. The chief of police asked the czar whether he was injured. "Thank God, I am fine. But look . . .," Alexander said, pointing at a boy who lay dying on the sidewalk. "Is it thanks to God?" interjected Rysakov. "A fine one," the czar muttered, looking the man up and down. At this point, another assassin, Ignacy Hryniewiecki, stepped forward and threw a second bomb at the czar. According to a witness, the blast was "so strong that all the glass was blown out of the gas lights and the post itself was bent." Some twenty people were wounded in the explosion, and blood, clothing, splinters, body parts, and other debris littered the street. Hryniewiecki himself died as a result of the blast, and the czar's legs were blown to pieces.

Some cadets, who had been returning from the parade ground when the attack took place, covered the czar in a cape and lifted him onto a sled. Meanwhile, a third assassin, who had been waiting in the crowd ready to throw another bomb in case the others failed, rushed forward inexplicably and, with the instinct of human feeling, helped the cadets aid their fallen ruler. A little more than an hour later, the "Czar Liberator" was dead.[1]

The government was completely caught off guard by the assassination. Members of the czar's cabinet seem to have worried that a popular socialist uprising was under way, and it was said that the murdered czar's son and successor, Alexander III, "became a prisoner of the royal palace at Gatchina, literally looking under the bed in his private apartments for assassins."[2] The secret police quickly arrested the conspirators, and on April 3 five of the plotters were hanged in a public square filled with spectators. The assassination marked the end of an era of progressive reform. The new czar, Alexander III, would prove to be a strict autocrat who favored nationalism, state censorship, and a powerful secret police force.

Jews in Russia and across Europe were shocked by the news of the czar's death. In London, where much of the Anglo-Jewish population was of Polish-Russian origin, Jews had considered Alexander II an improvement over his predecessor. In a sermon at the Bayswater Synagogue in northwest London, the rabbi Dr. Hermann Adler declared, "His brethren, in common with the rest of civilized mankind, were penetrated with a feeling of horror and indignation at the infamous crime perpetrated in St. Petersburg."[3] On the day of the czar's interment, a funeral service was held at a synagogue in Catherine Wheel Alley, Bishopsgate, in the City of London, where "every inch of space in the . . . little synagogue was occupied, and even the stairs were thronged by a congregation consisting, with only one or two exceptions, of Russians and Poles." The walls were hung with black curtains on which was stitched in gold thread: "A grievous mourning of the Jews for the death of the Emperor Alexander." Under this was an eagle wearing the Russian crown and the words "Fear God and the King."[4]

Almost immediately, London's Jewish press began to express apprehension over the potential consequences of the situation in Russia. On March 18, the *Jewish Chronicle* reported:

> It is, we fear, unfortunately to be dreaded that in the reaction which is sure to ensue on the murder of the Czar, the Jews will lose some of the privileges gained during the reign of Alexander II. Such fear is augmented when we remember how persistently the Russian officials contend that the Nihilist movement is supported by the Jews. God help them if but the faintest shadow of suspicion rests upon any Jews for complicity in the Regicide conspiracy. When we reflect that the fate of the majority of existing Jews is thus hanging in the balance, we cannot but follow the course of events in Russia with breathless anxiety. The assassination of the Czar of all the Russias may, we fear, be an event of disastrous importance to the condition of Russian Jews.[5]

It was an insightful prediction. In fact, one young Jewish woman, Gesya Gelfman, had been involved in the assassination plot, although her role was minimal. Gelfman, a free-love practitioner and a revolutionary, was described in press accounts as a "stupid and unimportant follower of the ringleaders."[6] The fact that the rest of the conspirators were gentiles went by the wayside, and within the week, at least two

Russian newspapers, *Vilenskii Vestnik* and *Novoye Vremya*, had openly speculated that Jews were behind the assassination.[7] Both papers later retracted these statements, but the damage was done. It didn't help matters that the assassination took place on the eve of the Jewish Feast of Esther, and as the *Daily Telegraph* pointed out, "The Jews were charged with having made merry in anticipation of what was going to happen." By Easter, it was rumored (falsely) that the new czar had "issued a decree instructing the people to beat and plunder the Jews for having murdered his father and for exploiting the people."[8]

Beginning around the end of April, reports of large anti-Jewish riots began to filter through to the West. The first incident of *pogromy* (the Russian word for "devastation") occurred in April in the southwestern city Elizavetgrad. The immediate cause of the pogrom was not clear, and early reports only said, "The rioting arose out of a dispute between some Christians and Jews."[9] But as the *Jewish Chronicle* noted, "Bigotry, envy, and excitement combine to make the mind of the Russian peasant peculiarly inflammable just now, after the remarkable tragedy recently enacted at St. Petersburg."[10] Christian peasants from surrounding villages flocked into Elizavetgrad, where "one hundred houses were pillaged, a quantity of furniture being thrown into the streets."[11] After the pogrom, the town looked "as if it has been devastated by the elements."[12] According to reports, at least one Jew was killed, and hundreds of people were injured.[13]

After the Elizavetgrad riots, a veritable wave of pogroms was unleashed in numerous locations in the southwestern regions of the Pale, and a correspondent traveling through the area wrote that Judenhetze (Jewish agitation) had "assumed proportions of which Western Europe is not yet aware."[14] An officer who traveled for a time with the correspondent said that he had "seen things that sickened him to think of," and it was said that "unheard-of cruelties" were perpetrated by the mob.[15] Women and young girls were raped, and one report even claimed, "In many Jewish homes infants had been thrown out of windows into the street."[16] In Kiev, a huge crowd stormed through the streets, smashing the doors and the windows of Jewish houses and businesses and throwing all of the Jews' property into the street. The mob wrecked the synagogue, and the Torah scrolls were "torn to shreds, trampled in the dirt, and destroyed with incredible passion." The riots then spread to a suburb called Demiovka, where the mob demolished all of the Jewish saloons and set fire to Jewish residences. Then, "under the cover of night indescribable horrors were perpetrated," according to author Simon Dubnow. "Numerous Jews were beaten to death or thrown into the flames, and many women were violated."[17]

Police and army troops were dispersed to quell the riots, but they were unable to stop the carnage. In fact, in many instances, the police were more or less complicit with the rioters and "allowed the sanguinary acts of the rioters to proceed without check." In Kiev, soldiers were said to have "fraternized with the mob," and often the soldiers and the police "accompanied [the mob] from place to place, forming, as it were, an honorary escort."[18] When the Jews in Kiev appealed to the police for protection, they were told, "You Jewish hogs only get what you deserve."[19] In Odessa, a Jewish man was killed by a party of Cossacks, while the officer in command "almost choked himself with laughter to the consternation of the affrighted people." The man was later buried privately.[20]

Ultimately, two hundred or more attacks were made on Jewish communities in at least eight Russian provinces in the southwestern region of the Pale, and outbreaks were also reported in Germany, Romania, and Egypt. One modern source estimates that there were "some forty Jews killed, many times that number wounded and hundreds of women raped."[21] Thousands of Jews were financially ruined and left homeless. Many decided to flee the affected regions, and emigrants who arrived at the Austrian border reported, "A general massacre of the Jews in South Russia is imminent."[22] Romania and Prussia took steps to prevent an influx of refugees from crossing their borders.

Although the Russian government did not (apparently) have a direct role in instigating the riots, anti-Semitism was rife at the top levels of government, and many officials may have sympathized with the rioters in sentiment, if not in deed. Despite this, the government lived in fear of any popular disturbances and was worried that the peasants' anger might shift from the Jews to the landowners and then broaden into a general socialist uprising. As a result, the government was all too happy to frame the story in the usual manner. When the minister of the interior Nicholas Ignatiev set up regional commissions to investigate the pogroms, he did not ask *whether* Jewish exploitation was the cause—this was assumed. Instead, he merely asked the commissions which specific examples of Jewish exploitation had caused the peasants' anger.[23] The Russian government, in other words, turned to its tried-and-true formula and blamed the Jews themselves for instigating the attacks. Ignatiev ultimately concluded that the peasants were angry because the Jews had taken over trade, manufacturing, and also large amounts of land. Moreover, the "uncharacteristic violence" of the Russian peasants who plundered and destroyed the Jews' possessions was justified, it was argued, because the peasants "were merely appropriating property that did not rightly belong to the Jews."[24] The official sentiment of the government was perhaps best expressed by Czar Alexander III himself, who said, "I am glad in my heart when they beat the Jews, but it cannot be permitted."[25] Konstantin Pobedonistev, the czar's chief adviser on Jewish affairs, supposedly proposed the following solution to the Jewish Question: "One third of the Jews would emigrate, one third would be assimilated, and one third would die out."[26]

The pogroms of 1881 were the primary catalyst for a wave of Jewish emigration from Russia that would continue for decades. A veritable flood of penniless and frightened Jewish refugees streamed across the borders in search of safety. According to William Fishman, some 225,000 Jewish families left the country between April 1881 and June 1882 alone.[27] The majority ended up in America, but many thousands went to London. Among the latter group was Aaron Kozminski, a fifteen-year-old boy who, according to the head of Scotland Yard, would grow up to become the most famous murderer of all time.

3

The Victorian East End

I have seen the Polynesian savage in his primitive condition,
before the missionary or the blackbirder or the beachcomber
got at him. With all his savagery he was not half so savage,
so unclean, so irreclaimable, as the tenant of a tenement in
an East London slum.

—*Thomas Huxley*

London in the 1880s was the world's largest city and the capital
of the most far-reaching empire on the planet.[1] Yet despite
England's generally thriving economy, there was a vast dispar-
ity of wealth between the rigidly defined classes. The upper classes
lived in West London, where they enjoyed plays, fine dining, strolls in
Hyde Park, and the numerous fruits of a prosperous capitalist society.
The lower classes, by contrast, scratched out a tenuous existence in
the vast and violent East End, an area described by Arthur Morrison
as "an evil plexus of slums that hide human creeping things."[2] The
East End was plagued by disease, poor sanitation, poverty, excessive
drinking, and crime, and novelists and social commentators typically
wrote of the area in what can only be described as apocalyptic terms.

For example, in *The Anarchists*, the novelist J. H. Mackay likened the East End to a monster. "Like the enormous black, motionless, giant Kraken, the poverty of London lies there in lurking silence," he wrote, "and encircles with its mighty tentacles the life and wealth of the City and of the West End."[3] If London was the beating heart of the empire, then the East End was a festering sore, like a cancer, lurking menacingly at its core.

As recently as the early eighteenth century, the East End was a largely undeveloped area, with fields surrounding the area of Commercial Road. The region had historically been outside the old walls of the City of London and was a place for industries whose manufacturing processes were considered too noxious and/or dangerous to be performed within the city proper, such as leather tanning and gunpowder production. By the nineteenth century, however, the East End had developed into the overcrowded slum of dark alleys and criminality for which it gained a peculiar notoriety.

At the very stinking center of the area was Whitechapel, a district named after a small white parish church called St. Mary Matfelon. By the late nineteenth century, Whitechapel was the epicenter of crime in London, known for its brawling public houses (pubs), prostitution, robbery, and violence. At night it was dark, the back streets lit by a few sparsely located gas lamps, many of which were only partly working or not working at all. To outsiders, Whitechapel was a forbidding place, considered the breeding ground for countless varieties of immoral behavior. As the Reverend Samuel Barnett said, "Dark passages lend themselves to evil deeds."[4] Indeed, the whole East End was a veritable maze of alleys, courtyards, tunnels, and streets, and at night danger seemed to lurk everywhere. In one instance, when a Texas policeman visited Inspector Henry Moore in Whitechapel, presuming to give the experienced London detective advice on how to catch Jack the Ripper, Moore took his guest to one of the murder sites, a warren called Castle Alley. Once there, the Texan exclaimed, "I apologize. I never saw anything like it before. We've nothing like it in all America." Inspector Moore knew the area well and claimed that Whitechapel was called the "three F's district, fried fish and fights."[5] He was known to carry a cane painted to look like maple—it was actually made of iron.

By 1888, the year of the Ripper murders, Great Britain had been in a state of economic depression for more than a decade, and falling food prices had caused thousands of poor rural farm workers to move to the cities in search of jobs. Poverty and unemployment hit hardest in the East End. In 1887–1889 in Whitechapel, Spitalfields, Mile End, and the Docklands, more than 150,000 residents, or 35 percent of the population, scraped out a meager existence "on or below the level of subsistence."[6] The legions of unemployed fought a daily battle to survive, and thanks to a weak labor market, those who had work did not fare much better. Many of the East End's inhabitants toiled away in low-paying jobs at match mills, chemical plants, distilleries, gasworks, and breweries, while others worked as tailors, carmen, factory workers, or bootmakers. Thousands of others were casual dock laborers, who would show up at the docks every morning to stand in a crowd of desperate job seekers, each hoping to get chosen for a day's work. Others worked in one of the area's many slaughterhouses. Such work lent an air of savagery to the district, as a letter by Reverend Samuel Barnett to the *Times* illustrated. "At present animals are daily slaughtered in the midst of Whitechapel," he wrote, "the butchers with their blood stains are familiar among the street passengers, and sights are common which tend to brutalize ignorant natures."[7] Although working conditions across the board were generally abominable, industrial capitalists profited from the situation by exploiting the cheap labor and intense competition for jobs. Labor-organizing and unionist tendencies were suppressed, until by the 1880s, there was a general distrust of capitalism by the East End's working classes.[8]

On the other side of the great divide, the propertied classes of London's West End (much like their counterparts in Russia) were becoming increasingly worried about the perceived threat of social revolution. Such fears seemed about to become a reality in February 1886, when a protest meeting in Trafalgar Square by a group called the Social Democratic Federation (SDF) got out of hand, and rumors spread that East End socialists and the unemployed were descending on Westminster to wreak vengeance on the upper classes. This caused a brief terror in the West End, but the rumors turned out to be exaggerated. Another protest by the SDF and large numbers of unemployed Irish in November 1887 degenerated into a riot, which was so violently

suppressed by Foot Guards and Life Guards that it became known as
Bloody Sunday.[9] Class tension was an ever-present facet of London
life in this period, and more clashes between the police and "vagrants"
were to follow.

Unmarried women were also in the labor market, working to
supplement the income of families that were supported tenuously by
underemployed and poorly paid men who worked as casual laborers.
Some women had jobs that were characterized by seasonal or intermit-
tent employment, in which they toiled away in dreary shops for long
hours to earn "starvation wages" under the supervision of a middleman,
or "sweater." The novelist Margaret Harkness described the girls who
applied for such factory work as follows:

> A more miserable set of girls it would be difficult to find
> anywhere. They had only just escaped the Board School, but
> many of them had faces wise with wickedness, and eyes out
> of which all traces of maidenhood had vanished. . . . "[T]he
> universal adjective" fell from their lips as a term of endear-
> ment, whilst the foulest names were given to girls they did
> not like, also blows and kicks by way of emphasis.[10]

In July 1888, a strike by young women working at the Bryant and
May's match factory in Bow drew the public's attention to the wretched
conditions for female workers in the East End. The women were appall-
ingly underpaid, and their plight received the support of various local
unions. After two weeks, the factory's management gave in and agreed
to higher wages and some improvement in working conditions. Yet
despite such "bright spots," there was a vast labor surplus compared
to the available number of women's jobs, and hundreds of applicants
often competed for the same job. As writer Helen Ware suggested, an
unemployed woman on her own had to choose between "starvation,
the workhouse, or the streets"—in other words, prostitution.[11]

Prostitution was one trade, at least, that was booming in the East
End. An 1868 survey revealed that there were 623 prostitutes of a "low"
class "infesting" the neighborhoods of H Division (Whitechapel).
Whitechapel alone had 128 brothels and an additional 11 described
as "coffee houses or other places where business is ostensibly carried on, but which are known to the Police as Brothels or places of

accommodation for prostitutes." K Division (Stepney, including Mile End) was even worse—it had some 932 prostitutes in total and a staggering 350 brothels.[12] By 1881, London police were sending nearly 6,000 women to trial for the crime each year, and in 1887, the Lancet medical journal estimated, incredibly, that there were more than 80,000 prostitutes in London, 3 percent of the total population of 2,360,000.[13]

The "low prostitutes" of the East End (commonly referred to as unfortunates) survived on the very fringes of society, spending their sad and drunken lives in doss houses and on the streets. They solicited their clients in pubs or on the streets and typically serviced them outdoors, standing against a wall in some dark alley or courtyard. Most were alcoholics living a hand-to-mouth existence, turning tricks so they could afford to buy food and gin and pay for a bed to sleep in. Many women worked as only occasional prostitutes, whenever desperation drove them to it. As Charles Booth noted, "There are in each class some who take to the life occasionally when circumstances compel: tailoresses or dressmakers, for example, who return to their trade in busy times; girls from low neighborhoods who eke out a living in this way; or poor women, neglected wives, or widows, under pressure of poverty."[14]

As late as the 1880s, many reformers still ignored the obvious connection between poverty and prostitution and instead believed that prostitution was a result of moral weakness, which was generally associated with the perceived immorality of the lower classes. The East End was seen as a breeding ground for incest, prostitution, and other forms of degenerate sexual behavior, and it was thought that overcrowded living conditions, in which entire families often lived in a single room and family members often slept in the same bed, "made the cultivation of chastity impracticable."[15] Social institutions were established to combat the scourge of prostitution and to encourage "civilized domestic values" in the East End by rewarding the so-called deserving poor. But civilized domestic values were, broadly speaking, too expensive for the district. Marriage and respectability were often out of the question, as a fireman in Jack London's People of the Abyss explained:

> I'll tell you wot I'd get on four poun' ten—a missus rowin',
> kids squallin', no coal t' make the kettle sing, an' the kettle
> up the spout, that's wot I'd get. Enough t' make a bloke

bloomin' well glad to be back t' sea. A missus! Wot for? T'
make you mis'rable? Kids? Jest take my counsel, matey, an'
don't 'ave 'em. Look at me! I can 'ave my beer w'en I like,
an' no blessed missus an' kids a-cryin' for bread.[16]

Prostitution existed in the Jewish community as well. In Russia's
Pale of Settlement, Jewish prostitution in the cities had been a problem
since at least the 1870s. In Warsaw by 1872, 17 percent of registered
prostitutes were Jewish, and in Vilna in 1873, a full 50 percent of prostitutes were Jewish.[17] By 1889, a survey would find that Jews ran 203 of
the 289 registered brothels in the Pale of Settlement.[18] To an extent,
the practice carried over to London's East End, and by the mid-1880s,
as the social researcher Beatrice Potter noted in her diary, "Prostitution
among Jewesses was becoming a problem."[19] As Dr. Hermann Adler,
chief rabbi of the British Empire, explained to the Home Office,

It is an admitted fact that in former years, one rarely, if
ever, heard of an unchaste Hebrew maiden in this country.
I grieve to be obliged to say that this happy state of things
no longer exists. The extension of the social evil to my
community may be directly traced to the overstocked labor
market and to the Russian persecutions continuing to this
day which cause thousands of Jewish girls to arrive at these
shores without any means of subsistence.[20]

As everywhere, the social evil of prostitution was an outcropping of
poverty and hopelessness, to which young Jewish women were not
immune.

In March 1885, a Jewish Ladies Society for Preventative and
Rescue Work (after 1889, it was renamed the Jewish Association for
the Protection of Girls and Women [JAPGW]) was formed to battle
Jewish prostitution. The organization opened a refuge in Mile End
called Charcroft House, where fallen women were prescribed healthy
doses of laundry work and prayer. They were taught how to read and
cook, and were otherwise prepared for a life of housekeeping, as either
a wife or a domestic servant. Members of the JAPGW's Gentlemen's
Committees went to the docks to protect unwary girls from procur-
ers for the "white slave trade"—essentially, an international trade in

prostitutes, who were largely "recruited" from Eastern Europe. The fact that Jews were among the foremost participants in white slavery was a great embarrassment to the established Anglo-Jewish community. The trade was largely run from London, and prostitutes (often Jewish) were shipped off to work in British colonies or other distant lands, from whence they were usually never heard of again.

In January 1888, the Ladies Society report gave a "terrible account of the gross immoralities of the Jewish people in the East India Dock Road."[21] In October of that same year, in the midst of the Ripper murders, a letter printed in the *Jewish Chronicle* from a Michael Zeffertt noted, "The amount of immorality daily growing among the women is a blot upon our community at large." Still, in the overall scheme of things, Jewish involvement in prostitution in the East End was comparatively minimal—or, at least, primarily confined to work indoors, in brothels. The vast majority of the area's street prostitutes were British natives.

Overcrowding in the East End was another problem. Between 1871 and 1901, the number of houses in Whitechapel had dropped from 8,264 to 5,735, even though the population rose by about four percent.[22] The overcrowding led to an increase in the cost of rent, worsening things still further.[23] Often an entire family would live in one room, sharing beds or sleeping on the floor. In a widely publicized article titled "The Bitter Cry of Outcast London," the Reverend Andrew Mearns wrote, "Every room in these rotten and reeking tenements houses a family, often two. In one cellar a sanitary inspector reports finding a father, mother, three children, and four pigs!"[24] And as Jack London described in *People of the Abyss*, "Not only was one room deemed sufficient for a poor man and his family, but I learned that many families, occupying single rooms, had so much space to spare as to be able to take in a lodger or two."[25]

Unemployed vagrants could find a night's sleep in the casual ward of the local workhouse, but space was limited. First-comers would receive a bed in exchange for doing a certain amount of hard labor, and the rest were turned away. Those who had a bit of money could stay in one of the East End's many common lodging houses (or doss houses). Others didn't have a bed at all, and they slept on the streets, under bridges and archways, or anywhere else they could. As Mearns wrote, "Hundreds cannot even scrape together the two pence required to secure them the privilege of resting in those sweltering common sleeping rooms, and so they huddle together upon the stairs and landings, where it is no uncommon thing to find six or eight in the early morning."[26] A bleak portrayal of the hardships faced by the homeless was given in a memoir published anonymously in 1885 by someone who referred to himself only as "One of Them." The author recounted his memories of sleeping in the niches of Blackfriars Bridge, where on one occasion he counted 215 homeless people sheltering from a cold, driving rain.

Various charities were established to address the problems of overcrowding and homelessness in the East End, but these were often either mismanaged or entirely insufficient in the face of the overwhelming destitution of the area. As London wrote, "The quarters of the Salvation Army in various parts of London are nightly besieged by hosts of the unemployed and the hungry for whom neither shelter nor the means of sustenance can be provided."[27] In October 1883, Queen Victoria herself penned a letter to the prime minister, William Gladstone, expressing her distress on reading about "the deplorable condition of the houses of the poor."[28] A report of the Royal Commission on the Housing of the Working Classes in 1884 determined, according to author Alan Palmer, that too much "was left to charity: too little imposed by firm paternalistic central government." Critics condemned the report as "state socialism."[29]

As much as anything, the Jack the Ripper murders would focus the world's attention on the horrific living conditions and the crime that had long existed in the East End. One year after the murders, Police Superintendent Thomas Arnold of H Division (Whitechapel) admitted, "There can be no doubt whatever that vice in its worst forms exists in Whitechapel."[30] His statement was in response to a scathing letter in the *Times* by the Reverend Samuel Barnett, who complained of "houses in which men and women live as beasts, where crime is protected, and where children or country people are led on to ruin."[31] Barnett pointed to the cheap lodgings where prostitutes lived with men who "partially if not wholly subsist on their wretched earnings"—in other words, pimps—and added that the district frequently had "rows in which stabbing is common" and "fights between women stripped to

the waist, of which boys and children are spectators." He concluded
that reform would be possible only "when public opinion will condemn
as offenders those who directly or indirectly live on the profits of vice."

Theft and robbery were also rampant, as noted by Dr. Jacqueline
Banerjee of King's College, London:

> Mugging, with its associated violence, was rife. A hanky
> dipped in chloroform might be used to subdue someone
> before robbing him, or a man's hat might be tipped over his
> face to facilitate the crime (this was called "bonneting").
> Another ruse was to lure men down to the riverside by using
> prostitutes as decoys. The dupes would then be beaten up
> and robbed out of sight of passers-by.[32]

The police must have felt overwhelmed in such a vicious environment, and Superintendent Arnold apparently thought the police of
H Division were unfairly blamed for their inability to enforce law and
order in the wake of the Ripper murders. He admitted that brawling
and fighting did take place but "not nearly to such an extent as might
be expected and is generally believed by persons non resident in the
district." Arnold concluded that the only remedy was to clear out the
lodging houses and replace them with "improved dwellings with better
supervision."[33] Police Commissioner James Monro disagreed with this,
pointing to a larger problem. "Behind the whole question lies the larger
matter of street prostitution generally," Monro said, "and until that is
taken up and regulated (objectionable as this may appear to a public
which confuses between liberty and licence) the mere multiplying of
comfortable lodging houses will not have any appreciable effect in
diminishing the number of and evils resulting from a class who do not
want comfortable lodging houses, and the scene of whose operations
is on the street."[34]

Monro's statement touched on an important problem, which would
become all too apparent during the Ripper murders—specifically, that
the prostitutes' own methods played right into the hands of the killer.
As Inspector Henry Moore later said, "It is not as if he had to wait for
his chance; they make the chance for him."[35] The prostitutes of the
East End typically conducted their business in dark and deserted courtyards and alleys where they could service their clients without being

seen by anyone, least of all by the police. Such locations were ideal for illicit sex, but they were also ideal for murder. As Monro wrote in a May 1889 letter to the Home Office, "The only wonder is that [the Ripper's] operations have been so restricted. There is no lack of victims ready to his hand, for scores of these unfortunate women may be seen any night muddled with drink in the streets & alleys, perfectly reckless as to their safety, and only anxious to meet with anyone who will help them in plying their miserable trade."[36] The prostitutes of Whitechapel were in a rather hopeless position, because they had to work to survive, and large numbers of them continued to work out of desperation, even while they knew a killer was on the prowl. When Inspector Moore tried to frighten the prostitutes off the streets, they would laugh and say, "I ain't afraid of him. It's the Ripper or the bridge with me. What's the odds?"[37]

4

Jewish Tailors in the East End

Aron Mordke Kozminski was born in Kłodawa (pronounced kwo-dava), a small village to the east of a bend in the Warta River, about midway between Poznan and Warsaw. In the late eighteenth and early nineteenth centuries, this region was passed back and forth between countries as the booty of war and conquest, until 1865, the year of Kozminski's birth, when Congress Poland was officially absorbed into Russia. The village was then located in the westernmost part of the Pale of Settlement, just thirty miles from the Prussian border. (Ten miles to the west of Kłodawa is the village of Kolo—oddly enough, the hometown of another Jack the Ripper suspect, Severin Klosowski, later known as George Chapman.)

There had been a Jewish presence in Kłodawa since the fifteenth century. Then in 1547, the Jewish residents were chased out of town after a blood libel accusation against some Jews for the supposed ritual murder of two Christian children.[1] Jews would not return until the early 1800s, when they began to resettle in a quarter of the village called Dziadowice. By 1862, there were 621 Jews in Kłodawa, slightly less than 25 percent of the total population of the town.

Aron's father, Abram Josef Kozminski, was a tailor from the village of Grzegorzew, seven miles southwest of Kłodawa. (The exact year of Abram's birth is unknown and is based on estimates of his age from

later documents.) At the age of twenty-two, Abram married Golda
Lubnowski, a twenty-three-year-old woman from Kłodawa, who was
the daughter of a butcher named Wolek and his wife, Ruchel.[2] The
couple then lived in Grzegorzew for a brief period before moving to
Kłodawa around 1845. During the next twenty years, Abram and Golda
had a total of seven children. Pessa, their first daughter, was born in
December 1845 but died before reaching three years of age. A second
daughter, Hinde, was born in November 1848; then a son, Iciek (later
called Isaac), was born in 1851. A third daughter, Malke (later called
Matilda), was born in 1854; Blimbe, another daughter, was born in
1857; then another son, Wolek (later called Woolf), was born in 1860.
Aron Mordke Kozminski, the youngest child, was born on September
11, 1865, by which time Golda was almost forty-five years old.[3]

In 1867, two years after Aaron's birth, the Russian government
revoked Kłodawa's municipal charter, probably as a punishment for the
town's support of the January Uprising. This caused a sort of economic
crisis in the village—no longer officially a town, Kłodawa "became a
quiet place without further development," enlivened only by "a few
fairs each year and a big religious celebration of the Virgin Mary."[4]
In 1871, Aaron's oldest brother, Iciek, then twenty years old, was the
first member of the family to leave Russia for England. The reason for

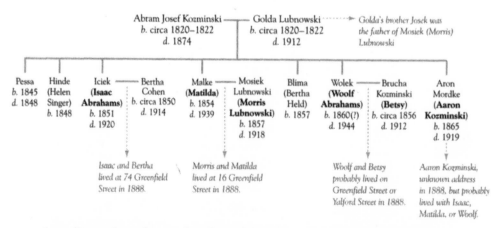

Aaron Kozminski was born in the village of Kłodawa in the westernmost part of Russia's
Pale of Settlement. The decade of the 1870s, when Aaron was an adolescent and a
young teenager, witnessed a rise in anti-Semitism in Russia. Woolf, Betsy, and Aaron left
Russia shortly after the outbreak of pogroms in the spring of 1881.

Iciek's departure is not known, but it is likely that he left simply to escape the crushing poverty and hopelessness that were endemic in the Pale. When Aaron Kozminski's father, Abram, died three years later, he left "after himself a widowed wife Golda and three children." This statement, recorded on Abram's death certificate, apparently means that he left three dependent children living at home, in all likelihood, Blima (age sixteen), Wolek (age fourteen), and Aron (age eight). The cause of Abram's death is not known.[5]

Apart from the bare facts outlined previously, very little is known about the Kozminski family's life in Poland. An undated entry in Kłodawa's Book of Residents lists the six Kozminski siblings as "petty bourgeois" and "unmarried."[6] The three boys, Isaac, Woolf, and Aaron, are described as tailors, and the means of support for the three daughters, Hinde, Malke, and Blima, is given as "with brother," which suggests the entry was made after Abram's death. Because it was common for Jewish children in the Pale to work at a young age, it should come as no surprise that Aaron Kozminski was employed as a tailor when he was only around ten years old or even younger. Still, the Kozminskis were probably in a rather difficult situation, financially speaking. Because Isaac had already moved to England by the time of Abram's death, the eldest "brother" responsible for supporting the family must have been Wolek Kozminski, who was then only fourteen years old.

In the late 1870s, Aaron's sister Malke (Matilda) married a boot-maker named Mosiek (Morris) Lubnowski.[7] Mosiek was in fact the son of Golda Lubnowski's brother Josek, a shoemaker. In other words, Malke and Mosiek were cousins.[8] Cousin marriage was common at the time, and as a descendant of the Lubnowskis acknowledged, "It is well known in the family that Morris and Matilda were cousins."[9] The young couple moved to Germany, where their first two children were born.[10] Then, shortly after the outbreak of pogroms in the spring of 1881, Wolek Kozminski likewise married his second cousin Brucha Kozminska and they promptly left Russia for England, bringing fifteen-year-old Aron Kozminski with them.[11] Wolek, Brucha, and Aron thus joined the thousands of Jewish refugees fleeing Russia and heading to London.

For most Jews, the seven-hundred-mile journey to England was a harrowing and dehumanizing ordeal, during which they were repeatedly robbed and swindled by border guards and other unscrupulous vultures. The passage across the North Sea, according to William Fishman, typically consisted of travelers spending two or three days on a ship similar to a cattle-boat, crammed together and sleeping on dirty, rank-smelling blankets. As a British Board of Trade report described it, "Men, women, and children were lying on the bare boards partly undressed. . . . Young men lay abreast of young unmarried women, chatting jocularly and acting indecently, and young children were witnesses of all that passed."[12] Such was the style in which the Kozminskis traveled to their new home, the East End of London.

Jews from Eastern Europe had in fact been arriving in London for years, but the wave of immigration after the Russian pogroms of 1881 was akin to a tsunami, and by the middle of summer hundreds of Jewish immigrants were arriving at London's docks daily. It was not a warm welcome. On arrival, the Russian Jews found themselves in an unwelcoming, unfriendly, and unfamiliar ghetto that afforded little in the way of either housing or employment, and it was said that on debarking the men were so enfeebled that they looked "nearer seventy than thirty." Some of the new arrivals hoped that a distant relative or someone they knew from home might give them refuge.[13] The scene at the docks was utter mayhem. Many of the newcomers were robbed almost immediately after arrival, while young unaccompanied women were in constant danger of being stolen away to a bordello by a "white slave" agent. Beatrice Potter described the ensuing chaos as follows:

> A little man with an official badge (Hebrew Ladies Protective Society) fights valiantly in their midst for the conduct of unprotected females and shouts or whispers to the others to go to the Poor Jews Temporary Shelter in Leman Street. For a few moments it is a scene of indescribable confusion: cries and counter cries; the hoarse laughter of the dock loungers at the strange garb and broken accent of the poverty-stricken foreigners; the rough swearing of the boatmen at passengers unable to pay the fee for landing. In another ten minutes eighty of the hundred new comers are dispersed in the back slums of Whitechapel; in another few days the majority of these robbed of the little they possess are turned out of the free lodgings destitute and friendless.[14]

The police were not always sympathetic to the newcomers. As George Sims noted, "When I explain to one that a gesticulating Pole wants to give the boatman into custody for refusing to give up his bundle without the sixpence is paid, the policeman grins and says 'Lor now, does he?'"[15] The majority of the Jews who marched up into the city, "like a gang of convicts marching to the mines," Sims observed, would "presently be working as tailors and bootmakers in the den of the sweater."[16] In their eyes was the "indescribable expression of hunted, suffering animals."[17] Things had not changed much by the time Sam Dreen arrived in London in 1900. "We walked through a rough area, where the inhabitants hated immigrants and threw stones at us all the way to Leman Street."[18]

Even London's established Anglo-Jewish community was not particularly welcoming to the newcomers. Anglo-Jewry had fought long and hard to overcome the undercurrents of anti-Semitism in Britain, while various restrictions on full citizenship rights were gradually removed during the course of the nineteenth century. The influx of poverty-stricken Jewish refugees in the 1880s threatened everything that the Anglo-Jewish residents had gained. London's "Anglicized" Jewish establishment regarded the immigrants as a lower caste of radical Jews, "fit only to receive alms," and they feared "social retrogression" through association with them. As an editorial in the *Jewish Chronicle* put it, "Our fair fame is bound up with theirs; the outside world is not capable of making minute discrimination between Jew and Jew, and forms its opinion of Jews in general as much, if not more, from them than from the Anglicized portion of the Community."[19]

Still, the majority of native Londoners, Jew and gentile alike, were initially sympathetic to the plight of the refugees. Compared to life in the Pale of Settlement, London was a vast improvement, and the immigrants found themselves with previously unimagined freedoms and opportunities. Various Jewish social programs assisted the new arrivals in finding jobs and places to live, and, as William Fishman noted, the Eastern Jews' "compulsive tenacity proved an inbred asset for survival."[20] A Poor Jews Temporary Shelter was eventually established, in 1885, to assist the destitute newcomers; it provided two warm meals a day, a vapor bath, prayer services, and a bed for a maximum stay of two weeks. Opponents of unrestricted immigration claimed that the shelter's address was "bought and sold" in eastern Europe.[21]

Yet as the decade wore on, immigration continued and the economy worsened, and rising unemployment, combined with a general mistrust of foreigners, led to a backlash against the Jews. For the Kozminski family and thousands of other Jewish immigrants, the situation in England gradually evolved into a mirror image of the anti-Semitic environment they had just escaped. It was a case of out of the frying pan, into the fire.

When Aaron's brother Iciek had arrived in London's East End in 1872, he followed the common practice of Jewish immigrants to English-speaking countries and changed his foreign-sounding Jewish name to one that was thought to be easier to spell and pronounce. Hence, Iciek Kozminski became Isaac Abrahams. When the rest of the family arrived in 1881, they settled in the same neighborhood where Isaac had already been living for nearly a decade.[22] Following Isaac's lead, they likewise adopted more English-sounding first names. Wolek Kozminski became Woolf Abrahams; Wolek's wife, Brucha, became Betsy; and Mosiek and Malke became Morris and Matilda Lubnowski. We must also assume that fifteen-year-old Aaron Kozminski became Aaron Abrahams at this time. As we shall see, however, Aaron continued to use the name Kozminski, at least on some occasions, although the reason he did so is unknown.

By December 1885, all four Kozminski siblings were living on Greenfield Street, just south of Whitechapel Road and St. Mary Matfelon. Greenfield Street was lined with two- and three-story brick houses and was said to be comparatively respectable for the district. According to Charles Booth's 1888 survey of the area, it was inhabited by "a rather superior class of people." The great majority of those in the street were Jewish, Booth noted. "A few fairly well off. Others poor, but tolerably comfortable."[23] Both of Aaron's brothers, Woolf and Isaac, were ladies' tailors in the business of making jackets and outer garments called mantles. As with many tailors in the East End, it was probably a somewhat tenuous existence. Woolf especially, it seems, struggled to make ends meet. From 1881 until 1887, he moved several times and lived at four different addresses, all on Greenfield Street.[24]

In April 1886, Woolf's house at 62 Greenfield Street was broken into, as reported in the *Illustrated Police News*:

> John Isaacs, seventeen, has been charged, at the Thames Police court, with burglariously entering the premises of Woolf Abrahams of Greenfield street, Whitechapel, and attempting to steal therefrom various articles, value 12 pounds, on the previous night. The prosecutor stated that when he and his brother-in-law entered the front room they saw the prisoner lying under the bed. As soon as he saw witness he said, "Be quiet. Your watch and chain are under the bedstead. I did not mean to do anything. Let me go." They pulled him out from under the bedstead and then sent for a constable. When the prisoner was searched at the station a silver watch, some matches, a piece of candle, a knife, and 6d were found in his possession.[25]

This article unfortunately does not tell us very much. The brother-in-law mentioned must have been Morris Lubnowski, who lived just down the street at the time. Woolf then moved again sometime around 1887 and lived (apparently briefly, in either 1888 or 1889) on Yalford Street, a narrow street parallel to Greenfield Street that was described as being the residence of "very poor class Polish Jews."[26] At some time prior to February 25, 1890, he relocated once more, this time to 3 Sion Square, another poor area, characterized by "chronic want."[27]

Aaron Kozminski's sister Matilda and her husband, Morris, likewise lived at various addresses in the area before moving into a two-story brick row house at 16 Greenfield Street in December 1885.[28] They would stay at this address for the next five years, until early 1891. Morris was a bootmaker, and he probably had a workshop in the house. It was most likely a cramped situation, and by 1888, Morris and Matilda had four young children living with them. (After arriving in England, Morris and Matilda Lubnowski changed their last name to Lubnowski-Cohen and later simply to Cohen.)

Directly across the street from Morris and Matilda's house was 74 Greenfield Street, a modest brick row house that was the home of Aaron's other brother, Isaac, who, as previously mentioned, had been living in the East End since 1872. By the middle of the 1880s, Isaac had established himself as a prosperous ladies' tailor, making dresses and mantles as a subcontractor for wholesale manufacturers in the West End or in the area around St. Paul's. A description of Isaac's business can be gleaned from Charles Booth's survey of East End tailors in 1887–1888. Booth, the son of a Liverpool cotton merchant, was a dedicated philanthropist who, from 1886 until 1903, conducted extensive surveys into poverty, industry, and religion in London, with the intention of providing a statistical basis for understanding social and economic issues in the East End. The result of his undertaking was *Life and Labour of the People in London*, the third edition of which (1902–1903) was a staggering seventeen volumes long. Booth's inquiries included the study of various trades, such as a survey of the tailoring industry in the East End, which consisted of data from questionnaires and interviews with workers, trade union leaders, and employers. By 1888, Isaac Abrahams had fourteen employees, and it would appear that he was reasonably well off. He appeared in Booth's survey as follows: "Abrahams / 74 Greenfield St / III. B. 1. Grade B. Garment: C."

> Good Work. Ladies coats.
> First class work. Employs about 14 men. Gets an average price of 12/- per coat. Of this the men get 6/-, & he takes 6/-, out of wh. he pays 1/3 for machining & B.H., making 4/9 profit. Some of the men employ an assistant, & the firm can turn out 20 coats a day. In busiest season (May, June, July) he can make £40 a week.[29]

Isaac's workshop was located in the yard behind his house. The building was about thirty-five feet long, with a long skylight, which extended the length of the ceiling. The one large room would have been filled with several tables and chairs, a number of sewing machines, and piles of fabric of different types and colors. Beatrice Potter commented on this type of "garden workshop" in 1887. "Between factories proper and home work lie a class of home workshops," she wrote. "These are usually built in the yard or garden behind the dwelling house."[30] Booth's survey noted that there were fifteen "nice garden workshops" of similar construction on the east side of Greenfield Street.[31] Some of these were described in the survey. For example, the workshop of a Mr. Solomon at 83 Greenfield Street was described as "similarly built to the others in this street but longer being 38 ft long."[32] Another interview, with a Mr. Goldstein at 70 Greenfield Street, noted, "Workshop a counterpart of Mr. Rosen's (No. 71) and this is the type of shop on this side (east) of Greenfield St." Mr. Rosen's shop was described in some detail and probably gives some idea of what Isaac's shop was like:

> It is about 28 ft by 24 ft and is lighted by a large skylight extending the whole length of the room and fitted with six ventilators. The walls are matchboarded & polished. A comfortable shop & one that appears to meet all sanitary requirements. Coke fire was situated in the furthest corner & the brick stove appeared to be built back into the wall. When I first saw the shop these hands were all at work and Mr. R was at his table. The four machines were ranged along the side of the shop. The two pressers tables were at the further end of the shop. In the centre the baisters boards were placed and adjoined the masters table, while the girls were seated at a low table at the side nearest the door.[33]

Tailoring was the leading profession practiced by immigrant Jews in the Victorian East End. It was a highly competitive trade, in which workers struggled to meet the needs of a "huge and constantly increasing class" with "wide wants and narrow means."[34] The 1870s had seen the emergence of a market for British-made, tailored ladies' clothing, especially ladies' jackets and mantles, typically elaborate and frilly outer garments worn over the shoulders as a barrier against chilly temperatures. All ladies' tailoring prior to the 1870s had been done abroad, mostly in Germany and France. But by 1890, the East End mantle- and jacket-making industry was well established, and by 1895 it employed more than a thousand workers. According to Morris Cohen (no relation to Aaron's cousin and brother-in-law, Morris Lubnowski, later Morris Lubnowski-Cohen or Morris Cohen), the man generally credited with being the first ladies' tailor in London, the trade was entirely created by Jewish immigrants. In his testimony before the alien commission, Cohen said that there were no English ladies' tailors in London prior to 1870. As he exclaimed in an 1898 interview, "Why! English ladies' tailors? Are you aware of their existence? . . . The English tailor . . . is all right in his place," Cohen said. "That is in the men's trade, where solidity and durability is the chief quality required." The ladies' trade, by contrast, required "something smart in appearance, something to catch the eye. This quality you will not find in an English tailor. It is not in him. You might as well expect water from a rock."[35] A letter from the wholesale clothing firm Hitchcock, Williams, and Co. confirmed this statement. When asked why they employed foreign laborers in their factory, they replied, "Our experience shows that these foreign Jewish tailors do a class of work which our workers cannot undertake with success, and earn a high rate of pay."[36]

Large clothing manufacturers around St. Paul's and in the West End had initially employed workers in-house, but they soon found it to be more profitable to contract work out to East End Jewish tailors, who could produce garments more cheaply by employing foreign workers. This system, in which work was farmed out to middlemen whose employees toiled away in workshops or in their own homes, was referred to as "the sweating system." The workers were typically forced to work long hours for low pay, and thus the term "sweater" came to mean "any sub-contractor or middleman who squeezes a profit out of the labour of the poor."[37] Isaac, as a subcontractor running a small tailoring workshop, would have been called a sweater. In fact, Woolf Zeitlin, the secretary of the Jewish branch of the Amalgamated Society of Tailors, specifically referred to Isaac Abrahams as a sweater in an interview conducted for the Booth surveys. Zeitlin claimed, "He had worked in the 'sweaters' workshops, and thought that as a rule they make very good profits, though some of them were poor." The interview noted, "Another example given by Mr. Zeitlin (No. 96—Abrahams) will be found in the general notes on list." (No. 96 was Isaac Abrahams.)[38]

The influx of poor Jewish immigrants in the 1880s had severely weakened an already cheap labor market. Large numbers of unskilled or semiskilled Jewish immigrants known as "greeners" were desperate for work and were willing to work long hours in often unsanitary workshops for starvation wages. "They would bring with them the scantiest means of existence," wrote Myer Wilchinski in 1882, "some married and with families and all with that enquiring, beseeching look, that half starved, helpless, hopeless beings must of necessity possess." The greeners would stand in the employment market known as the chazar mark (literally "pig market") on Goulston Street and try to get work with the master tailors. There they would wait, looking like "unwashed corpses," "with barely any clothes to cover them, and without a penny in the pockets."[39] As described by William H. Wilkins,

> To call the place where these transactions are carried on a "slave-market" is perhaps an abuse of terms, since, in a strictly legal sense, nobody buys and nobody sells; but that it is a traffic in human beings cannot be denied. Almost any Sunday morning during the spring, summer and autumn months, at the corner of Goulston Street, Whitechapel, for instance, may be seen a varying number of men drawn up in a line against the wall. In front of them stands a man who engages—I will not say sells—them to the sweater, who gets his victims to sign a paper, binding them to work for so many weeks and at so much money in the sweating dens. It is a pitiful sight.[40]

An 1884 article in the *Poilishe Yidl* noted, "When you come to London, on Sabbath take a stroll to the well known . . . chazar mark and you will see masters (you can distinguish them by their fat bellies!) scuttling about like a plague of mice between the poverty stricken workers [calling], 'Jack, are you a machiner? John! I need a presser!'"[41] The journalist George Sims later described the sweating system as "little better than the importation of foreign slaves."[42]

Greeners were often compelled to work for "bare keep"—no money, but a little food and a place to sleep—ostensibly in exchange for learning the trade. Then after a few months, they would be offered a pitiful wage, which, out of desperation, they would accept. The Jewish master tailor who employed greeners was thus able to be more competitive than those who employed English tailors. Such an arrangement pushed down wages generally, and, as a result, sweaters, especially in the tailoring industry, came under great scrutiny for unfair labor practices. By 1884, antisweating forces were mobilizing on multiple fronts. In March, a factory inspector who spoke at a meeting of the Amalgamated Society of Tailors said, "The Factory Laws have socially raised every trade which has been subjected to them, and have given independence to workers in every case, save for the one degraded and wretched trade of East London tailoring!"[43] Then in May, the *Lancet* published a "Report of the Lancet Special Sanitary Commission on the Polish Colony of Jew Tailors," exposing the "unwholesome, overcrowded" conditions of sweatshops and evasion of the Factory and Workshop Act. The article cited a workshop in Hanbury Street, where eighteen workers were found "crowded in a small room measuring eight yards by four and a half yards and not quite eight feet high." In one room in the building, "the window frame was almost falling into the street; in another the floor was broken and the fireplace giving way." The *Jewish Chronicle* suggested that the evils of the sweating system "are to be cured by the pressure of public opinion acting upon the unscrupulous masters, and by a combination among the work people themselves."[44]

Simultaneously, a vocal group of immigrant Jewish socialists, mostly of Russian and Polish origin, started trying to organize workers into unions, to fight exploitation by the "masters," whom they saw as being emblematic of capitalist exploitation in general. This was especially troubling to members of London's established Anglo-Jewish population, who worried that any association with socialism would lead to further prejudice against the Jews in general. The year 1885 saw the first appearance of a new monthly socialist newspaper, called *Arbeter Fraint* ("Worker's Friend"), printed in Yiddish. The paper would become a powerful soapbox for East End unions and workers. By June 1886, the *Arbeter Fraint* had been taken over by the International Workingmen's Educational Club, a conglomerate of socialists and anarchists who waged war on capitalist oppression and the exploiting "masters" from their headquarters in an "old wooden two storey building" at 40 Berner Street. The paper attacked the Jewish religion, both by ridiculing its holidays and "superstitions," and by endlessly criticizing the Orthodox Jews' main representative in the East End, Dr. Hermann Adler, assistant to the chief rabbi of the British Empire. Unfortunately, such blasphemous rantings alienated large numbers of "simple" Jews who may have otherwise been sympathetic to the workers' cause. Aaron Kozminski's family on Greenfield Street, only a few minutes' walk from the Berner Street club, was thus in the very heart of socialist and anarchist territory. In fact, at the south end of Greenfield Street near the intersection with Commercial Road was a "squalid-looking" coffee house "much patronized by the great bulk of the poorer East End Anarchists and Socialists who live in the district."[45] A sign in the window read (in Yiddish), "Here can be had coffee."

By the middle of the 1880s, the British East Enders increasingly resented what they perceived to be a Jewish invasion of their turf. Native English tailors blamed both the sweating system and the constant influx of newly arrived greeners for creating an unfair advantage for Jewish tailors and devaluing labor in the middle of a depression. Jewish workers were accused of "blacklegging" by accepting lower living standards and of undermining the unions by working as scabs. As the flood of immigration continued, Jews took over entire streets and neighborhoods, and, as Alan Palmer noted, the immigrants were additionally blamed "for pushing up rents by accepting overcrowded conditions, thereby forcing native East Enders to move out."[46]

The result was a sort of pressure cooker, which led to a backlash against Jews in general. By the mid-1880s, anti-Semitism was on the rise, and British nationalists encouraged anti-Semitic and antiforeign sentiments in the district. As early as October 1884, the *Poilishe Yidl* (the predecessor to the socialist journal *Arbeter Fraint*, also printed in Yiddish) was forecasting a change in the wind:

> Go any Sabbath afternoon to Whitechapel and stand for a few moments in a doorway near where some English workers lounge with their pipes in their mouths, and you will hear, every time a Jew passes by, the lovely calling "Bloody Jew!" Is this a token of love?
>
> At the same time in Brick Lane you will often see dolled up Jewish women, girls with golden rings on their fingers sitting outside in the street. Look in the eyes of the passing Englishmen and can't you discern the look—which is already half indicative of a pogrom. . . . A pogrom in Brick Lane, in the crossroads of Commercial Road can be a more bloody and terrible affair than one in the Baltic.[47]

The prediction was ominous. By February 1886, an article in the
Pall Mall Gazette, which was widely considered an anti-Semitic newspaper by most Jews, warned, "Foreign Jews of no nationality whatever
are becoming a pest and a menace to the poor native-born East Ender."
The article went on to say that "fifteen or twenty thousand Jewish refugees of the lowest type . . . have a greater responsibility for the distress
which prevails there than probably all other causes put together."[48]
Anti-Semitism became increasingly overt as the decade wore on.
One typically hateful article in the *Contemporary Review* noted, "The
foreign Jews are filthy in their lives, and present a substantial similarity
to the Mongolian type of character."[49]

By 1887, unemployment had peaked, and an article in March in
the *Pall Mall Gazette* warned, "We shall have an anti-Jewish riot in
the East End quite as serious as the anti-Chinese riot in California,
if we don't look out."[50] This was a reference to the "Rock Springs
massacre"—a bloody incident that had occurred in a small coal-mining
town in Wyoming (not California, as the article claimed). Like the
Jews in Whitechapel, the Chinese in the American West were considered "alien in blood, habits, and civilization." The white, mostly
immigrant, miners considered the importation of Chinese laborers a
"system worse than slavery" and blamed the lower-paid immigrants
for driving down their wages. The clash came on September 2, 1885,
when 150 men armed with Winchester rifles entered Rock Springs'
Chinatown and shot several Chinese miners, then proceeded to wreak
havoc on the residents of the village. At night, the white miners
burned down seventy-nine Chinese camp houses. A memorial presented to the Chinese consul in New York noted that dead bodies
were "thrown into the flames," and that some of the Chinese were
"burned alive in the houses."[51] All told, the massacre resulted in
twenty-eight deaths and property damage of approximately $150,000.
Anti-Chinese riots then spread to other areas in the West. President
Grover Cleveland was appalled at the violence but thought that anti-
Chinese feeling was so deeply entrenched that the immigrants would
never be able to assimilate.

In effect, the *Gazette's* reference to this incident was tantamount
to a threat of violence against the Jews in the East End. The situation
was rapidly deteriorating. In April 1887, a meeting of residents in Mile

End petitioned for the exclusion of pauper immigrants from the district. Then in May, the St. James's Gazette suggested that the majority of the immigrants were "nihilists and anarchists of the worst type"— this was exactly the type of propaganda that London's established Anglo-Jewish population had worried about.[52] The nationalist Arnold White emerged as a mouthpiece for native Englishmen, who he claimed were being speedily displaced by foreign intruders. A letter by White published in the Times in November 1887 declared, "The time for inquiry is over. The hour for action has arrived," and demanded whether "our own kith shall be sacrificed to an obsolete shibboleth and the bloodthirsty operation of an artificial competition."[53] By 1888, forty-three unions were officially opposed to unrestricted immigration, including the Docker's Union, the Master Tailors' Association, and the Shoemakers' Association.

As a result of these gathering forces, the government agreed to conduct an inquiry into the question of Jewish immigration, and members of a Commons Committee on Immigration were appointed by February 10, 1888.[54] A separate Parliamentary committee in the House of Lords was established to examine the effects of the sweating system in tailoring and other trades.

By early 1888, just before the Ripper murders began, Jewish sweaters in the tailoring industry were under attack from three, albeit related, directions. Anti-Semitic British nationalists and disgruntled unemployed locals were the most directly threatening enemies. Jewish socialists were likewise attacking the master sweaters in frequent bitter diatribes published in the Arbeter Fraint, in an attempt to mobilize the workers to unionize and strike. And finally, two looming government inquiries were bearing down on Jewish immigrants in general, and on Jewish sweaters specifically. On March 3, 1888, the East London Advertiser noted in an editorial, "The swarms of foreign Jews who have invaded the East London labour market, are chiefly responsible for the sweating system and the grave evils which are flowing from it—the brunt of the hardship involved (falling) with tenfold severity upon the English men and women."[55]

Around this same time, Booth's researchers were conducting interviews with Jewish tailors, including some of Isaac Abrahams's neighbors on Greenfield Street. In one interview, a master tailor named Mr. Goldstein of 70 Greenfield Street said that "there was not much trade," and that "much harm had been done by newspaper men." There was not enough work to go around, the tailors reported, and the wholesalers took advantage of the situation by offering contracts that paid less for each item of clothing produced. The sweaters had no choice but to compete for such low-paying contracts, and as a result, prices were dropping across the board. In effect, the master tailors were struggling. In one interview, Mr. Rosen of 71 Greenfield Street noted, "There was much more competition to get work than formerly and the employers had taken advantage of this. Prices had been reduced about 10 per cent." Another tailor, named Mr. Solomon, at 83 Greenfield Street, claimed that prices had fallen even further than this and added that, in his opinion, "the men were better off than the masters."[56] These interviews were conducted on March 1, 1888, just two weeks before the first meeting of the House of Lords Committee on the Sweating System.

According to a *Jewish Chronicle* article by J. A. Dyche titled "A Trade Created by the Jewish Immigrants" (1898), the harsh criticism leveled at Jewish sweaters was largely unjustified. Dyche defended the sweaters, noting that "in the ladies' mantle trade the foreign 'sweater' is not only a first-class workman, but also a designer and an artist in his trade." Dyche laid the blame at the door of the wholesale manufacturers, who he said generally know "little more about the technical part of the trade than the man in the street. . . . To become a 'manufacturer' in this industry only a little capital is required." In other words, the so-called manufacturers were little more than wholesale dealers of clothing entirely produced by subcontracted labor.

"The British Christian manufacturers who exploit the Jewish 'sweater,'" Dyche wrote, "can and do amass wealth; their voices are heard on public platform and in Parliament. But it is the Jewish 'sweater' who is dragged before the public by the sensational journalist and the public orator as a social plague." In Dyche's opinion, the sweater who came under such harsh scrutiny was being squeezed himself and was merely struggling to survive by responding to the pressures of the market. Yet in the court of public opinion, such theories went by the wayside. It didn't seem to matter that the large manufacturers of the West End and in the area of St. Paul's were apparently at least as responsible as the sweaters for exploiting the weakened labor market for their own financial gain. Dyche added, "The Christian British public throw up their hands and thank heaven they are not as bad as these foreigners. Yes:—Das ist eine alte Geschichte, Doch bleibt sie immer neu. (This is an old story, however, it remains ever new.)"[57]

The social researcher Beatrice Potter (later Beatrice Webb) was one of the researchers who worked on Charles Booth's labor surveys of the 1880s and the 1890s. Potter studied the tailoring industry and the Jewish community firsthand, walking the East End streets and visiting Jewish homes, workshops, and synagogues, and her research, interestingly enough, roughly coincided with the Ripper murders. In April 1888, Potter went undercover in a sweatshop to get an insider's view of the operation. Dressed in shabby clothes and affecting a working-class accent, she toiled away as a trouser finisher in a hot and crowded workshop at 198 Mile End Road. In one rather humorous incident, when disgruntled workers threatened the master's wife with calling the factory inspectors, Potter politely assured the missus, "You have nothing to fear from the factory inspector; you keep the regulations exactly."[58] So much for undercover work. By the following day, the woman was remarking that Potter was different from the other girls and should get married to a nice respectable man. On November 28, 1888, a little more than two weeks after the final and most ghastly of the Ripper's murders, Potter recorded in her diary that she was still "Hard at work at 'The Jewish Community,' seeing Jews of all classes, all day long."[59]

Potter's conclusions about sweating essentially confirmed Dyche's view. She found that Jewish sweaters were only a small part of the problem and noted that Jewish workers were "confined to the manufacture of certain commodities, which had not been produced in the locality before."[60] This was largely in line with Morris Cohen's assertion that the manufacture of ladies' coats, for example, was an industry entirely created by immigrant Jews. Potter concluded that "if every foreign Jew resident in England had been sent back to his birthplace, the bulk of the sweated workers would not have been affected, whether for better or for worse."[61]

Likewise, Charles Booth, in *London: A Portrait of the Poor at the Turn of the Century*, claimed that the criticism of the small masters in the sweated trades was largely unfounded. He wrote:

> It is remarkable that the larger type of sweating master should have been seized upon by the public imagination as the central figure of a monstrous system. It is difficult, not to say impossible, to prove a negative—to prove that the monster sweating master of the comic papers has no existence. I can only say that I have sought diligently and have not found. If a specimen exists, he has nothing to do with the troubles we are investigating. . . . The sweating master I have found, and who is connected with the troubles under investigation, works hard, makes often but little more, and at times somewhat less, than his most skilled and best paid hands. He is seldom on bad terms, and often on very kindly terms, with those who work under him.[62]

None of this mattered much. In practice, the blame fell squarely on the Jewish sweater, because he was the most visible target. Rising unemployment was coincident with Jewish immigration into the area, so it was not hard for the locals to identify the source of the problem. As William Fishman pointed out, "A ready-made scapegoat was available."[63] And as Booth noted, the attack on the sweating masters was "prompted by indignation at the hardships suffered by the poor, and seeking a victim on which to vent its anger, but at times compounded largely of lower motives."[64] These lower motives were fear, hatred, and mistrust of the alien intruder. As Reverend G. S. Rainey said in Arnold White's racist propaganda piece *The Destitute Alien in Great Britain* (1892), "When visiting the poor when times were bad, I often heard the complaint, 'It's them Jews.'"[65]

The House of Lords Committee on the Sweating System met for the first time on March 16, 1888. Among the members on the thirteen-person committee was the twenty-sixth Earl of Crawford, James Ludovic Lindsay, a man who will appear later in our narrative as the author of a letter to Sir Robert Anderson concerning the Ripper murders. Testimony in the committee was given by tailors, antialienists, and social researchers, including Beatrice Potter. The committee found that tailors' wages in the 1880s were decreasing not only because of the competitive labor market, but also because of an increase in productivity—among other reasons, due to the increased use of Isaac Singer's newly affordable sewing machine.[66] Various examples of low wages were given, including "an establishment where cloaks are now made for 4s. 6d, and six or seven years-ago were paid 8s."[67] The only workers who were able to compete with Jewish tailors for the low-paying jobs were English women, who were already accustomed to being underpaid. Desperation sometimes drove workers to suicide or, more often, to crime.

The committee also heard testimony about the working conditions in sweatshops, which were described as "deplorable in the extreme." A Mr. Munro described a workshop as follows: "Three or four gas jets may be flaring in the room, a coke fire burning in the wretched fire-place, sinks untrapped, closets without water, and altogether the sanitary condition abominable."[68] Workers frequently slept in the shops where they worked. One witness, for example, stated, "In a double room, perhaps 9 by 15 feet, a man, his wife, and six children slept, and in the same room ten men were usually employed, so that at night eighteen persons would lie in that one room."[69] The same witness alluded to the "want of sanitary precautions and of decent and sufficient accommodation, and declared that the effect of this, combined with the inadequate wage earned, had the effect of driving girls to prostitution." Sanitary conditions, especially associated with the bathrooms, were described as indecent. "It is easy to imagine what follows on such contamination," the report stated.[70]

Yet by far the most damning aspect of the committee's findings concerned the number of hours worked per day. "The trade is governed by no rules at all," the committee's report stated. "The hours are anything a sweater likes to make them; each sweater has his own method of engaging and paying his workers. The question as to what is a day, or half a day, is differently interpreted by different masters. It is the usual thing for seven and a-half, eight, and nine hours to be regarded as half a day."[71] The report cited, "Evidence tends to show much evasion of the Factory Acts and overtime working of females."[72] Proper hours were in theory thirteen to fourteen hours a day, but some men were found to work for as long as eighteen to twenty-two hours at a stretch, from six in the morning until midnight or later. As Myer Wilchinski reported, "I had to get up in the morning about half past five, and we finished at night between ten and eleven."[73] One worker even testified to working forty hours in a row. There was no holiday, even on the Sabbath, and one witness testified that on the Sabbath, the curtains were simply pulled down. Employers often tried desperately to deceive factory inspectors, in order to circumvent hour limitations enforced by the Factory Act, prompting Potter to remark, "The evil cannot be uprooted by official visits paid in broad daylight; it must be dealt with by the same methods as those employed in the detection of crime."[74]

In conclusion, the committee admitted that its findings were "of an extremely contradictory nature," and that conditions were variable, depending on the class of work.[75] To the antisweating contingent, it was clear that the government was not going to do anything and that the workers would have to take matters into their own hands. On June 27, 1888, the London Tailors' Association met at a hall on Goulston Street to address a large audience about the evils of the sweating system. The association president, Herbert Burrows, referred to the Sweating Committee's findings and concluded that the only solution was for the workers to take control of the means of production and establish cooperative workshops—a suggestion that, he conceded, was socialist in nature. At the end of the meeting, those in attendance passed a resolution stating that they considered "the method of production known as the sweating system, inhuman and barbarous," and that "no workshops be open for more than eight hours during every twenty-four."[76]

The House of Lords Committee on the Sweating System, while not coming to any specific conclusions, did give an air of official recognition to the English workers' seething disdain of foreigners, whose animosity was not directed solely at master tailors, but instead was a xenophobic hatred of the Jews in general, especially those who worked in the sweated industries. Such were the times that in September 1888, when a man appealed to a court of justice on behalf of a Polish tailor whose master (a Jewish tailor) refused to pay him, the judge replied, "The Pole has no business in this country. He is taking the bread out of the mouths of Englishmen. You may have a summons, but I hope you won't succeed."[77]

By early 1889, the workers in the tailoring industry began to mobilize. The socialists and the anarchists of the Berner Street club realized that the time for action had finally arrived, so the *Arbeter Fraint* announced a workers' parade of Jewish Unemployed and Sweaters' Victims "to demand work, bread and the eight-hour day."[78] On March 16, some two thousand men gathered at the International Workingmen's Educational Club on Berner Street and then marched to Duke Street, where they intended to hold an open-air meeting in a courtyard called Mitre Square, directly behind the Great Synagogue. But the police refused to allow the mob to convene in that location, so the throng relocated to the Mile End Waste. After numerous speeches the meeting dispersed, and many of the participants returned to Berner Street, where a large force of police was waiting for them. According to one report, Police Commissioner Monro had sent "some of his men, without any pretext, to break into [the club],"[79] whereupon they proceeded to smash up the place and beat up anyone who was there. Numerous club members came out in defense "armed with sticks," and a vicious street battle erupted. Three club members were arrested, among them a man named Louis Diemschutz. A pamphlet was circulated that sought funds for the club members' legal defense; it noted, "The wealthy Jews and the sweaters, both Jews and Gentiles, wish to see these men in prison and their club destroyed."[80]

By August, a committee headquartered in the White Hart pub on Greenfield Street had organized a "Great Strike of London Tailors & Sweater's Victims." The tailors and the tailoresses met en masse outside the baths on Goulston Street and then marched to Victoria Park, where they listened to speeches demanding "hours be reduced to 12 with an interval of one hour for dinner and half-hour for tea."[81] A contemporary source described the strikers: "A more abject and miserable set of men it would have been impossible to have seen anywhere. Ill clad, dirty, unwashed, haggard and ragged, they looked in the bright sunlight, a picture of abject misery."[82] Some six thousand workers went on strike for three weeks, during which time 120 shops were temporarily shut down. The *East London Observer* remarked, "The strike of the East London tailors bids fair to make 'The White Hart' public house in Greenfield St, Whitechapel, almost as famous as 'The Wades Arms' which formed the headquarters of the Strike Committee during the dockers' agitation."[83] The *Jewish Chronicle* noted the "questionable policy" of tailors allowing themselves to be led by "men conspicuously associated with Socialist movements," which it feared might provoke further prejudices against the Jews in a broader sense.[84]

Finally, the Jewish MP (Member of Parliament) for Whitechapel, Samuel Montagu, met with strikers at the Working Men's Club in Great Alie Street, then with members of the Master Tailors' Protective and Improvement Association at Christ Church parish hall on Hanbury Street, and brokered a deal that ended the strike. The result was that Parliament passed the Factory and Workshop Act (1891) and the Public Health Act (1891), which improved conditions somewhat for workers.

It is now time to move on to the more grim chapters of our narrative. The stage has been set, and some of the locations and the characters discussed in this chapter will already be familiar to readers who are well versed in the story that follows. The International Workingmen's Educational Club on Berner Street, the Great Synagogue adjacent to Mitre Square, and the chazar mark for Jewish tailors on Goulston Street held significance to Jews in the East End, but they would also be sites of great significance in the story of the Ripper murders. And in the middle of it all was the White Hart pub, the headquarters of the Great Strike of Sweater's Victims, just a few houses north of Aaron Kozminski's brother's sweating workshop on Greenfield Street.

Indeed, it would be impossible to consider Kozminski as a suspect in the Jack the Ripper murders without understanding the rising tide of anti-Semitism in the East End of London in the years prior to the murders. By 1888, the year of the murders, anti-Jewish sentiment had been building up in the East End for almost a decade, and political agitators were giving expression to what William Fishman referred to as "the irrational hatred festering in the mind of the slum dweller."[85] There was a distinct possibility that pogroms and riots would break out in East London, and the Jewish sweaters who ran tailoring workshops were in the firing line, being turned into scapegoats by anti-Semites and Jewish socialists alike. All of this is arguably significant in considering the type of environment that nurtures the intense anger and hatred that give rise to a serial killer.

We will later examine an FBI survey of serial killers that found that the desire to kill was motivated in part by an "ineffective social environment." As the study noted, "The child's memories of frightening and upsetting life experiences shape his developing thought patterns." Such factors included a "perception of unfair treatment by adults and authority figures."[86] As we have seen, Aaron Kozminski lived in hostile anti-Semitic environments for his entire life. In considering him as a suspect in the Ripper murders, it may be argued that the tension between Jews and gentiles in the East End, which appeared to be at a breaking point in late 1887 and early 1888, laid the groundwork for the unleashing of violence that would soon follow.

On February 21, 1888, the *East End News* printed an interview with Captain Colomb, MP for Bow and Bromley, who stated, "I object to England with its overcrowded population, being made a human ashpit for the refuse population of the world." Three weeks later was the first meeting of the House of Lords Committee on the Sweating System, the reports of which would bring even more pressure to bear on the East End's most popular scapegoat, the "social plague" known as the Jewish sweater. As had happened earlier in Russia, government committees again seemed poised to attack, ready to blame the Jews—this time for unfair labor competition and for being a general "pest and a menace to the poor native-born East Ender."[87] The social atmosphere was volatile. Given such mounting pressure, it seemed inevitable that something was sure to break.

In fact, it already had.

Alexander II of Russia, "the Czar Liberator." His emancipation of the Russian serfs in 1861 was called "a piece of philanthropy never equaled in the history of man."

Gesya Gelfman, a member of the revolutionary group Narodnya Volya (the People's Will). Gelfman was the only Jew involved in the assassination plot, and her role was greatly exaggerated in the Russian press.

The assassination of Alexander II on March 13, 1881. Ignacy Hryniewiecki stepped forward and threw a bomb that blew the czar's legs to pieces. A little more than an hour later, the czar had bled to death. The assassination sparked a wave of anti-Jewish pogroms in southwest Russia.

Beginning in April 1881, anti-Jewish pogroms broke out in more than two hundred locations in the southwestern regions of the Pale of Settlement. One officer who traveled for a time with a correspondent of the *Jewish Chronicle* said that he had "seen things that sickened him to think of."

A street devastated by the pogroms. The total destruction of property was estimated as high as 100 million rubles. After the pogrom in Elizavetgrad, the town looked "as if it has been devastated by the elements. Whole streets have been literally razed."

Aaron Kozminski was born
in this small village in 1865.
These photos are circa 1910.

A photo from my trip to Kłodawa in May 2008. It is a small village in western Poland
that seems detached from the modern world.

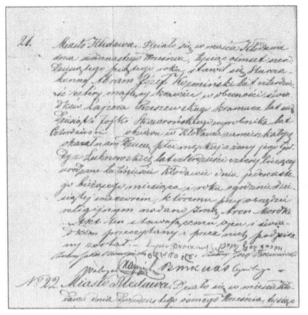

Aaron Kozminski's birth certificate. Aaron Mordke Kozminski was born on September 11, 1865, a son of Abram Josef Kozminski (tailor) and Golda Lubnowski (Goldy Lubnowskicz). Abram died when Aaron was nine years old.

The Vampire of the Sweatshop, frontispiece of *Songs of Labour* by Morris Rosenfeld (1914). "The sweatshop at midday, I'll draw you the picture: a battlefield bloody."

A tailoring workshop on Christian Street, circa 1900. Isaac Abrahams's workshop on Greenfield Street probably looked similar to this. Like the shop pictured above, Isaac's shop also had a skylight and the same number of employees.

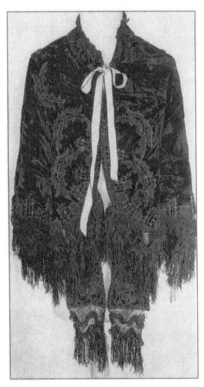

A late Victorian–era mantle, circa 1880s.

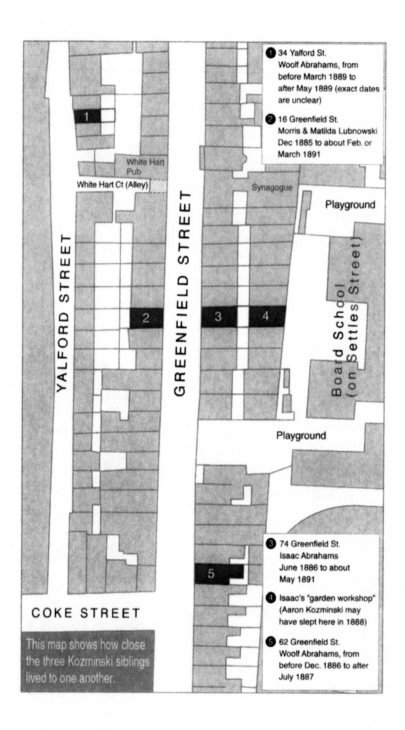

1 34 Yalford St.
Woolf Abrahams, from
before March 1889 to
after May 1889 (exact dates
are unclear)

2 16 Greenfield St.
Morris & Matilda Lubnowski
Dec 1885 to about Feb. or
March 1891

White Hart
Pub

White Hart Ct (Alley)

YALFORD STREET

GREENFIELD STREET

Synagogue

Playground

Board School
(on Settles Street)

Playground

3 74 Greenfield St.
Isaac Abrahams
June 1886 to about
May 1891

4 Isaac's "garden workshop"
(Aaron Kozminski may
have slept here in 1888)

5 62 Greenfield St.
Woolf Abrahams, from
before Dec. 1886 to after
July 1887

COKE STREET

This map shows how close
the three Kozminski siblings
lived to one another.

58

Greenfield Street today, looking north. None of the original buildings remain on this street. The arrow points to the approximate location of 74 Greenfield Street, where Aaron's brother Isaac lived, with the "garden workshop" in the backyard.

Another shot of Greenfield Street, looking south. Isaac lived on the left, and Morris and Matilda lived directly opposite at number 16 (on the right).

What used to be Yalford Street is now just an alley off Fieldgate Street. Number 34 Yalford Street was the address of Woolf Abrahams. The houses on this street were described as "without water supply or dustbins" and with the woodwork "rotten through filth." "The stones of the yard exuded when trodden upon damp filth," and "overpowering smells, from the condition of the houses, pervaded the interiors."

The "White Hart" pub on Greenfield Street in the 1880s, headquarters of the Anti-Tailor Strike Committee. This pub was just six doors north of Isaac's tailoring workshop. The entrance to White Hart Court can be seen next to the ladder. This alley led to Yalford Street, where Woolf Abrahams lived.

Christ Church, on Commercial Street in March 1909. The church was then, and still remains, the dominant architectural feature of the district. Next door was the Ten Bells, a pub frequented by several of the Ripper's victims. In 1976, it was briefly renamed the "Jack the Ripper."

Whitechapel High Street with St. Mary Matfelon Church in the distance in the 1890s. This thoroughfare would have been Kozminski's most direct route home after the Eddowes murder, but because it was such a busy street, he probably avoided it. St. Mary Matfelon was close to the geographical center of the murders. Emma Smith claimed that she was accosted by some youths who were hanging around in front of St. Mary's, and Polly Nichols was last seen alive drunkenly walking down the street across from it. Kozminski lived about one minute's walk from the church.

Wentworth Street in modern days. This street was parallel to and north of Whitechapel High Street and was quite possibly Aaron Kozminski's route home after the Eddowes murder.

PART TWO

1888

5

The Murders Begin

Homo sum, humani nil a me alienum puto. [I am a man and reckon nothing human alien to me.]

—*Publius Terentius Afer, second century* B.C.

On February 25, 1888, a woman named Annie Millwood was admitted to the Whitechapel Infirmary with numerous stab wounds in the "legs and lower part of the body." According to a newspaper report, she had been the victim of a "most violent and brutal attack . . . by a man who she did not know, and who stabbed her with a clasp knife which he took from his pocket."[1] The article added, "No one appears to have seen the attack, and as far as at present ascertained there is only the woman's statement to bear out the allegations of an attack, though that she had been stabbed cannot be denied."[2] It is not clear where the attack took place, whether indoors or out, but Millwood's address was in the middle of what would later be the territory of Jack the Ripper. Annie's condition "progressed favourably," and she was transferred to South Grove Workhouse about a month later.

Just a month after the attack on Millwood, another unusual attack occurred two miles to the east, in Mile End. At 12:30 a.m. on

Wednesday, March 28, several "screams for help were heard" from a house on a small thoroughfare called Maidman Street.[3] Two women nearby heard the screams and ran to Mile End Road, where they found two police constables of K Division standing outside the Royal Hotel. The police rushed back to 19 Maidman Street, where they "found a young woman, named Ada Wilson, lying in the passage, bleeding profusely from a fearful wound in the throat." Little is known about the nature of this wound, but, as Wilson's neighbor Rose Bierman said, it "must have been deep, I should say, from the quantity of blood in the passage." A doctor arrived shortly afterward and bandaged the wound, then sent Wilson to the London Hospital, "where it was ascertained that she was in a most dangerous condition." At the hospital, Wilson soon recovered enough that she was able to describe the attack. According to Wilson, she had been about to retire to bed when "a total stranger" knocked on her door and told Wilson to give him money, warning, "if she did not at once produce the cash she had but a few moments to live." When Wilson refused, the man took a clasp knife out of his pocket and stabbed her twice in the neck, then ran off, apparently frightened away by Wilson's screams. Wilson described her "would-be murderer" as about five and a half feet in height, thirty years old, with a sunburned face, a dark coat, and a "wide-awake" hat, similar in style to a cowboy hat. Although it was initially thought "impossible that the injured woman can recover," Wilson's condition gradually improved, and she was discharged as "cured" a month later.[4]

The details of the attack came entirely from Wilson herself, but there is some evidence to suggest that she may have been lying. Bierman made a statement the day after the attack that was printed in the *Eastern Post and City Chronicle*. "I knew Mrs. Wilson as a married woman," Bierman said, "although I had never seen her husband. Last evening she came into the house accompanied by a male companion, but whether he was her husband or not I could not say."[5] Bierman added that Wilson was "under notice to quit" her lodgings at the time the attack occurred. Her statement continued,

> Well, I don't know who the young man was, but about mid-
> night I heard the most terrible screams one can imagine.
> Running downstairs I saw Mrs. Wilson, partially dressed,

wringing her hands and crying, "Stop that man for cutting my throat! He has stabbed me!" She then fell fainting in the passage. I saw all that as I was coming downstairs, but as soon as I commenced to descend I noticed a young fair man rush to the front door and let himself out. He did not seem somehow to unfasten the catch as if he had been accustomed to do so before.[6]

Bierman's statement suggests the possibility that Wilson was in fact a prostitute, and that the man was a client in her house. Ripperologist Quentin Pittman has theorized that Wilson might have lied for reasons of "pride and appearance." Pittman argued, "Being robbed was one thing, but admitting you were an unfortunate [a Victorian term for a 'low prostitute'], and your client had savagely wounded you was quite another offence altogether."[7] The attack took place on the first day of Passover. As Mrs. Bierman, whom the newspaper described as "a young Jewess," said, "I am now 'keeping the feast,' and how can I do so with what has occurred here?"[8]

By an odd coincidence, Wilson's house on Maidman Street was only a few hundred yards from South Grove Workhouse, where at the time of the attack Annie Millwood was recuperating from her own stabbing that occurred a month earlier. The doctors seemed to think that Millwood was recovering well, but suddenly, on March 31, she was "observed to fall, and on assistance being given it was found that she was dead."[9] The coroner's inquest ruled that Millwood's death was due to "natural causes."[10] A report of her death was printed in the *Eastern Post and City Chronicle* on Saturday, April 7. By then, however, yet another brutal attack had taken place.

The previous Tuesday, April 3, at around four or five in the morning, a prostitute named Emma Smith stumbled into her lodgings on George Street. She had been severely beaten, her right ear was nearly torn off, and she was holding a bloody woolen wrap between her legs. Smith told the deputy of the lodging house that she had been "shockingly ill-treated by some men" and was "badly injured in the region of the abdomen."[11] After she was rushed to the London Hospital, it was discovered that the blood between her legs came from a torn peritoneum, the thin membrane that lines the abdominal wall and covers most of the organs of the body. Smith was able to describe the attack to the house surgeon Dr. G. H. Hillier, before slipping into a coma. Smith "was reticent with regard to the details but distinctly denied having addressed the men in solicitation."[12] She died the following day. Dr. Hillier made a postmortem examination of the body and determined that death had been caused by peritonitis resulting from injuries to the abdomen, the peritoneum, and the perineum. He noted that Smith "appeared to know what she was about," but that she had been drinking.[13]

Emma Smith was a forty-five-year-old widow, rumored to be a "common prostitute of low type." It was said that she often went out at night and returned at "all hours, sometimes very drunk," and that she "acted like a madwoman when in that state."[14] She had been last seen at 12:15 that Tuesday morning, a Bank Holiday, at the corner of Farrance Street and Burdett Road, Limehouse, talking to a man who wore dark clothes and a white scarf. The woman who saw Smith noted that she herself had been "struck in the mouth a few minutes before by some young men," and added, "the quarter was a fearfully rough one."[15] Smith was later returning home when two or three young men, one of whom Smith described as a youth of about nineteen, began to follow her from St. Mary Matfelon Church on Whitechapel Road. Near Taylor's Cocoa Factory at the corner of Brick Lane and Wentworth Street, the youths beat her, and then one of them, horrifically, rammed some sort of "blunt instrument," apparently with great force, into her vagina. She was robbed and left to die.[16]

Somehow, Smith made it back to her lodgings and was taken to the hospital by the deputy lodging house–keeper, Mary Russell, and other lodgers, who claimed, for some reason, that they "didn't think it necessary to report the circumstances to the police."[17] As a result, the police did not learn about the attack until three days later, when they were informed that an inquest was to be held. The police inquiry of the murder was put in the hands of a forty-two-year-old "clever East End detective" named Edmund Reid, who in 1887 had replaced Frederick Abberline as the local inspector of H Division (Whitechapel). Unfortunately, Reid's investigations went nowhere. At the inquest, conducted by the East Middlesex Coroner Wynne E. Baxter, it was determined that Smith had been murdered by "some person or persons unknown." "It was impossible to imagine a more brutal and dastardly assault," Baxter said.[18]

From what little we now know, it seems probable that Emma Smith fell victim to a violent gang of youths. Yet there are some curious aspects to the story. For one thing, the newspaper report of the inquest states that Smith "seemed unwilling to go into details, did not describe the men nor give any further account of the occurrence to witnesses."[19] In addition, Smith apparently did not want to notify the police about the attack. These facts may suggest that she, like Ada Wilson, invented the story about the gang to conceal the fact that she was a prostitute and to cover her shame at being attacked by a customer, who then beat and sexually assaulted her. But such speculations must be left for the time being.

In an interesting coincidence, another rather brutal attack occurred the same night Smith was assaulted. The details are vague, but it appears that a thirty-four-year-old woman named Malvina Haynes was stabbed in the vicinity of the Leman Street railway station. A police constable, alerted by her screams, found Haynes lying in a pool of blood with a "scalp wound of rather an extensive character." When she was later asked about the details of the assault, Haynes replied, "I cannot remember, my mind is gone."[20] Very little is known about this incident or about the nature of her wounds.

Most researchers dismiss the notion that Jack the Ripper committed any of the attacks mentioned here. By contrast with the Ripper's later technique, the modus operandi in all cases appears to have been clumsy, and all of the victims were left alive by their attackers. Yet the possibility remains that any of these crimes may have been early Ripper attacks, and I will reexamine them later in the book. Still, horrific as they were, the events of early 1888 were just an opening act. Four months after the murder of Emma Smith, an even more ferocious and mysterious murder occurred, again on the night of a bank holiday and a mere hundred yards from the spot where Smith had been attacked.

6

Martha Tabram

On Saturday, August 4, 1888, the actor Richard Mansfield presented London with the first stage performance of Robert Louis Stevenson's popular story *The Strange Case of Dr. Jekyll and Mr. Hyde* at the Lyceum Theatre in Westminster. The story concerned Dr. Henry Jekyll, an upper-class doctor who is repeatedly transformed into the sadistic monster Mr. Hyde after drinking a potion concocted in his lab. The *Times*'s review of the play was not very positive, although the reviewer did admit that Mansfield's performance was "morbidly fascinating." The *Daily News*, on the other hand, described the performance as a work of genius. "Whenever Mr. Mansfield becomes Hyde," the reviewer said, "his savage chuckles, his devilish gloating over evil, his malignant sarcasms, his fierce energy of hate and revelling in all sinful impulses awaken strange sensations in the spectator."[1] Like the notorious twentieth-century serial killer Ted Bundy, Jekyll was "constantly haunted with a horror of the crimes of his other self." The theatrical effort, coming as it did in the middle of a rather "dull period of the dramatic calendar," was judged to be a good omen. Luckily for the dullness of the theatrical season, a much more compelling drama soon began to unfold on the streets of the East End.

That following Monday was a rather gray bank holiday, characterized by a "dull leaden sky" and "more or less rain."[2] Thousands of

London's residents visited the city's various indoor attractions, including Madame Tussaud's, the Zoological Gardens in Regent's Park, the Tower of London, and the People's Palace. In the evening, they went out on the town, attending the theaters and the music halls, before returning home in a damp rain.

In Whitechapel, it was another typically rough night, and two "very noisy and quarrelsome" brawls reportedly took place on Wentworth Street. According to a newspaper account, a Mr. and Mrs. Reeves reported that a disturbance started at "the dead wall of Leterworth Buildings, in George Street. The first row commenced about 11:30 p.m., followed by another at 12:20 a.m., when both Mr. and Mrs. Reeves asserted they heard cries of 'Police!' 'Help!' and terrible screaming." Sometime after 1 a.m., more fights broke out. Then at 2 a.m. more piercing screams were heard. The article added, "Only a few roughs seemed to constitute this crowd, which seemed to be moving in the direction of George Yard."[3] Nothing more is known about these street brawls, but such incidents were not uncommon, given the "desperate character of the neighbourhood."

At 4:45 a.m., a dock laborer and a tenant of nearby George Yard Buildings named John Saunders Reeves was leaving home to look for work when he discovered a woman lying on her back in a pool of blood on the second-floor stone-staircase landing.[4] Reeves rushed off to get help and soon returned with P.C. (police constable) Thomas Barrett of H Division. Barrett found the woman lying with her arms at her sides with her fists clenched, her legs spread open, and her clothes pulled up, exposing her abdomen and genitals.[5] She had been dead for at least an hour. Another tenant in the building, a cabdriver named George Crow, had actually stumbled across the body at around 3:30 a.m., but it had been too dark to see, and Crow assumed that the woman was a passed-out drunk, because he was "accustomed to seeing people lying about there."[6] Earlier that night, a little before 2 a.m., another resident, Mrs. Mahoney, passed the same spot with her husband and saw no one. The superintendent of George Yard Buildings, Mr. Francis Hewitt, later pointed out that although his room was a mere twelve feet from the spot of the murder, he had heard nothing on the night in question.[7] In short, no one had seen or heard any disturbance at all.

P.C. Barrett sent for Dr. Timothy Killeen in nearby Brick Lane. Killeen arrived by 5:30 a.m., at which time he estimated that the woman had been dead for about three hours. The body was then taken in an ambulance (in those days, a hand-pushed carriage) to what served as Whitechapel's "mortuary"—in fact, just a shed in the yard of the Whitechapel Workhouse Infirmary in Eagle Place, off Old Montague Street.

On August 9, the deputy coroner George Collier initiated an inquest into the woman's death at the Working Lads' Institute on Whitechapel Road. At that time, the identity of the victim—a heavy-set woman, about five feet three inches in height, who appeared to be in her forties—was still a mystery. As the superintendent of George Yard Buildings noted, however, "Although the deceased is not known by name, her face is familiar. She is undoubtedly an abandoned female."[8] Collier took the testimony of several witnesses and then adjourned the inquest for a fortnight. Detective Inspector Edmund Reid was again left in charge of the investigation.

By August 16, Henry Tabram of East Greenwich had identified the murdered woman as his wife, Martha.[9] Tabram, a foreman packer at a furniture warehouse, claimed that he and his wife had separated thirteen years earlier. When asked why, Tabram replied, "Drink, sir; she drank."[10] Martha Tabram was a thirty-seven-year-old "common prostitute," who in many respects matched the profile of the majority of the Ripper's later victims. One witness at the inquest, Mrs. Mary Bousfield of Commercial Road, claimed that Martha was an occasional street hawker, who dealt in "needles, pins, menthol cones, &c," and added, "she would rather have a glass of ale than a cup of tea."[11] Bousfield added that the deceased woman was her lodger and that she went by the name Turner. In fact, Martha had been living with a carpenter named Henry Turner on and off for the last twelve years, and the couple had separated only three weeks previously.

The murder inquiry seemed to get off to a good start, because the police had a promising lead to follow up. The lead came from none other than P.C. Barrett himself. Barrett had been on duty in George Yard on the night of the murder, and about 2 a.m. he encountered a grenadier of the Tower Guards in Wentworth Street at the north end of George Yard, who claimed to be "waiting for his mate who had gone away with a girl."[12] Barrett later described the soldier as age twenty-two to twenty-six years, five feet nine or ten inches, with dark hair and a small mustache turned up at the ends. Furthermore, Barrett said that he would recognize the man again. Thus, on the morning after the murder, Inspector Reid arranged an identity parade of guardsmen at the Tower of London. Unfortunately, the identification proved to be a confused affair, and the guardsman whom Barrett ultimately identified was able to provide a solid alibi. Inspector Reid was forced to conclude that the young constable had "made a great mistake."[13]

Then another witness came forward. Two days after the murder, a large and somewhat manly looking prostitute named Mary Ann Connelly (aka "Pearly Poll" or "Mogg") informed the police that she and Tabram had been drinking at several pubs on Whitechapel Road with two soldiers between 10:00 and 11:45 p.m. on the night in question. The women then took the soldiers off to separate locations for "immoral purposes." Connelly went into Angel Alley with one of the soldiers, a man she called "the corporal," and Tabram went into George Yard with the other, apparently a private. "We parted all right," Connelly said, "and with no bad words; indeed we were all good friends. I know nothing of what became of [the] deceased after we left her."[14] Some thirty or forty minutes later, Connelly and her client went their separate ways near the corner of George Yard, and the "corporal" walked off toward Aldgate.

Connelly told the police that she would recognize the soldiers if she saw them again, so Inspector Reid arranged a second lineup at the Tower the next morning.[15] Connelly didn't show up for the identification, but she was eventually tracked down and agreed to attend an identity parade on Monday, August 13. A description of the incident was reported in the Echo:

> "Pearly Poll" was asked, "Can you see here either of the men you saw with the woman now dead?" "Pearly Poll" in no way embarrassed, placed her arms akimbo, glanced at the men with the air of an inspecting officer and shook her head. This indication of a negative was not sufficient. "Can you identify anyone?" she was asked. "Pearly Poll" exclaimed, with a good deal of feminine emphasis, "He ain't here."[16]

Connelly then informed Inspector Reid, somewhat belatedly, "They are not here they had white bands around their hats."[17] This meant the soldiers were likely Coldstream Guards, so Reid arranged for yet another identification to take place at the Wellington Barracks in Pimlico on August 15. On this occasion, Connelly picked out two privates and declared that she was positive of her identification. One of them was a man named George, whom Connelly referred to as "the corporal." The other was a man named Skipper, who, according to Connelly, was the man who went off with Tabram. Skipper was shown to have returned to the barracks by 10 o'clock on the night of the murder. George, on the other hand, had indeed been away from the barracks on the night of Tabram's murder and, as stated in the *Echo*, "that circumstance, coupled with the fact of 'Pearly Poll's' certainty as to his features, at first placed him in rather an awkward position." But George was able to prove his whereabouts on that night "beyond doubt."[18] Inspector Reid concluded that Pearly Poll was an unreliable witness and that her evidence was worthless.

In any case, it seems unlikely that the soldiers Connelly described had anything to do with the murder. The evidence suggests that Tabram was murdered between 2:00 and 3:30 a.m., and, as Chief Inspector Swanson wrote in a report on the murder, "two and a quarter hours had elapsed" between the time Tabram went off with the soldier and the earliest time she could have been murdered. As Swanson pointed out, "A close inquiry did not elicit that she had been seen with any one else than the soldier, although from the lapse of time, it is possible she might have been."[19]

Tabram's wounds were frightful. Dr. Killeen's postmortem found that Tabram had been stabbed numerous times in an apparently frenzied attack targeting the chest, the upper abdomen, and the neck. "On examining the body externally I found no less than thirty-nine punctured wounds," Killeen reported, mostly in the torso and the neck.[20] In addition, there was one larger and deeper wound to the heart, which apparently penetrated the breastbone. According to Killeen, this wound must have been caused by some sort of "sword-bayonet or dagger," whereas the rest of the wounds might have been done with a "penknife." The building superinten-dent, Mr. Hewitt, who saw the body in situ, described this wound specifically. There was "blood flowing from a great wound over her heart," he said. "There were many other stab wounds of a frightful character on her."[21] As the *Echo* pointed out, the one stab to the heart was sufficient to kill, and "if the lesser wounds were given before the one fatal injury, the cries of the deceased must have been heard by those who, at the time of the outrage, were sleeping within a few yards of the spot where the deed was committed." The paper added, "Unless the perpetrator were a madman, or suffering to an unusual extent from drink-delirium, no tangible explanation can be given of the reason for inflicting the other thirty-eight injuries."[22]

The exact nature of Tabram's wounds is difficult to determine, because the newspaper reports of Dr. Killeen's inquest testimony varied somewhat in details. For example, a report printed in the *Evening News* on August 10 stated, "Dr. Kaleene [*sic*] . . . found 39 punctured wounds on the body and legs."[23] Of all of the papers that covered the inquest, this is the only mention of any wounds in "the legs." Most of the newspaper accounts listed twenty-one puncture wounds in the organs—five in the left lung, two in the right lung, one in the heart, five in the liver, two in the spleen, and six in the stomach. Yet one newspaper, the *East London Observer*, noted the existence of an additional wound: "The lower portion of the body was penetrated in one place, the wound being three inches in length and one in depth."[24] The exact location of this three-inch cut "in the lower portion of the body" is not given, but Chief Inspector Donald Swanson, in his summary report of the murder, noted that there were "39 wounds on body, and neck, and private part."[25] This mention of a wound in the "private part" is almost certainly a reference to the same wound that the *Observer* claimed was in the "lower portion of the body."[26] The fact that the other newspapers did not remark on the wound at all suggests that they deemed this detail of Killeen's testimony too obscene to print. The *Observer* also noted that "there was a deal of blood between the legs, which were separated"—this was another detail that was not specified in any of the other newspaper accounts.[27] In other words, both the *Evening News*'s mention of a wound in the "legs" and the *Observer*'s comment on a wound in the "lower portion of the body" were both probably referring to the same wound and were simply euphemisms for "genitalia." In this respect, it is perhaps important to remember that the victim

Annie Millwood was described as having "numerous stabs in the legs and lower part of the body."[28]

To illustrate the point, we need only compare two similarly worded extracts of Killeen's testimony in the *East London Observer* and the *East London Advertiser*, both of which were printed on August 11. In each version, Killeen's testimony is given in the same sequence, and both papers use almost the same wording to describe the twenty-one specific puncture wounds to the organs. Then, the *Observer* continued, "The lower portion of the body was penetrated in one place, the wound being three inches in length and one in depth. From appearances, there was no reason to suppose that recent intimacy had taken place."[29]

Whereas the *Advertiser* wrote only, "Dr. Keeling then described where the wounds had been made, and in answer to questions stated positively that there were no signs of there having been recent connexion [sexual intercourse]." It is perhaps also relevant to point out that the coroner "thanked Dr. Keeling for the very careful way in which he had given his testimony."[30]

Evidence also seemed to indicate the possibility that Tabram was strangled. The *Illustrated Police News*, for example, reported that Tabram was "throttled while held down, and the face and head so swollen and distorted in consequence that her real features are not discernible."[31] Thus, it seems likely that the attacker first strangled Tabram and then intended to kill her with a stab to the heart, followed by multiple stabs in the torso and the throat.

The jury returned a verdict of "murder by a person or persons unknown," and Inspector Reid informed the court, "Careful inquiries are still being made with a view to obtain information regarding the case." In his closing comments at the inquest, the coroner remarked, "For a poor defenceless woman to be outraged and stabbed in the manner which this woman had been was almost beyond belief."[32]

In the aftermath of this latest horror, the citizens of the district began to worry that there was a madman on the loose. On August 10, the *Echo* reported on the similarity between the murders of Martha Tabram and Emma Smith, who, the paper said, had been killed by some miscreant "thrusting a walking-stick or other blunt weapon into her body with great violence." "For ferocity, the two cases are somewhat analogous," the report concluded, "and some of the Scotland-yard experts in tracing criminals and fathoming crime incline to the opinion that one man is responsible for the two crimes."[33] Tabram's murder was indeed remarkable for its viciousness, even for the violent East End. "No crime more brutal has ever been committed in the East-end," said an unnamed officer of the Criminal Investigation Department (CID) on the day of the inquest.[34] The *East London Advertiser* reported on August 11, "The virulent savagery of the murderer is beyond comprehension." And Mr. Collier, the deputy coroner at the inquest, noted, "It is one of the most terrible cases that anyone can possibly imagine. The man must have been a perfect savage to have attacked the woman in that way."[35]

Unfortunately, Inspector Reid's inquiries went nowhere. Then another violent murder, three weeks later, seemed to confirm everybody's worst fears.

7

Polly Nichols

Mary Ann ("Polly") Nichols was forty-three years old and somewhat short, with brown hair that was turning gray and a number of front teeth missing. When Polly, the daughter of a blacksmith, was only eighteen, she married a printer named William Nichols. The couple had five children, but according to William, his wife was "much given to drink," and by 1880, the marriage was in shambles.[1] The couple separated, and Polly left the children with her husband. For a few years, she lived with a blacksmith named Thomas Drew, but then she separated from him as well. After that, Polly's life appears to have taken a downward turn, and by 1888 she was living in the East End and scraping out a meager living as a prostitute.[2] In fact, as Neal Shelden noted in his book *The Victims of Jack the Ripper*, "It is difficult to know how long she had lived the life of a streetwalker," and it is possible that Nichols had been working on and off as a prostitute since about 1880.[3]

By August 1888, Polly Nichols was sharing a bed in a common lodging house at 18 Thrawl Street with another prostitute, named Emily Holland (aka Jane Oram). Around August 24, Nichols moved to the White House, a "doss" amid the rookery of Flower and Dean Street.[4] Flower and Dean Street was described as "perhaps the foulest and most dangerous street in the whole metropolis," and it was said that the police were afraid to venture too far into this den of crime at night.[5] One who did "was threatened by a man standing on a kerbstone, who held a large stone in his hand and said 'If you come a step further, I'll knock your brains out with the stone!'"[6]

On the rain-swept night of August 30–31, Nichols had some drinks at the Frying Pan Public House on Brick Lane, then returned to her previous lodgings at Thrawl Street, where she sat in the kitchen, somewhat drunk and completely broke. Around 1:30 a.m., the deputy of the lodging house kicked Nichols out because she did not have money to pay for a bed. Polly told the deputy to save a bed for her. "Never mind! I'll soon get my doss money," she said. "See what a jolly bonnet I've got now."[7]

About an hour later, Emily Holland ran into Nichols at the corner of Whitechapel High Street and Osborn Street, "nearly opposite the parish church." According to Holland, Polly was "much the worse for drink and staggering against the wall."[8] Holland tried to convince Nichols to go back to the lodging house and share her bed, but Polly declined, stating, "I've had my doss money three times today and spent it." She added, "It won't be long before I'm back."[9] After Holland left, Polly wobbled off down Whitechapel Road, heading east.

The spot where Nichols spoke to Holland—"nearly opposite the parish church" (that is, St. Mary Matfelon)—was very close to the same location where Emma Smith had passed the two or three young men who then followed and attacked her. It was also only a two-minute walk from the site of the Tabram murder. Walking east down Whitechapel Road, Nichols would soon pass the Whitechapel Bell Foundry at the corner of Fieldgate Street, where the American Liberty Bell had been cast in 1752. The foundry, just 250 yards from where Nichols was last seen, was less than a one-minute walk from Greenfield Street, where Aaron Kozminski was probably living at the time. Nichols was unaware that she was walking into the hunting grounds of a predator.

Forty-five minutes later, at 3:15 a.m., P.C. John Neil of J Division (97J) was patrolling his beat along a "narrow, cobbled, mean street" named Buck's Row, just half a mile east of where Nichols was last seen. Buck's Row was a dark and gloomy street, dimly lit by only one gas lamp at its far end. On its south side were "dirty little houses of two stories," and opposite were "the high walls of warehouses which at night would shadow the dirty street in a far deeper gloom than its own character would in broad day light suggest."[10] At the west end of the street was the black, looming shape of a board school. P.C. Neil noticed nothing out of the ordinary at the time and continued on his beat.

Half an hour later, at approximately 3:40 or 3:45 a.m., a carman (a person who drove a horse-drawn vehicle for delivering goods) named Charles Cross was walking west down Buck's Row on his way to work when he noticed a dark shape that looked like a tarpaulin, lying in front of a locked gateway that led to a small stable yard. As Cross got closer, he saw that the shape was in fact a woman. He hesitated, unsure of what to do, and then out of the silence heard footsteps approaching behind him. It turned out to be another carman, named Robert Paul, also on his way to work. "Come and look over here," Cross said. "There is a woman lying on the pavement." The two men approached the body, but it was too dark to see much of anything. Cross felt the woman's hands, which were cold and limp, and said, "I believe she is dead." Paul then put his hand on the woman's chest. "I think she is breathing, but very little if she is."[11] The woman's dress was pulled up almost to her stomach, and Cross thought it looked like she had been "outraged and gone off in a swoon." Paul pulled down the woman's clothes.

Cross and Paul were both "behind time" (that is, late for work) and didn't want to stop very long, so they continued down the street, hoping to find a policeman along their way. About eight hundred feet away at the corner of Baker's Row and Hanbury Street, they encountered P.C. George Mizen and informed him of what they had seen. "She looks to me to be either dead or drunk," Cross said. "But for my part I think she is dead."[12] Mizen left to investigate. It was a little before 4 a.m.

A few minutes earlier, P.C. Neil's beat had taken him back into Buck's Row, where he then also came across the woman lying on the side of the street. He stooped down to lift the woman up, assuming she was drunk, but then in the light of his lantern, noticed that her throat was cut "almost from ear to ear." As Neil stated later, "I examined the body by the aid of my lamp, and noticed blood oozing from a wound in the throat. She was lying on her back, with her clothes disarranged."[13] The woman's legs were extended and a little bit apart.

Various policemen soon arrived on the scene. P.C. John Thain had been walking along Brady Street when Neil signaled to him with his bull's-eye lantern. Neil sent Thain to fetch the local surgeon, Dr. Rees Ralph Llewellyn. When P.C. Mizen arrived, Neil sent him for an ambulance. Meanwhile, Neil went across the street to Essex Wharf to inquire whether anyone had seen anything, but no one had. About this same time (4 a.m.), a night watchman named Patrick Mulshaw was guarding a worksite in Winthrop Street, just one street south of Buck's Row, when a man passed by and said, "Watchman, old man, I believe somebody is murdered down the street."[14] When Mulshaw went into Buck's Row, he saw three or four policemen and a number of other men standing around the body.

When Dr. Llewellyn arrived at approximately 4 a.m., he noted that the body was still warm and estimated that the woman had been dead for no more than half an hour, placing the time of death at sometime around 3:30 a.m. Because a small crowd was starting to gather, Llewellyn ordered that the body be taken to the Whitechapel infirmary mortuary, where a further examination could be conducted. The police constables carted Polly's body off to the Whitechapel mortuary, and it was not until her corpse had been undressed and placed in a black coffin at the mortuary that attendants noticed that her abdomen had been mutilated.

Dr. Llewellyn's postmortem examination revealed that Nichols had been savagely butchered. In his inquest testimony, Llewellyn stated that Nichols had "severe injuries to her throat"—specifically, two parallel incisions cut from left to right. One of these, an eight-inch-long gash, "completely sever[ed] all the tissues down to the vertebrae. The large vessels of the neck on both sides were severed."[15] Llewellyn also made the manifestly obvious point that he was "quite certain that the injuries to her neck were not self-inflicted." His testimony continued:

There were no injuries about the body till just about the lower part of the abdomen. Two or three inches from the left side was a wound running in a jagged manner. It was a

very deep wound, and the tissues were cut through. There
were several incisions running across the abdomen. On the
right side there were also three or four similar cuts running
downwards. All these had been caused by a knife, which had
been used violently and been used downwards.[16]

Here we see the first real evidence of the Ripper's signature abdominal mutilations, as there was one long, deep cut in the lower abdomen,
from which the woman's intestines were protruding. In some respects,
Nichols's wounds seem to have been similar to those of the previous
victim, Martha Tabram. The nature of the cuts, with a knife, "which
had been used violently and been used downwards," seems to suggest
a stabbing motion. Also, there were "two small stabs on [the] private
parts," which, as before, were not mentioned in newspaper accounts.[17]
In addition, the long gash in the lower abdomen sounds at least
somewhat similar to the three-inch-long cut in the lower portion of
Tabram's body.

The murders were fast becoming a sensation, and newspapers all
over the world picked up the story, drawing attention not only to
the murders themselves but also to the deplorable conditions and
the depravity of the East End. A letter printed in the Echo noted,
"Thousands who read the Echo have not the faintest idea of the terrible state of things which exist in these parts."[18] The author claimed
that the number of "fallen" women in the district was increasing
greatly. "The drink houses are the great attraction for these wretched
women. Is it not high time that something be done to check this
sad state of things?" In the aftermath of the Nichols murder, some
attention was focused on a "High Rip" gang as the likely perpetrator
of this and the previous murders. Yet the police, although briefly
considering this possibility, soon began to think otherwise. As the
Times reported, the murder had "so many points of similarity with
the murder of two other women in the district—one Martha Turner,
as recently as August 7, and the other less than 12 months previously—that the police admit their belief that the three crimes are
the work of one individual." The report added, "The investigation
into the George-yard mystery is proceeding hand-in-hand with that
of Buck's-row."[19]

Polly Nichols's funeral was held on September 6, and large crowds came out to see her funeral cortege as it passed through Whitechapel. According to the *Echo*, "The hearse and two mourning coaches were followed by a concourse of people for a considerable distance along the Whitechapel-road."[20] The crowd was augmented by a large number of Jews who were observing the holiday of Rosh Hashanah and were thus not at work that day. In all likelihood, Aaron Kozminski watched as the funeral procession went somberly along Whitechapel Road past St. Mary's church.

8

The Police

To my great joy I was posted to "H" division, which meant—
Whitechapel. The dread of most young constables, it was my
father's wish. "If ever you do join the Force," he once said, "I
hope they send you to Whitechapel. It will make a policeman of you." And it did!

—*Ex-detective sergeant Benjamin Leeson*

By September 4 or 5, newspapers began to report that the police
were on the lookout for a thug with the ominous-sounding
name "Leather Apron." According to a CID report, Leather
Apron became a suspect in the murders "on account of his alleged
levying blackmail on prostitutes and assaulting them if they did not
comply with his request."[1] The newspapers' descriptions were frightening. An American reporter who ventured into the East End to ask the
locals' opinion on the murders was told that the murders had likely
been committed by "a 'wild looking man, wearing a leather apron,'
who had been seen about in Whitechapel lately, and was believed
to be an escaped lunatic."[2] A report in the *Star* claimed that Leather
Apron was "a Jew or of Jewish parentage, his face being of a marked

Hebrew type," and "a more ghoulish and devilish brute than can be found in all the pages of shocking fiction."[3] News of the creature quickly spread across the Atlantic, where the *Atchison* (Kansas) *Daily Globe* described Leather Apron as "half way between Dickens' Quilp and Poe's baboon."[4] By September 6, the police were still attempting to arrest Leather Apron, who was now described as a "crazy Jew," but they were unable to locate him.

Leather Apron's real name was Jack Pizer, as noted in a report submitted to Scotland Yard by Inspector Joseph Helson of J Division: "A man named Jack Pizer, alias Leather Apron, has for some considerable period been in the habit of ill using prostitutes in this, and other parts of the Metropolis."[5] Pizer was a Jewish thirty-eight-year-old boot finisher of Polish extraction, who stayed at various lodging houses in the district. When he discovered that he was the prime suspect in the case, and fearing a lynch mob, Pizer went into hiding at his stepmother's house on Mulberry Street.

It is easy to see why Pizer was afraid. The press reports clearly played into the East End locals' fear and resentment of Jews, and the implied racism in the articles is self-evident—indeed, they made Pizer sound more like a monster from a cheap horror novel than a human being. It was after the appearance of the newspaper reports putting forth Leather Apron as a suspect that a truly violent anti-Semitism began to fester in the East End.

By this time, the unsolved murders were becoming a real headache for the police. The investigation was the responsibility of London's Metropolitan Police Force (aka the MET), the jurisdiction of which included the vast majority of London and the East End. The only area in London outside of the MET's territory was the City of London, the so-called square mile that included the old portion of London that had been inside the city's fortresslike walls. This area was under the control of a completely separate City of London Police Force, which was (up to this point) not involved in the murder inquiries. The MET consisted of 23 police divisions, 30 superintendents, approximately 800 inspectors, 1,350 sergeants, and roughly 12,000 police constables (P.C.'s).[6] The P.C.'s were generally divided into beat constables, who patrolled circular beats, and fixed-point constables, who stood in one location so as to be readily located in case of trouble. The duties of the MET roughly broke down to two main functions: the prevention of crime, which was the responsibility of uniformed police constables, and the investigation of crimes already committed, which was the responsibility of detective inspectors under the direction of the Criminal Investigation Department or CID. At the time of the Whitechapel murders in 1888, the head of the MET was Commissioner Sir Charles Warren, an ex-army officer who had previously been the administrator of various British colonial interests. Directly under Warren was James Monro, an ex-inspector general of police in India, who was both assistant commissioner in charge of the CID, and director of the Special Irish Branch, a small but highly secretive unit of spies within the MET that collected intelligence on terrorist threats from Irish Fenian groups. Up to that point, the Whitechapel murder inquiries had been in the hands of H Division inspector Edmund Reid, a capable and well-respected detective with sixteen years' experience. After the Nichols murder, however, the investigation was ramped up, and the ground inquiries were delegated to Inspector Frederick Abberline of Central Office CID and Inspector Joseph Helson of J Bethnal Green Division. Abberline was assigned to the case because of his previous experience as an inspector in Whitechapel and his knowledge of crime in the East End, which was said to be unsurpassed. The force of police constables in H Division was also augmented by men drafted in from other divisions, as well as by a team of plainclothes detectives especially assigned during the murders.

In the late 1880s, there was a great deal of friction between the Metropolitan Police and the Home Office—the former wishing to operate without interference, the latter concerned that the police were not always forthcoming with information—and both were regularly excoriated by the press for their perceived shortcomings. Home Secretary Henry Matthews regularly clashed with Police Commissioner Charles Warren, who in turn micromanaged the affairs of his underlings to such an extent that CID chief James Monro noted in his unpublished memoirs that the Home Office et al., "nearly drove me frantic . . . attempting to direct a police inquiry instead of letting the responsible police officers do the duty."[7] Warren was also frustrated that Monro, his subordinate at the MET, was able to circumvent the chain of command due to his double role as head of the Special Branch. The two men did not get along, and had divergent views on police procedure. As a result of such frustrations, Monro resigned his four-year tenure as head of CID at the end of August 1888, just prior to the murder of Polly Nichols. His replacement in the job was a forty-seven-year-old Irish ex-barrister and spymaster named Robert Anderson.

Anderson came to head the CID in a rather roundabout fashion. In his early twenties, after spending some time in law school, he had flung himself into the "long life of a Christian witness," traveling around Ireland as part of a small team of faith missionaries and trying to convert the uninitiated to the ways of Christ and the Gospel. Anderson seems to have enjoyed his work as a lay-preacher and noted many "happy blessings" in his diary from this period. In one entry he wrote, "A gentleman said that a week ago he was the vilest wretch in the county, but now saved." The missionaries preached in church buildings or, when that was not available, "in schoolrooms, court-houses or jury-rooms, in private houses, cottages or barns, once at least in a ballroom, at times in the open air."[8] "We are living in the pilgrim fashion," he wrote to his sister. Anderson later reminisced about this period of his life, noting that he was "greatly humbled by the record of the work there."[9] He would remain devoted to religious study throughout his life and wrote numerous well-received, yet controversial, books on biblical exegesis and interpretation.

Anderson, however, was not destined to remain a missionary. Through family connections, he gradually "drifted into Secret Service work," first by writing a summary of the history of the militant Irish Fenians who were dedicated to the mission of overthrowing British rule in Ireland and establishing an independent Irish Republic. To achieve their goal, the Fenians employed both politics and terrorism, frequently bombing various locations in central London, including Scotland Yard itself. Anderson's expert knowledge of Fenian organizations eventually became known in high official circles, and he was called to London to deal with Irish terrorist threats to domestic security and to report to the Home Office on political crime in general.[10] In this role, Anderson was given access to the detective department of the MET, where he soon "got to know all that was worth knowing about their work."[11] Among other things, Anderson's responsibilities included interrogating prisoners and infiltrating the ranks of London's Fenians by planting informants within their numbers.

One of Anderson's top spies was a man named Thomas Beach. British by birth, Beach was drawn to a life of adventure and wandering, and at the outbreak of the Civil War in America, he crossed the Atlantic and enlisted in the Northern Army under the assumed name Henri Le Caron. It was during this time that Le Caron (as he would henceforth be known) made the acquaintance of John O'Neill, who would later become head of the American Fenians. Through O'Neill, Le Caron learned of various Fenian plots, and after the war he decided to serve his country by infiltrating Fenian organizations as a spy for England. Le Caron initially wrote about the Fenian plots in letters to his father. When the letters were shown to a local Member of Parliament, Le Caron was put in touch with the Home Office, where he met Robert Anderson. Le Caron would serve as a British spy for the next twenty years, until he was finally outed as a spy during the Parnell Commission, a judicial inquiry that gravely damaged Anderson's reputation and threatened a scandal at a high level of government.

Anderson ran in elite circles, hobnobbing with the rich and powerful. He was invited to become a member of "Gossett's Room," a social club whose membership was generally limited to members of Parliament. In addition to advising the Home Office on political crime, Anderson served in other capacities, including as secretary of the Royal Commission on Loss of Life at Sea and secretary of the Prison Commission. He also was on the Royal Observatory of Edinburgh Commission, and in this capacity Anderson came to befriend the committee chairman, James Ludovic Lindsay, the twenty-sixth Earl of Crawford. The two men shared an interest in astronomy.

By 1880, Anderson had begun lose interest in Secret Service work, and, as he later wrote, he had "openings for other work, both literary and professional, which would have made me independent of it."[12] But then an increase in Fenian bombings in London led to the creation of a new intelligence organization called the Special Irish Branch. At the request of the Home Secretary, Sir William Harcourt, Anderson was "drawn back into Secret Service work," both advising the Home Office on the creation of the new department and acting as a liaison in daily conference with its head, Adolphus Williamson.[13] In the following years, James Monro took over as head of the Special Branch and as chief of the CID and was in both capacities at the start of the Ripper murders in 1888. After Monro's resignation in August of that year, Anderson was appointed to the post of assistant commissioner (crime) of the Metropolitan Police and chief of the CID.

Operationally speaking, the Special Irish Branch was a suborganization within the MET, which employed many of the same detective methods as the CID—namely, the use of informants, the collection of information on suspected Fenians, and surveillance of suspected members. Monro, who retained his role as head of the Special Branch after his resignation from CID, maintained ties with his previous office in an unofficial capacity. The two departments were closely intertwined, and their functions often overlapped. Thus, it is highly likely that Monro was kept abreast of developments in the Ripper case, even though the case was not handled by his department.

Likewise, with his extensive background as a spymaster and an expert on Fenian activities, Robert Anderson was well acquainted with the inner workings of intelligence agencies such as the Special Branch. The Ripper murders would be his trial by fire. At the time of his appointment, however, Anderson was in such a state of fatigue from overwork that his doctor ordered him to take sick leave on the continent to recuperate. And thus, with notoriously bad timing, Scotland Yard's new head of CID departed for a holiday in Switzerland on September 7, leaving the department without effective leadership just as the Ripper murders were getting under way. The day after Anderson's departure, while Leather Apron was still in hiding from both the police and the East End mobs, another murder occurred. Anderson's holiday was destined to be shorter than planned.

9

Annie Chapman

Annie Chapman was a middle-aged prostitute, short and stout, with dark hair, a thick nose, and a pale face. She was born Annie Eliza Smith in 1840 or 1841, the daughter of George Smith, a private in the 2nd Regiment of Life Guards.[1] In 1864, when Annie was in her early twenties, her father committed suicide, coincidentally by cutting his own throat. Five years later, Annie married a coachman named John Chapman. The couple had three children. The oldest daughter, Emily, died of meningitis at the age of twelve, and a son named John was born a cripple in 1880. After this, Annie started drinking heavily. Eventually, she and her husband separated, apparently because Annie's drinking and "immoral ways" forced the couple to move off the estate where he was employed. Also, it seems that Annie was stealing from her husband's employer.[2]

After the separation, Chapman moved to Spitalfields and began to work as a prostitute. As her friend Amelia Palmer put it, Chapman "was not very particular what she did to earn a living."[3] By June 1888, Chapman had taken up residence in "Crossingham's," a lodging house at 35 Dorset Street that was run by a man named Timothy Donovan. Dorset Street was in contention with Flower and Dean Street as one of the most criminal locations in the entire East End. "It was a street of whores," Ralph Finn wrote in his memoirs, which "teemed with nasty

characters—desperate, wicked, lecherous, razor-slashing hoodlums."[4]
By the late 1880s, Chapman had become involved with a bricklayer
named Edward Stanley. The two were together only on weekends, but
Stanley frequently paid for Chapman's bed at Crossingham's and told
Donovan to kick her out if she tried to enter the lodging house with
any other man.[5]

Around September 1, 1888, Chapman got into a fight with a woman
named Eliza Cooper, another prostitute who was said to be a rival for
Stanley's affections. It seems that an argument broke out between
the two women at the Britannia pub, where they were drinking with
Stanley and another man, called Harry the Hawker. Then later, back at
Crossingham's, Chapman slapped Cooper in the face and said, "Think
yourself lucky I did not do more." In retaliation, Cooper punched
Chapman, giving her a black eye. When Donovan later noticed the
black eye, Chapman remarked, "Tim, this is lovely, ain't it."[6]

For the next few days after the fight, Chapman did not stay at
Crossingham's, and her whereabouts during this time are unknown.
When Amelia Palmer ran into Chapman on September 3 on Dorset
Street, Chapman showed her the bruises from the fight with Cooper and
said she was feeling sick. The following day, Palmer again saw Chapman
near Christ Church on Commercial Street, and Chapman again said
that she felt sick and wanted to go to the casual ward (a free clinic).
Annie claimed that she had not eaten anything that day, so Palmer gave
her two pence for a cup of tea. "Don't have rum," Palmer said.[7]

The next day, Palmer encountered Chapman on Dorset Street.
She claimed that "she felt too ill to do anything." "I must pull myself
together and go out and get some money," she said, "or I shall have no
lodgings."[8] By 11:30 that night, Annie was somewhat "the worse for
drink" and returned to Crossingham's, where she sat in the kitchen
and shared a beer with another lodger. She then went to the Britannia
pub and continued to drink, but within two hours she was back at
Crossingham's, eating a baked potato. The night watchman asked
Chapman for money for her bed, but she didn't have it. She went to
see Tim Donovan and told him, "I have not any money now, but don't
let the bed; I will be back soon." "You can find money for drink, but
not for your bed," Donovan chided her. When Chapman left around
2 a.m., she told the night watchman, "I won't be long, Brummy. See

that Tim keeps the bed for me." Her whereabouts for the next three and a half hours are unknown.[9]

Just a five-minute walk north of Crossingham's was Hanbury Street, described as a "foul, stinking neighborhood where the children are stunted little creatures with vicious faces, old features, and where the women's faces would frighten one."[10] At 4:45 a.m., a man named John Richardson entered 29 Hanbury Street, where his mother, Amelia, a packing-case maker, both lived and had a workshop in the basement. The front door led from the street into a hallway that went to the back door, which opened onto a fenced-in yard about fifteen feet square. Both the front and the back doors were normally unlocked, and after a recent break-in, Richardson had been in the habit of stopping by to make sure the basement was secure and to throw out prostitutes who used the first-floor landing and the yard for "immoral purposes." After checking the basement door (the entrance of which was off the yard), he sat on the steps at the back door to cut away a piece of leather that was protruding from his boot. He later said that he had seen nothing unusual at the time.[11]

About a half-hour later, just as the sun was rising, a woman named Elizabeth Long was walking along Hanbury Street toward Spitalfields Market, when she passed a man and a woman standing on the sidewalk, close against the shutters in front of number 29. The man was turned away from Long, but the woman was facing her, and Long later identified the woman as Annie Chapman. The man and the woman were talking loudly, and Long overheard the man ask, "Will you?" to which Chapman replied, "Yes."[12] "I did not see the man's face," Long later said, "but I noticed that he was dark. He was wearing a brown low-crowned felt hat. I think he had on a dark coat, though I am not certain. By the look of him he seemed to me a man over forty years of age. He appeared to me to be a little taller than the deceased." She described the man as "what I should call shabby-genteel," and added, "He looked like a foreigner."[13] "Foreigner" was a euphemism meaning "Jew."

Next door to 29 Hanbury Street was the residence of a carpenter named Albert Cadosch. Around 5:20 a.m. Cadosch went into his backyard, apparently to use the outhouse. A wooden fence, five and a half feet tall, separated his yard from the yard of number 29, and when Cadosch was returning to the back door of his house, he heard a voice from the other side of the fence say, "No!" Cadosch went back inside, then reentered the yard three or four minutes later. This time he heard "a sort of fall against the fence." Unfortunately, Cadosch did not look over the fence. Instead, he went back inside and then left for work. When he passed the clock at Spitalfields Church, it was 5:32.[14]

It was shortly after 5:45 a.m. when a resident at 29 Hanbury Street named John Davis entered the backyard and made a shocking discovery. Sprawled between the steps and the fence was the severely mutilated body of a woman. The woman was lying on her back with her clothes disarranged and her legs drawn up, and there was blood everywhere. Davis was terrified and ran out of the house. He returned with some men who had been working at a packing-case maker's a few houses down, but the men were too afraid to go into the yard and instead went off to find a police officer. When Inspector Joseph Chandler of H Division showed up, it was about 6:15, and there were several people standing in the passage. Chandler briefly surveyed the situation and then sent for the divisional surgeon, Dr. Bagster Phillips, who lived only a few minutes away in Spital Square. After Dr. Phillips arrived, Chandler carefully examined the crime scene and searched the yard. The body was then taken to the Whitechapel mortuary in the same ambulance that had carted Polly Nichols's body there a little more than a week ago.

Word of this new murder sent the residents of the East End into a panic. "The excitement in the neighborhood of Whitechapel this morning is intense," an article in the *Echo* stated. "The discovery of this terrible crime, following as it does so rapidly upon the murders in George-yard and Buck's-row, seems to have paralyzed the inhabitants with fear. All business in the vicinity of the scene of the murder, has, apparently, for the time, been stopped. The streets were, this morning, swarmed with people."[15] The newspapers did a roaring business selling the latest editions, and it was not long before everyone was discussing all of the gory details of the latest crime. One woman reading a newspaper account of the murder was apparently so affected that she collapsed "in a fit" and died a few days later. She had been "killed by emotion," the *Star* reported.[16]

The inquest, which began two days later, only served to increase the panic. Dr. Phillips's testimony on the third day of the inquest made it clear that not only had Chapman been brutally mutilated, but the killer had apparently tried to decapitate her. "There were two distinct clean cuts on the body of the vertebrae on the left side of the spine," Phillips stated. "They were parallel to each other, and separated by about half an inch. The muscular structures between the side processes of bone of the vertebrae had an appearance as if an attempt had been made to separate the bones of the neck."[17] According to Phillips, the cause of death was a severed carotid artery resulting from a jagged left-to-right incision across the throat. Phillips thought that Chapman had been "partially strangled" before her throat was cut, and he pointed out, "The tongue protruded between the front teeth, but not beyond the lips. The tongue was evidently much swollen." Phillips also noted that "The small intestines and other portions were lying on the right side of the body on the ground above the right shoulder, but attached."[18]

Phillips then mentioned "various other mutilations of the body" but added that these were so gruesome that it would be too "painful to the feelings of the jury and the public" to describe them. He argued that he did not see any point in detailing the postmortem mutilations at all, because his descriptions up to that point were already sufficient for the court to determine cause of death. Coroner Wynne Baxter accepted this line of reasoning, apparently satisfied that the doctor had a record of the wounds. Baxter subsequently changed his mind and recalled Dr. Phillips several days later, telling him that it was necessary that "all the evidence the doctor had obtained from his post-mortem should be on the records of the Court for various reasons which he need not then enumerate, however painful it might be."[19] The two men argued back and forth for a few minutes, until Dr. Phillips finally agreed to describe the mutilations, but only after all of the women and the children had been cleared from the inquest chamber.[20] The evidence he gave was omitted from the *Times* report of the inquest, because it was deemed "totally unfit for publication," and several people in the inquest chamber apparently fainted as he gave it.[21] The following summary was reported in the *Lancet*:

> Mr. Phillips . . . stated that the mutilation of the body was of such a character as could only have been effected by a practised hand. It appears that the abdomen had been entirely laid open; that the intestines, severed from their

mesenteric attachments, had been lifted out of the body, and
placed on the shoulder of the corpse; whilst from the pelvis
the uterus and its appendages, with the upper portion of the
vagina and the posterior two-thirds of the bladder, had been
entirely removed. No trace of these parts could be found,
and the incisions were cleanly cut, avoiding the rectum,
and dividing the vagina low enough to avoid injury to the
cervix uteri.[22]

Phillips's opinion that the mutilations indicated "a practised hand"
led the police to wonder whether the murderer might be a doctor or
someone with rough anatomical knowledge, such as a butcher. The
question of whether the Ripper had anatomical knowledge was later
debated by other doctors, and it has been a controversial topic among
Ripper scholars ever since.

Without a doubt, however, the most shocking aspect of Phillips's
testimony was that the killer had removed the "uterus and its appendages with the upper portion of the vagina and the posterior two thirds
of the bladder" and had taken the organs with him. Today, it is known
that such behavior—taking body parts as "souvenirs" of a murder—is
not uncommon among serial killers. Yet in Victorian times, there was
little awareness of serial murder at all, either by the public or by the
police. "What kind of monster could do such things?" people wondered. Naturally, people looked for a theory to explain what seemed
unexplainable. The Telegraph, for example, warned that the East End
was prowled by "beings who look like men, but are rather demons,
vampires."[23] Some people suggested that the murderer was a religious
maniac or a member of a cult, and that the murders were part of some
sort of bizarre ritual.

Right from the start, one of the most common theories was that
the murderer was a madman who had escaped or been recently released
from a lunatic asylum. "This angle of investigation was pursued relent-
lessly," wrote Metropolitan Detective Chief Inspector Walter Dew in
his memoirs. "Inquiries were made at asylums all over the country,
including the Criminal Lunatic Asylum at Broadmoor, with the object
of discovering whether a homicidal lunatic had been released as cured
about the time the Ripper crimes commenced."[24] Inspector McWilliam

of the City of London CID likewise noted in a *Report to the Home Office* (October 29) that officers had been sent "to all the lunatic asylums in London to make enquiry respecting persons recently admitted or discharged: many persons being of the opinion that these crimes are of too revolting a character to have been committed by a sane person."[25] It is likely that such inquiries covered both asylums and workhouses, and that officials at these institutions were instructed to contact the police if any promising suspects turned up.

Yet in the eyes of many East End residents, there was an even more likely suspect: the Jew. As we have seen, anti-Semitism in Whitechapel had already reached a dangerous level even before the murders, and thus the East End Jewish immigrant fell under suspicion from very early on. The immigrant Jew presented a perfect scapegoat for the locals' need to lay blame for the murders on some outside, mysterious, and incomprehensible alien entity. The Leather Apron scare only increased the locals' suspicions, and the result, inevitably, was a further dramatic increase in anti-Semitism in the East End. After Annie Chapman's murder, crowds of native British locals began to assume a much more openly threatening manner toward Jews in the East End and said they would lynch the murderer if they found him. In fact, a riot very nearly broke out on the day after the murder, as reported in an article titled "A Riot against the Jews" in the *East London Observer*:

> On Saturday in several quarters of East London the crowds who had assembled in the streets began to assume a very threatening attitude towards the Hebrew population of the district. It was repeatedly asserted that no Englishman could have perpetrated such a horrible crime as that of Hanbury-street, and that it must have been done by a Jew—and forthwith the crowds proceeded to threaten and abuse such of the unfortunate Hebrews as they found in the streets. Happily, the presence of the large number of police in the streets prevented a riot actually taking place.[26]

As *Lloyd's Weekly* reported, "Bodies of young roughs raised cries against the Jews, and many of the disreputable and jabbering women sided with them. This state of things caused several stand-up fights, thus putting a further and serious strain on the police, many of whom began to express their fears of rioting."[27] Noisy crowds roamed the streets, shouting "Down with the Jews!" and the police had a difficult time keeping things under control. Three days later, the *Evening News* printed a letter from a City police constable named George Henry Hutt under the heading "Slaughtering the Jews":

> I found it difficult to traverse the streets in the vicinity of the Whitechapel, without observing in almost every thoroughfare, knots of persons (consisting of men, women and children), and overhearing their slanderous and insulting remarks towards the Jews, who occasionally passed by. With justice to my countrymen, I mention that the foul epithets was made use of by people of the most ignorant and dangerous class, promoted by the information they had casually obtained that a man known as "Leather Apron" had a Jewish appearance, and was wanted for the recent Whitechapel murders.[28]

Whether Leather Apron was the Ripper or not, his mere existence was like an open wound that aggravated the tension between the East End's Jews and gentiles. The police must have been at least somewhat relieved, therefore, when on September 10, the day before Hutt's letter was printed, Leather Apron was finally arrested at his stepmother's house by Detective Thicke.

After the arrest, the police thoroughly investigated Pizer's alibis and found that they checked out. Ultimately, the police discovered absolutely no evidence connecting Pizer with the murders, and they had no option but to release him. The police then allowed Pizer to give testimony at the inquest, apparently in the hopes of defusing any threats of mob vengeance against both him and the Jews in general. When asked why he went into hiding, Pizer declared, "I will tell you the reason why. I should have been torn to pieces."[29] After Pizer testified as to his whereabouts on the night of the Chapman murder, the coroner added, "I think it only fair to say that this statement can be corroborated." Pizer then sat down next to Sergeant Thicke, looking "somewhat pale and worried." When Pizer later exited the building, he was "recognized at once," according to the *East London Advertiser*, and "the murmurs and mutterings from the crowd which greeted his appearance boded no good." Sergeant Thicke walked him home.[30]

Pizer was thus exonerated, and the name "Leather Apron" quickly faded from the public's attention. As George Sims put it, "Most people are beginning to see that Leather Apron has probably as much to do with the Whitechapel murders as the Archbishop of Canterbury or the Baroness Burdett-Coutts."[31]

By September 14, the tensions had eased somewhat, and the *Jewish Chronicle* reported that within the last week, "the foreign Jews in the East End of London have been in some peril—though happily averted."[32] The article drew parallels to the pogroms of Eastern Europe, noting, "It is so easy to inflame the popular mind when it is startled by hideous crime, that sensation-mongers incur a fearful responsibility when they add to the excitement by giving currency to every idle rumour." But if the police thought that Pizer's exoneration would put an end to the anti-Semitic tensions in the East End, they were mistaken, and the newspapers continued to report on various "clues" that seemed to point to a Jewish killer. As noted in the *Jewish Standard*, "So inflamed was the popular mind, so convinced was it that 'Leather Apron' was the murderer, that had he been captured by the crowd Lynch Law would have almost certainly been put into operation. As Piser plaintively said, he would have been torn in pieces. And not only so, but the whole Jewish quarter would have been in danger of attack."[33] The Jewish community, sensing the impending danger of the situation, rallied together in solidarity with their English neighbors, to show that they were as eager as anyone to discover the culprit. The Jewish MP for Whitechapel, Samuel Montagu, offered a reward for the capture of the criminal, and the Mile End Vigilance Committee, which had been formed to "strengthen the hands of the police" and patrol the streets, seconded the offer. The Vigilance Committee, headed by a man named George Lusk, was largely made up of Jewish tradesmen.[34]

On September 10, just two days after Chapman's murder, the *Daily Telegraph* reported that the police were looking for a man "with a foreign accent" who had "entered the passage of a house at which the murder was committed with a prostitute at 2 a.m., the 8th." The source of this story is a bit of a mystery. According to several newspaper reports, a woman named Emily Walton accompanied a man into one of the backyards on Hanbury Street at 2:30 a.m. on the eighth—just three hours before Chapman was murdered. Once in the yard, the man began to treat Walton roughly, until her screams scared the man off. It is not clear if there was any truth to this story, however, and it may well be a false lead, as Walton did not appear at the inquest. Whatever the source of the police telegram, more damage had been done, since the description of the man "with a foreign accent" cast further suspicion on the Jews.

Then, on September 19, Elizabeth Long gave her evidence at day four of the inquest, and it was revealed that the man she saw with Annie Chapman on the morning of the murder "looked like a foreigner."[35] It was now on record that the murderer might have been a Jew.

During this period, the police kept busy chasing down leads and arresting suspects, but ultimately, they all seemed to go nowhere. And because the new head of CID, Robert Anderson, was still on vacation, overall command of the investigation was still effectively in the hands of his subordinate, Chief Constable Adolphus Williamson. As the panic increased, and the press continued to comment on the absence of Scotland Yard's leader, Commissioner Warren decided to give responsibility for the entire investigation to Chief Inspector Donald Sutherland Swanson. A letter from Warren to the acting assistant commissioner of CID (in Anderson's absence) instructed,

> [Swanson] must be acquainted with every detail. I look upon him for the time being as the eyes and ears of the Commr. in this particular case. He must have a room to himself, & every paper, every document, every report every telegram must pass through his hands. He must be consulted on every subject. I would not send any directions anywhere on the subject of the murder without consulting him. I give him the whole responsibility.[36]

Thus it was that on September 15, Donald Swanson was put in charge of what would become the most famous murder investigation in history. Four days later, Commissioner Warren was forced to admit to the Home Office, "No progress has as yet been made in obtaining any clue to the Whitechapel murderers. A great number of clues have been examined & exhausted without finding any thing suspicious."[37] And then on September 27, the Central News Agency received a letter written in red ink, in a neat cursive hand, from a person claiming responsibility for the crimes.

> Dear Boss,
>   I keep on hearing the police have caught me but they wont fix me just yet. I have laughed when they look so clever and talk about being on the right track. That joke about Leather Apron gave me real fits. I am down on whores and I shant quit ripping them till I do get buckled. Grand work the last job was. I gave the lady no time to squeal. How can they catch me now. I love my work and want to start again. You will soon hear of me with my funny little games. I saved some of the proper red stuff in a ginger beer bottle over the last job to write with but it went thick like glue and I cant use it. Red ink is fit enough I hope ha. ha. The next job I do I shall clip the ladys ears off and send to the police officers just for jolly wouldn't you. Keep this letter back till I do a bit more work, then give it out straight. My knife's so nice and sharp I want to get to work right away if I get a chance. Good Luck.
>   Yours truly
>   Jack the Ripper
>   Dont mind me giving the trade name
>
> PS Wasnt good enough to post this before I got all the red ink off my hands curse it No luck yet. They say I'm a doctor now. ha ha[38]

From the standpoint of those who wished to sell newspapers (and eventually books and movie tickets), the name Jack the Ripper was a godsend. It was like throwing a match into a vat of gasoline, igniting an interest in the case that has scarcely died down in the hundred and twenty years since the murders took place.

10

Elizabeth Stride

On September 30, around 12:45 a.m., a Hungarian immigrant named Israel Schwartz was walking home along Berner Street when he witnessed a disturbing scene unfold on the sidewalk before him. A "broad-shouldered" man ahead of him suddenly attacked a woman who was standing near the entrance to a dark courtyard called Dutfield's Yard. Schwartz was frightened and didn't want to get involved, so he crossed to the other side of the street, where he then noticed a second man standing at the corner lighting a pipe. The broad-shouldered man by this time had noticed Schwartz and shouted out something that sounded like "Lipski!" Schwartz hurried onward. He then began to think the "pipe-man" was following him, so he ran until he was safely away.[1]

A short time later, around 1 a.m., a man named Louis Diemschutz was driving his costermonger's barrow along this same stretch of Berner Street and turned into Dutfield's Yard—the same spot where Schwartz had witnessed an attack only fifteen minutes earlier. Dutfield's Yard was a narrow courtyard between two buildings. On the south side of the yard was a brick house, and farther back were several "terraced cottages, occupied by sweat shop tailors and cigar makers."[2] On the north side was 40 Berner Street, the two-story building that housed the International Workingmen's Educational Club, where Diemschutz was steward and manager. As mentioned earlier, the IWEC was a club of Jewish socialists and anarchists, mostly of Russian and Polish origin, and was the nexus of the assault on the capitalist exploitation by "sweaters" in the tailoring industry. A meeting of socialists had in fact ended shortly before Diemschutz arrived, and a number of people were lingering in the upstairs meeting room, talking and singing in Russian.

Diemschutz could not see much of anything as he steered his cart into the dark courtyard, but suddenly his pony recoiled and pulled to the left, apparently frightened by a shape lying next to the wall of the club. Diemschutz prodded the shape with his whip, then got down off his cart to investigate. He lit a match and briefly saw the figure of a woman before the wind blew out the match. Diemschutz rushed into the club and told his wife and several other club members that there was a woman lying in the alley but "that he was unable to say whether she was drunk or dead."[3] He grabbed a candle and rushed back to the yard with a man named Isaac Kozebrodsky. In the dim candlelight, the men saw that the woman was indeed dead and lying in a pool of blood.[4] Diemschutz's wife followed the men as far as the club door, and when she saw the woman's "ghastly" face and the blood trickling through the yard, she screamed. Diemschutz and Kozebrodsky ran off for help, shouting, "Police!"

Several people in the upstairs room went down to the yard to find out what was happening. One club member named Morris Eagle ran off with a companion in the direction opposite from that taken by Diemschutz and Kozebrodsky. On Commercial Road, the men found two police constables, P.C. Henry Lamb and P.C. Edward Collins, and returned with them to Dutfield's Yard. When P.C. Lamb arrived, he shone his lantern on the body. The woman was lying on her side with her knees drawn up in a sort of fetal position, and her throat had been cut. According to Lamb, "She looked as if she had been laid quietly down."[5] Lamb sent P.C. Collins to call for a doctor and then told Eagle to report the murder at the Leman Street police station. By this time, some twenty or thirty people had gathered in the yard, many of them from the club. Lamb tried to keep the crowd away from the body, because he didn't want anyone to get blood on his or her clothing. Then he closed the gate and stationed a constable outside to see that no one entered or left the yard.[6]

When Dr. Frederick Blackwell arrived around 1:16 a.m., he noted that the woman's face was still slightly warm, and he estimated that she had died only twenty or thirty minutes earlier. The woman's right hand was smeared with blood and lay across her breast, and her left hand, lying partly closed on the ground, "contained a small packet of cachous [breath fresheners] wrapped in tissue paper."[7] She was wearing a checked scarf around her neck, the knot of which was turned to the side and "pulled tightly," which gave Blackwell the impression that the killer had pulled the woman backward with the scarf, perhaps choking her so that she couldn't scream.[8] As the postmortem examination would later reveal, the woman's throat had been deeply cut from left to right. Unlike the previous victims, however, she had no abdominal mutilations. The police took down the names of the club members and then conducted inquiries at the crime scene until 5 a.m., by which time news of the murder had spread, and an excited crowd had gathered in front of the club.

The victim this time was Elizabeth Stride, a forty-five-year-old occasional prostitute from Gothenburg, Sweden, known locally as "Long Liz." For three years prior to her murder, Liz Stride had been in a relationship with a waterside laborer named Michael Kidney, who lived on Devonshire Street, Mile End. Kidney was said to have beaten Stride on occasion, apparently because he objected to her lifestyle, and as a result, the pair separated frequently. The last separation was only five days before Stride's murder, when the couple broke up after a "row." When Stride was not staying with Kidney, she frequently slept at 32 Flower and Dean Street in a doss house run by a woman named Elizabeth Tanner. According to Tanner, Stride was a charwoman by profession, and in the months prior to her murder, she had been "at work among the Jews" cleaning houses. Tanner claimed that Stride was a sober and quiet woman, but in reality she was an alcoholic who had been fined a number of times for drunk and disorderly behavior at Thames Magistrate Court.[9] Like many downtrodden women living in the East End, Stride resorted to prostitution when she couldn't find work.

There were several witnesses to events in the vicinity of the Stride murder. One witness, fifty-seven-year-old Matthew Packer, claimed that at 11 p.m. he sold some grapes to a man and a woman from the window of his house at 44 Berner Street, just south of Dutfield's Yard. The man had the look of a young clerk, Packer said, with broad shoulders, and a quiet but rough voice. He was age twenty-five to thirty and was about five feet seven inches tall, with a long, black, buttoned up coat, and a soft felt hat. "They passed by as though they were going up Commercial Road," Packer said in his October 4 police statement. "But—instead of going up they crossed to the other side of the road to the Board School, & were there for about 1/2 an hour till I should say 11.30, talking to one another. I then shut up my shutters."[10]

Packer was later taken to the mortuary, and he identified Stride as the woman he saw. There are problems with Packer's testimony, however. When he was originally questioned on the morning after the murder, Packer did not mention the incident at all but instead told the police, "I never saw anything suspicious or heard the slightest noise and know nothing about the murder until I heard of it in the morning." As Chief Inspector Donald Sutherland Swanson wrote in a report, Packer had "made different statements" and therefore "any statement he made would be rendered almost valueless as evidence."[11] Most Ripperologists likewise dismiss Packer as a credible witness.

Another witness, William Marshall, claimed to have seen a man and a woman "kissing and carrying on" around 11:45 p.m. on Berner Street between the intersections with Fairclough Street and Boyd Street, one block south of the murder location. The man was described as middle-aged, about five feet six inches, stout, and wearing a short black cutaway coat and a "round cap with a small peak," like a sailor's hat. It was dark, however, and Marshall did not get a good look at the man's face, although he thought the man looked like "he was in business, and did nothing like hard work." Marshall overheard the man say, "You would say anything but your prayers," to which the woman laughed. After talking for about ten minutes, the couple sauntered off toward Ellen Street, away from Dutfield's Yard.[12] After the murder, Marshall was taken to the mortuary, where he positively identified Stride as the woman he had seen. In any case, Marshall had witnessed this couple an hour before the probable time of the murder, so his evidence may be of little relevance.

Around 12:30 a.m., only fifteen or twenty minutes before the murder, P.C. William Smith, a twenty-six-year-old beat constable whose patrol included Berner Street, saw a man and a woman standing on the sidewalk opposite Dutfield's Yard. "I have seen the deceased in the mortuary," Smith later said at the inquest, "and I feel certain it is the same person."[13] The woman was talking to a man who was about twenty-eight years old, five feet seven inches tall, with a dark complexion and a small dark mustache. The man had a respectable appearance; was wearing dark clothes, an overcoat, and a hard dark felt deerstalker hat; and was carrying a newspaper-wrapped parcel approximately eighteen inches long by seven inches wide.[14] About ten minutes later, at 12:40 a.m., twenty-four-year-old Morris Eagle returned to the Workingmen's Club after walking his girlfriend home. He tried the front door but, finding it locked, walked around and entered the club through the side door in Dutfield's Yard. Eagle did not see anybody in or near the yard at this time, which is important, because he walked right through the dark portion of the yard where Stride's body was found only twenty minutes later. This suggests that the murder must have occurred after 12:40 a.m.[15]

Around the same time Eagle returned to the club, a dock laborer named James Brown left his house on Fairclough Street and walked to a shop at the corner of Fairclough and Berner streets to get his supper. When Brown left the shop three or four minutes later, he saw a man and a woman standing against the wall of the board school at the corner. Brown estimated that it was then around 12:45 a.m. but admitted that he had not looked at a clock recently. He overheard the woman say, "No, not tonight, some other night."[16] The man was about five feet seven inches and of average build, with a long dark overcoat that reached almost to his heels. Brown later claimed that he was "certain the woman was the deceased."[17] It seems, however, that he was incorrect in this identification, because the couple was later tracked down and questioned. As reported in the *Evening News*, "When the alarm of murder was raised a young girl had been standing in a bisecting thoroughfare not fifty yards from the spot where the body was found. She had, she said, been standing there for about twenty minutes, talking with her sweetheart, but neither of them heard any unusual noises."[18]

To add to the confusion, we have one final witness—Mrs. Fanny Mortimer. In a report printed in the *Daily News*, Mortimer claimed that she stood in the doorway of her house at 36 Berner Street, just a few doors north of the Workingmen's club, "nearly the whole time between half-past twelve and one o'clock this (Sunday) morning, and did not notice anything unusual."[19] She added, "A young man and his sweetheart were standing at the corner of the street, about 20 yards away, before and after the time the woman must have been murdered, but they told me they did not hear a sound."[20] This was probably the same couple seen by Brown at 12:45 a.m..

Mortimer's story is difficult to interpret, because she claimed to be outside for upward of a half hour between 12:30 and 1 a.m. but did not see anything, including the assault that Israel Schwartz witnessed at 12:45, practically right next door. Yet a report in the *Evening News* gave a slightly different version of the story. The report stated that Mortimer went outside shortly before 12:45 a.m., after hearing "the measured heavy stamp of a policeman passing the house on his beat," and then stood in the doorway for only about ten minutes. "The quiet and deserted character of the street appears even to have struck her at the time," the report added. Mortimer then went back inside and got ready for bed. A few minutes later, she heard Diemschutz's cart roll by, and then, shortly afterward, she heard all of the commotion following the discovery of Stride's body.[21]

It is difficult to make sense of all of this seemingly contradictory testimony, and as a result, the murder of Elizabeth Stride is now one of the most hotly debated aspects of the entire case. The crux of the problem is the testimony of Israel Schwartz, who saw a man attacking a woman (later identified as Stride) in front of Dutfield's Yard, only about fifteen minutes before Stride's body was discovered just a few yards away. It is a distinct possibility that Schwartz actually witnessed the Ripper in the act of committing a murder. The police seemed to think this was the case, and they clearly considered Schwartz an important witness. But our knowledge of the event is complicated by the fact that Schwartz did not appear at the public inquest into the Stride murder. Instead, Schwartz's testimony was apparently recorded in private proceedings, probably because the police did not want his description of Stride's attacker published in the newspapers. Their caution was futile, however, because a reporter from the *Star* newspaper tracked Schwartz down and got the story anyway.

The fact that the broad-shouldered man shouted "Lipski!" was a point of interest to the police. The use of the term "Lipski" was in all likelihood a reference to a widely publicized murder that had occurred a year previously in Batty Street, one street over from Berner Street. Israel Lipski was a Jewish immigrant umbrella salesman who had been convicted and hanged in 1887 for murdering a young pregnant woman named Miriam Angel by forcing her to consume nitric acid. As Detective Frederick Abberline pointed out, after the murder trial, "Lipski" was used as a sort of derogatory slang term in the East End in reference to Jews.[22] As an article in the Yiddish paper Die Tsukunft (The Future) from the time of the trial noted, "When Lipski is sentenced to death, the ordinary people taunted other Jews 'Lipski'!"[23] One theory, therefore, was that the broad-shouldered man shouted "Lipski!" as a taunt or a threat because of Schwartz's Jewish appearance. This might seem to suggest that the attacker was not himself Jewish. As it turns out, however, a recently discovered article has shown that Jews used the term Lipski as a derogatory insult as well, so we cannot assume that Stride's broad-shouldered attacker was not Jewish.

Many Ripperologists have accepted the theory that the Ripper was interrupted during the murder, thus explaining the notable lack of abdominal mutilations to Stride's body. Specifically, it has been proposed that Louis Diemschutz interrupted the Ripper at his bloody work when his cart rolled into Dutfield's Yard. Yet the problem with this theory is that there is a fifteen-minute gap between the assault witnessed by Schwartz at 12:45 and the discovery of the body by Diemschutz at 1 a.m.—ample time for the Ripper to have performed his typical postmortem mutilations. This conundrum has led some researchers to conclude that the broad-shouldered man was not the Ripper. Moreover, they argue, the attack witnessed by Schwartz was too clumsy and heavy-handed to have been committed by the Ripper.

There is a better explanation. The theory that the murderer was interrupted is probably correct, but in all likelihood, the interruption was not by Diemschutz, as is commonly argued, but instead by a much more obvious candidate—Schwartz himself. If the broad-shouldered man was the Ripper, then what Schwartz witnessed was almost certainly a murder in progress. The attacker must have been worried that Schwartz would return with the police, and he may also have feared that Stride's screams would attract attention, either from the people inside the club or from the young sweethearts Fanny Mortimer claimed were standing "at the corner of the street, about 20 yards away."[24] Clearly, it was not an ideal situation for committing a murder and then lingering about to perform postmortem mutilations on the body. Still, the Ripper must have realized that he could not let Stride live to identify him. He probably waited until Schwartz left, dragged Stride into the alley, and killed her quickly, then left the scene immediately afterward. This would place the murder around 12:45 a.m. or shortly thereafter—in agreement with Dr. Blackwell's estimate of the time of death as between 12:46 and 12:56 a.m.

The only problem with this scenario is that Mortimer claimed that she went outside shortly before 12:45 a.m., after which time she didn't see anybody at all. Of course, as with every witness that night, Mortimer's estimate of the time might not have been accurate. She claimed that she went outside after she heard the "measured heavy stamp of a policeman passing the house on his beat," and some researchers have suggested that this might have been P.C. Smith, patrolling his beat on Berner Street. But Dave Yost, in his article "Elizabeth Stride: Her Killer and Time of Death," proposed that "the idea that she heard a constable is not necessarily correct." Yost argued that the footsteps Mortimer heard might not have been those of P.C. Smith but instead were those of the murderer leaving the scene of the crime.[25] This suggests the possibility that Mortimer went outside shortly after the murder occurred and after the murderer left.

In summary, despite some lingering confusion over the exact sequence of events that night, we must endeavor to draw the simplest and most logical conclusions from the facts as we know them. Was Liz Stride a victim of Jack the Ripper? In my opinion, she almost certainly was. Other than the lack of abdominal mutilations, the Stride murder was generally consistent with the Ripper's modus operandi. The killer severed Stride's left carotid artery with a deep left-to-right cut and may have incapacitated her through strangulation.

In my opinion, it is also very likely that the broad-shouldered man seen by Israel Schwartz was Jack the Ripper. It is important to note that the man seen by Schwartz was very similar in description to the man described by P.C. Smith. Schwartz described the man he saw as "about 30; ht, 5 ft 5 in; comp[lexion] fair; hair, dark; small brown moustache, full face, broad shouldered; dress, dark jacket and trousers, black cap with peak, and nothing in his hands."[26] Whereas P.C. Smith described a man who was about twenty-eight years old, 5'7" tall, with a cleanshaven and respectable appearance, wearing dark clothes, an overcoat, and a hard dark felt deerstalker hat.[27] Schwartz and Smith may well have been describing the same person.

These descriptions also matched that of a man who was seen wiping his hands shortly after the murder. According to the October 1 *Star* newspaper, "A man, when passing through Church Lane at about half past one, saw a man sitting on a doorstep and wiping his hands. As everyone is on the lookout for the murderer the man looked at the stranger with a certain amount of suspicion, where upon he tried to conceal his face. He is described as a man who wore a short jacket and a sailor's hat." Church Lane was adjacent to St. Mary Matfelon, near the spot where Emma Smith was accosted and where Polly Nichols was last seen alive. The "short jacket" and "sailor's hat" essentially matches the broad-shouldered man's dark jacket and black peaked cap.

But more important, the above descriptions also matched the description of a man witnessed near the scene of a second murder that took place later the same night. For after Stride's murder, the Ripper was apparently unsatisfied and struck again, less than one hour later.

I I

Kate Eddowes

Some five hours before the murder of Liz Stride, a woman named Kate Eddowes was making a drunken spectacle of herself somewhere in the vicinity of St. Botolph's Church before passing out in a heap on the sidewalk on Aldgate High Street. Eddowes was another fairly typical East End prostitute. She was forty-six years old and had had a number of children with her common-law husband, Thomas Conway, before the two separated in 1881. The all-too-familiar reason given for the separation was Kate's drinking habits. After the split, Kate moved in with a man named John Kelly at a lodging house on Flower and Dean Street. Eddowes sometimes earned a living by hawking goods on the street, and also, like Liz Stride, she reportedly did "cleaning amongst the Jews."[1]

At 8:30 p.m., City P.C. Louis Robinson came across Eddowes lying on the sidewalk near the Bull Inn, smelling "very strongly of drink," with a crowd gathered around her. The constable asked if anyone knew the woman's name or where she lived. No one answered, so he picked up the woman and tried to sit her against the wall, but she fell down sideways. Robinson and another constable then took her to Bishopsgate Police Station. Eddowes was so drunk that she couldn't stand up without assistance, and when asked her name, she replied, "Nothing."[2] She was put in a cell to sober up. She remained asleep for several hours, but when the jailer George Henry Hutt checked on Eddowes shortly before midnight, she was awake and singing a song to herself. At 12:30 a.m., when Hutt checked on her again, Eddowes asked when she could be released. "When you are capable of taking care of yourself," Hutt said. "I can do that now," Kate replied. Hutt finally decided to release her a few minutes before 1 a.m. Eddowes asked what time it was. "Too late for you to get anything to drink," Hutt told her.

"Well, what time is it?" she persisted.

"Just on one," Hutt answered.

"I shall get a damn fine hiding when I get home," Kate said.

"And serve you right," Hutt said, opening the door to her cell. "You had no right to get drunk."

Eddowes was brought into the office to see the sergeant on duty, where she gave her name, falsely, as Mary Ann Kelly of 6 Fashion Street. Hutt then opened the door to the outside passage. "This way, missus. Please pull it to." "All right," Kate said. "Goodnight, old cock."[3] She left the Bishopsgate Police Station and stepped out into the black night.

Half an hour later, three men had just exited a Jewish club called the Imperial at 16–17 Duke Street and stepped outdoors into a rainy night. Joseph Lawende, a traveling salesman in the cigarette trade, Joseph Hyam Levy, a butcher, and Henry Harris, a furniture dealer, stood outside, facing the Great Synagogue, a large blockish building with high arched windows that stared down at them from across the street. Originally founded in 1690 as the first Ashkenazi synagogue in London, the Great Synagogue was probably the most important Jewish landmark in the entire East End. It was, according to historian Toni L. Kamins, "not only a synagogue, but also the community's center and its heart, and it was known throughout the world."[4] The synagogue was the domain of Hermann Adler, assistant to the chief rabbi of the British Empire, who (as previously mentioned) was one of the primary targets of ridicule by the antireligious socialists of the Berner Street Club and the *Arbeter Fraint* newspaper.

When Lawende, Levy, and Harris left the Imperial around 1:35 a.m., they noticed a man and a woman standing across the street from them, near the entrance of Church Passage, a narrow alley that ran alongside the synagogue. Levy turned to Harris and remarked, "Look there, I don't like going home by myself when I see those characters about." He added, "The court ought to be watched."[5] Levy later said he assumed that "persons standing at that time in the morning in a dark passage were not up to much good." Despite the fact that the couple was only fifteen feet away, Levy and Harris admitted that they took little notice of them. Lawende, however, apparently got a better look. He later gave a description of the man to the police and claimed that Kate Eddowes was dressed the same as the woman he saw that night.

At the other end of Church Passage, directly behind the synagogue, was a dark and desolate courtyard called Mitre Square. The court was roughly sixty feet square and dimly illuminated by only two lights—one freestanding gas lamp stood in front of the Kearley and Tonge tea and grocery warehouse on the west side of the square, and a second fixed lamp was attached to a building at the end of Church Passage in the east corner. Mitre Square was even darker than normal on this night because the freestanding lamp was deficient, either because "the quality of the gas supplied to the lamp was poor, gas pressure was low, or the mantle had corroded."[6] The southern corner of the square, a place frequently used by prostitutes, was blanketed in deep shadow.

Mitre Square was just within the easternmost boundary of the City of London and was thus under the jurisdiction of the City of London Police Force. Two City Police constables patrolled beats that went into the square. One of these, a City P.C. named Edward Watkins, walked a circuitous beat that took him through Mitre Square about every fourteen minutes. A second P.C., named James Harvey, walked an adjacent beat that took him along Duke Street past the Great Synagogue and then to the end of Church Passage facing Mitre Square. When P.C. Watkins entered the square at 1:30 a.m., he did not see anything unusual. Likewise, when P.C. Harvey walked down Church Passage around 1:40 and briefly looked into the square, he noticed nothing out of the ordinary and went back up the passage to continue his beat. (Harvey's estimate of the time came from the clock that was hanging outside the Postal Telegraph Office, Money Order, and Savings Bank at the corner of Duke Street.)

Watkins's beat took him back into Mitre Square at roughly 1:44 a.m. After entering from Mitre Street, he then turned right to continue counterclockwise around the square's perimeter. When Watkins turned his bulls-eye lantern toward the dark southern corner of the square, he saw a sight that would stay with him for the rest of his life. It was the body of a woman, horribly mutilated. "I saw her throat was cut and her bowels protruding," Watkins later said. The woman's stomach had been "ripped up, [and] she was lying in a pool of blood."[7]

Watkins ran across the square to the Kearley and Tonge warehouse, where he found the night watchman George Morris inside cleaning offices. "For God's sake, mate," Watkins cried, "come to my assistance!"

"Stop till I get my lamp," Morris replied. "What is the matter?"

"Oh, dear," Watkins said. "Here is another woman cut to pieces."[8] The two men went out into the square and briefly looked at the body, then Watkins told Morris to run and get help. The night watchman took off, blowing his whistle as he went up Mitre Street. In nearby Aldgate High Street, Morris found P.C. Harvey and told him about the murder, which undoubtedly came as a shock to Harvey, because he had looked into Mitre Square from the end of Church Passage only three or four minutes earlier. Harvey signaled to a second police constable across the street, and the three men returned to Mitre Square. Harvey then dispatched the other constable to fetch Dr. George William Sequeira in nearby Jewry Street.

News of the murder spread quickly, and by about 2 a.m., two doctors and numerous detectives and police constables, some of whom had heard Morris's whistle, were converging on Mitre Square.[9] Dr. Sequeira was one of the first to arrive on the scene, at just five minutes before 2 a.m. City Detective Daniel Halse had been standing with two other detectives near St. Botolph's Church on the corner of Houndsditch when they heard about the murder a little before 2 a.m. The three detectives ran to Mitre Square and arrived only a few minutes after Dr. Sequeira. Halse gave "instructions to have the neighborhood searched and every man examined"; then he and several other detectives and constables spread out to search the surrounding area for clues and suspicious characters.[10]

Dr. Frederick Gordon Brown arrived with his assistant at 2:18 a.m. and did an on-site examination of the body. Eddowes was lying in the all-too-familiar position of the Ripper's other victims: she was on her back, with her legs apart, and her right leg bent at the knee. Her clothes were drawn up, exposing the abdomen and the genitals, and the upper part of her dress was torn open. She was even more viciously mutilated than Annie Chapman had been—as P.C. Watkins later put it, "She was ripped up like a pig in the market."[11] Her throat had been deeply cut, and there was a long incision from the abdomen to the rectum, which cut through the vagina. In addition, her intestines, "smeared with some feculent matter," had been removed and placed over her right shoulder. There were also cuts through her eyelids, cheeks, lips, nose and one earlobe. In addition, both the left kidney and the uterus had been removed and apparently taken by the killer.[12]

At 2:55 a.m., P.C. Alfred Long discovered an important clue in Goulston Street, a largely Jewish thoroughfare just a few minutes east of Mitre Square. The street was the site of an outdoor market where Jewish merchants sold food and clothing from stalls, and, as such, it "formed part of the commercial centre of the Jewish East End."[13] As P.C. Long was walking along the northern end of the street, he noticed a rag smeared with blood and fecal matter lying inside the entrance to 108–119 Wentworth Dwellings, a "model dwelling" building largely inhabited by Jews, many of whom were secondhand clothing dealers at the open-air market. The rag turned out to be a piece of Eddowes's apron, which the killer had apparently severed "by a clean cut," then used to wipe the blood from his hands and knife. Above the apron, scrawled in chalk "in a good schoolboy hand" on the inside of the entryway was an enigmatic message: "The Juwes are the men that will not be blamed for nothing."[14]

Long made a quick search of the staircases and then, after informing adjoining beat constables of his discovery, went to the Commercial Street Police Station and gave the bloody rag to the inspector on duty.[15] As word of the discovery spread, members of both the City and the Metropolitan Police forces went to Goulston Street. The fact that the cryptic message was directly above the discarded bloody apron seemed to suggest it had been written by the murderer himself, and the police considered the writing an important clue. Inspector James McWilliam, head of the City Police Detective Department, was at the crime scene in Mitre Square when he first learned of the graffito, and he immediately relayed instructions that the writing should be photographed. Detective Halse, by then in Goulston Street, received the order and sent for a photographer.

Shortly before 5 a.m., Commissioner Warren arrived at Leman Street Police Station to consult with H Division police superintendent Thomas Arnold. Arnold had already seen the graffito in person and was concerned that if the writing was left much longer the public would catch wind of it, and a riot against the Jews might ensue. He proposed to Warren that the writing should be erased, but insisted that Warren had to make the decision, so Warren decided to go to Goulston Street to assess the situation himself.

According to Detective Halse, by the time the police commissioner arrived on Goulston Street, the people were already "bringing out their stalls, which they did very early on the Sunday morning."[16] As Warren later wrote in a report to the Home Office,

> There were several Police around the spot when I arrived. . . . A discussion took place whether the writing could be left covered up or otherwise or whether any portion of it could be left for an hour until it could be photographed, but after taking into consideration the excited state of the population in London generally at the time the strong feeling which had been excited against the Jews, and the fact that in a short time there would be a large concourse of the people in the streets and having before me the Report that if it was left there the house was likely to be wrecked (in which from my own observation I entirely concurred) I considered it desirable to obliterate the writing at once, having taken a copy.[17]

The message was copied down, but there was no time to photograph it, and the writing was wiped out at 5:30 a.m.[18] Warren came under harsh criticism for his decision. City Inspector James McWilliam, for example, reportedly told Warren that the erasure of the message was "a fatal mistake." In his report to the Home Office, Warren defended his decision and added, "I do not hesitate myself to say that if the writing had been left there would have been an onslaught upon the Jews, property would have been wrecked, and lives would probably have been lost."[19] The extent to which the police went to suppress an anti-Jewish "onslaught"—essentially destroying one of the few actual clues in the entire case—is telling. The threat of pogroms had again reared its ugly head.

The Goulston Street graffito is one of the most frequently debated aspects of the Whitechapel murders case. Some people have naturally suggested that the graffito had nothing to do with the murders at all, and that it was merely a coincidence that the Ripper had dropped the apron near it. In Chief Inspector Swanson's summary report of the Eddowes murder, the chalked writing was described as "blurred," which led some researchers to speculate that it was not very recent.[20] On the other hand, Detective Halse said at the inquest that "he assumed that the writing was recent, because from the number of persons living in the tenement he believed it would have been rubbed out had it been there for any time."[21] In any case, the police took the writing very seriously, and both Sir Robert Anderson and Henry Moore believed that the message had been written by the killer.[22] Today we know nothing more about the matter than the police did at the time, and the debate continues.

The intended meaning of the graffito was a subject of much debate. Commissioner Warren believed that the graffito was "evidently written with the intention of inflaming the public mind against the Jews" but admitted that the wording of the message was difficult to interpret. "The idiom does not appear to be English, French, or German," he wrote, "but it might possibly be that of an Irishman speaking a foreign language. It seems to be the idiom of Spain or Italy."[23] In short, Warren thought the author of the graffito was someone whose native language was not English.

Among the police, the two main interpretations of the message were that either it was written by a Jew boasting about committing the murders, or that it was written by a gentile as a deliberate ruse, to cast blame for the murders on the Jews. For example, as Samuel Montagu wrote in a letter to the *Jewish Chronicle*, "If the 'handwriting on the wall' was done by the monster himself, can there be any doubt of his intention to throw the pursuers on the wrong track, while showing hostility to the Jews in the vicinity?" Given that the wording of the message is so vague, it is important to note that in either of these interpretations, the author of the message was ostensibly a Jew, bragging about committing the murders.

"The Juwes are the men that will not be blamed for nothing." We might consider the implications of such a message from the perspective of someone like Aaron Kozminski. The Russian Jewish immigrants in the East End were a group that had been unfairly blamed for years. In Russia, they had been blamed for numerous social problems and were accused of being leeches who exploited the Russian peasants. They were blamed for both the assassination of the czar and for the anti-Jewish pogroms that followed in its wake. After arriving in London, this same group was once again blamed for various social ills in the East End, including unfair competition (most notably, in the tailoring trade) and taking jobs from the native-born English residents. After the murder of Annie Chapman, the Jews were again, predictably, blamed for the Ripper murders. In all of these instances, arguably, the Jews were wrongly blamed. In 1888, an East End immigrant Jew might very well have said, "We are being blamed for nothing!"

The message was located in a spot where it may have been calculated to do the most damage. As noted, Goulston Street was a site of particular relevance to Jews. Just one street to the west was Petticoat Lane, the largest Jewish market in London, described as "a seething, boiling, bubbling mass of poor humanity."[24] Goulston Street was the site of the chazar mark, the Jewish employment market where master tailors went to find "greeners" for their workshops. The street was also the site of a major antisweating meeting in early 1888. If the murderer was an immigrant Jew, then the message may have been intended as a defiant statement that the Jews had been wrongly made into scapegoats (blamed for nothing). Was the murderer essentially saying, "Now I will give you something to blame the Jews for . . . we will not be blamed for nothing"? Interpreted thus, the graffito is a chilling statement, both irreverent and wicked.

In the end, despite the confusion about the meaning of the graffito, one thing at least is certain—Jack the Ripper left the bloody apron in Goulston Street after murdering Kate Eddowes in Mitre Square. This gives us one of the few real clues in the entire case, because it indicates the direction the killer walked after committing the murder—in other words, his probable "getaway" route and, in all likelihood, the direction of his home. I will discuss this later in a chapter on modern geographic profiling. For now, suffice to say, the apron was deposited along the most direct route toward Aaron Kozminski's home on Greenfield Street.

12

Lonesome October

As morning dawned on September 30, talk of the murders spread like wildfire throughout the East End, and the streets once again became packed with people. Large crowds gathered in Berner Street and Mitre Square, and police guarded both crime scenes and let no one in to see them. The murder sites had by then become a tourist attraction even to the more fashionable residents of London. Denizens of West London took "a lively interest in the doings of the Whitechapel murderer," the *Observer* reported, and "a very large number of cabs and private carriages containing sightseers have visited the scenes of the tragedies."[1]

On the following day, the Central News Agency received a second correspondence signed "Jack the Ripper"—this time it was a postcard, again written in red ink, and in the same handwriting as the letter. It read,

> I wasnt codding dear old Boss when I gave you the tip. you'll hear about Saucy Jackys work tomorrow double event this time number one squealed a bit couldnt finish straight off. had not the time to get ears for police thanks for keeping last letter back till I got to work again.
> Jack the Ripper[2]

The fact that the writer of the postcard seemed to have an intimate knowledge of several details of the murders made the police take both this correspondence and the previously received "Dear Boss" letter very seriously. Both were clearly written by the same person, and the statement "number one squealed a bit couldn't finish straight off" sounded like an accurate description of the Stride murder. For several reasons, however, the police at once doubted the authenticity of both letters, and as Commissioner Charles Warren wrote to the Home Office, "At present I think the whole thing is a hoax but of course we are bound to try & ascertain the writer in any case."[3] Likewise among modern researchers, the general consensus is that both letters were hoaxes. For one thing, it has been pointed out that a hoaxer could have learned the details of both murders from the newspapers. In fact, according to both Robert Anderson and Inspector John Littlechild of the Special Branch, the police discovered the hoaxer's identity. As Anderson later wrote, the letters were "the creation of an enterprising London journalist."[4] Littlechild suggested that the author of the "Dear Boss" letter was either Tom Bulling or Charles Moore, both of the Central News Agency, and he noted, "It was a smart piece of journalistic work."[5] In the weeks and months to come, the police would receive numerous letters from people claiming to be the murderer. Almost all of them were considered to be hoaxes. Meanwhile, the new murders provided ample fodder for the press, and accounts of both inquests were reported extensively in several papers. As before, the papers sold like hotcakes.

The month of October seems to have been a crucial time for the investigation, and there was a growing sense that the police were on the verge of a breakthrough. In the days immediately after the double event, the Metropolitan police conducted thorough house-to-house inquiries in the immediate vicinity of Berner Street and distributed handbills to residents asking for information. As noted by authors Stewart Evans and Donald Rumbelow, these house-to-house inquiries "undoubtedly, took in the adjoining streets."[6] Thus, it is likely that they included the homes of Isaac Abrahams at 74 Greenfield Street and Matilda and Morris Lubnowski at 16 Greenfield Street, just one block north of the site of the Stride murder on Berner Street. The police may have interviewed members of the Kozminski family in October, as a matter of procedure, and if so, they probably first came across Aaron Kozminski at this time. In any case, Kozminski's family certainly would have seen one of the thousands of police handbills asking for information regarding "any person to whom suspicion is attached."

Sometime around October, Robert Anderson finally returned to London to take charge of his duties as head of the CID.[7] "On my return," Anderson later wrote, "I found the Jack the Ripper scare in full swing."[8] It is likely that Inspector Donald Swanson briefed Anderson on the status of the investigation, then Anderson undertook "reinvestigating the whole case," as he put it. When Anderson met Commissioner Warren and Home Secretary Henry Matthews for a conference on the investigation, Matthews told him, "We hold you responsible to find the murderer." Anderson declined the responsibility but replied that he would hold himself "responsible to take all legitimate means to find him."[9]

By this time, there was considerable pressure on the Home Office to solve the case, and it had been repeatedly suggested that the government should offer a reward for information leading to the murderer's capture. Yet the Home Secretary refused to do so. Matthews would come under attack for this position, but he never changed his mind. The City Police, on the other hand, did offer a reward, and on October 5 the *Police Gazette* reported that "A reward of £500 will be paid by the Commissioner of the City of London Police, to any person (other than a person belonging to a Police Force in the United Kingdom) who shall give such information as shall lead to the discovery and conviction of the murderer or murderers."[10] Additional rewards were offered by a variety of institutions, groups, and private individuals, until a total of close to £1,500 was available to anyone who could provide information that would lead to a conviction of the Ripper. As a result, the police found themselves inundated with "clues" and tips submitted by concerned citizens, who claimed to have knowledge pointing to the perpetrator of the crimes.

On October 8, the day of Kate Eddowes's funeral, a large crowd assembled outside the mortuary on Golden Lane in the City of London. The streets were filled with so many people that the road was effectively blocked, while other spectators looked on from windows and the rooftops of adjoining buildings. At 1:30 p.m., the funeral procession emerged. Eddowes's polished elm coffin was carried in an open glass car, followed by a mourning coach in which rode Eddowes's boyfriend, John Kelly, and four of the victim's sisters. Thousands of people followed the cortege as police conducted the carriages with some difficulty to the City of London boundary, then along Whitechapel Road past St. Mary's church, where another large crowd was assembled, and continuing through Mile End, Bow, and Stratford. All along the eight-mile route, people stood to watch and express their sympathy for the Ripper's latest victim, and it was said that some five hundred mourners attended the interment at Ilford Cemetery.

Because the Eddowes murder had occurred within the boundary of the City of London, the crime fell to the jurisdiction of the City Police Force. Both the MET and the City Police were now working the Ripper case together, for better or worse. James McWilliam, the head of the Detective Department for the City of London Police, wrote, "The department is co-operating with the Metropolitan Police in the matter, and Chief Inspector Swanson and I meet daily and confer on the subject."[11] Swanson likewise noted that the Metropolitan Police "have daily acquainted the City Police with the subjects and natures of their enquiries."[12] Several liaison officers, including a City detective named Robert Sagar, were deputed for daily meetings between the City Police and the Metropolitan Police at Leman Street Station.

On October 9, the Metropolitan Police commenced a massive house-to-house inquiry of a large part of the East End, including "some of the worst slums of Whitechapel and Spitalfields."[13] The search was confined to an area north of Whitechapel Road, roughly centered on Commercial Street. According to Swanson, the search area was "bounded by the City Police boundary on the one hand, Lamb St Commercial St. Great Eastern Railway & Buxton St. then by Albert St Dunk St. Chicksand St and Great Garden St. to Whitechapel Rd and then to the City boundary."[14] The police questioned residents and lodgers at doss houses and again distributed handbills asking for information about "any person to whom suspicion is attached."

Meanwhile, anti-Semitic tension continued unabated in the East End. The fact that Stride had been murdered next to the Jewish socialists' club in Berner Street and Eddowes just behind the Great Synagogue did not lessen the public's suspicions that the murderer was a Jew. Then on October 2, the *Times* irresponsibly stirred the pot by printing a dispatch from a Vienna correspondent that drew attention to "a crime of an exactly similar kind" that had occurred near Krakow. The article stated,

> A Galician Jew named Ritter was accused in 1884 of having murdered and mutilated a Christian woman in a village near Cracow. The mutilation was like that perpetrated on the body of the woman Chapman, and at the trial numbers of witnesses deposed that among certain fanatical Jews there existed a superstition to the effect that if a Jew became intimate with a Christian woman he would atone for his offence by slaying and mutilating the object of his passion.[15]

The correspondent conceded there was "no doubt that the man was innocent" but added, "the superstitions prevailing among some of the ignorant and degraded of his coreligionists remains on record and was never wholly disproved." This was, of course, merely a variation of the blood libel myth, the traditional form of Judenhetze that had been leveled against Jews for centuries. The fact that the "Vienna correspondent" admitted that Ritter was innocent in no way mitigated the irresponsible nature of the article, given the explosive tension that existed in the East End at the time.

On October 3, the *Times* published two letters expressing anger and frustration over the article. A letter from Hermann Adler expressed the "profoundest concern" and noted "the experience of many centuries as to the falsehood of such and similar charges."[16] A second letter, from Moses Gaster, a lecturer at Oxford and the chief rabbi of the Sephardic communities in England, was even angrier and expressed the author's "utter amazement and stupefaction" at the Vienna correspondent's letter. "Has the writer never seen and never heard that all those depositions and quotations were clumsy fabrications?" he asked. "That the absurd fable—the legend of the blood—has been 'wholly disproved' by a host of eminent writers? . . . I cannot find expressions strong enough to condemn these atrocious crimes; but it makes man still more despair of the progress of mankind when one sees this revival of absurd legends disposed of long ago."[17] Gaster concluded with a stern warning: "Baseless and without foundation as these legends are, they are dangerous even in normal times; how much more in abnormal? Who can foresee to what terrible consequences such a superstition might lead, when the people frantic with rage and terror, get hold of it and wreak their vengeance on innocent men?"

At the time when the Vienna correspondent's letter on the Ritter case was published, the public had not yet learned of the Goulston Street graffito. By October 9, however, word of the graffito had leaked to the press, and the *Evening News* printed a story boldly titled "Is the Whitechapel Murderer a Jew?" The article noted, "'Shall the Jews be blamed for nothing,' was the inscription alleged to have been written on the wall in Goulston street by the perpetrator of the Mitre square murder."[18]

The proxy war continued with an anonymous "important letter" signed only "A Butcher," speculating that the murders had been committed by a Jewish slaughterman. The writer theorized that "Only a man having a perfect knowledge of how to deliver a cut so effectually and with such certainty as in these cases must know exactly the kind of knife to use, and I know of no more suitable instrument than the knife used by a 'Jewish cutter' when slaughtering sheep or oxen."[19] Jewish slaughtermen, he pointed out, cut the throat, causing death "quickly and noiselessly," after which, a second man called a "searcher" would then cut open the abdomen and reach his hand into the abdominal cavity to examine the internal organs by touch to determine whether the animal was "fit for Jewish consumption." The publication of this letter obviously did not help matters. The police briefly examined the Jewish slaughterman theory, as much for damage control as anything else. On October 12, the *Jewish Chronicle* printed an article stating that Dr. Gordon Brown "has examined the knives used by the Jewish slaughterers, all of which have been submitted to him by the City detectives, and he is thoroughly satisfied that none of them could have been used."[20]

There was extensive reporting of day 2 of the Eddowes inquest on October 11. The star witness that day was Joseph Lawende, one of the three men who had witnessed Kate Eddowes talking to a man on Duke Street just a few minutes before she was murdered. His testimony was reported in the *Daily Telegraph*:

Joseph Lawende: On the night of Sept. 29, I was at the Imperial Club, Duke-street, together with Mr. Joseph Levy and Mr. Harry Harris. It was raining, and we sat in the club till half-past one o'clock, when we left. I observed a man and woman together at the corner of Church-passage, Duke-street, leading to Mitre-square.

The Coroner: Were they talking?

Lawende: The woman was standing with her face towards the man, and I only saw her back. She had one hand on his breast. He was the taller. She had on a black jacket and bonnet. I have seen the articles at the police-station, and believe them to be those the deceased was wearing.

Coroner: What sort of man was this?

Lawende: He had on a cloth cap with a peak of the same.

Mr. Crawford: Unless the jury wish it, I do not think further particulars should be given as to the appearance of this man.

The Foreman: The jury do not desire it.

Mr. Crawford (to witness): You have given a description of the man to the police?

Lawende: Yes.

Coroner: Would you know him again?

Lawende: I doubt it. The man and woman were about nine or ten feet away from me.[21]

The police obviously considered Lawende an important witness. According to the *Evening News*, this fact was "borne out by the police having taken exclusive care of Mr. Joseph Levander [*sic* Lawende], to a certain extent having sequestrated him and having imposed a pledge on him of secrecy." The police were said to be paying Lawende's expenses, and "one if not two detectives are taking him about." It seems that the police requested the same oath of secrecy from Joseph Levy, because the *Evening News* reported that he "is absolutely obstinate and refuses to give us the slightest information."[22]

Lawende's description of the suspect was presumably held back at the Eddowes inquest for the same reason that Israel Schwartz did not appear at the Stride inquest—the police did not want his description to be publicized. But again, it somehow got out anyway, and Lawende's description of the alleged killer was published in the *Police Gazette* on

October 19. The man was described as "age 30, height 5 ft. 7 or 8 in., complexion fair, moustache fair, medium build; dress, pepper-and-salt colour loose jacket, grey cloth cap with peak of same material, reddish neckerchief tied in knot; appearance of a sailor."[23]

It is interesting that this description so closely matches the description of the "broad shouldered" man seen by Schwartz less than an hour earlier on the same night. Schwartz's man was "about 30; ht, 5 ft 5 in; comp[lexion], fair; hair, dark; small brown moustache, full face, broad shouldered; dress, dark jacket and trousers, black cap with peak, and nothing in his hands." Both descriptions also generally fit the description of the man seen on Berner Street by P.C. Smith: "about 28, 5'7" tall, with a cleanshaven and respectable appearance. The man was wearing dark clothes and a hard dark felt deerstalker hat." In other words, Lawende, Schwartz, and P.C. Smith may have all seen the same person.

The particulars of the Eddowes murder were described in detail in all of the major London papers, and as the *Times* reported, "The revelations made at the inquest on the Mitre-square victim have caused a profound sensation in the East-end of London." On October 11, the same day that Lawende testified at the inquest, the *Pall Mall Gazette* berated Warren for erasing the Goulston Street graffito, while simultaneously gloating over the reason. Even more troubling was the *Gazette's* completely false suggestion that "Juwes" was a spelling used in the Yiddish language.

> [Warren] feared that if the words remained on the wall, a crowd might assemble and there might be an attack on the Jews! So, rather than take the trouble of covering them up with a cloth and preventing access to the spot until the inscription was photographed, he rubbed it out, all out, refusing even to be content with erasing the one word "Juwes," as it appears to have been written in Yiddish, and so perished the only clue which the murderer has left us by which he might be identified.[24]

The *Evening News* likewise reported,

The language of the Jews in the East-end is a hybrid dialect, known as Yiddish, and their mode of spelling the word

"Jews" would be "Juwes." This the police consider a strong indication that the crime was committed by one of the numerous foreigners by whom the East-end is infested.[25]

A Star reporter called on the Jewish Chronicle to find out whether this was true and discovered that it was not. "The Yiddish word for Jew is Yiddin," the Star reported, adding, "Much indignation is felt amongst the Jews at these repeated and unjustifiable attempts to fasten the responsibility for the dastardly crimes on them."[26] The same day, the Jewish Chronicle again pointed out, "There are not wanting signs of a deliberate attempt to connect the Jews with the Whitechapel murders."[27]

Sir Charles Warren likewise wrote to Rabbi Hermann Adler to ask whether the Yiddish word for Jew was in fact "Juwes." Adler's response was a definite no: "I was deeply pained by the statements that appeared in several papers today, the 'Standard,' 'Daily News,' etc., that in the Yiddish dialect the word Jews is spelled 'Juewes.' This is not a fact. The equivalent in the Judao-German (Yiddish) jargon is 'Yidden.' I do not know of any dialect or language in which 'Jews' is spelled 'Juewes.'" He added that "in the present state of excitement it is dangerous to the safety of the poor Jews in the East to allow such an assertion to remain uncontradicted."[28] Three days later, Commissioner Warren issued a statement that was printed in various papers. "With reference to a statement in various journals that the word 'Jews' is spelt 'Juwes' in the Yiddish jargon, the Commissioner of Police has ascertained that this is incorrect. It is not known that there is any dialect or language in which the word 'Jews' is spelt 'Juwes.'"[29]

Yet it was too late to close the barn door. Judenhetze had already achieved its desired results. By the middle of October, the Jewish residents of the East End must have noted a similarity between the anti-Jewish "demonstrations" of Eastern Europe and the situation that now presented itself in their new home. It was in the middle of this tense and combustible situation that the story of the "Batty Street lodger" first began to appear in the press.

13

The Batty Street "Lodger"

The first movie inspired by the Jack the Ripper murders was Alfred Hitchcock's 1927 silent film *The Lodger*. Based on Marie Belloc Lowndes's 1913 novel of the same name, the plot concerns a series of murders committed by "the Avenger," a mad killer who roams London's foggy streets, targeting young girls with "golden hair." In the midst of the crimes, a mysterious lodger moves into an apartment upstairs from a family with a young daughter. The man's strange behavior—he goes out late at night and has a map of the murder sites—soon arouses the suspicion of his landlord. In the end, it is revealed that the lodger's sister was the Avenger's first victim; the poor man has been roaming the streets trying to catch the killer, which explains both his obsession with the case and his rather odd behavior. Not surprisingly, Hitchcock hated this ending and thought that the lodger should have been guilty, but the studio demanded a happy ending.

Lowndes's novel was possibly inspired by a true event in the Ripper case, which was reported in London newspapers in the middle of October 1888. The story, in brief, was that a lodger staying at a house in the East End dropped off some laundry to his landlady, saying that he was going away for a few days. When the landlady later examined the man's clothing, she found that one of his shirts was covered in blood.

The lodger, predictably, was never seen again. This story—neatly packaged and almost charming in its simplicity—appeared in several papers. As it turned out, however, the initial report of the incident was grossly misreported and apparently based on neighborhood gossip. Yet several follow-up articles corrected many of the errors in early reports, and something closer to the truth slowly emerged from the muck of bad reportage.

The first version appeared on October 15, when the *Echo* printed the following:

EAST END TRAGEDIES.
A MYSTERIOUS LODGER.
HIS BLOODSTAINED CLOTHES.
WHAT HIS LANDLADY SAYS.
The police are, writes a Correspondent this morning, watching with great anxiety a house in the East end, which, it is believed, was the actual lodging made use of by someone connected with the East end murders. From various statements made by the neighbours, the landlady had a lodger, who, since the Sunday morning of the murder, has been missing. It appears, according to the statements made by the landlady to her neighbours, her lodger returned home early on the Sunday morning, and she was disturbed by his moving about. She rose very early, and noticed her lodger had changed some of his clothes. He told her he was going away for a little time, and he asked her to wash the shirt he had taken off, and get it ready for him by the time he came back. When she took the shirt she was astonished to find the wristbands and part of the sleeves completely saturated with wet blood. Acting on the advice of some of her neighbours, she gave information to the police and showed them the shirt. They then took possession of it, and obtained from her a full description of the lodger. A reporter visited the house early this morning. He had a conversation with the landlady, a German, who appeared very reticent. She, however, stated that a detective and two police officers had been in the house ever since information was given.[1]

This article is the version of the Batty Street lodger story that is most often repeated in Ripper books. As such, it is important to note that the article was based primarily on information gathered from the landlady's neighbors, not from the landlady herself. The landlady was described as "very reticent" in speaking to the reporter and did not say much, apart from corroborating the fact that "a detective and two police officers had been in the house ever since her information was given." As would soon become apparent, though, the article was wrong in the most important detail—specifically, there was never a missing lodger at all.

In a continuation of the same article, the *Echo* gave a somewhat different version of the incident:

GERMAN ARRESTED AND DISCHARGED

A strange and suspicious incident in connection with the Whitechapel murders has just been explained by the arrest, late on Saturday, of a German whom the police had every reason to suspect as being connected with the murder of Elizabeth Stride, at Berner street. The affair has until now been kept a profound secret; but the matter was, it is asserted, regarded at first as of such importance that Inspector Reid, Inspector Abberline, and the other officers engaged in the case, believed that a clue of a highly important character had been obtained. It appears that Detective Sergeants W. Thicke and S. White, of the Criminal Investigation Department, made a house-to-house inquiry in the locality of the Berner street murder. They then discovered that on the day after that crime a German left a bloodstained shirt with a laundress at 22 Batley (sic) street—a few yards from the seat of the tragedy—and remarking, "I shall call in two or three days," departed in a hurried manner. His conduct was deemed highly suspicious. Detectives Thicke and White, who probably know more of the East end criminals than any other officers, arrested the man suspected on Saturday night. He was conveyed to Leman street Station, and inquiries were immediately set on foot. These resulted in the man's release this morning. Our representative made an inquiry respecting the above incident this afternoon, and ascertained that the shirt had a quantity of blood on the front and on both sleeves.[2]

This second part of the story contained several elements that seemed to contradict the lodger story. For starters, there was no mention of the "lodger" at all. Instead, the item speaks only of "a German" who "left a bloodstained shirt with a laundress at 22 Batley (sic) street" on the day after the murders. The police discovered the incident as a result of the "house to house inquiry in the locality of the Berner street murder," and then Detectives Thicke and White arrested "the man suspected" on Saturday night—presumably, the previous Saturday, October 13. The suspect was questioned by police and then released "this morning" (that is, Monday morning, October 15).

The following day, the *Evening News* essentially reprinted the *Echo's* article, with a few small additions. The German landlady "speaks very bad English," the report declared, and was "not inclined to give much information." The article added that the house had "rather a dingy and uninviting appearance" and concluded, "The police have in their possession a series of most important clues, and that his [the killer's] ultimate capture is only a question of time."[3]

The next day, the *Echo* printed a much more extensive follow-up to the story:

EAST-END ATROCITIES.
SUSPECTED MURDERER TRACKED.
EXPECTED CONFESSION.
There are indications in official circles that at no period during the search for the miscreant has there been so much chance of an arrest as at the present moment. From more than one source the police authorities have received information tending to show that the criminal is a foreigner, who was known as having lived within a radius of a few hundred yards from the scene of the Berner-street tragedy. The very place where he lodges is asserted to be within official cognisance. If the man be the real culprit, he lived some time ago with a woman, by whom, he has been accused.

Her statements are, it is stated, now being inquired into. In the meantime the suspected assassin is "shadowed." Incriminating evidence of a certain character has already been obtained, and, should implicit credence be placed in the woman already referred to, whose name we will not transpire under any circumstances until after his guilt is prima facie established, a confession of the crimes may be looked for at any moment. The accused is himself aware, it is believed, of the suspicions entertained against him.

In addition, the article noted,

The laundress at 22, Batty-street, where a German left a blood-stained shirt, is Mrs. Kuer, also a German. The man, who was arrested, as already stated, and liberated, explained the blood-stains by the fact that he was with a friend who was cutting his corn, when the knife slipped and inflicted a wound, when the injured man stanched the cut by using the sleeves of his companion's shirt. There were, however, extensive stains upon the front of it as well, and this the man asserts was done by the blood spurting on to it. Mrs. Kuer denied that she gave information to the police, who were told of the circumstances by a neighbour. Mrs. Kuer says the man had occasionally called with a shirt to be washed. She feels certain she says that the man is entirely innocent of any such offence as was at first suggested by the police. Inspector Reid, Inspector Helson, and other detective officers are pursuing their investigation. A man was arrested and taken to Commercial-street Police-station last night, but was released shortly afterwards.[4]

The article states that the police arrested "the German" who dropped off and picked up the shirts. According to the man's story, however, the blood actually came from someone else—a man described as a "friend" who accidentally wounded himself while cutting his corn. Strangely, "the injured man" did not get blood on his own shirt but instead "stanched the cut by using the sleeves of his companion's shirt." The "extensive stains" on the front of the shirt were explained by "blood spurting onto it." This story sounds a bit fishy, because it seems odd that a person would stanch the flow of blood from a cut using the sleeves of someone else's shirt. Clearly, the police may have suspected that "the German" was lying. And they certainly would have wanted to interview the man who cut himself—but did they?

According to the *Echo's* initial report, the man who dropped off the shirts was arrested on Saturday night (October 13) and then released on Monday morning (October 15). Yet this was contradicted by a report in the *Daily News* that said the man was arrested "last Saturday" (again, October 13), then "taken to the Leman-street Police-station, where he was questioned, and within an hour or two released, his statement being proved correct." If this version of the story is correct, then who was released on Monday morning? Was a second man also arrested? This would seem to be supported by the *Echo's* October 17 report that stated, "A man was arrested and taken to Commercial-street Police-station last night, but was released shortly afterwards." In other words, it seems that at least two separate people were arrested—one on Saturday and another sometime later, although it is not really clear when.

The *Echo's* October 17 report also discussed "a German named Ludwig, residing in the Leman-street district, who has already been in custody on suspicion of being concerned in the murders, and who was released after an exhaustive inquiry." The article added, "The police are keeping him under surveillance at present." This was a reference to a German hairdresser named Charles Ludwig, who had been arrested almost a month earlier, on September 18, for threatening to attack a prostitute and another man with a knife. The police were initially very interested in Ludwig as a suspect in the Ripper murders, but Ludwig had nothing to do with the story of the man who dropped off the shirts at Batty Street. Nor was Ludwig the Ripper, because he was in police custody when the Stride and Eddowes murders took place. Ludwig was brought before the Thames Police Court on October 2 and then released.[5] Yet sometime around October 16 or 17 (in other words, around the time that the previous article was printed), Ludwig was again seen "flourishing a knife and acting in a suspicious manner," and it was said that the police were keeping him under surveillance.[6] In short, it seems that the papers confused two separate stories, apparently assuming that the bloody shirt story had something to do with Ludwig. This might explain the *Echo*'s statement that it was a "German" who dropped off the bloody laundry. In fact, it seems possible that the police may have intentionally misled the press about this, essentially using the Ludwig story as a red herring, to draw public attention away from their real quarry.

By this time, the *Echo* had conceded that its first reports of the story were largely incorrect or, as the paper put it, "not altogether devoid of foundation." The article also added that the police denied the story's veracity immediately after publication, "presumably because they were anxious to avoid a premature disclosure of facts of which they had been for some time cognisant." It went on,

> The police have taken exceptional precautions to prevent a disclosure, and while repeated arrests have taken place, with no other result than that of discharging the prisoner for the time being in custody they have devoted special attention to one particular spot, in the hope that a few days will suffice to set at rest the public anxiety as to further deeds of murder in the district.

The article added that the police had the bloody shirt in their possession and that they were "evidently convinced that [the shirt] was left in a house in Batty-street by the assassin after he had finished his work." In conclusion, the article stated,

> The police during Saturday, Sunday, and Monday answered negatively all questions as to whether any person had been arrested, or was then in their charge, there is no doubt that a man was taken into custody on suspicion of the missing lodger from No, 22, Batty-street, and that he was afterwards set at liberty. The German lodging-house keeper could clear up the point as to the existence of any other lodger supposed to be absent from her house under the suspicious circumstances referred to, but she is not accessible, and it easy of understanding that the police should endeavour to prevent her making any statement.[7]

Clearly, the police wanted to keep Mrs. Kuer from talking to the press, presumably because they were afraid that any additional publicity would further disrupt an ongoing undercover investigation. The overall picture that emerges from these reports is an interesting one. It seems clear that an important investigation was under way, and that the police were endeavoring to keep quiet about it. It also seems obvious that a suspect was under surveillance and that the police were watching "one particular spot" in the East End. The *Daily News* picked up the story the following day. In this report, the man who dropped off the shirts was referred to as a "foreigner" (but not as a German), and it was said that the incident "occurred more than a fortnight ago."[8] The paper still seemed confused about whether Ludwig had anything to do with the bloody laundry incident, because the article referred again to a foreigner, residing in the Leman Street district, who was seen "flourishing a knife, and acting in a suspicious manner in the neighbourhood."

Then on October 18, the *Evening News* printed a letter from Carl Noun, a man who was himself a lodger in the house on Batty Street. His letter would put the "lodger" myth to bed, once and for all:

> SIR—Referring to your issue No. 2227, I beg of you to publish a contradictory statement respecting the Whitechapel murder; in fact, your reporter has been wrongly informed, or else it his own suggestion.
>
> The police are not in the house, nor has the woman had a lodger who is now missing, but a stranger brought the shirts, and when he fetched them, he was detained by the police, and after inquiries discharged. As regards our house, it is not as your report describes it, for it is a most respectable house and in good general condition; although it is certainly not Windsor Castle. There are only two lodgers, one a drayman, name of Joseph, who works for the Norwegian Lager Beer Company, and the other a baker, name of Carl Noun, who has been at work in Margate, and only returned on the 6th of this month after the season was over. I trust you will publish these statements as I put it to you, in fact it may injure the poor woman in her business.—Respectfully. C. NOUN (a lodger in the house).[9]

This letter provides us with the likely explanation for the origin of the lodger myth in the first place. Apparently, Mrs. Kuer showed the bloodstained shirt to a neighbor, probably on September 30 or October 1, and the neighbor assumed (possibly as a result of Mrs. Kuer's bad English) that the shirt belonged to Kuer's lodger Carl Noun, who was then out of town doing business in Margate. The police heard about the incident via this gossiping neighbor during a house-to-house search "in the locality of the Berner street murder" in the days immediately after the murders, and the press probably got their original information from the same source. Noun was understandably worried that he might be mistaken for the "missing" lodger and hence for the killer. To clarify matters, the *Evening News* followed up Noun's letter with an interview with the landlady, Mrs. Kuer:

> A Press representative had an interview, yesterday, with the landlady of the house, 22, Batty-street, Whitechapel, which place was alleged to be the resort of the owner of the blood-stained shirt. The lodging-house is kept by a German woman, the wife of a seaman. She denied that the man for whom the police were searching was one of her lodgers, and asserted that he simply had his washing done at the house. He was a ladies tailor, working for a West-end house, and did not reside in the Leman-street district. She explained the presence of blood on the shirt by saying that it was owing to an accident that occurred to a man (other than the one taken into custody) who was living on the premises, and that the police would have known nothing of it but for her having indiscreetly shown it to a neighbour. The woman denies that the detectives are still in possession of her house.[10]

Here, Mrs. Kuer reiterates Noun's assertion that the man who dropped off the shirts was not a lodger but instead was a man who "simply had his washing done at the house." She then says that the man who dropped off the shirts was a "ladies tailor" and "explained the presence of blood on the shirt by saying that it was owing to an accident that occurred to a man (other than the one taken into custody) who was living on the premises." This confirmed the earlier report that said the man who dropped off the shirts "explained the blood-stains by the fact that he was with a friend who was cutting his corn, when the knife slipped and inflicted a wound." It also suggested that the suspect the police were interested in was, in all likelihood, someone "other than the one taken into custody."

This article deserves close inspection, especially since it came directly from the landlady herself. Mrs. Kuer said that the man who had the accident was "living on the premises," but what does this mean? Clearly, "the premises" cannot be 22 Batty Street, because both Mrs. Kuer and Noun denied that the suspect was a lodger in the house. The fact that the statement follows a sentence about a ladies' tailor, whose residence was "not in the Leman-street district," seems to imply that Kuer means the premises of the ladies' tailor. Of course, both of Aaron Kozminski's brothers—Isaac and Woolf Abrahams— were ladies' tailors. Could "the premises" be a reference to Isaac's workshop on Greenfield Street? Recall that it was said that the police received information that the criminal was "a foreigner, who was known as having lived within a radius of a few hundred yards from the scene of the Berner-street tragedy," and that the "very place where he lodges" was "asserted to be within official cognisance." Obviously, Kozminski was a foreigner, and Isaac's shop at 74 Greenfield Street was approximately three hundred yards from the site of the Stride murder. The *Echo's* October 17 article also stated that the police had received information "from more than one source," and that the suspect "lived some time ago with a woman, by whom, he has been accused." We know Kozminski lived with his sister Matilda in 1890, and it is likely that he lived with her at other times in the 1880s.

The ladies' tailor, according to Mrs. Kuer, worked for a West End house. The question is, did Isaac or Woolf Abrahams work for a West End house? As we have seen, the master tailors of the East End were sweaters or middlemen, who typically did contract labor for wholesale clothing firms in the West End and the area around St. Paul's Cathedral. Of course, it is not known for certain that Isaac worked for a West End house, but it seems highly probable that he did. And whereas a journey-man tailor would probably have been described as working in a local shop, a master tailor would be described as "working for" a West End manufacturer. This suggests that the ladies' tailor mentioned in the Kuer interview was a master tailor (that is, a sweater) such as Isaac Abrahams.

Mrs. Kuer finally noted that the man who dropped off the shirts "did not reside in the Leman-street district." This was almost certainly in reply to a direct question to clarify whether the man was the German hairdresser Charles Ludwig and is further evidence that the Ludwig story and the "lodger" story were confused in early reports. Clearly, Ludwig was not the man who dropped off the shirts, nor was he the suspect in question.

As early as September 19, the Home Office had expressed concern over the enormous amount of press attention given to the Ripper case. A memo by J. S. Sanders, the assistant to Evelyn Ruggles-Brise, the private secretary to the Home Secretary, Henry Matthews, noted that Commissioner Charles Warren remarked on the "great hindrance" caused by the press attention:

> These "touts" follow the detectives wherever they go in search of clues, and then having interviewed persons with whom the police have had conversation and from whom inquiries have made, compile the paragraphs which fill the papers. This practice impedes the usefulness of detective investigation and moreover keeps alive the excitement in the district & elsewhere.[11]

Such was clearly the case on October 20, when the *Echo* reported, "The police complain that their work is increased, and morbid excitement created, by the statements made as to alleged arrests of an important character." Needless to say, the *Echo* was undeterred by this and, in the same article, added more information about the inquiry in question:

> There is a clue upon which the authorities have been zealously working for some time. This is in Whitechapel, not far from the scene of the Berner-street tragedy, and the man is, indeed, himself aware that he is being watched; so much so, that, as far as observation has gone at present, he has scarcely ventured out of doors. The police called on Mr. Packer, of 44, Berner-street, yesterday morning; and later on an *Echo* reporter also saw him as to what had transpired. Mr. Packer was rather reticent; but, when asked his opinion as to where

the murderer lodged—for he had seen him several times before the fatal night—remarked, "In the next street." It is considered he is not far wrong in his conjecture; but the police do not deem it prudent to say what steps are being taken in the matter.[12]

The police were clearly trying to suppress the story, but press attention was making it difficult for them to conduct surveillance on the suspect, who was "aware that he is being watched" and, as a result, now "scarcely ventured out of doors."[13] In fact, the visit to Matthew Packer may have been an attempt by the police to convince him to stop talking to the press. The *Echo* reporter spoke to a "reticent" Mr. Packer after the police talked with him. It even seems possible that the police may have contacted newspapers such as the *Echo* and the *Daily News*, to ask them to stop reporting on the Batty Street incident. In any case, after October 20, there was no further mention of the suspect until October 29, when the *Echo* suddenly reported not only that the suspect "has been exonerated," but also that he was "a resident of Batty Street. . . . Though certain suspicious circumstances needed explanation, his innocence has been established." The article then continued, somewhat strangely, by specifically declaring that the murderer was not a lunatic. "If he's insane," an unnamed medical authority was quoted, "he's a good deal sharper than those who are not."[14] This report has a somewhat suspicious ring to it. It almost seems as if the police planted the *Echo* story to divert attention from their real suspect, who quite possibly was insane, and who did not live on Batty Street. In other words, the story may have been intended as bait, to induce their real suspect to venture out of doors, in the hopes that he might be trailed by detectives.

So, was Aaron Kozminski the suspect in the Batty Street inquiry? It seems possible. Kozminski was a foreigner, whose brother Isaac was a ladies' tailor living "within a radius of a few hundred yards from the scene of the Berner-street tragedy." Moreover, the suspect was said to have been kept under police surveillance—and as Chief Inspector Donald Swanson would later write, "Kosminski" was identified by a witness, then after his "return to his brother's house in Whitechapel he was watched by police (City CID) by day & night."[15] Also, as we will later see, Assistant Commissioner Robert Anderson implied that the Ripper was discovered as a result of "a house-to-house search" that investigated every man who could "go and come and get rid of his blood-stains in secret."[16] Was this a reference to the bloodstained shirt? A clue that was discovered as the result of a house-to-house search conducted while Anderson was still on sick leave on the continent?

Unfortunately, we will probably never know. The extant police files make no mention of the Batty Street inquiries at all. And even if Kozminski became a suspect as early as October 1888, he was still only one of many individuals the police were investigating at the time. As Chief Inspector Swanson stated in an October 19 report to the Home Office, "About 80 persons have been detained at the different police stations in the Metropolis & their statements taken and verified by police."[17] On October 23, Anderson confessed to the Home Office that the police were without "the slightest clue of any kind."[18] Ultimately, it seems that the inquiry into the Batty Street suspect reached a dead end.

Meanwhile, the police were keeping busy, thanks to numerous tips from the public, and Swanson reported that the police had conducted inquiries into "sailors on board ships in [the] Docks," Asians, butchers and slaughtermen, gypsies, and "Cowboys" belonging to Buffalo Bill's American Expedition, which was playing at Earl's Court in West Brompton. In all, the police acted on tips concerning some three hundred suspected individuals.[19] Among several proposed detection methods, the police were also contemplating the use of bloodhounds to track the murderer in case he should strike again. While all of this was going on, there was a new, rather morbid, turn of events. On October 16, George Lusk, the chairman of the Whitechapel Vigilance Committee, received a small cardboard parcel containing what appeared to be half of a human kidney, along with a letter, written in red ink, with messy handwriting and several spelling errors. It read:

> From Hell
>   Mr Lusk,
>   Sir
>   I send you half the

Kidne I took from one women
prasarved it for you tother piece I
fried and ate it was very nise. I
may send you the bloody knif that
took it out if you only wate a whil
longer.
Signed Catch me when
you can
Mishter Lusk[20]

Lusk assumed that the letter was some sort of sick joke, but members of the Vigilance Committee convinced him to submit the kidney to the pathological curator of London Hospital, Dr. Openshaw, for analysis. Openshaw examined the kidney under a microscope and determined that it was a human kidney that had been preserved in spirits of wine. He then brought the package to the police station at Leman Street, after which the kidney was passed around like a hot potato. Detective Frederick Abberline gave it to the City Police, and then Inspector James McWilliam submitted it to City Police surgeon Dr. Frederick Gordon Brown for a second analysis.

When Dr. Brown was interviewed by the *Sunday Times*, he stated that the kidney was certainly from a human adult, but he could not say whether it came from Catherine Eddowes. On the one hand, Dr. Brown noted that there was "no substantial reason that this portion of kidney should not be the portion of the one taken from the murdered woman." On the other hand, he added, "The probability is slight of its being a portion of the murdered woman in Mitre Square." Because the kidney had no remaining piece of the renal artery attached to it, Brown said, he was unable to match it to "the portion of the body from which it was cut."[21] In short, it might have been Eddowes's kidney, but Brown doubted it. Still, even if Brown had concluded that the kidney was from Eddowes, it is likely that he would have kept this information from the press. As Inspector McWilliam wrote in a report, "It is not desirable that publicity should be given to the doctor's opinion, or the steps that are being taken in consequence."[22]

The "From Hell" letter is the only letter that some researchers now believe might have been by written by the actual murderer, although there is still much debate over the issue. Either way, the reference to eating half of the kidney ("tother piece I fried and ate it was very nise") presented a gruesome new facet of the case. Such behavior would have been consistent with a "trophy taker" like Jack the Ripper. Cannibalism is an example of a paraphilia practiced by a subtype of serial killer called a "lust murderer" or a postmortem mutilator. It is theorized that some cannibalistic serial killers may feel that by consuming their victims, they are gaining power over them. The notorious Milwaukee serial killer Jeffrey Dahmer, for example, claimed that he ate body parts because he believed that his victims would live again inside him. Another example was Albert Fish (aka "the Gray Man" or "the Brooklyn Vampire"), who at the age of fifty-seven was gripped by what he called a "blood thirst." Fish confessed to killing and eating two children and later described how he killed one boy and cut the "meat" from his body to take home and cook. When asked why he did it, Fish rather blandly said, "I never could account for it."[23]

14

Mary Kelly

By the first week of November, there had been no murders in more than a month, and people were starting to wonder whether perhaps the killer had moved away or died. Things seemed to be returning to normal, and the residents of London turned their attention to other news. On October 31, Princess Mary Adelaide of Cambridge visited the East End, accompanied by the Queen's oldest daughter, Princess Victoria, for the opening of the King Edward Institute and Schools on Hanbury Street, which was gaily decorated for the occasion. At the opening ceremony, Samuel Montagu declared, "Her Royal Highness had brought sunshine into Whitechapel at the period of its greatest gloom and depression."[1] In other news, Dr. Debenham of the London Hospital reported that a diphtheria epidemic was under way, centered around Hackney and the surrounding districts.

In the absence of any fresh Ripper news, the papers continued to fill their pages with lurid tales of violence. On November 3, it was reported that an underemployed tailor in Marylebone attempted to shoot his wife, firing three rounds at her while chasing her around the house. The shots missed, however, and the man committed suicide instead.[2] A few days later, an actor in the stage play *The Armada* at the Drury Lane Theatre "accidentally discharged a carbine loaded with blank cartridge in the face of an opponent instead of firing the weapon in the air."[3]

Such incidents lacked both the punch and the sales potential of the Ripper murders, but the papers tried their best.

On November 5, Guy Fawkes Day was celebrated in various parts of London, and crowds carried stuffed effigies of recently unpopular or otherwise notorious figures, including both Jack the Ripper and Leather Apron.[4] At Clerkenwell Green, it was rumored that a large crowd of unemployed men was planning to burn an effigy of Commissioner Charles Warren, and in anticipation of trouble, the police turned out in force, armed with billy clubs. An inspector informed one of the mob leaders, "I'll allow no bonfire tonight; and, if you try it, we shall go for you." Eventually, the "guy" appeared—not surprisingly, it was "an artistic production representing a stalwart policeman with his baton raised over the head of a workman." Due to the large number of police in attendance, however, the crowd decided not to burn it.[5] Later that night, there was some excitement when a crowd mistakenly believed that the police had arrested a Ripper suspect, but, as it turned out, the man, who was wearing blackface, was arrested merely for some "guying" activities.[6]

Yet the biggest news of the week was the much-anticipated Lord Mayor's Day parade, which was scheduled to take place on Friday, November 9. The police would be directing traffic and performing crowd control duties all along the parade route, which was to begin at Guildhall and meander for several miles through the City of London. Afterward, a "substantial meat tea" was to be given in the Tower Hamlet's Mission Hall for up to two thousand destitute people, followed by an "amusing entertainment" for three thousand people.[7]

As it turned out, though, the Lord Mayor's Day celebrations were upstaged by a much more thrilling East End affair, for in the early morning hours of November 9, Jack the Ripper struck again in a most brutal fashion. At 10:45 a.m., just as the parade was setting off, the horribly mutilated body of a young prostitute named Mary Kelly was discovered in a small room on one of East London's worst streets. The event was well timed. Indeed, it seemed almost as if the killer had a sense of the dramatic potential of the situation. This was to be the last of the murders definitely ascribed to Jack the Ripper. It would go down as one of the most heinous murders on record in the history of crime.

Mary Kelly was said to be a vivacious young woman, "possessed of considerable personal attractions." She was twenty-five years old and had blue eyes, a rather pale complexion, and "a very fine head of hair" that reached almost to her waist.[8] According to a neighbor, Kelly was "on good terms with everybody." A friend named Caroline Maxwell described her as a "pleasant little woman" who "spoke with a kind of impediment," adding, "she never associated with anyone much, beyond bowing 'Good morning.'" But Kelly frequently got drunk and then became "quarrelsome and abusive" and "would go about singing."[9] As Mary's boyfriend, Joseph Barnett, put it, "When in drink she had more to say."[10]

Kelly was born in Limerick, West Ireland, sometime around 1863 or 1864, and when she was very young she moved with her family to Carmarthen, Carmarthenshire, in southern Wales, where her father, John Kelly, got a job as a foreman in an iron works.[11] At the age of sixteen, Mary Kelly married a coal miner named Davies and then lived with him for a year or two until he was killed in a pit explosion. After her husband's death, Kelly briefly lived in Swansea before migrating onward, as always in an easterly direction, toward the great capital. She eventually arrived in London around 1884 and found work as a prostitute in an upscale West End "gay house" run by a French woman. Kelly later claimed that during this time, she led the life of a lady and frequently drove around in a carriage. At some point, she went to live in France with a "gentleman" but didn't like it there and returned to London after only a week or two.[12] For the next few years, Kelly lived in the vicinity of the Ratcliffe Highway, where she probably worked on and off as a prostitute.

By April 1887, Kelly was staying in Cooley's Common Lodging house on Thrawl Street, Spitalfields, and living as a prostitute. On April 8 of that year, she met a man named Joseph Barnett on Commercial Street, and the two had some drinks together. Barnett was a thirty-nine-year-old London-born Irishman who worked at the Billingsgate Fish Market as a fish porter. They arranged to meet the following day and then decided to move in together. By early 1888, the two were living in a dingy room at 13 Miller's Court, Dorset Street. Miller's Court was a narrow and dimly lit courtyard that contained six "two-story, 'one up, one down' slum houses" of single-room apartments, accessible via a thin and unlit arched passage, less than a yard wide, that ran between two three-story buildings at 26 and 27 Dorset Street.[13] A few yards from the archway was a partly torn down poster advertising a reward for the capture of the murderer, and just down the street was Crossingham's Lodging House, where Annie Chapman had stayed on the night of her murder.

On the ground floor of 27 Dorset Street was a chandler shop run by John McCarthy, and there were some rented rooms upstairs. McCarthy owned the apartments in the courtyard out back, thus Miller's Court was also known as "McCarthy's Rents." Number 26 Dorset Street was another lodging house, also owned by McCarthy, with seven rented rooms on the two upper floors. The ground floor in the front of the house had been converted to a "shed" for storing costermongers' barrows, with a gate entrance onto the street. According to a report in the *Daily Telegraph*, this shed had until recently been "the nightly resort of poor homeless creatures, who went there for shelter."[14] What had once been the back parlor of the house had been partitioned off— apparently, by nailing a door shut and possibly covering it with a thin layer of plaster or wallpaper—creating the small one-room apartment known as 13 Miller's Court, where Kelly and Barnett lived.[15] The room was about twelve feet square and sparsely furnished with a bed, two tables, and a cupboard. Opposite the door, which opened off the end of the arched passage, was a fireplace, over which hung a print titled *The Fisherman's Widow*, which had been reproduced in the *Illustrated London News* some years earlier. Two windows looked out onto the courtyard in back.

Kelly and Barnett seem to have lived together amicably, although they sometimes quarreled. On one occasion, Kelly broke one of their two windows, and the pane was never fixed. The couple relied on Barnett's "hard earnings" to get by, and during their time together (according to Barnett), Kelly did not work the streets. But sometime around August 1888, Barnett lost his job, and Kelly returned to her former occupation as a prostitute. Barnett did not approve of this, but there was nothing he could do about it. He earned a little money by selling oranges in the Billingsgate and Spitalfields markets, but it was not enough to support the two of them, and by November, Kelly and Barnett were six weeks behind on their rent.

Kelly was worried about the killings and always asked Barnett to read her newspaper accounts of them. "I used to bring them all home and read them," Barnett said. "If I did not bring one she would get it herself, and ask me whether the murderer was caught. I used to tell her everything that was in the paper."[16] Possibly because of the murders, Kelly started to let other prostitutes sleep in her room. Barnett said that she allowed the prostitutes to stay with them because "she was good hearted and did not like to refuse them shelter on cold bitter nights." Yet Barnett objected to the new arrangement, and the couple separated. On October 30, Barnett moved out and took up lodgings on New Road.

On Thursday, November 8, Mary mentioned to her upstairs neighbor Elizabeth Prater, also a prostitute, that she was hoping for fine weather that Friday. "I want to go to the Lord Mayor's Show," she said. Unfortunately, the prospect for "fine weather" was bleak, because the entire week had been gloomy and dark, with winds blowing "with some considerable violence."[17] The forecast for that night called for strong winds, a rapidly dropping temperature, and cold rain. Kelly passed most of the afternoon with her friend (and fellow prostitute) Maria Harvey, a "laundress" of 3 New Court, who had spent both Monday and Tuesday sleeping in Kelly's room.

At 7:30 or 7:45 p.m., Joe Barnett visited Mary Kelly at Miller's Court. When he arrived, he found Mary sitting with her friend Lizzie Albrook. Albrook got up to leave, saying, "Well, Mary Jane, I shall not see you this evening again." Lizzie later claimed that one of the last things Kelly said to her was "Whatever you do don't you do no wrong and turn out as I have."[18] Barnett and Kelly spoke amicably for about fifteen minutes, then Barnett left. As he was leaving, Barnett told Kelly that he had no work and was sorry he had no money to give her.

Mary Kelly's movements for the remainder of the night are unclear, but she apparently went out drinking again. At 11:45 p.m., Kelly's neighbor Mary Ann Cox, another prostitute, was returning home and followed Kelly and a man as they walked up the court through the arched passage. Kelly's companion was a man about five feet five inches tall, stout, about thirty-six years of age, and shabbily dressed in a dark overcoat and a round black billycock hat. The man was carrying a pot of ale and had "blotches" on his face and a carroty mustache, with a clean-shaven chin. As Cox passed, she said, "Goodnight, Mary." Kelly didn't turn around but drunkenly slurred, "Good night, I am going to have a song." The man shut the door behind them. A few minutes later, Cox heard Kelly singing a song called "A Violet from Mother's Grave." When Cox went back outside around midnight, Mary was still in her room singing. There was a light on, but the blinds were drawn.[19]

By 1 a.m., it was raining hard, and Cox returned to her room to warm her hands. A short time later, she went back out again and heard Kelly still singing. Also around 1 a.m., Prater returned home and stood near the entrance of Miller's Court on Dorset Street waiting for a young man—presumably, either a boyfriend or a client. Prater waited twenty minutes, but the man never showed up, so she went into the chandler's shop and told McCarthy, "Say to my young man that I had gone to my room."[20] She then entered a door off the arched passageway that opened onto a staircase leading to the upstairs rooms in number 26. This staircase abutted the partition on the other side of Kelly's bedroom wall. "I should have seen a glimmer of light in going up the stairs if there had been a light in deceased's room," Prater later said, "but I noticed none. The partition was so thin I could have heard Kelly walk about in the room." Prater's room was on the floor above Kelly's, apparently at the front of the house, facing Dorset Street. She barricaded the door to her room with two tables, then lay down on the bed in her clothes and fell asleep. It was around 1:30 a.m., and the courtyard was quiet.[21]

A man named George Hutchinson later claimed that at 2 a.m. he saw Kelly back on Commercial Street, presumably looking for more clients. Hutchinson's statement was written down by Sergeant Edward Badham of H Division:

> About 2 am 9th I was coming by Thrawl Street, Commercial Street, and saw just before I got to Flower and Dean Street I saw the murdered woman Kelly. And she said to me Hutchinson will you lend me sixpence. I said I cant I have spent all my money going down to Romford. She said Good morning I must go and find some money. She went away toward Thrawl Street. A man coming in the opposite direction to Kelly tapped her on the shoulder and said something to her. They both burst out laughing. I heard

her say alright to him. And the man said you will be alright for what I have told you. He then placed his right hand around her shoulders. He also had a kind of a small parcel in his left hand with a kind of strap round it. I stood against the lamp of the Queen's Head Public House and watched him. They both then came past me and the man hid down his head with his hat over his eyes. I stooped down and looked him in the face. He looked at me stern. They both went into Dorset Street I followed them. They both stood at the corner of the Court for about 3 minutes. He said something to her. She said alright my dear come along you will be comfortable He then placed his arm on her shoulder and gave her a kiss. She said she had lost her handkercheif he then pulled his handkercheif a red one out and gave it to her. They both then went up the court together. I then went to the Court to see if I could see them, but could not. I stood there for about three quarters of an hour to see if they came out they did not so I went away.

Description age about 34 or 35. height 5ft 6 complexion pale, dark eyes and eye lashes slight moustache, curled up each end, and hair dark, very surley looking dress long dark coat, collar and cuffs trimmed astracan. And a dark jacket under. Light waistcoat dark trousers dark felt hat turned down in the middle. Button boots and gaiters with white buttons. Wore a very thick gold chain white linen collar. Black tie with horse shoe pin. Respectable appearance walked very sharp. Jewish appearance. Can be identified.[22]

A later version of the same story that was printed in the newspaper added that the man was carrying a "parcel" about eight inches long, covered in dark cloth, with a strap around it. We will return to Hutchinson's statement shortly.

At 2:30 a.m., a laundress named Sarah Lewis was walking along Commercial Street after having had a fight with her husband. She was going to visit her friend Mrs. Keyler at Miller's Court. On her way there, she noticed a suspicious-looking "gentleman" standing near the Britannia pub, at the corner of Dorset and Commercial streets. In fact,

Lewis had run into this same man just the night before, when she was walking with a female friend on Bethnal Green Road. The man had been carrying an ominous-looking shiny black bag about nine inches long and had approached the two women to ask whether one of them would follow him into an entryway. "I don't like the look of this man," Lewis's friend said. "Come away." The man put down the bag and then picked it up again. "What are you frightened about? Do you think I've got anything in the bag?" he asked. He then undid his overcoat and began to reach for something, at which point the two women ran off without looking back.[23] When Lewis saw this man again at the Britannia, she was frightened and hurried past. The man looked up, but Lewis could not tell whether he recognized her. She later described him as about forty, short and pale-faced, with a small black mustache, a high round hat, a black coat, and salt-and-pepper trousers.

After turning into Dorset Street, Lewis noticed a second suspicious-looking man standing across the street from Miller's Court, "looking up the court" as if he was "waiting or looking for someone." In all likelihood, this was George Hutchinson himself, because, according to his statement, he waited outside Miller's Court "for about three quarters of an hour," between 2:00 and 2:45 a.m. Lewis continued up the court, then went into the room of her friend Mrs. Keyler, directly across from Mary Kelly's room, and dozed off in a chair.[24]

By around 3 a.m., Hutchinson gave up on waiting for Kelly on Dorset Street and left. Around the same time, Mary Ann Cox returned home. This time, the lights in number 13 were out, and Cox heard no noise coming from the room. She went to her room at the far end of the court, but she was worried because she had not paid her rent, and she could not sleep.

Sometime between 3:30 and 4:00 a.m., Elizabeth Prater, upstairs in number 26, was awakened by her cat, Diddles. "I had a little black kitten, which need to come on to my neck," she said. "It woke me up from 3.30 to 4.00, by coming on to my face, and I gave it a blow and knocked it off." Just as the cat jumped to the floor, Prater heard a cry of, "Oh, murder!" She later described the sound as "a faintish one, as though some one had woke up with a nightmare." The cry seemed to come from the court in back of the house, but Prater paid little attention to it. Such cries were common in Dorset Street.[25] Sarah

Lewis, at number 1 Miller's Court, was also awake at this time. She had dozed off in the chair at Mrs. Keyler's but then woke up, heard the clock strike 3:30 a.m., and could not fall back asleep. Around four o'clock, Lewis heard a woman's voice cry, "Murder!" Unlike Prater, who said she only heard the cry faintly, Lewis described it as a "scream" or a loud shouting. But like Prater, Lewis was not particularly alarmed by the cry, "especially as a short time before there had been a row in the court," she said.[26] If the cry of "Murder!" actually came from Mary Kelly, it gives a good idea of the time of her death—specifically, sometime around 4 a.m. or shortly before. The difference in the perceived volume of the cry as heard by Lewis and by Prater is not very hard to explain. Lewis was sitting up, wide awake, in a ground-floor room, only about ten feet from Kelly's room, whereas Prater was probably half-asleep, in a room that was apparently above the storage space in the front part of the house.

At 7:30 a.m., another neighbor, Catherine Picket, was leaving the court to buy flowers at the market and went downstairs to borrow Kelly's pelerine (a kind of cape), because her "poor shawl" was "thin as a cobweb," and it was still raining.[27] She knocked repeatedly at Kelly's door, but there was no answer. Picket assumed that Kelly was still sleeping and left.

At 10:45 a.m., John McCarthy sent his servant, Thomas Bowyer (aka Indian Harry), to collect the rent from "Mary Jane," because she was 29 shillings in arrears. Bowyer went to number 13 and knocked on the door. Getting no answer, he knocked again. When he still received no response, Bowyer walked around to the corner by the gutter spout to look in Kelly's window. He reached through the hole in the broken glass and pulled the curtain aside. What Bowyer saw was so hideous that he must not have believed his eyes—there were "two lumps of flesh" lying on a table near the door. Bowyer recoiled, then looked again, this time noticing "the body of somebody lying on the bed, and blood on the floor." Bowyer rushed back into the shop. "Governor, I knocked at the door, and couldn't make anyone answer," he stammered. "I looked through the window and saw a lot of blood." "Good God!" McCarthy responded, "do you mean to say that, Harry?" Both men returned to Kelly's room, and McCarthy looked through the window. What he saw stunned him so badly that he was momentarily unable to speak. "Harry, don't tell anyone," he said. "Go for the police." Bowyer ran off toward Commercial Street Police Station. McCarthy then changed his mind and ran off after him.[28]

At the time, Detective Constable Walter Dew was in the Commercial Street Police Station talking with Walter Beck, the inspector in charge. Suddenly, Bowyer came charging into the station, panting. According to Dew, "The poor fellow was so frightened that for a time he was unable to utter a single intelligible word." Eventually, Bowyer managed to stammer, "Another one . . . Jack the Ripper . . . awful . . . Jack McCarthy sent me." The inspectors ran to the court, collecting constables along the way. Beck sent someone to fetch Dr. George Bagster Phillips in nearby Spital Square, then dispatched a telegram to Scotland Yard, informing his superiors that the crime scene was undisturbed, in case they wanted to use their bloodhounds to try to track the culprit. Beck closed off the court, and no one was allowed to enter or leave.[29]

Dr. Phillips arrived at Miller's Court around 11:15 a.m., and, seeing that the door was locked, looked in the window to determine whether there was anyone inside who required medical attention. The scene before him was all too plain. As Phillips later said, I "satisfied myself that the mutilated corpse lying on the bed was not in need of any immediate attention from me." Beck and Phillips agreed that they should wait for the bloodhounds before opening the door, and when Detective Frederick Abberline arrived at 11:30 a.m., he was informed that they were still waiting for the bloodhounds, which were supposedly on the way.[30] At 1:20 p.m., however, Superintendent Arnold arrived and informed everybody that the order had been canceled, and the bloodhounds were not coming. He gave the order to break down the door, and McCarthy proceeded to tear it open with a pickax.

The men entered the room and saw the horrific sight that was to be the Ripper's most gruesome crime of all. Mary Kelly's body had been savagely mutilated. Inspector Henry Moore later said that the murderer "cut the skeleton so clean of flesh that when I got here I could hardly tell whether it was a man or a woman." Kelly was lying on her back, inclined to the left side of the bed, with her legs wide apart. Her throat had been severed, and then her body had apparently been moved to the middle of the bed and eviscerated. Much of the skin had been removed from her thighs, and her breasts had been cut off by circular incisions. One of her breasts was near her right foot and the other was under her head. Her intestines were by her left side, her liver was between her feet, and on the table next to the bed were large flaps of skin and muscle that had been removed from her abdomen and her thighs. Her face had been mutilated "beyond recognition."

Before anything was disturbed, the police took at least two photographs of the body in situ. Detective Abberline then searched the room for clues. There had evidently been a large fire in the fireplace, and the ashes were still warm—in fact, as Abberline noted, the fire had been "so large as to melt the spout off the kettle." The ashes were later carefully examined, and it was discovered that "a large quantity of women's clothing had been burnt." Abberline speculated that this was done "to make a light for the man to see what he was doing," because, as Abberline pointed out, the only other light in the room came from "one small candle . . . on the top of a broken wine-glass." Abberline also found a pipe, which turned out to belong to Joseph Barnett.[31]

After receiving news of the murder, Assistant Commissioner Robert Anderson sent word to Dr. Thomas Bond, the police surgeon for A (Whitehall) Division, to proceed to the scene. Anderson then rode to Miller's Court in a cab and arrived at ten minutes before two. Meanwhile, news of the murder had reached the public. When the crowds cheering the Lord Mayor's show got wind of it, as Walter Dew later recounted, "The cheers died in their throats; the smiles left their faces."[32] Throngs of curiosity seekers made their way to Dorset Street, only to find, to their disappointment, that the police had closed off the entire length of Dorset Street, with "a cordon of constables drawn across each end."[33] Four doctors—Dr. Phillips, Dr. Bond, Dr. Gordon Brown of the City Police, and Dr. John Rees—conducted examinations in the room until 4 p.m., when a horse-drawn cart arrived to remove the body. As reported in the *Times*,

> The news that the body was about to be removed caused a great rush of people from the courts running out of Dorset-street, and there was a determined effort to break the police cordon at the Commercial-street end. . . . Ragged caps were doffed and slatternly-looking women shed tears as the shell,

covered with a ragged-looking cloth, was placed in the van. The remains were taken to the Shoreditch Mortuary.[34]

The windows to Mary Kelly's room were then boarded up, and the door to number 13 was padlocked.

On November 10, at 7:30 a.m., a postmortem examination conducted at the mortuary next to the Whitechapel Church by Dr. Phillips, Dr. Bond, Dr. Brown, and Dr. William Dukes of Spitalfields concluded that as in the other cases, death had resulted from a severed carotid artery. The neck was severed down to the bone, and there were notches cut in the vertebrae of the spine, as with two of the previous victims. The throat had been slashed so many times that it was impossible to determine the direction of the cuts.

On November 12, an inquest was held in a small committee room on the ground floor of the Shoreditch Town Hall, conducted by Dr. Roderick McDonald, MP, the coroner for the North-Eastern District of Middlesex. Superintendent Arnold of H Division, Detective Abberline of CID, and Inspector James Nairn, who had been imported from N Division to work the case, were in attendance representing the police, and large crowds gathered both inside and outside the hall. The fifteen jurymen were taken to view the body at the mortuary and then went to inspect Kelly's room. After an hour, they were back in the inquest chamber, and the first witness, Joseph Barnett, was called. When handed the Bible, as reported in the *Morning Advertiser*, "he at once kissed it, and on being checked by the officer he said, 'Oh, well, I don't know nothing about such things.'"[35]

In his inquest testimony, George Bagster Phillips gave only a very limited description of Kelly's wounds and did not describe the mutilations at all. Coroner McDonald then said, "It was clear that the severance of the artery was the immediate cause of death, and unless the jury otherwise desired, this was all the evidence Dr. Phillips proposed to give that day." The jury acquiesced. By the end of the afternoon, the inquest was over, and the jury had passed verdict of "Wilful murder against some person or persons unknown."[36]

The funeral was held on November 19, and, as before,

[A]n enormous crowd of people assembled at an early hour, completely blocking the thoroughfare. . . . As the coffin

appeared, borne on the shoulders of four men, at the principal gate of the church, the crowd was greatly moved. Round
the open car in which it was to be placed men and women
struggled desperately to touch the coffin. Women with faces
streaming with tears cried out "God forgive her!" and every
man's head was bared. The site was quite remarkable, and
the emotion natural and unconstrained.[37]

Kelly was interred at St. Patrick's Roman Catholic Cemetery in
Leytonstone. No members of her family could be located to attend,
and because neither Barnett nor any of Kelly's friends had any money
to speak of, Mr. H. Wilson, a sexton of St. Leonard's Church in
Shoreditch, generously paid the funeral costs. Barnett knelt in the clay,
weeping as Kelly's coffin was lowered into the ground.

Thus ends the story of Mary Kelly. A year after the murder,
Inspector Henry Moore took an American journalist on a tour of the
murder sites, and the pair visited 13 Miller's Court. By then, there was
a new couple living in Kelly's old room, but the woman invited "Mister
Inspector" and his guest inside to look around. A man was lying in the
bed, but he obligingly got up and pointed out the bloodstains that were
still visible as dark streaks on the wall. When the man turned his face
to the wall to go back to sleep, Moore wished him "pleasant dreams."[38]

Before moving on, I will take a moment to discuss the statement of
George Hutchinson. Because Hutchinson gave such a detailed description of the man seen with Kelly at 2 a.m., and because he said he could
identify the man again, the police took his statement very seriously.
Detective Abberline, for one, was of the opinion that Hutchinson
was telling the truth and regarded him as an important witness. Yet
there are several aspects of Hutchinson's statement that seem bizarre
and somewhat questionable. The main problem is the great amount of
detail Hutchinson noticed about the man, right down to a gold watch
and chain, a horseshoe pin, and gaiters. In addition, Hutchinson did
not give his statement to the police until November 12, three days after
the murder and after the inquest was completed. He did so, quite possibly, in order to clear himself as a suspect after he learned that Sarah
Lewis stated that she had seen a man standing across from Miller's
Court at 2 a.m. on the night of the murder. Thus, Hutchinson's motive

for giving the statement in the first place makes his description of the man he allegedly saw a bit suspicious.

Several parts of his statement seemed to fit, however. Like P.C. William Smith, who saw a man on the night of the Berner Street murder carrying a "newspaper parcel 18 × 7 inches," Hutchinson claimed that the man he saw had a "small parcel in his left hand with a kind of strap round it."[39] Other aspects of Hutchinson's description, such as the man's age, height, and complexion, also generally match the descriptions given by Smith, Israel Schwartz, and Joseph Lawende, and the fact that Hutchinson said that the man was Jewish tallies with Elizabeth Long's description of the "foreign"-looking man seen at the Chapman murder. But the well-dressed "toff" seen by Hutchinson did not match any of the other witness statements, which generally described a man who was more or less shabby-genteel and dressed like either a clerk or a sailor. In the end, it is impossible to know what to make of Hutchinson's statement. Many Ripperologists think Hutchinson fabricated the story to deflect attention from himself as a potential suspect.

In any case, even if Hutchinson was telling the truth, perhaps the man he saw with Kelly was not the killer. Hutchinson claimed that he saw Kelly on Commercial Street at approximately 2 a.m. and then stood outside the entrance to Miller's Court until around 3 a.m. Yet it is entirely possible that Kelly got another client after this time. Recall that both Sarah Lewis and Elizabeth Prater heard a cry of "Murder!" sometime around 4 a.m. It seems unlikely that the well-dressed toff would have waited around in Kelly's room for some two hours before killing her. Again, however, the evidence is open to various interpretations.

15

The Curtain Falls

The day before Mary Kelly was murdered, Sir Charles Warren tendered his resignation as commissioner of the Metropolitan Police Force. Warren resigned ostensibly because of his frustration at being censured by Home Secretary Henry Matthews for writing an article titled "The Police of the Metropolis" that appeared in *Murray's Magazine*, but the department's failure in the Ripper case must have factored into his decision. Warren stayed on as commissioner until November 27 and then was replaced by James Monro, Anderson's predecessor as head of the CID.

In the days and weeks following Kelly's murder, the Home Office and the police were under great pressure to make progress in the case, but they were still apparently getting nowhere. The day after Kelly's murder, Queen Victoria gave notice that the government would grant a full pardon to any accomplice "who shall give such information and evidence as shall lead to the discovery and conviction of the person or persons who committed the murder," the only condition being that the accomplice was not "a person who contrived or actually committed the murder."[1] It was a desperate attempt to do something, anything really, to deflect the public's anger at the fact that the murderer was still on the loose.

On November 16, 1888, just one week after the murder, Dr. Hermann Adler gave a special Sabbath address to an assembly of

Jewish workingmen and workingwomen, imploring them not to do anything "which would be calculated to raise the breath of calumny against their homes." "These were troublous times," Adler said, and "it was only necessary (Heaven forbid it) for an unconscientious person to make a false but terrible accusation, and a riot might ensue." Adler entreated the assembly to "obey the directions of the police, especially in their house-to-house investigations."[2] It is unclear why Adler felt it necessary to ask his congregation to cooperate with the investigations then under way, although it may imply that some segments of the Jewish population were being less than helpful to the police.

The death of another prostitute on December 20, 1888, in Poplar, a few miles east of Whitechapel, briefly caused concern that the killer had returned. The murdered woman was named Catherine "Rose" Mylett. On the night of her death, Mylett was seen around 8 p.m. with two sailors on Poplar High Street near Clarke's Yard. According to a witness, Charles Ptolomey, the sailors were acting in a strange manner—one was speaking to Mylett, while the other was "walking up and down." Ptolomey heard Mylett cry out, "No! no! no!" and later said he took notice of the incident because he thought they "were there for no good purpose."[3] Several hours later, at 2:30 a.m., a woman named Alice Graves saw a drunken Mylett in the company of two men outside of the George public house on Commercial Road.

Mylett's body was found in Clarke's Yard about two hours later. She was lying on her side, her left leg stretched out in front of her, and her right leg drawn up, but her clothes were not disarranged. The police who investigated the matter found no signs of violence either on the body or at the crime scene and apparently did not think the woman had been murdered at all. When the divisional surgeon Dr. Matthew Brownfield conducted a postmortem examination, however, he discovered a thin white line around the woman's neck and noticed "impressions of the thumbs and middle and index fingers of some person plainly visible on each side of the neck." Brownfield concluded that the woman had been strangled to death. Yet for some reason, he did not bother to inform the police of this; instead, he told a reporter, and the results of his postmortem were printed in the *Star* newspaper. Dr. Brownfield's conclusions on the matter came as a great surprise to the police, and Robert Anderson claimed that the first he heard of the opinion that the woman had been murdered was in the newspaper. Commissioner Monro was furious, and, hesitant to accept Brownfield's conclusions, he sent Anderson to personally investigate the woman's death. Monro also ordered Dr. Alexander O. MacKellar, the chief surgeon of the Metropolitan Police, to make a second examination of the body. But Dr. MacKellar seconded the opinion of Dr. Brownfield, forcing Monro to concede that the case was indeed one of murder, although it was "murder of a strange and unusual type."[4]

Anderson's investigations into the matter went so far as to his personally examining the body. Dr. Bond, the police surgeon for A (Whitehall) Division, also eventually examined the body and decided that death was from "accidental strangulation," a conclusion that was shared, if not suggested, by Anderson. In a letter to Monro, Anderson suggested that Mylett's death had resulted from some combination of a tight-fitting collar and the woman's "drunken habits"—specifically, he thought the woman had fallen down in a drunken stupor, and "the weight of her head against the collar of her dress compressed the larynx and caused suffocation." Anderson claimed that this theory was backed up by Dr. Bond, Mr. Wontner, and the coroner Wynne Baxter, who declared, "There is no evidence to show that death was the result of violence." Anderson told Monro that despite the inquest verdict of "wilful murder," he "did not intend to take any further action in the matter."[5]

In comparison to the previous murders, this was a rather dull affair, and an article in the Star noted that the murder "failed to create any excitement even in the neighborhood," adding, "The police themselves appear to have shared the general feeling of non-interest."[6] The press briefly speculated that the Ripper had returned but had changed his methods. One theory was that the Ripper had in fact strangled all of the victims with a thin cord, but the white line that would have shown evidence of strangulation was obliterated by the subsequent knife cuts. Ultimately, however, the questions raised by Mylett's death were not answered, and the case was never solved.

By the beginning of 1889, active pursuit of the Ripper inquiry had started to dwindle. In late January 1889, Commissioner Monro decided that the extra plainclothes officers who had been drafted into Whitechapel to work the case were no longer needed, and told the Home Office that he was "gradually reducing the number of men employed on this duty as quickly as it is safe to do so."[7] By March 15, the extra plainclothes patrols had been phased out entirely, and in a letter to the Secretary of State, Monro said, "This duty has now ceased."[8] That same month, Detective Frederick Abberline was sent back to Scotland Yard to work on other cases, and Inspector Henry Moore took charge of ground inquiries in the Ripper case.

Six months went by. Then in July 1889, just when things seemed to be back to normal, there was another murder, in Spitalfields. The victim this time was Alice McKenzie, a middle-aged woman who had lived in a lodging house at 52 Gun Street with a laborer named John McCormack on and off for about six or seven years. According to Betsy Ryder, the deputy of the lodging house, McKenzie was "much addicted to drink" and "was in the habit of staying out all night if she had no money to pay for her lodging." Ryder added that the police considered McKenzie to be a prostitute. Like two of the previous victims, McKenzie was said to have "worked hard for the Jews."[9]

Around 8:30 p.m. on the night of Tuesday, July 16–17, 1889, Ryder saw McKenzie leave the lodging house with some money in her hand. McKenzie had been drinking and had not paid for her lodgings. Three hours later, she was walking briskly along Brick Lane, where she passed by an acquaintance named Margaret Franklin. Franklin asked McKenzie how she was getting on, to which McKenzie replied, "All right I can't stop now."[10]

At 12:15 a.m., P.C. Joseph Allen of H Division was "partaking of his supper" under a street lamp in Castle Alley, a narrow passageway that ran parallel to Goulston Street. He stood there eating for about five minutes and later said that the alley was completely deserted at the time. Just as Allen was leaving, P.C. Walter Andrews entered the street and stayed for about three minutes, during which time he saw nothing unusual. Half an hour later, Andrews's beat took him back into Castle Alley. It had been raining for about five minutes, and he was walking near the back of the public baths, "trying the doors," when he saw a woman lying on the pavement next to some carts. He touched the body and noted that it was quite warm, then blew his whistle for assistance. Sergeant Edward Badham, who had spoken to Andrews just a few minutes earlier, heard the whistle and rushed to Castle Alley. Andrews met Badham and told him, "Come on quick, here's another murder," and the two went back to look at the body. Badham instructed Andrews to stay at the murder site, while he went off to send information about the murder to the police station and call for a doctor.[11] Detective Inspector Edmund Reid, Superintendent Thomas Arnold, and a number of police constables from adjoining beats arrived on the scene shortly afterward. Arnold directed several of the constables to search the immediate surroundings and inquire whether any suspicious-looking characters had been seen entering the local common lodging houses and coffee houses. When Commissioner Monro heard of the crime at 3 a.m., he immediately set off to examine the spot in person, for the purpose of "assisting at the inquiry."

When Dr. George Bagster Phillips arrived around 1:10 a.m., he found the woman lying on her back with a pool of clotted blood under her head. The woman's clothes had been pulled up, exposing her abdomen and genitals, and her throat was cut. Phillips's postmortem examination report described the victim's wounds, which were in this case decidedly less extensive than those in the previous murders. Yet there were similarities. The cause of death was a "division of the vessels on the left side" of the throat, which had been cut from left to right. There was also a seven-inch-long wound on the right side of the abdomen, but the cut was not very deep. There were several other scratches in the lower abdomen that cut through the top layers of the skin, one of which "became deeper over the pubis."[12]

Phillips noted that "The clothing was fastened round the body somewhat tightly & could only be raised so as to expose about 1/3 of the abdomen," and concluded that the "scoring and cuts of skin on Pubis were caused through the endeavor to pass the obstruction caused by the clothing." In other words, it appeared that the killer struggled to get the woman's clothes off to expose the abdomen but ultimately failed to do so. In addition, because the ground under McKenzie's body was dry, it seems that the murder had been committed sometime between approximately 12:23 a.m., when Andrews left Castle Alley, and around 12:45 a.m., when it started raining. If the attack happened nearer to the end of this period, it is possible that Andrews's arrival in

Castle Alley scared the killer off. These facts may explain the lesser degree of mutilation in this case. Still, Dr. Phillips concluded that it was not a Ripper murder, although he pointed out that he did not take into account "what I admit may be almost conclusive evidence in favour of the one man theory if all the surrounding circumstances & other evidence are considered." Phillips stressed that his conclusion was based solely on "his own observations"—in other words, a comparison of McKenzie's wounds with those of the previous victims.[13]

Dr. Thomas Bond also examined the body, a day after Phillips did, but by this time "decomposition had fairly begun," and, what's more, Phillips's postmortem had disturbed the original condition of the wounds, which by then had been sewn up. Phillips was with Bond at the time of this second examination, and he described the original condition of the wounds and his various conclusions about them, to which Bond was in general agreement. As Bond stated, "In order to inflict the wound which I saw on the abdomen the murderer must have raised the clothes with his left hand & inflicted the injuries with his right." Unlike Phillips, Dr. Bond concluded, "I am of the opinion that the murder was performed by the same person who committed the former series of Whitechapel murders."[14] Commissioner Monro also believed that McKenzie had been killed by the Ripper, as he wrote in a report to the Home Office, stating that "Every effort will be made by the Police to discover the murderer, who, I am inclined to believe is identical with the notorious 'Jack the Ripper' of last year." Monro admitted that once again, the assassin had "succeeded in committing a murder and getting off without leaving the slightest clue to his identity."[15]

Alice McKenzie's murder would go unsolved, and today it is still debated whether she was a victim of the Ripper. But the horrors were not yet over.

On September 8, 1889, the one-year anniversary of the murder of Annie Chapman, a man named John Cleary walked into the offices of the *Herald* newspaper just after 1 a.m. and declared that Jack the Ripper had murdered another woman in the East End. Cleary claimed that a police inspector who was an acquaintance of his told him that the mutilated body of a woman had been found at 11:20 p.m. in Backchurch Lane. Cleary added that he hoped to get a reward for supplying this information and gave his address as 21 White Horse Yard, Drury Lane.[16]

Two *Herald* reporters decided to go to the East End to investigate, and they asked Cleary to accompany them. Cleary declined, however, saying that it was too far from his home, so the reporters decided to go without him. After the reporters finally managed to locate Backchurch Lane, they "made a thorough search of the neighborhood" but found no mutilated body and no crime scene.[17] They approached two policemen and asked whether there had been another murder in the area, but the constables knew nothing about it. Cleary, it seemed, was just another hoaxer.

Then strangely, three days later, the headless and legless body of a woman was found under a railway arch near the southern end of Backchurch Lane in Pinchin Street. There was no blood around the body, and the police thought that it must have been moved to the archway some time after the woman's death. Yet in the absence of a head, it was impossible to identify the victim. In fact, it was not even possible to determine whether the woman had been murdered at all or whether she had died of other causes. There were no mutilations, except for one long cut down the center of the body, extending from the chest to the genitals. No organs had been removed from the abdomen, and as Commissioner Monro wrote in a report of the incident, "The wound looks as if the murderer had intended to make a cut preparatory to removing the intestines in the process of dismemberment & had then changed his mind."[18] There was a mark around the waist, as if a rope had been tied around the body, and a postmortem examination determined that some sort of saw had been used to sever the bones of the neck and the legs. Doctors estimated that the woman had died at least three or four days before the body was discovered—in other words, around the time that John Cleary went to the *Herald* office and reported a murder in that very location.

When the *Herald* reporters learned about the discovery, they immediately remembered Cleary and tried to locate him. They visited his supposed address at 21 White Horse Yard but were told that there was no one by that name living there. Eventually, it was discovered that Cleary's real name was John Arnold. Arnold admitted that he had reported a murder at the *Herald* office and said that he gave a false name to avoid complications involving his wife, from whom he was separated. He claimed that he heard the story from a man who was dressed as a soldier, and he described the man as about thirty-five or thirty-six years old, and about five feet seven inches tall, with a fair mustache. Little more is known about Arnold, although he was known to the police as a gambler and a drunk. The police attempted to pursue a line of inquiry to see whether Arnold could identify the "soldier" who told him the story, but it is not know whether anything ever came of it.

The police eventually concluded that the "Pinchin Street torso" was not a Ripper murder and instead suspected that it was related to a series of crimes that had taken place in Battersea and Rainham. The inquest returned a verdict of "wilful murder," and a CID report stated the police had no objection to the torso being buried, "if it will not interfere with our being able to fit the head to the trunk, if we ever get it."[19] But they never got it.

16

An Encore? The Murder of
Frances Coles

P.C. Ernest Thompson was a new addition to the Metropolitan Police Force. He joined H Division in late December 1890, then six weeks later was sent on his first night patrol in the vicinity of the Royal Mint. As luck would have it, the date was Friday, February, 13, 1891. About 2:15 a.m., while patrolling a typically lonely stretch of road named Chamber Street, Thompson heard footsteps somewhere ahead, "proceeding in the opposite direction towards Mansell Street." But it was dark, and Thompson "was not sufficiently close to discern the person," nor did he think much of it at the time. He then turned into a dark arched railway underpass called Swallow Gardens and was shocked by the sight of a woman lying on the ground. The woman's throat had been cut, and blood was still issuing from the wound, but Thompson thought he saw one of the woman's eyelids move. It was just a few streets west of the spot where the Pinchin Street torso had been discovered five months earlier.[1]

Thompson immediately blew his whistle, alerting police constables on adjoining beats who soon arrived at the scene. One of them went to fetch a local doctor named F. J. Oxley, who came in short order and pronounced the woman dead. When H Division Superintendent

Thomas Arnold showed up, he instructed that the surrounding area be searched and inquiries be made at all of the local lodging houses. None of the constables had seen anyone passing nearby at the time of the murder.

The victim was a twenty-five-year-old prostitute named Frances Coles. Since about the age of seventeen, Coles had "walked about the streets" and for several years previously had "given way to drunken habits," staying at various lodging houses in the neighborhood of Commercial Street. In the days prior to her murder, Coles had been on a sort of bender, drinking pretty much nonstop for two days and nights with a ship's fireman named Thomas Sadler. Sadler had been one of Coles's clients on a previous occasion, and as he admitted, "I used her for my purpose."[2] According to Sadler's police statement, he and Coles first got drunk on Wednesday, February 11, then spent the night together in a lodging house called Spitalfields Chambers on White's Row. They proceeded to get drunk the following day as well, visiting numerous pubs around Brick Lane. By that evening, Sadler was well "getting into drink." Sometime between 9 and 11 p.m., the two were walking down Thrawl Street when a woman in a red shawl struck Sadler on the head, and then two men beat and robbed him, while Coles stood by and did nothing. After that, the pair got into an argument because Sadler claimed that Coles should have helped him when he was being beaten. They parted on bad terms. Around 11:30 p.m., Coles returned to the lodging house in White's Row, where she sat in the kitchen and continued to drink.

After their argument, Sadler (according to his police statement) went to the docks, where he tried to gain admission on a boat that he had previously worked on called the S.S. *Fez*. He was in such a dazed and drunken state, however, that he was refused entry. He started cursing out a nearby policeman and some dock laborers, one of whom remarked that if the policeman would turn his back, "he would give [Sadler] a damned good hiding." The policeman sauntered off, and Sadler was immediately beaten and kicked severely by the men. Sadler then wandered around, trying to find a bed in a lodging house, but he was penniless and drunk and couldn't get in anywhere. He finally returned to Spitalfields Chambers, where he found Coles in the kitchen, "half dazed from drink." Neither of them had enough money for a bed, and Sadler was turned out around midnight. He left Coles there in the kitchen, passed out on a bench. Sometime later, Coles woke up, and she was kicked out as well. According to conflicting statements, she left the lodging house either at 12:30 a.m. or around 1:30 to 1:45 a.m.[3]

If we are to believe Sadler's police statement, he did not see Coles again after this. He claimed that after he left White's Row, he walked in the direction of the London Hospital, where he was stopped and questioned by a policeman who thought Sadler looked like he was "in a pretty pickle." The policeman asked where Sadler was going, and Sadler explained that he had "had two doings that night" and had been cut with a knife or a broken bottle. The policeman apparently misunderstood this and said, "Oh, have you a knife about you?" Sadler replied that he said he did not have a knife and hadn't carried a knife in years, but the policeman searched him anyway. Sadler then walked across the street to the London Hospital, where he was treated for a wound in his head and was allowed to lie down on a couch. The next day, Sadler was paid at the shipping office and went to a lodging house in Upper East Smithfield, where he stayed all day, feeling miserable.

After Coles was kicked out of Spitalfields Chambers, she was seen at 1:30 a.m. dining on mutton at Shuttleworth's eating house on Wentworth Street. She sat alone in the corner and was repeatedly asked to leave by Joseph Haswell, an employee who was trying to close up shop. "Mind your own business!" Coles said. Haswell then physically assisted her to the door. A short time later, Coles was on Commercial Street, soliciting a man in a cheesecutter hat, despite the fact that a friend had warned her that the man was violent. But Coles was desperate.[4]

A half-mile to the south, a laborer named Thomas Fowles was standing with his fiancée, Kate McCarthy, in front of her home on Royal Mint Street, wearing what he referred to as a "black pilot monkey jacket." At 2 a.m., the couple noticed some railway workers walk by, toward the south end of Swallow Gardens, followed by a man Fowles knew only as Jumbo, who was carrying a whip and was apparently very drunk. "Jumbo," whose real name was Carmen Friday, would later misidentify Kate McCarthy as Frances Coles and would also state that she was with a man who looked like a ship's fireman.[5]

Given that most of what we know about Sadler's whereabouts that night came from Sadler himself, we must regard his statements with some suspicion. Indeed, the evidence suggests that Sadler was lying. For one thing, it is clear that Sadler did see Coles again after they left Spitalfields Chambers. Sadler admitted as much in his police statement, when he said, "I forgot to mention that Frances and I had some food at Mrs. Shuttleworth's in Wentworth Street." This means that Coles and Sadler met up at Shuttleworth's sometime before 1:30 a.m. Another problem with Sadler's story is that it seems he went to the London docks after he left Coles at White's Row, not before, as he claimed. In any case, Sadler clearly did not proceed "towards London Hospital," as he claimed, because at approximately 2 a.m., Sergeant Wesley Edwards encountered Sadler in a drunk and bloody state on the pavement near the Royal Mint. Fifteen minutes later, Coles would be found murdered only a few hundred yards away. The fact that Coles and Sadler both ended up in the vicinity of Royal Mint Street around 2 a.m. strengthens the case against Sadler. One possibility is that Coles and Sadler separated after meeting at Shuttleworth's, with the intention of meeting up again later. Coles may have tried to find a client around Commercial Street, while Sadler went to the docks to try to get on the *Fez*. After they both failed, they may have met again (as planned) near the Royal Mint.

The police were extremely interested in Sadler as a suspect, not only for the murder of Frances Coles, but for the previous Ripper murders as well. Chief Inspector Donald Swanson interviewed Sadler's wife, who described her husband as a tempestuous and violent alcoholic, who "not only assaulted her and otherwise treated her cruelly, but he had repeatedly threatened to take her life."[6] On one occasion, Sadler wanted to take his wife to look at one of the Ripper murder sites, saying, "It was miraculous that any person could do such a thing and get off," but his wife did not care to visit the place. Yet the jury at Coles's inquest eventually found Sadler not guilty, in part because the jurors thought he was too drunk to have performed the murder. In addition, the testimony of Carmen Friday, a central witness in the case against Sadler, turned out to be a case of mistaken identification. Ultimately, the police failed to find any definite evidence that proved Sadler was guilty, and the charges were dropped.

So, was Frances Coles killed by Jack the Ripper? As in the previous murder, police opinion was divided, and today, most researchers do not seem to think Coles was a victim of the Ripper. For one thing, although Coles's throat was cut, her abdomen was not mutilated, nor were her clothes disarranged. In addition, there seems to be a good circum-stantial case in favor of Sadler being Coles's murderer. Yet Sadler was clearly not the Ripper, because his shipping records showed that he was at sea during several of the murders. In any case, by the time Frances Coles was murdered, Aaron Kozminski was already locked away in an asylum. So, although it will never be known for certain whether Coles was a victim of the Ripper, if she was, then Kozminski must be declared innocent of all Ripper crimes.

The intersection of Whitechapel Road and Osborn Street circa 1890, near where Emma Smith was attacked. This corner was almost directly across from St. Mary's Church. The site of the Tabram murder was just a few minutes' walk from here.

St. Botolph's Church, aka "the Prostitutes' Church," circa 1892. Kate Eddowes was passed out drunk near here when she was arrested.

Buck's Row, looking west, in
the 1930s. New Cottage can
be seen in the center of the
photo. An arrow points to the
site of the murder.

Polly Nichols's
mortuary photo.

Discovery of the body.

Annie Chapman's wedding photo, circa 1869.

Chapman's mortuary photo.

The backyard at 29 Hanbury Street. Chapman's body was found lying between the step and the wood fence.

The corner of Berner and Fairclough streets, as it looked in April 1909. The entrance to Dutfield's Yard is under the hanging wagon wheel. The International Working Men's Educational Club was in the tall building adjacent to the yard.

Liz Stride's mortuary photo.

The north end of Berner Street at the intersection with Commercial Road circa the 1890s. The south end of Greenfield Street was almost directly opposite.

172

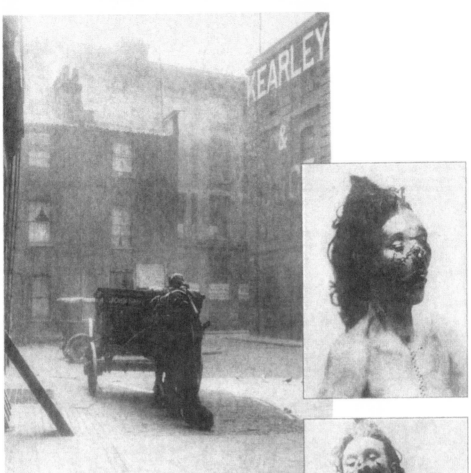

Mitre Square circa 1925. The darkest corner of
the square, where Eddowes was murdered, is to
the left behind the car.

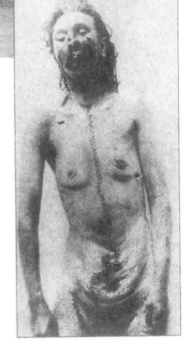

In situ drawing of Kate Eddowes by Frederick Foster.

Eddowes's mortuary photos.

173

Goulston Street cloth market in the early 1900s. Goulston Street was the site of the chazar mark, where Jewish master tailors went to hire "greeners." The infamous graffito was written in one of the entranceways of Wentworth Model Dwellings, the large building at the end of the street.

The Goulston Street graffito was scrawled in chalk in this doorway (this photo was taken in 1975), above a cut-off portion of Kate Eddowes's bloody apron. It read, "The Juwes are the men that will not be blamed for nothing." Ripperologists still debate whether this message was written by the killer.

The same entranceway in 2005.

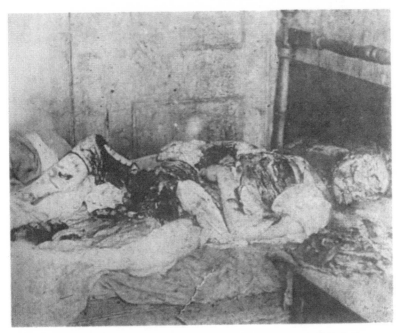

Mary Kelly's body, photographed on the day of her murder at 13 Miller's Court. She was the only victim to be photographed in situ at the murder site.

Photograph of Kelly's room taken on the day of the murder. The broken window can be seen on the right.

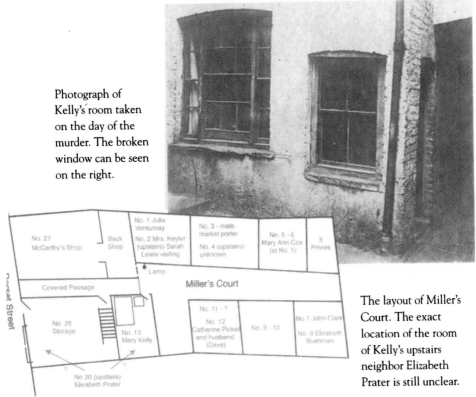

The layout of Miller's Court. The exact location of the room of Kelly's upstairs neighbor Elizabeth Prater is still unclear.

PART THREE

Aaron Kozminski

17

Downward Spiral

It was just one thing after another, Rodion Romanovitch,
my dear fellow! How could I avoid being brought to certain
ideas? From a hundred rabbits you can't make a horse, a hundred suspicions don't make a proof, as the English proverb
says, but that's only from the rational point of view.
—*Crime and Punishment*, Fyodor Dostoyevsky

Researching the life of Aaron Kozminski has proved to be a
difficult undertaking. There is no known photograph of him,
and what documentation has survived is riddled with apparent
contradictions. In a sense, he has slipped through the cracks, historically speaking.

Overall, one gets the impression of a man who seems to have barely
existed at all. In a sense, the paucity of information about Kozminski as
a suspect in the case seems a bit suspicious. Although he was arguably
Scotland Yard's top Ripper suspect, there is no dossier on him in the
extant police files on the case. Despite this, he is referred to as a suspect by at least three high-ranking Scotland Yard officials. Admittedly,
the explanation for this is probably an innocent one, because many

of the files were lost, destroyed, or "borrowed" over the years, and the documentation that did survive represents only a fraction of what once existed. But where did the files go? Was it merely an accident that files on Kozminski were "lost?" What about the fact that sixteen years of Kozminski's Leavesden Asylum file documentation seem to have disappeared? One begins to wonder whether this vanishing act was brought about by design—if the police made Kozminski disappear.

What remains of his story is an interesting one, however, and I will try to piece it together as best I can. Oddly enough, the only time Kozminski's name is known to have been in print during his lifetime was when he was arrested for the relatively innocuous charge of walking a dog without a muzzle.

In the 1880s, the residents of London had been growing increasingly concerned by the ever-present danger of being bitten by one of the countless ownerless dogs roaming the streets. The fear was rabies or hydrophobia, a horrible disease that in humans leads to mania, coma, and almost certain death. In 1885, there were twenty-seven recorded deaths from rabies in London, and by the 1890s, the police were seizing more than twenty thousand stray dogs each year.[1] The veterinary consensus was that muzzling would prevent dogs from biting one another and thus halt the spread of the disease. Yet the practice of muzzling was controversial, primarily because it was seen as being cruel to animals, so a select committee was set up to research the issue. In one rather comedic exchange, a member of the committee described an experiment in which he tried to drink while wearing a wire muzzle over his face. "I found it impossible," the man said. "There is a bar in front of the tongue." The chairman dryly responded, "With all respect, you are not a dog."[2] In the end, muzzling won out, and in July 1889, the Board of Agriculture passed a compulsory muzzling order that covered the entire London Metropolitan area and the City of London, which led to a rapid decline in rabies cases.

In December 1889, a few months after the passage of this new law, a City Police constable named Borer stopped a man who was walking an unmuzzled dog in Cheapside, a street in the City of London, described by Charles Dickens in 1879 as "the busiest thoroughfare in the world, with the sole exception perhaps of London-bridge."[3] The man gave his name as Aaron Kosminski and then gave what turned out to be a wrong address. Little else is known about the incident. It is not known what type of dog Kozminski was walking, although one might imagine it was similar to those Dickens described as "the poor vagrant homeless curs that one sees looking out for a dinner in the gutter."[4] Kozminski was ordered to appear in City Summons Court to answer for the charge. *Lloyd's Weekly News* reported the following on December 15, under the heading "Fined for Unmuzzled Dogs":

> Aaron Kosminski was summoned for a similar office— Police-constable Borer said he saw the defendant with an unmuzzled dog, and when asked his name gave that of Aaron Kosminski, which his brother said was wrong as his name was Abrahams—Defendant said that the dog was not his, and his brother said it was found more convenient to go by the name Abrahams, but his name was Kosminski.—Sir Polydore de Keyser imposed a fine of 10s. and costs, which the defendant would not pay as it was the Jewish Sunday, and it was not right to pay money on Sunday. He was given till Monday to pay.[5]

A second notice was printed in the *City Press* on December 18 under the heading "The Rabies Order":

> AARON KOSMUNSKI also appeared to a summons for having a dog unmuzzled in Cheapside. When spoken to by the police he gave a wrong name and address. Defendant: I goes by the name of Abrahams sometimes, because Kosmunski is hard to spell. (Laughter.) The defendant called his brother, who corroborated that part of the evidence which related to his name. The Alderman said he would have to pay a fine of 10s., and costs. Defendant: I cannot pay; the dog belongs to Jacobs; it is not mine. The Alderman: It was in your charge, and you must pay the fine, and if you have no goods on which to distrain you will have to go to prison for seven days.[6]

After the dog-muzzling incident, Kozminski disappeared from the record again, and nothing is known about his life for the next seven months.

By early 1890, East End life had basically returned to normal, and people were forgetting about the Ripper. The newspapers were then focusing on the "Cleveland Street Scandal," which revolved around a homosexual brothel in Fitzrovia that was said to be have been patronized by several prominent aristocrats and government figures, including "a gentleman of very high position"—apparently, Lord Arthur Somerset. The Metropolitan Police discovered the brothel in the summer of 1889 as a result of inquiries led by Detective Frederick Abberline, among others. Homosexuality at the time was illegal, and several trials followed. In February 1890, details were still unfolding, and the press was enthralled. The Ripper was the furthest thing from people's minds.

Then in June 1890, Commissioner James Monro gave a curious interview in *Cassell's Saturday Journal*, in which he stated that he had "decidedly" formed a theory about the Whitechapel murders. Monro declined to elaborate on this but added, "When I do theorize it is from a practical standpoint, and not upon a mere visionary foundation."

"Are you in possession of any clue at all?" the reporter asked.

"Nothing positive," Monro replied. "You see, crimes of this kind—when we consider the particular class of victims selected—are the most easy of all crimes to commit. The person entrapped is as anxious to secure secrecy as the murderer himself."[7]

On June 12, shortly after giving this interview, Monro tendered his resignation as Police Commissioner, apparently in protest over an issue related to police pensions. Years later, ex-CID chief Robert Anderson would refer to "a most painful incident which, on the eve of his [Monro's] resigning the Chief Commissionership of Police, broke up a close friendship of several years."[8] Yet Anderson does not explain what the "painful incident" was, and nothing more is known about Monro's "practical" theory. The timing is curious, however. Just one month after Monro's resignation, Kozminski was admitted to Mile End Old Town Workhouse, exhibiting signs of insanity.

Workhouses had existed in England ever since the reign of Queen Elizabeth I, when the Act for the Relief of the Poor made parishes responsible for taking care of their destitute citizens. In concept, the workhouse was a place where the poor could be put to work in exchange for receiving food and shelter. In an early reference from

1631, for example, the mayor of Abingdon, Berkshire, wrote, "Wee haue erected wthn our borough a workehouse to sett poore people to worke."[9] The earliest workhouses were much like ordinary houses, providing "out-relief" in the form of money, clothing, and food given to poor residents who lived in their own homes. By the eighteenth century, however, the workhouse had begun to evolve to an "in-relief" model, somewhat similar to a modern homeless shelter. In 1834, the Poor Law Amendment Act signaled an end to all out-relief and formed the parishes of England into Poor Law Unions, each of which had its own workhouse run by a Board of Guardians and paid for by local taxes levied on property owners.[10]

The new workhouses were larger in scale and could accommodate various types of paupers, including the mentally ill. They were notoriously plagued by unsanitary conditions, inadequate ventilation, untrained staff, defective equipment, and overcrowding. Such conditions were made repugnant by design. The "threat" of entering a workhouse was seen as a last option for the desperate and was regarded as the ultimate in degradation. As one anonymous writer put it, "As to the workhouse, it was literally burying one's self alive."[11]

Mile End Old Town was a large hamlet in the East End division of Stepney, just east of Whitechapel. In its southwest corner, the boundary of the hamlet jutted out like an arm reaching toward the very epicenter of the Ripper murders, and it was in this section that the Kozminski families lived. The Mile End Old Town workhouse on Bancroft Road was designed to house five hundred adults, with accommodations for casual paupers, infants, and the elderly and a separate "imbeciles block" for the mentally ill. In exchange for food and shelter, the casual poor were employed in breaking stones in the yard.

On July 12, 1890, Kozminski was brought to Mile End Old Town Workhouse by one of his brothers—probably Woolf Abrahams. It was a mile-and-a-half walk, because the Kozminskis lived in the farthest western part of Mile End Old Town, and the workhouse was in the farthest eastern part. It is not actually known why Kozminski was brought to the workhouse at this time, but presumably it was because he was exhibiting signs of insanity. On the admission papers, next to "Cause of Seeking Relief," the workhouse relieving officer Maurice Whitfield wrote, "Qy insane" ("query insane"), which was apparently a fairly standard procedure for pauper lunatics, because several other admissions had the same entry. Next to "Qy insane" Whitfield wrote "destitute." The admission recorded that Kozminski was born in 1865 and was single; his occupation was given as "hairdresser," his religion as Hebrew, and his class for diet as "able bodied man."[12] Kozminski's address was listed as 3 Sion Square, which was Woolf's address at the time. Next to "How Discharged; and, if by Order, by whose Order" was written "In care of brother." The entry gave no information about Kozminski's mental condition.

Kozminski was in the workhouse for four days, and, as far as we know, he was not examined by a doctor during this time. Then on July 15, he was discharged, and we must assume that he returned to live at Woolf's house in Sion Square.

Half a year later, on February 4, 1891, Kozminski was readmitted to the workhouse, this time from 16 Greenfield Street, the address of his sister, Matilda, and her husband, Morris Lubnowski. Kozminski's condition had apparently worsened by this time, and it seems that he was in a manic state when he was brought in. According to Chief Inspector Donald Swanson, Kozminski was brought to the workhouse with "his hands tied behind his back." The admission entry noted that Kozminski was "deemed insane." The informant was again listed as "Brother."[13] Two days after being admitted, Kozminski was examined by Dr. Edmund King Houchin and certified insane. The certification read as follows:

> In the matter of Aaron Kozminski of 16 Greenfield St Mile End E in the county of London Hair Dresser an alleged lunatic.
>
> I, the undersigned Edmund King Houchin do hereby certify as follows. 2. On the 6th day of February 1891 at the Mile End Old Town Workhouse in the county of London I personally examined the said Aaron Kozminski and came to the conclusion that he is a person of unsound mind and a proper person to be taken charge of and detained under care and treatment. 3. I formed this conclusion on the following grounds, viz:—(a) Facts indicating insanity observed by myself at the time of examination, viz.:—He declares

that he is guided & his movements altogether controlled by an instinct that informs his mind; he says that he knows the movements of all mankind; he refuses food from others because he is told to do so and eats out of the gutter for the same reason. (b) Facts communicated by others, viz.:—Jacob Cohen 51 Carter Lane St Pauls, City of London says that he goes about the streets and picks up bits of bread out of the gutter & eats them, he drinks water from the tap & he refuses food at the hands of others. He took up a knife & threatened the life of his sister. He says that he is ill and his cure consists in refusing food. He is melancholic, practises self-abuse. He is very dirty and will not be washed. He has not attempted any kind of work for years. 4. The said Aaron Kozminski appeared to me to be in a fit condition of bodily health to be removed to an asylum, hospital or licensed house

E. K. Houchin of 23 High St Stepney
Feb 6th 1891[14]

Much of what we know about Kozminski's mental state comes from this certification and from Houchin's personal examination of the patient. It is interesting to note that Dr. Houchin was a police surgeon with H (Whitechapel) Division, but whether his presence at the workhouse for Kozminski's certification had anything to do with the Ripper inquiry is unknown. Given that the police were on the lookout for insane suspects in the case, it seems possible that Houchin may have been installed at Mile End Workhouse in connection to the Ripper inquiries. Dr. Houchin had been certifying lunatics at Mile End since at least 1888; an article printed in the *Daily Telegraph* on October 18, 1888, noted, "Dr. Edmund King Houston [*sic*], divisional surgeon of police, H Division, and Mr. Slight, relieving officer, brought up a lunatic for the magistrate to examine, and presented the necessary papers for her removal to one of the county lunatic asylums."[15]

Some of the most important information in Houchin's certificate— that Kozminski was melancholic, practiced "self-abuse" (masturbation), and "took up a knife & threatened the life of his sister"—was provided by an "informant" named Jacob Cohen. At the time, Cohen was in a business partnership with Woolf Abrahams and another man, named Thomas Coughtrey Davies, running a "manufactory" that produced women's mantles under the name of Davies, Cohen, and Company. The business at 51 Carter Lane in the City of London was probably small and may have been little more than a subcontracting outfit. In any case, it was apparently an unsuccessful and short-lived affair, and a notice of the dissolution of the partnership was printed in the *London Gazette* on July 17, 1891.

The exact nature of the relationship between Cohen and Kozminski is unclear. Cohen obviously knew Kozminski well enough to supply detailed information about his insanity, and this may suggest that they were more closely acquainted than Kozminski's simply being the brother of Cohen's business partner. The two may have been related somehow. For example, it is possible that Cohen was somehow related to Kozminski's brother-in-law and cousin Morris Lubnowski, who changed his name to Cohen around this time. Another possibility is that Kozminski worked or maybe even lived at Cohen's mantle factory. It is interesting to recall that when Kozminski was arrested for walking an unmuzzled dog in Cheapside in December 1889, he claimed that the dog "belongs to Jacobs." This may have been a reporter's garbled transcription—for example, the alderman may have asked whose dog it was, to which Kozminski replied, "It is Jacob's." Indeed, the manufactory's business address at Carter Lane was only a few minutes' walk from Cheapside. The dog may have been a watchdog that guarded the premises. In the end, however, very little is known about the elusive Jacob Cohen, and attempts to find further information about him have been unsuccessful.

After Kozminski was certified insane at the workhouse, a Justice of the Peace named Harry Chambers wrote an order for Kozminski to be admitted to Colney Hatch Lunatic Asylum. On the back of the admission order was a "Statement of Particulars" written by Maurice Whitfield, Relieving Officer of the Hamlet of Mile End Old Town, which copied much of the information from Kozminski's Mile End admission records. In addition, it gave his "age on first attack" as "twenty five years," and the "duration of existing attack" as "six months." Whitfield also indicated that Kozminski was not epileptic, not suicidal, and, notably, not dangerous to others. Kozminski's residence was again listed as 16 Greenfield Street, and under "Names, Christian names, and full postal addresses of one or more relatives of the patient" was written "Wolf Kozminski, Brother, 3 Sion Square Commercial Road E."

Prior to the nineteenth century, insanity was poorly understood and was generally thought to be caused either by supernatural forces or by an imbalance of the four bodily humors. Because of the mysterious nature of the disease, the insane were typically subjected to arcane treatments such as bloodletting and emetics or even more bizarre therapies, such as "the douche bath (Chinese water torture), the 'bath of surprise' (plunging the patient unexpectedly into icy water), and the whirligig chair (for making patients sick with dizziness)."[16] The nineteenth century saw the first real progress in both understanding and treating mental disorders. The County Asylums Act of 1808 was the first law that officially recognized insanity as an illness of the brain that might be treated as other illnesses were. The act authorized the use of local taxes (rates) for the construction of county asylums, but the rate payment scheme was so unpopular that officials chose not to act on it, and no county asylums were constructed until more than twenty years later.

At the time, the majority of the insane poor in England were housed in either squalid and understaffed workhouse infirmaries or privately run licensed houses commonly referred to as madhouses. Generally speaking, madhouses were filthy places, characterized by a horrid lack of sanitation and a high death rate, where the insane were beaten and subjected to gross neglect. Because the private licensed houses endeavored to house the insane "with the least trouble [and expense] to the keeper," the mentally ill were generally "managed" by various forms of mechanical restraint, such as chains, leather straps, and cages. One popular form of restraint was the straitjacket or strait-waistcoat, which, according to the 1811 Grose Dictionary, was "used in madhouses for the management of lunatics when outrageous." The early "subscription" asylums were not much better. When a Yorkshire magistrate named Godfrey Higgins visited the notorious York Asylum in 1814, he reported finding horrifying conditions there: "I then went upstairs, and [the keeper] showed me into a room . . . twelve feet by seven feet ten inches, in which there were thirteen women who, he told me had all come out of their cells that morning. . . . I became very sick, and could not remain longer in the room. I vomited."[17]

In one room, Higgins found ten women "chained by one arm or leg to the wall, naked except for an unfastenable blanket gown." In another room, he discovered a sad character "in a dungeon, his body enclosed in a device of iron bars and chained to the trough where he lay." This man, a patient named James Norris, had been kept in chains continuously for nine years. "Subsequent investigations" at York, according to author Andrew Scull, revealed a regime "characterized by beatings, starvation, rape, and murder."[18] Conditions had not improved much by 1845, when the medical superintendent at York Asylum admitted that "flogging and cudgelling were systematically resorted to," although, he added, "this indeed, was denied at the time."[19]

Workhouses, on the other hand, were not originally intended as places for the sick or the insane at all but instead were meant to provide relief for the "able-bodied" poor. By the middle of the century, however, the role of the workhouse had evolved, and, as noted by researcher Peter Higginbotham, "The majority of those forced into the workhouse was not the work-shy, but the old, the infirm, the orphaned, unmarried mothers, and the physically or mentally ill."

In neither the workhouse nor the madhouse was there much intention of curing the mentally ill or even of treating them. Instead, the main idea was simply to unburden the family (and society) of the responsibility of dealing with their insane relatives. By the late 1820s, both institutions were considered woefully inadequate to the problem of housing the poor sick and the mentally ill. Finally, in 1827, the judiciary of Middlesex County decided it was time to act on the authority it had been granted by the 1808 County Asylums Act, and resolved to build a large asylum for the residents of London. The 1st Middlesex County Asylum at Hanwell opened in 1831. Yet the staff at Hanwell generally continued the same regimen of using mechanical restraint to control patients, until the asylum's third superintendent, John Connelly, pioneered various reforms that gradually shifted the focus from management of the insane to a system of nonrestraint and "moral treatment." As early as 1843, a report of the Visiting Justices noted the success of the system at Hanwell, remarking that "No harshness nor coercive cruelty should be used in any case, but that every patient, however violent, should be treated with uniform kindness and forbearance."[20]

The subsequent Asylums Act of 1845 made it mandatory for all counties to construct their own asylums. The law also gave a legal and medical definition for three classes of "insane" person. An "idiot" or "imbecile" was defined as a person who was non compos mentis (not of sound mind) from birth and incurable—in other words, a person with a mental disability or mental retardation; a "lunatic" was a person "who, though previously 'sane,' suffered from a temporary or permanent impairment of mental ability"; and finally, a "person of unsound mind" was defined as a "person who by reason of a morbid condition of intellect is incapable of managing himself and his affairs."[21] Right from the start, the use of such labels was problematic. For example, as author David Wright noted, the precise definition of a person of unsound mind was "murky and confusing," and "it was not unusual for the terms 'lunatic' and 'person of unsound mind' to be used more or less interchangeably."[22] Likewise, it is important to note that even though there was a fairly clear distinction between a lunatic and an imbecile, both were considered "insane" in the terminology of the day.

Although all insane people were qualified by the new law to receive care in county asylums, in practice, the Asylums Act focused largely on two types of patients: those who were dangerous or disruptive, and those who were thought to be curable. The medical superintendents of asylums generally did not want to clog their "therapeutic" asylums with incurable cases, and the Poor Law Guardians, well aware of their financial responsibility to the ratepayers in their districts, resisted sending incurables to the asylums. As a result, thousands of incurables, many classified as "idiots" and "imbeciles," were doomed to languish untreated in the workhouses.

Then a second, even larger, asylum opened in 1851. The Middlesex County Pauper Lunatic Asylum at Colney Hatch was a massive asylum located in what is now the London borough of Barnet. The building was designed "Italianate Style," and its cornerstone was laid by Queen Victoria's husband, Prince Albert of Saxe-Coburg and Gotha, a man whose grandson "Prince Eddy" would himself later be dubiously suggested as a suspect in the Ripper case. When it opened, Colney Hatch was the largest asylum in Europe, and, like Hanwell, it was envisioned as a "humane" alternative to the madhouse, dedicated to "non-restraint" and the notion of curing patients.

Unfortunately, by the late 1850s, both the county asylums and the workhouses had become severely overcrowded with chronic incurable patients. A Parliamentary Select Committee appointed in 1859–1860 to assess the situation advised that a separate set of asylums for "chronic harmless" patients should be constructed, as an "intermediate between union workhouses and the principle curative systems." This course of action was not immediately adopted. Instead, a new law, the Lunatics Amendment Act of 1862, dictated that harmless and chronic cases be sent back to the workhouses. By this time, many of London's workhouses (such as Mile End Old Town Workhouse, for example) had already built separate "imbecile wards" where the chronic incurable insane could be kept segregated from the rest of the workhouse population. In 1865, "inspectors" from the *Lancet* medical journal went to investigate accommodations for the insane in workhouses. "Their accounts," according to Peter Higginbotham, "painted a relentless picture of insanitary conditions, inadequate ventilation, poor nursing, defective equipment, and overcrowding."[23] Like the Parliamentary Committee, the *Lancet* proposed the construction of new asylums for chronic harmless patients.

Finally on March 14, 1867, Parliament passed the Metropolitan Poor Act, calling for the creation of three new institutions: the Imbeciles Asylum at Caterham in Surrey, the Imbeciles Asylum at Leavesden in Herfordshire, and Darenth Schools (for adolescent imbeciles) in Kent. Both Leavesden and Caterham officially opened their doors in the autumn of 1870. What followed was a massive shift of thousands of idiots, imbeciles, and other incurable patients to the new institutions.

The Imbeciles Asylum at Leavesden was a massive establishment laid out on a seventy-six-acre site, with eleven three-story patients' wards (five for men and six for women), each floor consisting of a large central hall with eighty dormitory-style beds and four lockable "Excitable Patients' Rooms," where difficult patients could be secluded. The sexes were "strictly segregated," according to Peter Higginbotham, "apart from the weekly dance and chapel service—even then, men sat at one side, and women at the other." Men who were capable of employment worked in the gardens, in the laundry, and in various shops as bootmakers, tailors, and upholsterers.

Although Leavesden and Caterham were nominally "Imbeciles Asylums," in reality, the criteria for admission had little to do with diagnosis—instead, the main requirement was that a patient be both incurable (chronic) and not dangerous. "I would be hesitant to see the purpose-built asylums as being overly concerned with labels," wrote David Wright. "That is, the Metropolitan Asylums Board [MAB] institutions (Leavesden, Darenth, Caterham) were meant . . . for chronic and harmless lunatics AND imbeciles/idiots, those for whom there was deemed to be no reasonable expectation of cure."[24] Yet even these criteria were not closely adhered to, because both Leavesden and Caterham apparently admitted acute cases as well. According to author G. M. Ayers, "The Poor Law Board regulations for MAB imbecile asylums—as they were called at this time—had stipulated that admission required a medical certificate to the effect that 'the pauper is a chronic and harmless lunatic, idiot or imbecile.' But, despite this rule, Leavesden and Caterham were soon filled with patients of all ages suffering from every type of mental disorder, acute and chronic."[25] Chronic patients, according to Leavesden superintendent Dr. Henry Case, were "often secluded for short periods as they're prone to noisy outbursts."[26]

Moreover, as pointed out by Paul Begg in *Jack the Ripper: The Facts*, Leavesden also admitted some patients who were violent and "destructive." According to Superintendent Case, such patients were "much more suited to treatment in an ordinary asylum." "In my opinion," he continued, "a case so bad as to need seclusion or restraint is not suitable for treatment here."[27] Another report noted that in one month, "No less than eleven of our cases have exhibited either suicidal or dangerous propensities."[28] Dr. Case himself was stabbed by a patient in 1894, and in another instance, after a lunatic named McDonald escaped from Leavesden, the local paper "warned against females about being out at night in the neighborhood, as this man was dangerous only to women."[29]

Between 1850 and 1890, the number of patients in licensed asylums, hospitals, and private homes had more than quadrupled, from 12,000 in 1851 to over 54,000 in 1891. The county asylums were largely seen as therapeutic failures, and the demand for accommodation continued to outpace supply. In effect, overcrowding in the asylums became such a problem that the imbecile asylums came to function like overflow containers. And a significant proportion of the insane never made it into the system at all but instead remained outside of the institutions, as burdens on the community. Like Edward Rochester's insane wife in *Jane Eyre*, difficult family members were sometimes managed by mechanical restraints within the home, and insane children and siblings were chained up or locked inside rooms.

By the 1880s, overcrowding was widespread, and conditions had deteriorated to the extent that the large county asylums such as Leavesden became "custodial warehouses for a thousand chronic incurables." The ostensible goal of "curing" patients thus shifted back to simply controlling and managing them, and asylum staff had no option but to resort to the use of straitjackets and other methods of restraint.

One popular method for controlling patients in this era was "chemical restraint," by which unruly patients were "kept in a state of permanent over-sedation" with drugs. Asylum doctors seem to have essentially used mental patients as guinea pigs in experiments with dozens of drugs, and in 1881, Daniel Tuck listed among treatments used in asylums "hypodermic injections of morphia, the administration of the bromides, chloral hydrate, hyoscyamine, physostigma (the poison from the calabar bean), canabis indica, amyl nitrate, conium (hemlock), digitalis, ergot, pilocarpine, the application of electricity, the use of the wet pack and the Turkish bath and other remedies too numerous to mention."[30] Some of these were administered as a form of punishment, by which patients were essentially "frightened into good behavior" through the threat of heavy dosages of unpleasant drugs. According to an article published by a Scottish asylum physician, "The restraining influence which the knowledge that medicine can be administered to them, whether they are willing or not, exercises over many of the insane is very potent."[31]

By the 1870s, the "workhorse of asylum pharmacology" was chloral nitrate, a drug so popular that it frequently made an appearance as a plot device in plays and literature of the era, where it was referred to as "knockout drops" or "Mickey Finns." A decade later, the powerful sedative-hypnotic drug hyoscyamine became the most commonly used method for restraining violent and homicidal cases. Hyoscyamine was said to be especially effective in curbing "maniacal excitement," because within half an hour of its use, a patient would be reduced to a state of "absolute helplessness." According to the *American Journal of Neurology and Psychiatry* (1883), "In cases of mania, or where there exists great excitement of an aggressive and destructive character, or rapidity of movement and speech, the use of the drug is the most effectual and rapid means of producing 'chemical restraint.'" The strength of the dosage was increased or decreased depending on the "violence of the patient," although, in practice, the use of hyoscyamine was still highly experimental, and there was "great uncertainty about the preparations."[32] One Pittsburgh doctor who personally experimented with the drug found himself in a state similar to deep intoxication, "oblivious to everything past, present, and future." He stumbled to bed with "marked incoordination" and fell into a "deep slumber or coma" that lasted eleven hours. When he finally awoke, he had difficulty concentrating, and everything he looked at seemed "tinged with yellow." Large dosages of hyoscyamine were often administered to manic patients with the intent of giving a shock to the system. The drug was not curative in any sense—on the contrary, its use was generally considered to be punitive, and the effect of the drug was described as "stupefying."[33]

The grim reality of the economic depression in England ultimately led to a decline in enlightened humane treatment and the emergence of a more pessimistic era. Thus, the age of idealism drew to a close. The Lunacy (Consolidation) Act of 1890 shifted the focus back to the issues of forced consignment and restraint, and "the asylum became less an institution of care or cure, more a prison . . . the emphasis was on locking up for life."[34]

Such was the state of affairs when Aaron Kozminski was admitted to Colney Hatch Asylum on February 7, 1891, as patient #11,190.[35] Kozminski's disorder was listed as "mania" with the symptom of "incoherence," and an observation noted, "On admission patient is extremely deluded. As mentioned in the certificate, he believes that all his actions are dominated by an 'Instinct.' This is probably aural hallucination. Answers questions fairly but is inclined to be reticent and morose. Health fair."

Much of the information on the admission form was simply copied from the Statement of Particulars written by Maurice Whitfield at Mile End workhouse. Thus, Kozminski was again listed as being not "dangerous to others." Likewise, the "duration of existing attack" was again given as "6 months," although this was later changed in red ink to "6 years." Presumably, the entry of six months merely indicated the time that had passed since Kozminski's previous admission to Mile End in July 1890. The updated "6 years" is therefore more accurate as an indication of when Kozminski actually first began to exhibit signs of insanity—in other words, in 1885, when he was twenty years old. The "Supposed Cause" of Kozminski's insanity was entered as "unknown," but in red next to this was an updated cause: "Self-Abuse," a nine-teenth-century colloquial term for masturbation, which was then widely thought to be the cause of a wide variety of disorders, including insanity.

Shortly after Kozminski's admission to Colney Hatch in February 1891, his sister, Matilda, and the rest of the Lubnowski family moved away from their home at 16 Greenfield Street, and by April 1891 they were living at 63 New Street, near the London Hospital. Then in May, Kozminski's brother Isaac also moved away from Greenfield Street. The timing here is curious. Why did both Kozminski's brother and his sister move away from Greenfield Street around the same time, shortly after Kozminski's admission to Colney Hatch? Researcher Chris Phillips has suggested that the Lubnowskis' move might have been motivated by "the imminent arrival of the twins Milly and Woolf in Spring 1891 . . . that might also explain why they wanted Aaron out of the house, if his behavior was giving cause for concern." But why did Isaac move as well? We will return to this question later.

Kozminski would remain at Colney Hatch Asylum for a little more than three years, and nine entries in the Colney Hatch Case Book give us some idea of his mental state between February 1891 and April 1894:

F. Bryan
    1891 Feb 10 Is rather difficult to deal with on account of the dominant Character of his delusions. Refused to be bathed the other day as his "Instinct" forbade him.

F Bryan

April 21 Incoherent, apathetic, unoccupied; still has the same "instinctive" objection to the weekly bath, health fair

Wm [?]

1892 Jan 9 Incoherent; at times excited & violent—a few days ago he took up a chair, and attempted to strike the charge attendant; apathetic as a rule; and refuses to occupy himself in any way; habits Cleanly; health fair.

Wm [?]

Nov 17 Quiet & well behaved. Only speaks German. Does no work.

Cecil F Beadles

1893 Jan 18 Chronic Mania; intelligence impaired; at times [?]noisy, excited & incoherent; unoccupied; habits cleanly; health fair.

Wm [?]

April 8 Incoherent, quiet lately, fair health

Cecil F Beadles

Sept 18 [Believes he is under protection of [?]Russian [?] Consulate—[deleted] Indolent but quiet, and clean in habits, never employed. Answers questions concerning himself.

Cecil F. Beadles

1894 April 13 Demented & incoherent, health fair.[36]

On April 19, 1894, Kozminski was transferred to Leavesden Asylum for Imbeciles, where he was entered as patient #7367. The reason for Kozminski's transfer is not known, although it is likely that he was moved simply because the asylum doctors had decided that his condition was incurable. At the time of his discharge from Colney Hatch, it was noted that Kozminski "has not recovered," and, on his transfer to Leavesden Asylum, his bodily condition was listed as "impaired," but no further explanation of this was given. His nearest relative was listed as "Mother, Mrs. Kozminski 63 New Street, New Rd, Whitechapel"— the address where Kozminski's mother, Golda, was by then living with Matilda and Morris and their children.[37]

Unfortunately, nothing is known about Kozminski's first sixteen years at Leavesden, because the registers that contained his case notes from 1894 to 1910 have either disappeared or been destroyed. We find Kozminski listed in the 1901 Census for Watford, Hertfordshire, at Leavesden as "Aaron Kozminski, patient, single, age 36, hairdresser, Mile End Old Town, London, lunatic."[38] Yet apart from this, nothing else is known about Kozminski until 1910, by which time he seems to have degenerated to a state of complete mental inability, and the nature of his illness had been changed from mania to "secondary dementia." Kozminski was then having both aural and visual hallucinations, and his physical condition had significantly deteriorated. The surviving Leavesden case notes are printed as follows:

September 10, 1910. Faulty in his habits, he does nothing useful & cannot answer questions of a simple nature. B. H. poor. [B.H. means "bodily health."]

September 29, 1911. Patient is dull & vacant. Faulty & untidy in habits. Does nothing useful. Nothing can be got by questions. B. H. weak.

April 15, 1912 Widal test negative [This was a test for typhoid fever.]

September 6, 1912 No replies can be got; dull & stupid in manner & faulty in his habits. Requires constant attention. B. H. weak.

January 16, 1913 Patient is morose in manner. No sensible reply can be got by questions. He mutters incoherently. Faulty & untidy in his habits. B. H. weak.

July 16, 1914 Incoherent & excitable: troublesome at times: Hallucinations of hearing. Untidy—B. H. fair.

February 17, 1915. Pat merely mutters when asked questions. He has hallucinations of sight & hearing and is very excitable at times. Does not work. Clean but untidy in dress. B. H. fair.

February 2, 1916 Patient does not know his age or how long he has been here. He has hallucinations of sight & hearing & is at times very obstinate. Untidy but clean, does no work. B. H. good.[39]

The case notes do not continue after this last date, thus we know of Kozminski's mental condition for only seven and a half years out of the total of almost twenty-eight years he was in both asylums. Some later notes briefly detailed Kozminski's physical deterioration—characterized by weight loss, diarrhea, and swollen feet—until his death on March 24, 1919, at the age of fifty-three. Although the death certificate gives the cause of death as "gangrene of the leg," as Philip Sugden said, some of Kozminski's physical symptoms "suggest that he may have been suffering from cancer." In any case, it seems likely that Kozminski's low weight at the end of his life (ninety-six pounds) was a result of disease and perhaps the refusal to eat and should not be taken as an indication of Kozminski's weight or build during the time of the Ripper murders, some thirty years earlier.

Among the papers in the Leavesden Asylum file was a document from G. Friedlander, a sexton and an officer of the Burial Society, St. James Place, Aldgate EC3, to A. J. Freeman at Leavesden Asylum, acknowledging receipt of Kozminski's death certificate. Another document (dated March 25, 1919) authorized the transfer of the "body of Aaron Kosminski" to Mr. Friedlander. This form was signed by I. & W. Abrahams, of "The Dolphin," Whitechapel E, London, whose relation to the deceased is given as "brothers"—in other words, these were Aaron's brothers, Isaac and Woolf Abrahams.[40] The form was originally mailed to Morris Lubnowski, then apparently filled out by (or on behalf of) Isaac and Woolf and given to the undertaker so that he could present it when collecting the body. The Dolphin was a public house located at 97–99 Whitechapel Road on the corner of Great Garden Street, where Isaac, Isaac's son Mark, and Mark's wife, Florence, lived at the time of Kozminski's death.

On March 27, 1919, Kozminski was buried in a Jewish cemetery in East Ham, for a cost of twelve pounds, five shillings. It is not known whether there was a funeral or whether any of Kozminski's relatives attended the burial. The grave still exists, but it has been badly eroded by the elements, and the inscription is barely legible. It once read:

In Loving Memory of
Aaron Kosminsky
Who Died 24th March 1919

Aged 54 Years
Deeply Missed By
His Brother, Sisters, Relatives
And Friends
May his dear
Soul Rest in Peace

An apparent problem with this is that both of Kozminski's brothers were still alive at the time he died, and so the inscription should read "Missed by His Brothers." But the likely explanation is that the gravestone wasn't cut until after Isaac's death a year later.

The next year, Isaac Abrahams suffered a brain hemorrhage on June 29 and was taken from the Dolphin to Whitechapel Union Infirmary, where he died two days later. Kozminski's other siblings, Matilda and Woolf, both lived for many more years—Matilda dying in 1939 and Woolf in 1944. All of Kozminski's family members were buried together in an East London cemetery, and the gravestones of Isaac, Woolf, and Golda all bear the name Abrahams. Aaron was buried elsewhere, and his grave was the only one marked "Kozminsky." Disassociated from the family by name, he was buried in a separate location, alone and apparently rejected by his family, in a cemetery two miles to the south.

18

Anderson's Suspect

Moral certainty: (n.) in a criminal trial, the reasonable belief (but falling short of absolute certainty) of the trier of the fact (jury or judge sitting without a jury) that the evidence shows the defendant is guilty. Moral certainty is another way of saying "beyond a reasonable doubt." Since there is no exact measure of certainty it is always somewhat subjective and based on "reasonable" opinions of judge and/or jury.

—*www.Law.com*

The police investigation of the Ripper murders has been much maligned over the years as an inept and disorganized affair that ultimately was responsible for the failure to solve the case. As head of the CID in 1888, Sir Robert Anderson was in overall command of all criminal inquiries in Metropolitan London, including the Ripper crimes, and thus much of the blame for this failure inevitably fell on him. Such criticism clearly rankled Anderson, and he seemed to have taken it personally.

As a matter of public record, a police "failure" in the case would seem hard to argue against. Yet Anderson's remarks on the matter

painted a somewhat different picture. Over the years, he made a number of comments about Jack the Ripper, first hinting at and then stating
outright that the killer's identity was known to the police, and that it
was a "definitely ascertained fact" that Jack the Ripper was a Polish
Jew who had been "caged in an asylum."[1] The suspect, according to
Anderson, had been "unhesitatingly identified" by "the only person
who had ever had a good view of the murderer," but unfortunately, the
witness refused to testify in court, and the police lacked sufficient evidence to convict the Ripper in a court of law. Despite this, Anderson
reiterated that it was "a simple matter of fact" that his Polish Jew
suspect was guilty. "It is not a matter of theory," he said.[2]

As a result of these statements, Robert Anderson has since become
perhaps the most controversial figure in all of Ripperology, and a
number of Ripperologists have dismissed his statements completely,
characterizing him as incompetent, boastful, and untrustworthy.[3] But
one wonders whether such criticism is based on an objective judgment
of Anderson's character or simply on a reluctance to accept that the
most fascinating and baffling of unsolved mysteries was indeed solved
more than a hundred years ago, with little applause or fanfare. Clearly,
Anderson's character would never have attracted the scrutiny it does,
were it not for his statements about the Ripper's identity. Indeed, the
criticisms of both Anderson's character and his abilities as leader of
the CID seem to fly in the face of his long tenure as assistant commissioner of the CID, his ability to effectively communicate with his
fellow officers, and a marked reduction in crime during his time with
the Metropolitan Police. By most accounts, Anderson was a competent
leader, highly esteemed by his colleagues, and especially accustomed
to dealing with sensitive matters regarding state security. In 1892, the
year after Aaron Kozminski's incarceration, Anderson was described
as "a tallish gentleman in the prime of life, of precise habits, of quiet
demeanor, and whose face is that of a deep student." As the reporter
noted, Anderson's "controlling hand and inspiring brain govern the
conduct of every investigation requiring delicacy and originality of
handling."[4] Surely, if any case ever required delicacy of handling, it
was the Ripper case.

Anderson did not make any public remarks implying that the
case was solved until several years after the canonical Ripper murders.

Indeed, in November 1889, a full year after the murder of Mary Kelly, Anderson commented on "our failure to find Jack the Ripper."[5] This would seem to imply that as late as November 1889, Anderson had not yet become convinced that he knew the Ripper's identity. By June 1892, however—a little more than a year after Kozminski had been admitted to Colney Hatch Asylum—Anderson had changed his tune. "There is my answer to people who come with fads and theories about these murders," he said. "It is impossible to believe they were acts of a sane man—they were those of a maniac revelling in blood."[6] The comment received little attention at the time. After all, Anderson may have been merely speculating that the murderer was a maniac and not speaking on any factual basis. In 1895, however, in an article in *Windsor Magazine* titled "The Detective in Real Life," Anderson's friend Major Arthur Griffiths stated the following: "Much dissatisfaction was vented upon Mr. Anderson at the utterly abortive efforts to discover the perpetrator of the Whitechapel murders. He has himself a perfectly plausible theory that Jack the Ripper was a homicidal maniac, temporarily at large, whose hideous career was cut short by committal to an asylum."[7]

This was the first definitive reference to Anderson's "theory," but, again, it lacked the stamp of authoritative declaration—everybody had a theory. Then, three years later, in an article titled "Mysteries of Police and Crime," Griffiths expanded on the topic:

> The police do not always admit that the perpetrators remain unknown; they have clues, suspicion, strong presumption, even more, but there is a gap in the evidence forthcoming, and to attempt prosecution would be to face inevitable defeat. . . . Sometimes an arrest is made on grounds that afford strong prima facie evidence, yet the case breaks down in court. . . . The outside public may think that the identity of that later miscreant, "Jack the Ripper," was never revealed. So far as actual knowledge goes, this is undoubtedly true. But the police, after the last murder, had brought their investigations to the point of strongly suspecting several persons, all of them known to be homicidal lunatics, and against three of these they held very plausible and reasonable grounds

of suspicion. Concerning two of them, the case was weak, although it was based on certain colourable facts. One was a Polish Jew, a known lunatic, who was at large in the district of Whitechapel at the time of the murder, and who, having afterward developed homicidal tendencies, was confined in an asylum. This man was said to resemble the murderer by the one person who got a glimpse of him—the police-constable in Mitre Court.[8]

In 1901, Anderson wrote an article titled "Punishing Crime," in which he noted that the Ripper was "a cause of danger only to a particular section of a small and definite class of women, in a limited district of the East End; and that the inhabitants of the metropolis generally were just as secure during the weeks the fiend was on the prowl as they were before the mania seized him, or after he had been safely caged in an asylum."[9] It was really just a rewording of what Griffiths had said in 1895, although the statement was somewhat less vague, because it now seemed clear that Anderson was referring to a specific suspect, as opposed to a general theory that the Ripper was probably a lunatic. Moreover, whereas Griffiths claimed that the police had strong suspicions about three suspects, Anderson was more or less declaring that the police knew the Ripper's identity. It is also relevant to note that Anderson's reference to "mania" corresponds with the diagnosis of mania noted on Kozminski's admission records at Colney Hatch asylum.

Anderson expanded on these vague hints in his 1907 book *Criminals and Crime: Some Facts and Suggestions*, when he alluded to "the fact of the fiend's detention in an asylum."

> When I speak of the efficiency [of the CID] some people will exclaim, "But what about all the undetected crimes?" I may say here that in London at least the undetected crimes are few. But English law does not permit of an arrest save on legal evidence of guilt, and legal evidence is often wholly wanting where moral proof is complete and convincing. Were I to unfold the secrets of Scotland Yard about crimes respecting which the police have been disparaged and abused in recent years, the result would be a revelation to the public. But that is not my subject here.[10]

The concept of "moral proof" (or "moral certainty") is one that Anderson mentioned several times when discussing the Ripper crimes. The statement here about "crimes respecting which the police have been disparaged and abused in recent years" is most likely a reference to the Ripper crimes, among others. As such, it is important to note that Anderson speaks of instances when the police were lacking sufficient legal proof to arrest a suspect, even though they had "complete and convincing" moral proof of his guilt. "Moral proof" refers to a concept in Aristotle's *Nicomachean Ethics* that is defined as a degree of "intuitive probability" that was, as Descartes put it, "sufficient to regulate the conduct of one's life even if it is in principle possible that we can be mistaken."[11] In other words, it implies a degree of probability sufficient for making practical decisions, if not quite an absolute certainty. On another occasion, Anderson again spoke of "moral proof," this time clearly in reference to the Ripper murders:

> Detractors of the work of our British Police in bringing criminals to justice generally ignore the important distinction between moral proof and legal evidence of guilt. In not a few cases that are popularly classed with "unsolved mysteries of crime," the offender is known, but evidence is wanting. If, for example, in a recent murder case of special notoriety and interest, certain human remains had not been found in a cellar, a great crime would have been catalogued among "Police failures"; and yet, even without the evidence which sent the murderer to the gallows, the moral proof of his guilt would have been full and clear. So again with the "Whitechapel murders" of 1888. Despite the lucubration of many an amateur "Sherlock Holmes," there was no doubt whatever as to the identity of the criminal, and if our "detectives" possessed the powers, and might have recourse to the methods, of Foreign Police Forces he would have been brought to justice. But the guilty sometimes escape through the working of a system designed to protect innocent persons wrongly accused of crime. And many a case which is used to disparage our British "detectives" ought rather to be hailed as a proof of the scrupulous fairness with which they discharge their duties.[12]

The crime writer Hargrave Lee Adam later echoed this, stating, "Robt. Anderson has assured the writer that the assassin [that is, the Ripper] was well known to the police, but unfortunately, in the absence of sufficient legal evidence to justify an arrest, they were unable to take him. It was a case of moral versus legal proof."[13] As Adam said, Anderson "never tired of referring to this, because he felt keenly the injustice done to the police when they failed to catch and convict a criminal against whom there was a lack of legal proof."[14]

That the police were hampered by legal procedures was clearly an important topic with Anderson, and it is a note that he hit over and over again. For example, in an interview published in the *Daily Chronicle* in 1908, he said, "No law hinders a police officer from going into a private house or private grounds to arrest a criminal. But the law gives him no right to enter for the investigation of the crime and the securing of evidence that may lead to the detection of the criminal." Anderson added that he told the Home Secretary, "I could not accept responsibility for non-detection of the Ripper crimes, for the reasons, among others, that I have given you."[15] Anderson later expanded on the overall gist of his complaint in his 1910 autobiography, where he wrote, "It sometimes happens that the murderer is known, but evidence is wholly wanting. In such circumstances the French Police would arrest the suspected person, and build up a case against him at their leisure, mainly by admissions extracted from him in repeated interrogations." Anderson went on to cite an example in which he attempted the "French procedure" in interrogating a murder suspect.

> I sent for the man, my ostensible object being to satisfy him that the Police were doing their duty. As I cross-examined him on the case he gave himself away over and over again. In any French court a report of that interrogation might have convicted the criminal. In an English court it would have raised a storm that might have brought my official career to a close! I never tried that game again.[16]

Anderson was clearly beating around the bush, eager to explain something that he was not supposed to be talking about. He made a similar statement in an article published in *The Nineteenth Century and After* in February 1908. In the article, titled "Criminals and Crime: A

Rejoinder," Anderson said, "The author of those murders [that is, the Whitechapel murders] was a lunatic, and if evidence had been available to bring him to justice he would have been sent to Broadmoor."[17] Broadmoor Asylum for the Criminally Insane was an institution "intended for the reception, safe custody and treatment of persons who had committed crimes while actually insane." It is important to note that in order for a person to be admitted to Broadmoor, he or she had to be found guilty of a crime. Anderson's quote contains three important points: the murderer was a lunatic; the police didn't have sufficient evidence to "bring him to justice"; and the Ripper was not committed to Broadmoor, as some researchers and press reporters later claimed.

Still, Anderson's statements up to this point were so nebulous that they attracted little attention, even though the ex-CID chief had certainly stated, on several occasions, that the Metropolitan Police knew the Ripper's identity. It wasn't until the publication of Anderson's autobiography in *Blackwood's Edinburgh Magazine* in March 1910 that he dropped the bomb.

One did not need to be a Sherlock Holmes to discover that the criminal was a sexual maniac of a virulent type; that he was living in the immediate vicinity of the scenes of the murders; and that, if he was not living absolutely alone, his people knew of his guilt, and refused to give him up to justice. During my absence abroad the Police had made a house-to-house search for him, investigating the case of every man in the district whose circumstances were such that he could go and come and get rid of his blood-stains in secret. And the conclusion we came to was that he and his people were low-class Jews, for it is a remarkable fact that people of that class in the East End will not give up one of their number to Gentile justice.

And the result proved that our diagnosis was right on every point. For I may say at once that "undiscovered murders" are rare in London, and the "Jack-the-Ripper" crimes are not within that category. And if the Police here had powers such as the French Police possess, the murderer would have been brought to justice. Scotland Yard can boast that not even the subordinate officers of the department will tell tales out of school, and it would ill become me to violate the unwritten rule of the service. The subject will come up again, and I will only add here that the "Jack-the-Ripper" letter which is preserved in the Police Museum at New Scotland Yard is the creation of an enterprising London Journalist.

In a footnote, Anderson added,

Having regard to the interest attaching to this case, I should almost be tempted to disclose the identity of the murderer and of the pressman who wrote the letter above referred to, provided that the publishers would accept all responsibility in view of a possible libel action. But no public benefit would result from such a course, and the traditions of my old department would suffer. I will only add that when the individual whom we suspected was caged in an asylum, the only person who had ever had a good view of the murderer at once identified him, but when he learned that the suspect was a fellow-Jew he declined to swear to him.[18]

Anderson's autobiography caused quite a scandal in the government when it was published, not for what he wrote about the Ripper case, but instead for his "indiscretions" in revealing other state secrets—most notably, that he was the author of one of a series of articles published in 1887 in the *Times* that had been written to smear the reputation of Charles Parnell, the head of the Irish Home Rule movement. The most contentious aspect of the articles was the reproduction of some letters supposedly written by Parnell, expressing sympathy with extremist Irish terrorist groups. The letters turned out to be forged, and Parnell successfully sued the *Times* for libel. The Irish nationalists believed (correctly) that the British government was collaborating with the *Times* in a covert attempt to discredit the Home Rule party. Anderson's revelation, some twenty-three years after the fact, that he was the author of one of the articles threatened to reopen an old and rather ugly wound. Scandal loomed. Anderson's participation was in fact limited to writing some of the less important articles, which as he later explained was done to expose and thus thwart "dynamite plots then hatching in America in view of the approaching 'Jubilee celebrations' in London." Such was the type of press manipulation regularly practiced by the secret service, but the exposure of such tactics was embarrassing. Because Anderson was the only member of the government who admitted to anything, he emerged as a scapegoat, and his "indiscretions" were lambasted in Parliament. As the Irish nationalist M.P. Jeremiah McVeagh charged, Anderson was "the connecting link between the government and the Times." In other words, he was only "one of the villains . . . there were other sinister figures in the background."[19]

The wolves were howling for blood, and several members of parliament suggested that Anderson should lose his pension. But the recently appointed Home Secretary, Winston Churchill, decided against such a drastic course of action. Churchill was in a difficult position, since he was clearly dealing with a person who was inclined to reveal whatever government secrets he thought the public had a right to know about. This meant that Anderson was a potentially dangerous figure. Denying his pension would have been like poking a tiger in its cage. Thus, Churchill decided merely to censure him. In the House of Commons, Churchill ridiculed Anderson's revelations in Blackwood's, noting, "They seem to me to be written in a spirit of gross boastfulness. They are written, if I may say so, in the style of 'How Bill Adams won the battle of Waterloo.' The writer has been so anxious to show how important he was, how invariably he was right, and how much more he could tell if only his mouth was not what he was pleased to call closed."[20] This got a round of laughter in the House. Churchill further described Anderson's revelations in Blackwood's as "the garrulous and inaccurate indiscretion of advancing years," noting that "it would be intolerable if ex-police officers and ex-agents of the service should be allowed after retirement to publish without fear of consequence, secrets which might have come into their possession." Such statements served the dual function of appeasing Anderson's enemies in Parliament and discrediting the ex-CID chief in the court of public opinion, calling into question the veracity of the claims he had made in Blackwood's magazine. None of this apparently had anything to do with Anderson's statements about Jack the Ripper, which Churchill apparently included among what he referred to as the "minor revelations" in the articles. But the statements of both McVeagh and Churchill effectively made Anderson seem like an unreliable and somewhat geriatric boaster and buffoon. The same statements would later be wielded against Anderson by Ripperologists, who seemed inclined to believe that Anderson's statements about the Ripper's identity were hogwash.

Anderson's claim that James Monro had authorized him to write the *Times* article was also ridiculed in the House of Commons—as Jeremiah McVeagh put it, it was "another of Anderson's Fairy Tales." When Monro was asked whether he had in fact authorized the article, he replied,

> I have no doubt that Mr. Anderson and I talked about [the articles], and I can quite imagine that I may have welcomed public interest being directed to the existence of a danger-ous conspiracy. But such an expression of opinion was a very different thing from authorising an agent of mine to give information to the public. Such a course would have been opposed to all my training in a Service where communica-tion on the part of officials with the Press was carefully limited. As a matter of fact, no such authority was asked by Mr. Anderson, and none was given to him by me. . . . A long time afterwards, Mr. Anderson informed me that he had written one or more of the articles, and I felt much annoyed.[21]

In short, Monro admitted that his "expression of opinion" might have inadvertently given Anderson the impression that he supported the writing of the article, even though he did not actually autho-rize it. Above all, Monro seems to have been angry at Anderson's indiscretions, because he firmly believed in the idea of keeping quiet about government secrets. Presumably, Monro likewise disapproved of Anderson's statements about the Ripper case, although he never mentioned them directly.

As Commissioner of the Metropolitan Police from November 1888 until June 1890, Monro must have been aware of all of the strong suspects in the Whitechapel murders case. As Andrew Morrison sug-gested, "It is possible that [Monro] was more informed about the case than most if not all his contemporaries. If anybody knew the truth about the events of 1888 it was him."[22] As Warren's successor to the post of commissioner, Monro was Anderson's boss between November 1888 and June 1890, at a time when Kozminski was probably "in the frame" as a suspect. It seems highly likely that Monro must have known all about Kozminski. And as we have seen, sometime prior to June 1890, Monro had "decidedly" formed an opinion on the case but was unwilling to elaborate on this to the press. Whatever Monro knew, he never publicly remarked on it, nor did he comment on Anderson's statements about the Ripper's identity.

Monro is said to have left some papers related to the Ripper case to his son Charles. The documents have never been found and were quite probably destroyed, but according to what Charles told his younger brother, Douglas, their father's theory on the case was "a very hot potato," a secret that he kept even from his wife. Monro's grandson Christopher later recalled his grandfather saying, "Jack the Ripper should have been caught."[23] What Monro knew (or believed) about Jack the Ripper is not known. Yet the "highly private" nature of his thoughts on the case seems to imply a carefully guarded secret. Indeed, if several top police officials at the MET in fact knew (or strongly suspected that they knew) the identity of the Ripper but, as Anderson suggests, were unable to secure a conviction, then the whole situation must have been considered a state secret. If the government had revealed not only that Jack the Ripper was a Jewish immigrant, but also that he got away scot-free because the police were unable to secure sufficient evidence for a conviction, there would have been (at the very minimum) a scandal and quite possibly riots and social upheaval in the East End. A "very hot potato" indeed.

Anderson's statements about the Ripper in his autobiography did not pass unnoticed. A harsh critic emerged in the form of Leopold Greenberg, the co-owner of the *Jewish Chronicle*. On March 4, 1910, Greenberg published an article in the *Chronicle* under the pseudonym "Mentor," in which he pointed out that Anderson supplied no proof to back up his claim that the Ripper was Jewish, and he criticized Anderson's "wicked assertion" that certain members of the "low-class" Jewish community would have protected the murderer from the police. The article read,

According to Sir Robert Anderson, the police "formed a
theory"—usually the first essential to some blundering injustice. In this case, the police came to the conclusion that
"Jack the Ripper" was a "low-class" Jew, and they so decided,
Sir Robert says, because they believe "it is a remarkable fact
that people of that class in the East End will not give up
one of their number to Gentile justice." Was anything more
nonsensical in the way of a theory ever conceived even in
the brain of a policeman? Here was a whole neighbourhood,
largely composed of Jews, in constant terror lest their wom-
enfolk, whom Jewish men hold in particular regard—even
"low-class" Jews do that—should be slain by some murderer
who was stalking the district undiscovered. So terrified were
many of the people—non-Jews as well as Jews—that they
hastily moved away. And yet Sir Robert would have us
believe that there were Jews who knew the person who
was committing the abominable crimes and yet carefully
shielded him from the police. A more wicked assertion
to put into print, without the shadow of evidence, I have
seldom seen. The man whom Scotland Yard "suspected,"
subsequently, says Sir Robert, "was caged in an asylum." He
was never brought to trial—nothing except his lunacy was
proved against him. This lunatic presumably was a Jew, and
because he was "suspected," as a result of the police "theory"
I have mentioned, Sir Robert ventures to tell the story he
does, as if he were stating facts, forgetting that such a case as
that of Adolph Beck was ever heard of. [Adolph Beck was
wrongly convicted of robbery in 1907 as a result of wrongful
identification.]

But now listen to the "proof" that Sir Robert Anderson
gives of his theories. When the lunatic, who presumably was
a Jew and who was suspected by Scotland Yard, was seen by
a Jew—"the only person who ever had a good view of the
murderer"—Sir Robert tells us he at once identified him,
"but when he learned that the suspect was a fellow-Jew he
declined to swear to him." This is Scotland Yard's idea of
"proof" positive of their "theory"! What more natural than

the man's hesitancy to identify another as Jack the Ripper so soon as he knew he was a Jew? What more natural than for that fact at once to cause doubts in his mind? The crimes identified with "Jack the Ripper" were of a nature that it would be difficult for any Jew—"low-class" or any class—to imagine the work of a Jew. Their callous brutality was foreign to Jewish nature, which, when it turns criminal, goes into quite a different channel. I confess that however sure I might have been of the identity of a person, when I was told he had been committing "Jack the Ripper" crimes and was a Jew, I should hesitate about the certainty of my identification, especially as anyone—outside Scotland Yard—knows how prone to mistake the cleverest-headed and most careful of people are when venturing to identify anyone else. It is a matter of regret and surprise that so able a man as Sir Robert Anderson should, upon the wholly erroneous and ridiculous "theory" that Jews would shield a raving murderer because he was a Jew, rather than yield him up to "Gentile justice," build up the series of statements that he has. There is no real proof that the lunatic who was "caged" was a Jew—there is absolutely no proof that he was responsible for the "Jack the Ripper" crimes, and hence it appears to me wholly gratuitous on the part of Sir Robert to fasten the wretched creature—whoever he was—upon our people.[24]

To an extent, Mentor's critique was valid, given that Anderson did not supply any proof for his allegations, and his vague wording was bound to suggest many different interpretations (or misinterpretations) of what he actually meant. Mentor's contention that the police came to the conclusion that the Ripper was a Polish Jew as the result of theory alone was almost certainly a misinterpretation of Anderson's words. The "theory" in Anderson's statement was that "One did not need to be a Sherlock Holmes to discover that the criminal was a sexual maniac of a virulent type; that he was living in the immediate vicinity of the scenes of the murders; and that, if he was not living absolutely alone, his people knew of his guilt, and refused to give him up to justice."[25] This is what would now be called a criminal profile, in other words, a deduced assumption about the murderer based on analysis of the case evidence. Then Anderson said, "The conclusion we came to was that he and his people were certain low-class Polish Jews," and "The result proved that our diagnosis was right on every point." Unfortunately, it is unclear whether Anderson meant that the police came to this "conclusion" as the result of theory or whether they discovered the Ripper by normal methods, and that the "result" (that is, the killer's identity) simply matched their profile. The difference is important. If the police thought that the Ripper was Jewish merely because of a theory or a profile, then Mentor's critique is entirely valid. If, however, the police discovered the Ripper's identity as a result of unbiased inquiry and detective work, then Mentor's critique falls flat.

Anderson responded to Mentor in an interview that was printed in the *Globe* on March 7, 1910:

> When I stated that the murderer was a Jew, I was stating a simple matter of fact. It is not a matter of theory. I should be the last man in the world to say anything reflecting on the Jews as a community, but what is true of Christians is equally true of Jews—that there are some people who have lapsed from all that is good and proper. We have "lapsed masses" among Christians. We cannot talk of "lapsed masses" among Jews, but there are cliques of them in the East End, and it is a notorious fact that there is a stratum of Jews who will not give up their people.
>
> In stating what I do about the Whitechapel murders, I am not speaking as an expert in crime, but as a man who investigated the facts. Moreover, the man who identified the murderer was a Jew, but on learning that the criminal was a Jew he refused to proceed with his identification. As for the suggestion that I intended to cast any reflection on the Jews anyone who has read my books on Biblical exegesis will know the high estimate I have of Jews religiously.[26]

The *Globe* added that "In connection with Sir Robert's assertion that the Whitechapel murderer was a Jew, it is of interest to recall that in one crime the culprit chalked up on a wall: 'The Jews are not the people to be blamed for nothing'." Anderson then responded to

Mentor's critique even more directly by writing a letter of apology to the *Jewish Chronicle*:

> TO THE EDITOR OF THE "JEWISH CHRONICLE."
>
> SIR,—With reference to "Mentor's" comments on my statements about the "Whitechapel murders" of 1888 in this month's *Blackwood*, will you allow me to express the severe distress I feel that my words should be construed as "an aspersion upon Jews." For much that I have written in my various books gives proof of my sympathy with, and interest in, "the people of the Covenant"; and I am happy in reckoning members of the Jewish community in London among my personal friends.
>
> I recognise that in this matter I said either too much or too little. But the fact is that as my words were merely a repetition of what I published several years ago without exciting comment, they flowed from my pen without any consideration.
>
> We have in London a stratum of the population uninfluenced by religious or even social restraints. And in this stratum Jews are to be found as well as Gentiles. And if I were to describe the condition of the maniac who committed these murders, and the course of loathsome immorality which reduced him to that condition, it would be manifest that in his case every question of nationality and creed is lost in a ghastly study of human nature sunk to the lowest depth of degradation.[27]

Mentor was not satisfied with this explanation and wrote a follow-up article claiming that Anderson had completely missed the point:

> I did not so much object to his saying that Jack the Ripper was a Jew, though so particular a friend of our people would have been well-advised, knowing the peculiar condition in which we are situated, and the prejudice that is constantly simmering against us, had he kept the fact to himself. *No good purpose was served by revealing it.* . . . What I objected to—and pace Sir Robert Anderson's explanations still

do—in his *Blackwood* article, is that Jews who knew that
"Jack the Ripper" had done his foul deeds, shielded him
from the police, and guarded him so that he could continue
his horrible career, just because he was a Jew. This was the
aspersion to which I referred and about which I notice Sir
Robert says nothing.[28]

Mentor's criticism was now leveled squarely at Anderson's statement that the Ripper's people were "low-class Jews" who "refused to
give him up to justice." Interestingly, Mentor said that he did not
object so much to Anderson's "saying that Jack the Ripper was a Jew"
(apparently conceding it might be true), although "a friend of our people would have been well-advised . . . had he kept the fact to himself."
This, of course, touched on a larger issue—specifically, whether members of the East End's Jewish community may have refused to cooperate
with the police, either out of a general distrust for authority or out of
fear that the Jewish community as a whole would be turned into scapegoats if it were revealed that Jack the Ripper was a Jew. This idea was
supported by Chaim Bermant, the Anglo-Jewish author and a frequent
contributor to the *Jewish Chronicle*: "If the Ripper was a Jew, then one
can be fairly certain that his fellows would have kept quiet about it for
the simple reason that the whole community could have been held
culpable for his deeds, and that the menacing mood of hostility which
surrounded them would have given way to outright violence."[29]
    We must recall that Anderson claimed that the witness refused
to testify after he discovered that the suspect was "a fellow-Jew."
Although Anderson does not elaborate on the point, it seems likely
that a Jewish witness must have been aware that if a Jew were convicted of the Ripper murders, all hell would break loose in the East
End. Given the climate of anti-Semitism and the prejudice that was
"constantly simmering" against the Jews in the East End, Mentor's
hesitancy to have Anderson "fasten the wretched creature . . . upon our
people" is understandable.
    Still, Anderson was treading on thin ice in more ways than one.
Among other things, he had made a rather public accusation that he
was unable to back up with proof. Whether Scotland Yard had any
other evidence against the suspect was a moot point, because Anderson

was not in a position to discuss the matter openly anyway. As he said, such a course would have violated the "unwritten rule of the service" not to "tell tales out of school." By the time *The Lighter Side of My Official Life* was published in book form later in 1910, Anderson had made a few changes. For starters, he changed the statement "his people were low-class Jews" to "his people were certain low-class Polish Jews." This was apparently to clarify that the Ripper was shielded only by certain Jews, rather than by the Jewish community as a whole. He also changed "when he [the witness] learned that the suspect was a fellow-Jew he declined to swear to him," to simply "he refused to give evidence against him." The statement that the identification took place "when the individual whom we suspected was caged in an asylum" was removed completely—possibly because Anderson realized that this was an error. Finally, Anderson added the following: "In saying that he was a Polish Jew I am merely stating a definitely ascertained fact. And my words are meant to specify race, not religion. For it would outrage all religious sentiment to talk of the religion of a loathsome creature whose utterly unmentionable vices reduced him to a lower level than that of the brute."[30]

It is important to note that despite the beating he took from Mentor, Anderson stood by his statement that Jack the Ripper was a "low-class" Polish Jew. It was, as he said, "a definitely ascertained fact." Yet after all of his hints and insinuations, in the end Anderson never actually revealed the name of the suspect in question.

19

Macnaghten and Swanson

Some forty years after the publication of *The Lighter Side of My Official Life*, a document surfaced that appeared to corroborate Sir Robert Anderson's story in many respects, but in other ways, it simply confused matters. In the 1950s, journalist Dan Farson discovered a copy of a Metropolitan Police memorandum that had been written by ex-chief constable Melville Macnaghten, Anderson's second-in-command at the CID in the years immediately following the Ripper murders. The document, now referred to as the "Macnaghten memorandum," was written in 1894 in response to a series of articles in the *Sun* newspaper that claimed the Ripper was a syphilitic and paranoid lunatic named Thomas Cutbush. The memorandum was apparently written in case the MET or the Home Office was asked to make a public statement about the *Sun* articles. The document was never released publicly, and it is not known whether it was ever submitted to the Home Office.

In the memo, Macnaghten wrote that there were three men, "any one of whom would have been more likely than Cutbush to have committed this series of murders." One of these suspects is described as

(2) Kosminski, a Polish Jew, & resident in Whitechapel. This man became insane owing to many years indulgence in

solitary vices. He had a great hatred of women, specially of the prostitute class, & had strong homicidal tendencies; he was removed to a lunatic asylum about March 1889. There were many circs. connected with this man which made him a strong suspect.[1]

An earlier draft of the memo, said to be in Macnaghten's handwriting, differed somewhat from the official version in the Metropolitan Police files. Luckily, Macnaghten's daughter Christabel Aberconway made a typed copy of the draft version sometime in the 1930s, before the original was somehow lost. The so-called Aberconway draft read,

> No. 2 Kosminski, a Polish Jew, who lived in the very heart of the district where the murders were committed. He had become insane owing to many years indulgence in solitary vices. He had a great hatred of women, with strong homicidal tendencies. He was (and I believe still is) detained in a lunatic asylum about March 1889. This man in appearance strongly resembled the individual seen by the City P.C. near Mitre Square.[2]

The suspects mentioned in the Macnaghten memorandum do not appear in any of the existing police files on the Jack the Ripper murders. Despite this, it is fairly certain that the police must have had dossiers on all three men, but the files are now gone, and they will probably never be recovered. In any case, Macnaghten disagreed with Anderson's theory, because he claimed to have received "private information" that convinced him that the number-one suspect was one of the other men described in the memo—specifically, a barrister named Montague John Druitt, who committed suicide shortly after the murder of Mary Kelly. Still, Macnaghten apparently was not entirely convinced of Druitt's guilt, referring to it only as a "more rational and workable theory, to my way of thinking," than the *Sun's* suggestion that Thomas Cutbush was the Ripper. As an alternative, Macnaghten also admitted the "less likely theory" that the murderer "was found to be so helplessly insane by his relatives, that they, suspecting the worst, had him confined to some lunatic asylum."[3] In other words, Macnaghten conceded that Kozminski may have been the Ripper, although he personally preferred Druitt as a more likely suspect. So despite the fact that Anderson was apparently certain of the Ripper's identity, there was no consensus about the matter within the CID.

When the Macnaghten memorandum was first discovered, few researchers made a connection between Anderson's suspect and the Polish Jew named "Kosminski" referred to by Macnaghten. Apparently, this was because it was assumed that Anderson was referring to another Jewish suspect, specifically John Pizer, aka "Leather Apron." With the benefit of hindsight, this seems a rather strange conclusion to have come to, because both Anderson's suspect and Macnaghten's "Kosminski" were Polish Jews who were admitted to an asylum. In addition, the fact that Macnaghten claimed that Kosminski "strongly resembled the individual seen by the City P.C. near Mitre Square" suggests that Macnaghten was aware that an identification of the suspect had been attempted, although (as we shall see) he was apparently wrong about the identity of the witness.

The Macnaghten memorandum is unfortunately riddled with errors, and we must therefore take it with a grain of salt as far as accuracy. For example, Macnaghten described one of the other two suspects, Montague John Druitt, as "a doctor of good family," whereas Druitt was actually a barrister and a teacher. As Paul Begg suggested, this "makes it abundantly clear that Macnaghten was relying on his memory and not working from written sources such as police reports." Regarding "Kosminski," one confounding aspect of the memorandum is the Aberconway version's reference to a "City P.C." witness. No researcher has ever found any evidence that there was a City P.C. witness at any of the Ripper crime scenes, and we must assume that this is another of Macnaghten's errors. In the official version of the memorandum, however, the reference to a "City P.C." was removed and replaced with "There were many circs. connected with this man which made him a strong suspect." This may indicate that Macnaghten realized his remark about a City P.C. witness was an error.

Some of Macnaghten's other statements about "Kosminski," while neither demonstrably correct nor incorrect, are not backed up by other sources. Specifically, these are the statements that Kozminski "had a great hatred of women, specially of the prostitute class, & had strong homicidal tendencies," and that "there were many circs. connected with this man which made him a strong suspect." While these statements seem to imply that the police knew much more about Kozminski than we do today, the source of the information is simply unknown. It might have come from interviewing Kozminski himself or from an interview with a family member or some other informer. Although these statements are obviously relevant to Kozminski's viability as a suspect in the case, we must look at them objectively. As researcher Chris Scott pointed out, "We are only seeing the tip of the iceberg. . . . There's a whole tranche of presumably once extant paperwork that we no longer have access to, so we simply don't know."[4] In any case, the Macnaghten memorandum still gave only the suspect's surname ("Kosminski"), again leaving researchers frustratingly in the dark. Nobody knew who he was talking about.

Then in 1987 another important discovery surfaced. This time, it was only a few penciled notes that had been written by Donald Sutherland Swanson in the margins of Swanson's personal copy of Anderson's autobiography. The so-called Swanson marginalia were revealed to the public on the centenary of the Ripper murders, when Swanson's grandson Jim decided to "put an end to all the fanciful conjecture concerning the killer," and reveal that the senior officials at Scotland Yard were convinced that they knew the Ripper's identity.[5] In the book, where Anderson had written that a witness "identified the suspect . . . but he refused to give evidence against him," Swanson penciled in "because the suspect was also a Jew and also because his evidence would convict the suspect and witness would be the means of murderer being hanged which he did not wish to be left on his mind." In the margin, Swanson added, "And after this identification which suspect knew no other murder of this kind took place in London." Swanson's commentary continued on a blank page at the end of the volume, where he wrote,

> Continuing from page 138, after the suspect had been identified at the Seaside Home where he had been sent by us with difficulty in order to subject him to identification, and he knew he was identified. On suspect's return to his brother's house in Whitechapel he was watched by police (City CID) by day & night. In a very short time the suspect

with his hands tied behind his back, he was sent to Stepney Workhouse and then to Colney Hatch and died shortly afterwards—Kosminski was the suspect—DSS[6]

Clearly, Donald Swanson simply jotted down the notes for his own private reasons and never intended to make his opinions on the matter public. In fact, Swanson never wrote publicly about the Whitechapel murders at all and was much more disciplined than Anderson in keeping his mouth shut about Scotland Yard's secrets. Indeed, an often-ignored aspect of the marginalia is that Swanson highlighted this sentence Anderson wrote: "Scotland Yard can boast that not even the subordinate officers of the department will tell tales out of school." He also underlined Anderson's sentence "It would ill become me to violate the unwritten rule of the service." Swanson undoubtedly recognized the irony here, because this was exactly what Anderson was doing.

In addition, just above Anderson's paragraph beginning "I am almost tempted to disclose the identity of the murderer and of the pressman who wrote the letter," Swanson penciled in "known to Scotland Yard head officers of CID," underlining the word "head" twice. Unfortunately, it is not exactly clear whether this was in reference to the author of the Ripper letter, which Anderson discussed in the preceding paragraph, or to "the identity of the murderer," which he discussed in the paragraph immediately following. Yet either way, it suggests that some aspects of the case were known only by the "head" officers at Scotland Yard and were kept even from the rest of the force working the case. Swanson, by comparison, knew how to keep his mouth shut, and, as noted in his obituary, his work was "decidedly a secret service."[7]

It is important to note that Swanson's penciled notes in general seem to corroborate Anderson's story. He does not contradict Anderson in any way, nor does he state that he agrees with Anderson's statement that the Ripper's identity was a "definitely ascertained fact." Yet as Ripperologist Andy Spallek has pointed out, Swanson "goes to great lengths to indicate that the suspect knew he was identified and as a result no further murders took place."[8] This seems to suggest not only that Swanson believed Kozminski was the murderer, but also that Kozminski stopped killing because he knew he was under police surveillance. And given that Swanson wrote the marginalia purely for himself, it seems likely that if he disagreed with Anderson about the Ripper's identity, he would have said so.

Most important of all, though, Swanson finally revealed the name of the suspect as "Kosminski," making it clear that Anderson's "low class Polish Jew" and the insane Polish Jew referred to by Macnaghten were the same person. Yet it was still not known which "Kosminski" they were all talking about.

Around the time that the "Swanson marginalia" were discovered, Martin Fido published a book called *The Crimes, Detection, and Death of Jack the Ripper*. Determined to figure out Macnaghten's vague reference to "Kosminski," Fido conducted an extensive search of asylum records, trying to find any lunatic named Kosminski (or some name of a similar spelling) who had been admitted to an asylum around March 1889. The only insane Kosminski he found was an immigrant Polish Jewish hairdresser named Aaron Kozminski.

In most respects, Aaron Kozminski seemed to fit the statements of Anderson, Swanson, and Macnaghten very neatly. He was an immigrant Polish Jew, who lived with a brother in Whitechapel and was admitted to Colney Hatch asylum. Kozminski also "lived in the very heart of the district where the murders were committed," within easy walking distance to all of the murder sites. In addition, the cause of insanity on Kozminski's asylum record was "self-abuse"—a Victorian euphemism for masturbation or "the solitary vice." This agreed both with Anderson's statement that the Polish Jew suspect was "a loathsome creature whose utterly unmentionable vices reduced him to a lower level than that of the brute," and Macnaghten's statement that Kosminski "became insane owing to many years indulgence in solitary vices."

Yet there were also several problems that caused researchers to wonder whether Aaron Kozminski was in fact the right "Kosminski." For starters, Swanson said that "Kosminski" was admitted to "Stepney workhouse," whereas Aaron Kozminski was in fact admitted to Mile End Old Town workhouse. If Swanson was confused here, however, the reason for it is understandable. By the time that Swanson wrote the marginalia, circa 1910, Stepney workhouse was no longer within the boundaries of the redefined Borough of Stepney but instead was in Poplar. The Mile End Old Town workhouse, on the other hand, was in Stepney. Swanson might have simply thought, It was at that workhouse in Stepney.[9] There were other problems, though. For one thing, Macnaghten wrote that "Kosminski" had been "removed to a lunatic asylum about March 1889"—whereas Aaron Kozminski was admitted to Mile End workhouse in July 1890 and then readmitted to Mile End and subsequently Colney Hatch asylum in February 1891. Even more troubling was Swanson's statement that "Kosminski" died shortly after his admission to Colney Hatch. As we have seen, Aaron Kozminski lived until 1919, some twenty-eight years after his admission, and he was probably still alive when Swanson penciled his marginalia.[10] In sum, these inconsistencies led Fido and others to conclude that Aaron Kozminski could not have been Anderson's suspect, and debate over this point continued (although largely abated) until the present day.

No one has ever really explained these problems. Of course, one likely explanation is simply that Macnaghten and Swanson made mistakes. As Ripperologist Stewart Evans has noted, the mistakes in the Swanson marginalia and the Macnaghten memorandum "are confined to demonstrable errors, not assumptions, and are few. Indeed if they can be explained the recollections of Anderson, Macnaghten and Swanson are remarkably accurate in relation to Kosminski, allowing for the effects of the passage of time on memory."[11] Macnaghten, for example, most likely had access to the police files on the case, but he probably did not have any direct involvement with Kozminski as a suspect. And, as he admitted in his autobiography, he never kept a diary or a notebook and wrote entirely from memory alone. Regarding Swanson's statement that Kozminski had died, it is perhaps possible that the MET simply lost track of him and somehow assumed that he had died after he was transferred to Leavesden Asylum in 1894. After all, the police lacked sufficient evidence to convict Kozminski, so, legally speaking, they couldn't touch him. They were obviously aware that he had been placed in an asylum, but they may not have bothered to check up on him there. We may speculate endlessly on various explanations for these two mistakes, but we will probably never know the answer.

In any case, such problems were of little interest to the press, which seemed to be champing at the bit to declare that the case was closed. In October 1987, Charles Nevin of the *Daily Telegraph* boldly suggested that the Jack the Ripper mystery was finally solved and that the guilty party was a destitute and insane hairdresser named Aaron Kozminski. As Nevin pointed out, the Swanson marginalia "would seem to deal a body blow to the deep and convoluted speculations about the Ripper's identity which have reached a new intensity with the approach of the centenary of the killings."[12] Still, the apparent solution to the most famous unsolved murder case of all time felt like a bit of a letdown. After all, the celebrated rogues' gallery of Ripper suspects included members of the royal family, Freemasons, and a black magic practitioner, and within a few years, both Lewis Carroll and the famous painter Walter Sickert would be added to the list. Compared to these exciting characters, a lower-class insane hairdresser was painfully dull and unglamorous. As Nevin wrote, "Truth has once again proved to be far more drab and far less entertaining than speculation."[13]

20

A Few Possible Leads

Given that Aaron Kozminski was a strong suspect in the Ripper case, we might expect to find additional sources that mention him, and indeed, there was at least one other person who did. George Sims was a journalist and a playwright who wrote extensively on the Ripper murders and on the East End in general. He was also a personal friend of Melville Macnaghten. In an article published in *Lloyds Weekly News* on September 22, 1907, Sims wrote, "It is betraying no state secret to say that the official view arrived at after the exhaustive and systematic investigation of facts that never became public property is that the author of the atrocities was one of three men."[1] Sims then went on to describe the same three suspects who were mentioned in the Macnaghten memorandum but without naming them.

> The first man was a Polish Jew of curious habits and strange disposition, who was the sole occupant of certain premises in Whitechapel after night-fall. This man was in the district during the whole period covered by the Whitechapel murders, and soon after they ceased certain facts came to light which showed that it was quite possible that he might have been the Ripper. He had at one time been employed in a hospital in Poland. He was known to be a lunatic at the

time of the murders, and some-time afterwards he betrayed such undoubted signs of homicidal mania that he was sent to a lunatic asylum.

The policeman who got a glimpse of Jack in Mitre Court said, when some time afterwards he saw the Pole, that he was the height and build of the man he had seen on the night of the murder.[2]

Sims's information clearly came from Macnaghten himself, so we can be certain that the suspect referred to here is Kozminski. Yet the article also contained some additional information that was not in the Macnaghten memorandum. For example, where Macnaghten said only that Kozminski "strongly resembled the individual seen by the City P.C. near Mitre Square," Sims said, "He was the height and build of the man he had seen on the night of the murder." Sims also said that "soon after [the murders] ceased certain facts came to light which showed that it was quite possible that he might have been the Ripper," adding that the man was not sent to the asylum until "some-time afterwards."[3]

Even more interesting is Sims's statement that the suspect "had at one time been employed in a hospital in Poland." It is not known whether this was true, and it might be argued that this idea seems to be contradicted by the Book of Residents for Kłodawa, which listed Kozminski as a tailor. Yet the date of the Book of Residents entry is uncertain, and it may have been entered when Kozminski was only about ten years old. Thus, it does not preclude the possibility that Kozminski may have worked as an assistant in a hospital at some later time. Of course, if Sims's statement were true, it would suggest that Kozminski might have had some degree of rough anatomical knowledge, as some doctors believed the Ripper had.

Finally, Sims's article claimed that Kozminski was "the sole occupant of certain premises in Whitechapel after night-fall" and that he "was in the district during the whole period covered by the Whitechapel murders, and soon after they ceased certain facts came to light which showed that it was quite possible that he might have been the Ripper." It would be fascinating to know what these "certain facts" were, but Sims does not say.

Although there are no other known sources that name Kozminski specifically, at least two other people referred to an unnamed suspect who may have been Kozminski. And given that Donald Swanson claimed that the City CID kept Kozminski under surveillance, it is especially interesting that both men were plainclothes City detectives, who spoke of conducting surveillance on a suspect who was apparently Jewish and was admitted to an asylum.

Ex-detective-inspector Robert Sagar of the City of London Police Force was, at the time of his death in 1924, described as "a man of outstanding ability in the detection of crime." Born in Lancashire, Sagar made a brief foray into the study of medicine as a young man, before becoming fascinated by the problem of criminology and the detection of crime. "His forte was the discovery of the criminal," his obituary noted. "To unravel the tangled skein of a complicated human problem gave him as much pleasure as even 'Sherlock Holmes' derived from his voluntary activities."[4] After the murder of Catherine Eddowes within the City of London boundary, Sagar was deputed as a liaison for the City Police Force in daily conferences regarding the Ripper crimes.

As noted in an article printed at the time of his death, Sagar "spent much time in trying to trace 'Jack the Ripper.'"[5] He is known to have made at least two separate references to conducting surveillance on an unnamed suspect who, as he said, "without a doubt, was the murderer." The first was in an article printed in the London City Press on January 7, 1905, at the time of Sagar's retirement. The article noted that Sagar's "professional association" with the Ripper murders was "a very close one," and added, "Mr. Sagar knows as much about those crimes, which terrified the Metropolis, as any detective in London." According to Sagar,

> It has been asserted that the murderer fled to the continent, where he perpetrated similar hideous crimes; but that is not the case. The police realised, as also did the public, that the crimes were those of a madman, and suspicion fell upon a man, who, without a doubt, was the murderer. Identification being impossible, he could not be charged. He was, however, placed in a lunatic asylum, and the series of atrocities came to an end. There was a peculiar incident in connection with those tragedies which may have been forgotten. The apron

belonging to the woman who was murdered in Mitre Square
was thrown under a staircase in a common lodging house in
Dorset Street, and someone—presumably the murderer—
had written on the wall above it, 'The Jewes are not the
people that will be blamed for nothing.'[sic] A police officer
engaged in the case, fearing that the writing might lead to an
onslaught upon the Jews in the neighbourhood, rubbed the
writing from the wall, and all record of the implied accusation was lost; but the fact that such an ambiguous message
was left is recorded among the archives at the Guildhall.[6]

In many respects, this sounds very much like Robert Anderson's
statements about Kozminski. The fact that Sagar said that identification was "impossible" seems to imply that he was aware that an
identification had been attempted but was not successful. Sagar insinu-
ated that after the identification, the suspect was "placed in a lunatic
asylum, and the series of atrocities came to an end." This parallels
Swanson's statement that "after this identification . . . no other murder
of this kind took place in London." It is also interesting that Sagar went
on to mention the Goulston Street graffito, and the police "fearing that
the writing might lead to an onslaught upon the Jews in the neighbourhood." This seems to hint that Sagar's suspect was Jewish.

Sagar's second reference to this suspect appeared in September
1946 in a *Reynold's News* article titled "Who Was Jack the Ripper?" by
Justin Atholl. The article read,

> More probable is the theory that the police knew the iden-
> tity of the Ripper but were never able to get evidence to
> arrest him. The crime committed by a maniac, completely
> without motive, is the most difficult on which to get evi-
> dence the law will accept.
>
> Inspector Robert Sagar, who died in 1924, played a lead-
> ing part in the Ripper investigations. In his memoirs he
> said: "We had good reason to suspect a man who worked in
> Butcher's Row, Aldgate. We watched him carefully. There was
> no doubt that this man was insane, and after a time his friends
> thought it advisable to have him removed to a private asylum.
> After he was removed, there were no more Ripper atrocities.[7]

In many respects, this statement also seems to fit Kozminski. Once again, it is suggested, "The police knew the identity of the Ripper but were never able to get evidence to arrest him."[8] The suspect was insane and "after a time" was removed to an asylum by "his friends." It is particularly interesting that Sagar, a City detective, said, "We watched him carefully," implying that the suspect was kept under surveillance by City detectives, which matches Swanson's statement that Kozminski was "watched by police (City CID) by day & night."[9]

Sagar claimed that the suspect worked in Butcher's Row, a section of Aldgate High Street that had historically been the location of butcher shops just outside the Old ("Ald") Gate of the City of London. Unfortunately, no documentation has been found to indicate that Kozminski ever worked in Butcher's Row, and it is not known whether he was employed at all in 1888. A review of trade directories for 1888–1891 by researcher Scott Nelson has revealed that there were three or four tailor shops in the area of Butcher's Row and at least one hairdresser's shop, Kallin & Radin, adjacent to St. Botolph's Church on the northwest corner of the block.[10]

An apparent problem with Sagar's statement is that he said the suspect was removed to a "private asylum." As far as we know, this does not fit with Kozminski, who was admitted not to a private asylum, but rather to the County Asylum at Colney Hatch. Again, it is possible that Kozminski was admitted to a private asylum, but no proof of this has ever been discovered. Despite these problems, it still seems possible that both of Sagar's statements might refer to Kozminski.

Another likely source was a man named Harry (or Henry) Cox. Like Sagar, Cox was a City detective, and an article published in the *Police Review* on the occasion of his retirement in December 1906 noted that it was "as a shadower of criminals that Mr. Cox did some of his best work."[11] The article described several of Cox's adventures shadowing criminals while wearing various disguises—one disguise was that of a painter, another that of a clerk "with a silk hat[,] umbrella, and evening paper." The same week this article came out, *Thompson's Weekly News* published an article titled "The Truth about the Whitechapel Mysteries, Told by Harry Cox." In it, Cox claimed to have conducted undercover surveillance on a suspect "not unlikely to have been connected with the crimes," who was insane, was apparently Jewish, and was later committed to an asylum. The article may well be a firsthand account of the surveillance of Kozminski, and we must assess it carefully. Because of this, I have excerpted the article at length, highlighting the more interesting points:

> We had many people under observation while the murders were being perpetrated, but it was not until the discovery of the body of Mary Kelly had been made that we seemed to get upon the trail. Certain investigations made by several of our cleverest detectives made it apparent to us that a man living in the East End of London was not unlikely to have been connected with the crimes. . . .
>
> The murderer was a misogynist, who at some time or another had been *wronged by a woman*. And the fact that his victims were of the lowest class proves, I think, that he was not, as has been stated, an educated man who had suddenly gone mad. He belonged to their own class.
>
> Had he been wronged by a woman occupying a higher stage in society the murders would in all probability have taken place in the West End, the victims have been members of the fashionable demi-monde.
>
> The man we suspected was about five feet six inches in height, with short, black, curly hair, and he had a habit of taking late walks abroad. *He occupied several shops in the East End*, but from time to time he became insane, and was forced to spend a portion of his time in an asylum in Surrey.
>
> While the Whitechapel murders were being perpetrated his place of business was in a certain street, and after the last murder I was on duty in this street for nearly three months.
>
> There were several other officers with me, and I think there can be no harm in stating that the opinion of most of them was that the man they were watching had something to do with the crimes. You can imagine that never once did we allow him to quit our sight. The least slip and another brutal crime might have been perpetrated under our very noses. It was not easy to forget that already one of them had taken place at the very moment when one of our smartest colleagues was passing the top of the dimly lit street.

The Jews in the street soon became aware of our presence. It was impossible to hide ourselves. They became suddenly alarmed, panic stricken, and I can tell you that at nights we ran a considerable risk. We carried our lives in our hands so to speak, and at last we had to partly take the alarmed inhabitants into our confidence, and so throw them off the scent. *We told them we were factory inspectors looking for tailors* and capmakers who employed boys and girls under age, and *pointing out the evils accruing from the sweaters' system* asked them to co-operate with us in destroying it.

They readily promised to do so, although we knew well that they had no intention of helping us. Every man was as bad as another. Day after day we used to sit and chat with them, drinking their coffee, smoking their excellent cigarettes, and partaking of Kosher rum. Before many weeks had passed we were quite friendly with them, and knew that we could carry out our observations unmolested. I am sure they never once suspected that we were police detectives on the trail of the mysterious murderer; otherwise they would not have discussed the crimes with us as openly as they did.

We had the use of a house opposite the shop of the man we suspected, and, disguised, of course, we frequently stopped across in the role of customers.

Every newspaper loudly demanded that we should arouse from our slumber, and the public had lashed themselves into a state of fury and fear. The terror soon spread to the provinces too. Whenever a small crime was committed it was asserted that the Ripper had shifted his ground, and warning letters were received by many a terror stricken woman. The latter were of course the work of cruel practical jokers. The fact, by the way, that the murderer never shifted his ground rather inclines to the belief that he was a mad, poverty stricken inhabitant of some slum in the East End.

Cox then described an evening of shadowing the suspect as he walked around the streets. The article concludes,

In the end, he brought me, tired, weary, and nerve-strung, back to the street he had left where he disappeared into his own house.

Next morning I beheld him busy as usual. It is indeed very strange that *as soon as this madman was put under observation, the mysterious crimes ceased,* and that very soon he removed from his usual haunts and gave up his nightly prowls. *He was never arrested for the reason that not the slightest scrap of evidence could be found to connect him with the crimes.*[12]

Many of the details here obviously fit with what is known about Kozminski. Cox's suspect lived in the East End, belonged to the lower class, and "from time to time he became insane, and was forced to spend a portion of his time in an asylum." But even more intriguing is that Cox said the suspect "occupied several shops in the East End," and that the detectives were apparently watching a workshop on a largely Jewish street. Moreover, Cox clearly implied that it was a tailor's workshop, because otherwise their cover story would not make any sense. In fact, it is likely that the detectives chose the "factory inspectors" cover story because of the close scrutiny that sweaters were under at the time, both by factory inspectors and by social researchers. In fact, in October 1888, one of Charles Booth's researchers, a man named Henry J. Bowsher, had been doing follow-up surveys on tailors on Yalford Street and Plumber's Row, both of which were adjacent to Greenfield Street, just one street to the west and the east, respectively.[13]

It was also in October 1888 that the police were conducting inquiries into the Batty Street laundry incident, in which the police were carrying out surveillance on a suspect who was "living on the premises" of a ladies' tailor's workshop, "within a radius of a few hundred yards from the scene of the Berner-street tragedy."[14] Now we have Cox saying that the suspect under City Police surveillance "occupied several shops in the East End." Likewise, George Sims referred to Kozminski as "the sole occupant of certain premises in Whitechapel after night-fall." All three statements may suggest that Kozminski was living "on the premises" of his brother Isaac's tailoring workshop at 74 Greenfield Street during the Ripper murders. This theory fits Swanson's statement, "On suspect's return to his brother's house in Whitechapel he was watched by police [City CID] by day & night."[15] Moreover, as Cox said, "We had the use of a house opposite the shop of the man we suspected, and, disguised, of course, we frequently stopped across in the role of customers." As we have seen, the house directly opposite from Isaac's shop was 16 Greenfield Street, where Kozminski's sister, Matilda, lived with her husband, Morris Lubnowski-Cohen. Is it possible that Kozminski's sister and her husband cooperated with the police, allowing undercover detectives to use their house for their surveillance? If this is true, then it seems likely that Morris and Matilda suspected that Kozminski was the murderer. Such a conjecture is well within the realm of possibility, especially since we know that Kozminski threatened to attack Matilda with a knife at one point. The motivation behind the attack is unknown.

The theory that Kozminski lived in the workshop behind his brother's house is indeed an intriguing one. Such an arrangement would not have been uncommon, because the East End was notoriously overcrowded, and "greeners" often lived in the shops where they worked. It would also make sense, because by 1888, Kozminski was probably exhibiting signs of delusional insanity, and his siblings may have considered him to be dangerous. As we have seen, those saddled with the responsibility of caring for insane and potentially dangerous family members often resorted to locking their mentally disturbed relatives in rooms or otherwise isolating them from the family. Whereas Woolf and Morris both probably lived in rather cramped quarters, Isaac had a large separate workshop in his backyard, where Kozminski could be kept away from the children. The arrangement might also fit with Robert Anderson's statement (or theory) that the Ripper lived in a place where he "could go and come and get rid of his blood-stains in secret."[16] Presumably, the workshop was accessible via a hallway leading directly from the front door of the house to the backyard, through which Kozminski could come and go without disturbing his family in the house.

Yet as usual, there are some problems with Cox's account. One problem, as noted in Evans and Rumbelow's *Jack the Ripper: Scotland Yard Investigates*, was that Kozminski "had not worked for years, which does not tie in with either Cox or Sagar's accounts."[17] The statement about Kozminski's unemployment comes from Edmund King Houchin's medical certification of Kozminski in February 1891, when Jacob Cohen claimed that Kozminski "has not attempted any kind of work for years."[18] Of course, February 1891 was more than two years after the murder of Mary Kelly, and thus we cannot deduce from Cohen's 1891 statement whether Kozminski was employed in 1888. Evans and Rumbelow's issue here seems to be based on the assumption that the surveillance of Kozminski took place a couple of years after the Ripper murders, most likely in either 1890 or 1891. Yet if Sagar and Cox were indeed referring to Kozminski, it seems that their surveillance took place much earlier than this, perhaps even as early as 1888. Cox, for example, said, "After the last murder I was on duty in this street for nearly three months." Cox also said, "It was not until the discovery of the body of Mary Kelly had been made that we seemed to get upon the trail" and, "as soon as this madman was put under observation, the mysterious crimes ceased." This implies that the City Police surveillance took place immediately after Kelly's murder. This, of course, would seem to contradict the possibility that Kozminski was the subject of the Batty Street laundry inquiries, which took place in October. Of course, Cox may have misremembered when the surveillance actually began. Or, Kozminski may have been under surveillance both before and after the Kelly murder. If Kozminski did initially come to the attention of the police in October 1888, he would have been only one name on a long list of suspects. And as we have seen, the Echo declared on October 20 that "the man is, indeed, himself aware that he is being watched; so much so, that, as far as observation has gone at present, he has scarcely ventured out of doors."[19]

There are many questions here but few answers. The problems with the Cox and Sagar accounts must remain unresolved for the time being. As Cox concluded, "[The suspect] was never arrested for the reason that not the slightest scrap of evidence could be found to connect him with the crimes." This obviously fits with Anderson's suggestion that the police did not have legal proof sufficient to convict Kozminski. If Cox's suspect was indeed Kozminski, then he gave the only known physical description of him, apart from a few brief notes about his weight in the asylum records. "The man we suspected was about five feet six inches in height, with short, black, curly hair."[20] Of course, this does not tell us much about the suspect's appearance, but in height, at least, the man generally matched the witness statements given by Joseph Lawende, Israel Schwartz, and Elizabeth Long.

21

The Identification, the Witness, and the Informant

"We are coming now rather into the region of guesswork," said Dr. Mortimer.

"Say, rather, into the region where we balance probabilities and choose the most likely. It is the scientific use of the imagination, but we always have some material basis on which to start our speculations."

—*Sherlock Holmes in* The Hound of the Baskervilles,
Arthur Conan Doyle, 1902

The identification of Aaron Kozminski by a witness is, on the face of it, one of the strongest pieces of evidence against him. Yet it is also a highly debated topic, and the circumstances of the incident are still largely unknown. When and where did the identification take place? Who was the witness? And what exactly happened? It is impossible to answer these questions with certainty. Again, we must try our best to interpret the sources.

According to Robert Anderson, Kozminski was identified by "the only person who had ever had a good view of the murderer."[1] Is it possible to determine who this person was? Swanson's statements clearly indicate that the witness was a Jewish man, so it must have been either Israel Schwartz or one of the three men (Joseph Lawende, Joseph Levy, and Henry Harris) who witnessed a man and a woman standing near the entrance of Church Passage on Duke Street. Yet Harris's testimony was hardly mentioned in the Kate Eddowes inquest at all, and Levy claimed, "I cannot give any description of either of them."[2] Therefore, we are left with Lawende and Schwartz as the two best possibilities.

Arguably, either of these men might have been the witness, but Lawende seems to be the more likely candidate. Melville Macnaghten did not explicitly mention the identification, but he did say that Kozminski "in appearance strongly resembled the individual seen by the City P.C. near Mitre Square."[3] As author Phillip Sugden has suggested, we might infer from this that Macnaghten was confused, and in saying "City P.C." he actually meant "City Police witness."[4] This suggests that the witness was Lawende, a City Police witness who testified at the inquest for a murder that took place in City Police jurisdiction. This might also explain why it was the City CID, as opposed to the Metropolitan CID, that conducted surveillance on a suspect who lived in Metropolitan Police territory. In addition, as noted by Stewart Evans, "Use of the City detectives for such observations would, of course, have been preferred as they would have been far less likely to have been recognised by the locals than the local CID."[5]

According to Anderson, "The only person who had ever had a good view of the murderer at once identified him"—in other words, the witness identified the suspect almost immediately after seeing him.[6] This does not mean that the witness was certain of his identification, although we may infer that that is what Anderson meant. Likewise, Donald Swanson told us that the suspect "had been identified," twice reiterating that the suspect "knew he was identified."[7] Again, this does not say much about the witness's degree of certainty as to his identification. Indeed, other sources suggest that the identification was somewhat shaky. For one thing, Macnaghten merely claimed that Kozminski "strongly resembled the individual seen by the City P.C. [sic] near Mitre Square."[8] Likewise, George Sims (whose source was almost certainly Macnaghten) said that Kozminski "was the height and build of the man" seen by the witness on the night of the Mitre Square murder.[9] (Sims does not actually name Kozminski, but we may assume that is who he is referring to.)

Indeed, it is difficult to imagine how the identification could have been anything but inconclusive at best. After all, in 1888 when Lawende was asked whether he would recognize the man again, he answered, "I doubt it."[10] He had only had a brief glimpse of the suspect, and as Levy noted, "The place was badly lighted."[11] Despite this, Lawende described the man he saw in considerable detail—"age 30, height 5 ft. 7 or 8 in., complexion fair, moustache fair, medium build; dress, pepper-and-salt colour loose jacket, grey cloth cap with peak of same material, reddish neckerchief tied in knot; appearance of a sailor"—and the police tried to keep his description out of the papers. This may suggest that Lawende got a better look at the man than he claimed, and it is clear that the police considered him an important witness, because they "sequestrated" him and "imposed a pledge on him of secrecy."[12]

Still, if we take Lawende's "I doubt it" at face value, as we probably should, it seems unlikely that he would have been able to positively identify Kozminski with any degree of certainty. Moreover, Lawende was aware that his identification was the linchpin of the whole case. As Swanson wrote, the witness refused to testify "because the suspect was also a Jew and also because his evidence would convict the suspect and witness would be the means of murderer being hanged which he did not wish to be left on his mind."[13] The police were clearly desperate for any evidence that might lead to a conviction, and Swanson and Anderson may have put pressure on Lawende to testify. Yet if Lawende had only a dim recollection of the man he saw that night and was unsure of his identification, he would have almost certainly declined to swear to it. Lawende may have said that Kozminski generally matched his vague recollection of the man—in height and build, for example—but that he was not sure about it. This, of course, would not have been good enough.

Both Anderson and Swanson would have been well aware of the power that a positive witness identification would have in court. Even today, eyewitness testimony is still among the most compelling evidence to juries. As University of California–Irvine professor Dr. Elizabeth Loftus remarked, there is "nothing more convincing [to a jury] than a live human being who takes the stand, points a finger at the defendant, and says 'That's the one!'"[14] Unfortunately, numerous studies have shown witness identifications to be notoriously inaccurate. According to the Benjamin N. Cardozo School of Law's Innocence Project, "Eyewitness misidentification is the single greatest cause of wrongful convictions nationwide, playing a role in more than 75% of convictions overturned through DNA testing."[15] Studies have shown, for example, that a person's recollection of events deteriorates significantly after even a short time. I tested this one afternoon when I was sitting with my friend John in a restaurant. The waitress came over to our table several times, first to take our drink order, then to deliver the drinks and take our lunch order, then to deliver the food, and then again to ask whether everything was okay. John looked at her several times as she stood next to the table, in a fairly well-lit environment. Toward the end of our lunch, I asked John if he thought he could identify the woman in a police line-up. He thought for a moment and replied, "Maybe, but I doubt it." The mind seems to forget such things almost immediately.

Of course, this does not mean the witness identification of Aaron Kozminski should be discounted. After all, both Swanson and Anderson said that Kozminski was identified, and if we take them at their word, the witness refused to testify only because he discovered the suspect was "a fellow Jew." As we have seen, this statement was harshly attacked in the *Jewish Chronicle* after the publication of Anderson's book. Still, as a Jew himself, Lawende must have been acutely aware that a positive identification of a Jewish Ripper suspect might lead to riots against the Jews in the East End. If he was in any way uncertain of his identification, it is easy to see why he might have refused to testify. It is perhaps unlikely that he would have explicitly said that he wouldn't testify because the suspect was Jewish. Instead, he probably said something like, "He looks like the man but I can't be sure of it. Moreover, if I testify, this man will be hanged, and all hell will break loose in the East End." Anderson and Swanson may have glossed over the subtle distinctions in such a statement when briefly summarizing the incident years later.

Despite this, Anderson was still for some reason convinced that Kozminski was the Ripper. It is possible that Kozminski's behavior, more than anything else, convinced Anderson (and perhaps Swanson) of his guilt. As Swanson said, Kozminski "knew he was identified."[16] It is even possible that the police told Kozminski that he had been positively identified, just to see how he would react. Anderson later described to author Hargrave Lee Adam a similar tactic he once used when he confronted a suspected murderer and informed him that "the murderer had been found." Anderson informed the suspect that an image of the murderer had been photographed from an impression left on the dead woman's retina—a bizarre method that was actually thought to have had some merit at the time. But Anderson was lying . . . he merely wanted to see the suspect's reaction. The man, according to Anderson, "turned deathly pale and trembled in his chair." "Then," he exclaimed, "I was morally certain that I had the murderer before me!"[17] A similar tactic may have been tried with Kozminski.

Ultimately, the witness identification should be considered just one aspect of a multifaceted "case" against Kozminski. And despite Anderson's strong belief in Kozminski's guilt, there was no consensus on the matter within Scotland Yard, because other police officials preferred suspects other than Kozminski. For example, John Littlechild, the ex–chief inspector and a former head of the Special Branch, wrote that Anderson "only thought he knew."[18] This suggests that Littlechild was aware of Anderson's "theory" but disagreed with it. We should probably conclude that Anderson's "definitely ascertained fact" was probably more along the lines of a strong belief in Kozminski's guilt, rather than definite proof of it.

Other aspects of the identification are equally vague. For example, it is not known where the identification took place. The only clue here is Swanson's statement that Kozminski was identified "at the Seaside Home where he had been sent by us with difficulty."[19] Several researchers have assumed that "the Seaside Home" was a reference to the Police Convalescent Seaside Home in Hove, a "small and ill-adapted" rented building at 51 Clarendon Villas, which opened in March 1890 as a retreat for policemen recovering from illness or disability. But if this was the Seaside Home Swanson was referring to, why did the identification take place there? After all,

Hove was more than fifty miles from central London. One theory is that the police wanted to keep the whole affair out of the prying eyes of the press. Yet is this reasonable? Surely, the police could have managed to conduct the identification somewhere in London without alerting the press about it. A more likely explanation is that someone—either the witness or a police official involved in the identification—was staying at "the Seaside Home," necessitating that the identification take place there.

Of course, Swanson did not say the identification took place at the Police Convalescent Home in Hove; he merely said "the Seaside Home." "I think this is really a conclusion that's been jumped to and clung to ever since," researcher Chris Phillips said, "even though there's no particularly strong evidence in its favour."[20] In fact, the Police Convalescent Seaside Home at Hove was only one of nearly seventy seaside convalescent homes for men, women, and children, most of which were located on the southern English coastline. Any of these might have been Swanson's Seaside Home. One possibility, for example, is the Metropolitan Convalescent Institution at Bexhill-on-Sea, a seaside resort town in the county of East Sussex. The Bexhill Seaside Home opened in 1881 and had a hundred beds available for "poor persons over 14 years of age in need of sea air and diet," convalescing from various infectious diseases and advanced consumption.[21] Another possibility, suggested by researcher Andy Aliffe, was the Morley House Seaside Convalescent Home for Working Men, which opened in 1883 in St. Margaret's Bay, near Dover. As Aliffe pointed out, Morley House reserved a certain number of beds for members of the City of London Police Force, and if the City Police were involved in the witness identification, it seems possible they would have used that location.

Debate over this point is relevant for one reason only: the Police Seaside Home at Hove officially opened on March 17, 1890. Therefore, if the identification took place there, it must have been *after* that date. Yet if the identification occurred in some other "Seaside Home," then it may have happened any time, including before March 1890.

This leads us to the last and, in some sense, the most confounding question of all: when did the identification take place? Perhaps the most likely scenario is that the identification was made around the time Kozminski was first admitted to Mile End on July 13, 1890. We might imagine that the workhouse staff informed the police about Kozminski's admission—after all, as an insane local resident Kozminski was the type of suspect the police were look-ing for. In this scenario, the police would have taken Kozminski to the Seaside Home (either in Hove or elsewhere) around July 14 or 15, conducted the identification, and then returned him to the workhouse by July 16 when he was discharged. The time line here is fairly reasonable.

It is possible, however, that the identification took place consider-ably earlier, around the time of the Mary Kelly murder or even before then. As Phillips pointed out, when Melville Macnaghten wrote his famous memorandum in 1894, he seemed to believe that Kozminski had been sent to an asylum or otherwise dealt with as a suspect in March 1889. Yet Macnaghten did not join the police force until after March 1889. As Phillips noted,

> That seems to imply that if Aaron came to the police's atten-tion and was investigated in 1890 or 1891, Macnaghten knew nothing about it at the time, or it was not significant enough for him to remember it when he came to write the memoranda in 1894 (and of course Macnaghten in his memoirs does profess a great interest in the Whitechapel Murders). The alternative is that Aaron Kozminski was suspected earlier on—in late 1888 or early 1889, before Macnaghten joined the force—that Swanson was confused about his dates, and that whatever the "Seaside Home" was, it wasn't the police one.[22]

The possibility that Kozminski was identified and kept under surveillance in late 1888 or early 1889 has rarely been consid-ered by Ripperologists, but several sources arguably support such a theory. As we have seen, Detective Robert Sagar, for example, spoke of conducting surveillance on a suspect who "was insane, and after a time his friends thought it advisable to have him removed to a private asylum. After he was removed, there were no more Ripper atrocities."[23] Admittedly, it is not known whether Sagar was referring to Kozminski, but if he considered Kelly to be the last of the "Ripper atrocities," it would seem that his surveillance began around November or December 1888. Likewise, according to Detective Henry Cox, "It was not until the discovery of the body of Mary Kelly had been made that we seemed to get upon the trail."[24] Cox discussed conducting surveillance on a suspect who lived on the premises of a tailor (or a cap maker), apparently on a largely Jewish street. This again seems to suggest that the City CID was shadowing a suspect shortly after Kelly's murder, in either November or December 1888. In addition, Cox noted, "It is indeed very strange that as soon as this madman was put under observation, the mysterious crimes ceased, and that very soon he removed from his usual haunts and gave up his nightly prowls. He was never arrested for the reason that not the slightest scrap of evidence could be found to connect him with the crimes."[25]

This mirrors Swanson's statement that "after this identification which suspect knew no other murder of this kind took place in London."[26] Both Cox and Swanson seem to imply that the suspect stopped killing because he knew he was being watched by the police.

"While the Whitechapel murders were being perpetrated his place of business was in a certain street," Cox said, "and after the last murder I was on duty in this street for nearly three months."[27] If we assume the "last murder" refers to Kelly's murder, Cox's surveillance would seem to have ended around February or March 1889—in other words, around the time that Macnaghten claimed that Kozminski "was removed to a lunatic asylum" (that is, March 1889). A hunch tells me that there is a crucial piece of the puzzle missing here. One possibility is that Macnaghten simply confused Kozminski's admission to Colney Hatch with an earlier admission to a private asylum as a voluntary patient. Remember that Sagar claimed that his suspect was admitted to a private asylum. And Cox said of his suspect, "From time to time he became insane, and was forced to spend a portion of his time in an asylum in Surrey."[28] As Chris Phillips pointed out, Cox's account "seems to suggest the suspect was in and out of an asylum, rather than simply being committed and staying there."[29] March 1889 is interesting for other reasons, because it was also around this time that the Ripper investigations were winding down.

By March 15, the plainclothes patrols were entirely phased out, and in a letter to the secretary of state, Monro said, "This duty has now ceased." Presumably, this included the termination of Cox's undercover surveillance duties. It was also in March 1889 that Frederick Abberline was moved off the case and that Home Office funding for additional police forces in the East End was not renewed. In sum, it seems likely that something happened around March 1889, but it is not clear what.

In June 1892, *Cassell's Saturday Journal* printed an interview with Sir Robert Anderson, in which he claimed that the Ripper murders had been committed by "a maniac revelling in blood." This was apparently Anderson's first hint that the police knew Jack the Ripper's identity, and we must assume that Kozminski was the "maniac" he had in mind. Anderson then added that "his department has a great thirst for information, and the public might often assist him very materially by communicating with him in confidence, for very often a small matter sets his officers in motion."[30] What was Anderson referring to here? Is it possible that the head of the CID had received confidential information that set his officers in motion, ultimately leading to the discovery of Jack the Ripper?

There are at least four references to informants—usually, female relatives—reporting their suspicions to the police. One of these, as we have already seen, was reported in the *Echo*, during the so-called Batty Street lodger incident, in October 1888:

> [The suspect] lived some time ago with a woman, by whom, he has been accused. Her statements are, it is stated, now being inquired into. In the meantime the suspected assassin is "shadowed." Incriminating evidence of a certain character has already been obtained, and, should implicit credence be placed in the woman already referred to, whose name we will not transpire under any circumstances until after his guilt is prima facie established, a confession of the crimes may be looked for at any moment.[31]

In fairness, we must treat this and other newspaper reports surrounding the Batty Street incident with caution. It is possible that the reference to a female informant was simply another case of shoddy journalism. Yet Aaron Kozminski almost certainly lived with female relatives, either his sister, Matilda, or his sisters-in-law, Bertha and Betsy Abrahams.

Another such reference was in a rather curious article titled "The Whitechapel Murderer—The Latest Police Theory," which appeared in the *Dublin Express* in December 1888:

> The *Dublin Express* London correspondent gives as the latest police theory concerning the Whitechapel murderer that he has fallen under the strong suspicion of his near relatives, who, to avert a terrible family disgrace, may have placed him out of harm's way in safe keeping. As showing that there is a certain amount of credence attached to this theory, detectives have recently visited all the registered private lunatic asylums and made full inquiries as to the inmates recently admitted.

Curiously, this article was published around the time, according to detective Harry Cox, that the police "seemed to get upon the trail" of the Ripper—that is, after "the discovery of the body of Mary Kelly." It is interesting that the article states that "to avert a terrible family disgrace," the suspect's family may have "placed him out of harm's way in safe keeping." Admittedly, this could mean almost anything, but one possibility, which I have already alluded to, is that Kozminski was locked up in his own home. As noted by author David Wright, in the absence of asylum care, lunatics were frequently cared for by family members, and "even 'occasional' or 'threatened' violence could force families to take pre-emptive action such as restraint or sequestration within the home."[32] It is also interesting that the article says, "Detectives have recently visited all the registered private lunatic asylums and made full inquiries as to the inmates recently admitted." This is reminiscent of detective Robert Sagar's statement that the suspect was removed to a private asylum sometime after the end of the murders.

Another interesting article, which appeared on July 29, 1890, in the *Galveston (Texas) Daily News*, claimed that the Ripper had been "arrested on the strength of information given by his own sister." The timing of this article is especially intriguing because it appeared only sixteen days after Kozminski's first admission to Mile End Old Town Workhouse. The article read,

JACK THE RIPPER'S VACATION

A Possible Explanation of the Suspension of Whitechapel Horrors

Halifax, N.S. July 28.

A curious story has got out here that if true explains the long rest which Jack the Ripper has been taking from his diabolical work in the Whitechapel district, London. A lady from this city visiting a distinguished official in London, states in a letter written to friends here that the Ripper has been under arrest in the London metropolis for some time. He is a medical student and was arrested on the strength of information given by his own sister.

The authorities, the letter states, have kept the matter a strict secret in order to work up the case against the prisoner, and they are said to have a very complete chain of evidence.

These statements are vouched for by the writer of the letter who came into possession of the facts accidentally. The person who makes the story public, however, refuses to divulge her name.[33]

As usual, the article is frustratingly vague, and there are problems to consider. Indeed, if there is any truth at all to the story, it may have been misinterpreted or garbled in translation somewhere along the line. The "distinguished official" who revealed this story to the unnamed "visiting lady" must have been aware he was letting the cat out of the bag, and he may have kept the details intentionally vague because, as the article notes, the authorities were keeping the matter a "strict secret." Obviously, it was not so much of a secret as to prevent it from being indiscreetly disclosed in what was probably very casual conversation. If Kozminski was identified by a witness (perhaps in July 1890), then several "distinguished officials" at Scotland Yard and the Home Office must have felt that they were very close to solving the case, and they were probably itching to tell somebody about it. One might imagine someone imprudently mentioning the exciting unfolding events in whispered tones at a dinner party.

A final reference to a female informant is perhaps most interesting of all. In 2001, a Ripperologist named Stephen Ryder discovered an intriguing letter in a collection of Anderson's surviving correspondence at Duke University in Durham, North Carolina. The letter, found in a folder marked "undated correspondence," read as follows:

> 2 CAVENDISH SQUARE
> W.
>
> My dear Anderson,
>
> I send you this line to ask you to see & hear the bearer, whose name is unknown to me. She has or thinks she has a knowledge of the author of the Whitechapel murders. The author is supposed to be nearly related to her, & she is in great fear lest any suspicion should attach to her & place her & her family in peril.
>
> I have advised her to place the whole story before you, without giving you any names, so that you may form an opinion as to its being worth while to investigate.
>
> Very sincerely yours,
> Crawford[34]

"Crawford" was the Twenty-sixth Earl of Crawford, James Ludovic Lindsay, a friend and a correspondent of Anderson's who took "a particular interest in the Ripper crimes." The identity of the woman, who was "supposed to be nearly related" to the Ripper, was not given, nor did Crawford know it. He wrote the note simply as a letter of introduction that "the bearer" could take to Anderson. Curiously, this is the only letter in Anderson's surviving correspondence that had anything to do with the Ripper crimes.

A woman "in great fear lest any suspicions should attach to her & place her & her family in peril" would certainly fit if the suspect were Jewish. Indeed, it is not difficult to understand why a Jewish woman at the time would be afraid to go to the police if she truly believed her relative was the killer. Of course, she would fear for her family's safety, and she would also be aware of the effect a disclosure of the truth might have for the Jewish community in general. Indeed, a Jewish East End woman who suspected a close relative of being Jack the Ripper would be faced with a terrible dilemma. She might want to go to the police but, at the same time, be afraid that her family would fall victim to mob justice, and that the entire Jewish community would be "in peril" of succumbing to the same fate—the target of anger, outrage, and violence.

The possibility that Kozminski was suspected of being the Ripper by members of his own family is supported by Melville Macnaghten's suggestion that the killer was "found to be so helplessly insane by his relatives, that they, suspecting the worst, had him confined to some lunatic asylum."[35] Such a predicament may have caused heated arguments among the family members. Some of them may have refused to believe that their relative was the killer, while others believed it but wanted to protect him anyway. When confronted with such a horrible dilemma, the family would be at a loss, unsure of what to do. None of the options would have seemed good. Perhaps this is why the woman mentioned in the Earl of Crawford letter went directly to the top of the police hierarchy, in the hopes that Anderson might devise a discreet solution to the problem and protect her family from violent reprisal by East End mob justice. The police, in other words, may have helped the family in having Kozminski committed and then hushed up the whole affair as best they could.

So, was the Crawford letter the key that led Sir Robert Anderson to the discovery of Aaron Kozminski as a suspect? Admittedly, it seems unlikely that an East End Jewish woman in such a predicament would have chosen to contact James Ludovic Lindsay, of all people, a member of the House of Lords, who lived in lavish surroundings in Westminster. On the surface of it, a meeting between two people from such completely opposite ends of the social spectrum may seem unlikely. Yet in 1888, Lindsay was a member of the Lords Committee on the Sweating System, and as such he had cause to interact with the sweaters of the East End, and he may have even traveled to the East End to inspect the sweatshops in person. It is unclear how, exactly, such a meeting might have taken place, but at the very least, the Earl of Crawford's membership on the Sweating Committee presents an intriguing possible point of contact between him and the Kozminski family.

Ultimately, it is difficult to come to any hard and fast conclusions about these disparate references to a female informant, and it is unclear whether any of them had anything to do with Kozminski. Trying to make sense out of the events in Kozminski's life is difficult, to say the least. We know a few things for certain, and others may be inferred or guessed at. These are the pieces of the puzzle. They give us a very general idea of what may have happened and in what sequence. Yet we simply do not know enough to form the complete and true picture.

Sir Robert Anderson. At the time of the Ripper murders, Anderson was the assistant commissioner (crime) and the head of the Metropolitan Police Criminal Investigation Department. He later wrote that Jack the Ripper's identity was a "definitely ascertained fact" known to the police.

Donald Sutherland Swanson circa early 1880s. Swanson was the man in charge of the Ripper inquiry and the author of the famous "Swanson marginalia" (see below).

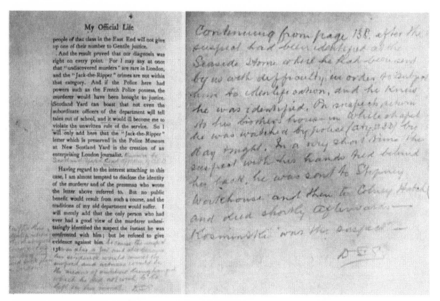

The "Swanson Marginalia," Swanson's penciled notes written in Anderson's autobiography. The annotations are on page 138 (left) and the notes on the endpaper (right). Anderson wrote that the identity of Jack the Ripper was known to the police, but he refused to name the suspect. On the endpaper, among other notes, Swanson penciled in, "Kosminski was the suspect."

248

The Police Seaside Convalescent Home at 51 Clarendon Villas, Hove, circa 1890. This was possibly where Aaron Kozminski was identified by a witness whom Donald Anderson described as "the only person who had ever had a good view of the murderer."

Melville Macnaghten's famous memorandum (above) claimed that Aaron Kozminski "had a great hatred of women, specially of the prostitute class, & had strong homicidal tendencies." Macnaghten added that "there were many circs connected with this man which made him a strong 'suspect.'" Despite this, Macnaghten did not agree with Anderson's "theory" that Kozminski was the Ripper.

Mile End
Old Town
Workhouse.

Aaron Kozminski's July 12, 1890, admission to Mile End Old Town Workhouse. His name is misspelled "Kosorimski."

On February 7, 1891, Aaron Kozminski was admitted to Colney Hatch Lunatic Asylum, suffering from "mania" and "incoherence." His medical certificate noted, "He declared that he is guided & his movements altogether controlled by an instinct that informs his mind." The "Supposed Cause" of insanity was entered as "unknown," but in red next to this was written "Self-Abuse"—a colloquial term for masturbation, then widely thought to be the cause of numerous disorders, including insanity.

Leavesden Asylum for Imbeciles. Although Leavesden was nominally an "Imbeciles' Asylum," the main criteria for admission were that a patient be both chronic and not dangerous—and even these criteria were not closely adhered to, because Leavesden admitted both acute cases and dangerous patients.

Leavesden Asylum Register of Patients, detailing Aaron Kozminski's physical decline. The entry at the top noted that Kozminski had "Hallucinations of sight and hearing [and] is very excitable and troublesome at times." On March 21, 1919, the night attendant S. Bennett noted, "Died in my presence at 5 AM."

251

Charles Booth, the son of a Liverpool cotton merchant, was a successful businessman and a dedicated philanthropist. From 1886 until 1903, he conducted extensive surveys into poverty, industry, and religion in the East End. In October 1888, at the height of the Ripper scare, one of Booth's researchers was doing follow-up surveys of tailors living on Yalford and Settles streets, in the neighborhood where the Kozminskis lived.

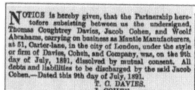

A notice of the dissolution of a mantle manufactory partnership between Woolf Abrahams and the elusive Jacob Cohen—the man who testified regarding Kozminski's insanity.

City detective Henry Cox spoke of conducting surveillance on a suspect who "occupied several shops in the East End, but from time to time he became insane." "The Jews in the street soon became aware of our presence," Cox wrote. "We told them we were factory inspectors looking for tailors and capmakers who employed boys and girls under age, and pointing out the evils accruing from the sweaters' system."

The Great Synagogue on Duke Street. It was under the street lamp (bottom left) at the entrance of Church Passage that Kate Eddowes was last seen alive. She was talking to a man, later apparently identified as Aaron Kozminski.

The Dolphin Pub was in this building at 97-99 Whitechapel Road (today occupied by the Islamic Bank of Britain). When Aaron Kozminski died in 1919, his brother Isaac was living upstairs with his son Mark and Mark's wife.

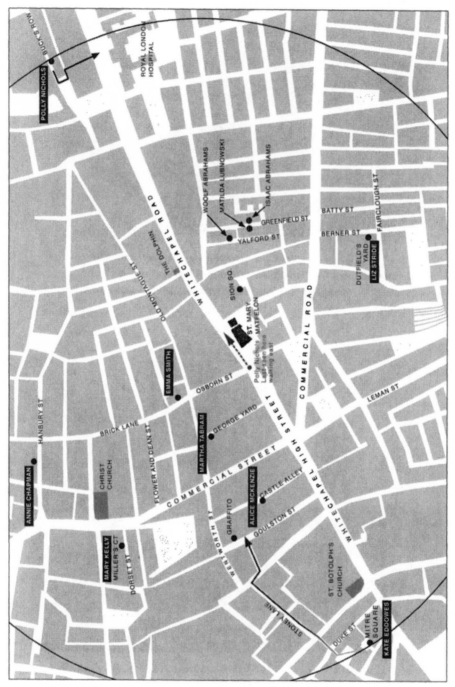

The center of the smallest circle containing the murder sites of the five canonic victims was a mere 350 yards from Aaron's likely residence on Greenfield Street. (Some of the noncanonic victims are also shown.)

Aaron Kozminski's grave. The headstone was made out of a soft sandstone. The inscription, now almost completely worn away, once read:

AARON KOZMINSKY
WHO DIED 24TH MARCH 1919
AGED 54 YEARS
DEEPLY MISSED BY
HIS BROTHER, SISTERS,
RELATIVES
AND FRIENDS

May his dear
Soul Rest in Peace

A theatrical version of Robert Louis Stevenson's *Dr. Jekyll and Mr. Hyde* premiered at the Lyceum Theatre on August 4, 1888, just two days before the murder of Martha Tabram. The *London Times*'s review of the play described Richard Mansfield's performance as "morbidly fascinating." Much like the twentieth-century serial killer Ted Bundy, Jekyll was "constantly haunted with a horror of the crimes of his other self."

PART FOUR

A Modern Perspective

22

Not Guilty?

"The fact is, we have all been a great deal puzzled because the affair is so simple and yet baffles us altogether."

"Perhaps it is the very simplicity of the thing that puts you at fault," said my friend.

—*"The Purloined Letter," Edgar Allan Poe*

When the Swanson marginalia were revealed in 1987, Charles Nevin of the *Daily Telegraph* penned an article declaring that "Sensational New Evidence" had emerged in the one-hundred-year-old case: "After all the increasingly bizarre suspects, and all the ingeniously constructed theories, a piece of hard evidence: nothing less than the identification of Jack the Ripper by the solid, stolid Scots Chief Inspector who investigated the Whitechapel murders." Nevin's article described Martin Fido's recent discovery of Aaron Kozminski in asylum records and briefly summarized what was known about the suspect, noting that among Ripperologists, "deep analysis has already started." He then put forth the million-dollar question "Is the case really closed?" For an answer, Nevin turned to author Donald Rumbelow, who was then arguably the world's leading Ripper expert. Rumbelow pointed out that the marginalia actually proved very little, except that the police suspected a man but did not have sufficient evidence to convict him. According to the article, Rumbelow could not "conceive of a serial sexual killer of increasing intensity who could survive without killing again between 1888 and 1891." In conclusion, he gave an explanation that would become a mantra to "anti-Andersonites" for years to follow. "We're dealing with old men's memories," he said. "The case is not closed."[1]

It was not long before the debate quickly degenerated into a muddled mess of obfuscation and confusion. In 1994, Philip Sugden wrote *The Complete History of Jack the Ripper*, widely and deservedly considered the best book yet written on the subject of the Ripper murders. In the book, Sugden referred to Kozminski as a "sad and pathetic suspect" and described Sir Robert Anderson's statements about the Ripper as "addle headed nonsense," based on "lapses of memory." Anderson had become senile and confused, Sugden argued, and was living in a sort of fantasy world—over the years, the ex-head of the CID gradually convinced himself that he had solved the case and wanted to boast of it. Of course, this meant that Donald Swanson must have been confused or lying as well, because he corroborated most of what Anderson wrote about Kozminski. The only logical explanation, in Sugden's opinion, was that both men were experiencing the same brand of revisionist self-delusional thinking. As Sugden put it, "Anderson and Swanson had come to inhabit a world of wish dreams."[2] Other Ripperologists followed Sugden's lead until eventually Anderson's "definitely ascertained fact" about the Ripper's identity had been rejected by the majority of experts in the case.

Given the apparent zeal with which Ripperologists chose to dismiss the unambiguous statements of the head of Scotland Yard's CID, one wonders how much "deep analysis" actually took place. In fact, it seems the main objection to Kozminski as a suspect was simply that in the minds of many Ripperologists, he just did not fit their "profile" of the Ripper. Yes, Kozminski was insane, and, according to Melville Macnaghten, he had homicidal tendencies and a "great hatred of women, specially of the prostitute class."[3] And yes, he threatened his sister with a knife and lived in the very heart of the Ripper's hunting ground. But his Colney Hatch admission also indicated that he was a compulsive masturbator and that he ate food out of the gutter. This clearly did not fit the popular image of Jack the Ripper as a suave and sophisticated killer, roaming the foggy London streets wearing a top hat and a tuxedo and carrying an ominously suggestive black leather bag.

An additional problem was that Kozminski's transfer to Leavesden Asylum for Imbeciles led many researchers to conclude that Kozminski was little more than a drooling idiot. Fido, for example, noted, "No sexual serialist had ever been an imbecile." Fido admitted that he did not pay much attention to Kozminski as a suspect and dismissed him almost immediately.[4] Likewise, Sugden referred to Kozminski as "a harmless imbecile." Kozminski's Leavesden case notes were cited in support of this theory. One entry, for example, stated that he was "Dull and stupid in manner," while another read that he "cannot answer questions of a simple nature."[5] Yet what is often ignored is that Kozminski's surviving Leavesden case notes begin in 1910, almost twenty years after the murders. Kozminski's Colney Hatch case notes, on the other hand, generally described him as "demented," "excitable," and "incoherent," which are symptoms that are consistent with his diagnosis of "mania."[6]

More important, the claim that Kozminski was an "imbecile" in any sense of the word is simply wrong. In the nineteenth century, the word *imbecile* was a strictly defined medical and legal term for one of three classifications of insanity. According to the Asylums Act of 1845, an imbecile was a person who was both non compos mentis from birth and incurable—this would now be referred to as mental retardation or an intellectual disability. The idea that Kozminski was an imbecile was apparently based on both an inaccurate understanding of the history of British asylums and a clumsy interpretation of Kozminski's medical records. It seems that Fido and Sugden simply assumed that all patients in Imbecile Asylums were actually imbeciles. As we have seen, however, the main criteria for admittance to Leavesden were that a patient be both incurable and not disruptive. As a result, Leavesden and other "Imbecile asylums" housed various categories of the sick poor, including both lunatics (insane people) and imbeciles (mentally handicapped people). The 1901 census of patients at Leavesden Asylum confirms this, for on the page listing Kozminski, almost half of the twenty-five patients were categorized as "lunatics" (48 percent), and the rest (52 percent) as "imbeciles." Kozminski was recorded as a "lunatic."[7]

In fact, there is no document that ever refers to Kozminski as an imbecile. On the contrary, both Dr. Houchin's medical certificate and Henry Chambers's committal order list Kozminski as a "person of unsound mind," another legally defined medical term that, according to author David Wright, was "used more or less interchangeably" with "lunatic."[8] Of course, this is consistent with Kozminski's probable diagnosis of schizophrenia. It is likely that Kozminski was admitted to Leavesden because his disease was clearly incurable and because by 1894 his schizophrenia had degenerated to the point where he was catatonic and thus not disruptive. In the asylums of the late nineteenth century, however, no one cared very much to differentiate between incurable lunatics and the mentally retarded. There was no treatment for any of them, so they were all simply thrown in together and managed.

Another common argument against Kozminski as a suspect in the Jack the Ripper murders is that as a schizophrenic, he would not have been able to engage his victims in conversation without arousing suspicion, nor would he be "together" enough to carry out the murders and avoid detection. The assumption, again, is that Kozminski was visibly and uncontrollably psychotic—essentially, a drooling idiot wandering around mumbling to himself. Such perceptions are based, at least in part, on Dr. Houchin's statement that Kozminski "refuses food from others because he is told to do so and eats out of the gutter for the same reason," and Jacob Cohen's statement that Kozminski "goes about the streets and picks up bits of bread out of the gutter."[9] Yet we must remember that Kozminski ate food from the gutter because his "instinct" told him to do so, which suggests that he may have been under the paranoid delusion that he was being poisoned. As we shall later see, if Kozminski was a paranoid schizophrenic (as opposed to a disorganized schizophrenic), he may have been more highly functioning and able to hide his disorder from others. Finally, keep in mind that Houchin's medical certificate was written more than two years after the last canonical Ripper murder, and Kozminski's behavior in February 1891 should not be taken to represent what he was like in 1888. The fact that Kozminski was able to speak in his own defense for the dog-muzzling charge in December 1889 supports this contention.

Another point raised against Kozminski as a suspect in the Ripper case is that he was listed as "not dangerous to others" in asylum records. Of course, the "nonviolent" aspect of Kozminski's admission entry appears to be contradicted by the fact that he had threatened to attack his sister with a knife. In addition, while at Colney Hatch, Kozminski was described as "at times excited & violent," and on at least one occasion he attempted to attack an asylum attendant with a chair. Yet we must remember that Kozminski was brought to Mile End Old Town Workhouse by his family, and it seems highly unlikely that they would have offered up any information that would incriminate Kozminski as the Ripper, especially since, according to Swanson, they had just gone through the ordeal of being under police surveillance. Along the same lines, it has been argued that if the police believed Kozminski was the Ripper, they would have informed the asylum staff that he was dangerous, regardless of what the family told the asylum officials. Despite what the police may have believed about Kozminski, however, they clearly lacked sufficient evidence to convict him, and it is unknown whether the police had any involvement in Kozminski's committal at all. Even if they did, the police would not have wanted the public to discover that they suspected they knew the Ripper's identity but were unable to convict him. The police may have decided that the best solution was to put the Ripper away quietly and hush up the whole affair. They must have been aware that if they had informed the asylum staff that Kozminski was a Ripper suspect, word would almost certainly have leaked out. As researcher Chris Phillips noted,

> If [the police] did communicate their suspicions to Colney Hatch, where would those suspicions have been noted? Given the sensitivity of the situation, would they necessarily have been entered in the documents that survive, which would have been routinely accessible to so many of the asylum staff? Or would they have been made known to senior staff, and communicated to others on a "need to know" basis?[10]

Much of the debate over these points is mere speculation, admittedly. We still do not know enough to answer these riddles. Still, if we step back from the fray and look at all of this with a fresh perspective, the widespread dismissal of Kozminski as a Ripper suspect may start to look surprising. After all, Anderson and Swanson were unarguably in a position to know more about the case than anybody else, and most Ripperologists (apart from Fido) now concede that Kozminski was almost certainly "Anderson's suspect." Aside from a few errors in the Swanson marginalia and the Macnaghten memorandum, the chain of reasoning is clear and scarcely disputed. So, why has Kozminski been dismissed as a suspect?

Again, it seems that the real issue is not the problems in the statements of the police officials or even the gaps in our knowledge about him. Instead, it boils down to whether Kozminski fits the profile of a serial killer, and specifically, whether he fits the profile of Jack the Ripper. For example, even though Fido was happy to accept the truth of Anderson's statements when applied to his own preferred suspect, Nathan Kaminsky, when the same statements were applied to Aaron Kozminski, Fido claimed that Anderson's theory was "barmy." Fido recently added that "if it is ever shown that Anderson really did mean Kosminsky [sic], then I dismiss Anderson and his theory as dead wrong. Kosminsky's record shows that he wasn't the sort of self-controlled figure who could rein himself in like the Green River murderer for a period of years."[11] It is not clear exactly what in Kozminski's asylum record supports this view. But the statement reveals Fido's main objection—specifically, that he thinks Kozminski simply doesn't fit the profile of a serial killer.

This begs the obvious question—does Kozminski fit the profile of a serial killer? In the next chapter, I will attempt to answer this question by comparing the known facts about Kozminski to the generic profile of a serial killer as defined by the FBI and other sources. We may find that a more thorough examination of the fragmentary evidence will vindicate Anderson after all and lead us, as it led him, to a moral certainty of Kozminski's guilt.

23

A Modern Take on Serial Killers

I was born with the devil in me. I could not help the fact that I was a murderer, no more than the poet can help the inspiration to sing. I was born with the evil one standing as my sponsor beside the bed where I was ushered into the world, and he has been with me since.

—*Herman Webster Mudgett (aka H. H. Holmes), serial killer*

Sometimes I feel like a vampire.

—*Ted Bundy*

It seems likely that serial killers have been in existence for centuries, if not for the entire course of human history. Indeed, as author Peter Vronsky argued in his book *Serial Killers: The Method and Madness of Monsters*, it is even possible that serial killers served as the foundation for some of the more notable monster myths. Vronsky proposed that people would not have been able to conceive that ordinary humans were capable of committing the types of heinous murders routinely committed by serial killers and would have instead imagined that such crimes were committed by vampires or werewolves roaming in the

265

streets or in the woods. One interesting example along these lines was the 1603 case of Jean Grenier, a fourteen-year-old boy in France who admitted to eating several children after he was transformed into a werewolf. Physicians at Grenier's trial determined that the boy did not in fact turn into a werewolf but that he was instead insane.

Cases of serial murder in the distant past have not generally survived in documentation, except when the killer was a notable figure in government or the nobility. One such example was Gilles de Montmorency-Laval (aka Gilles de Rais), a wealthy aristocrat who killed hundreds of children in fifteenth-century France. At his trial, de Rais described how he tortured and sodomized both boys and girls and claimed that he "caused their bodies to be cruelly opened and took delight in viewing their interior organs." As he admitted, "I committed [the crimes] solely for my evil pleasure and evil delight." De Rais and two accomplices were excommunicated and then hanged for their crimes.[1] Another extraordinary example was Erzsébet Báthory, a Hungarian countess who may well have been the most prolific serial killer in history. Báthory was said to have tortured and killed upward of six hundred young women in the gynaeceum of Cachtice Castle and at several other properties she owned in Hungary. The torture she inflicted included extended beatings, burning, mutilation of hands and genitalia, starvation, and eating flesh off her victims. (The story that the countess bathed in the blood of her victims in order to maintain a youthful beauty was apparently a myth, invented more than one hundred years after her death.)

Various accounts of serial murder began to crop up in the nineteenth century. In 1808, the "Bavarian Ripper" Andreas Bichel was arrested for murdering several young women who came to his house seeking employment as servants. Referring to the murder of one victim, Bichel said, "I opened her breast and with a knife cut through the fleshy parts of the body. Then I arranged the body as a butcher does beef, and hacked it with the axe into pieces. I may say that while opening the body, I was so greedy that I trembled and could have cut out a piece and eaten it."[2] Another example was Vincenzo Verzeni, the so-called Strangler of Women, who killed and mutilated two women (and attacked several more) in Italy in the 1870s. Vincenzo was said to have been completely ignorant of sexual intercourse and admitted, "It never occurred to me to touch or look at the genitals and such things. . . . To this very day I am ignorant of how a woman is formed." Instead, he derived pleasure from killing and sucking blood from his victims. "I have really butchered some of the women," he admitted, "and I have tried to strangle a few more, because I take immense pleasure in these acts. The scratches found in the thighs weren't the product of my nails, but of my teeth, because after the strangulation I bit her and sucked the blood that dripped out, which I enjoyed very much."[3]

Despite such notable cases, by the late nineteenth century, the concept of serial murder was still practically unheard of, and the phenomenon of so-called motiveless murder was discussed only in obscure academic publications, such as Richard von Krafft-Ebing's *Psychopathia Sexualis* (1886). Krafft-Ebing pointed out a connection between lust and the desire to kill—citing, for example, the case of a prostitute killer named Phillipe, who stated, "I am fond of women but it is sport for me to strangle them after having enjoyed them." Krafft-Ebing theorized that a great number of lust murderers were driven by a combination of "hyperaesthesia and paraesthesia sexualis," in other words, a sort of hypersensitivity of the skin of the sexual organs, characterized by a tingling sensation, possibly caused by nerve damage.[4] Such an idea may seem strange today, but it was consistent with the nineteenth-century tendency to connect criminal behavior with various biological and physiological abnormalities. It was the age of phrenology and physiognomy, and many people believed that criminality was an inherited trait, which could be identified by physical defects known as stigmata—sloping foreheads, asymmetric facial features, and so on. In 1876, the Italian criminologist Cesare Lombroso published *L'uomo Delinquente* (The Criminal Man), essentially arguing that criminals were atavistic throwbacks to an earlier, more primitive state of human evolution—animals, basically.[5]

Modern Advances in Criminology

Today, the understanding of criminal behavior and serial murder is obviously somewhat more advanced than this. Researchers from a variety of disciplines, including sociology, psychology, and biology, have studied serial killers from numerous angles, in an attempt to understand what makes them tick. Over the years, several predictive models and classification systems have been proposed, but most have proved to be insufficient in some way or another. In short, it is difficult to put serial killers into any one box, and many of the assumptions about serial killers have turned out to be wrong.

Despite this, it has been shown that there are some traits and behaviors that seem to be common to a large percentage of serial killers. Two of the first people to apply statistical analysis to the study of serial killers were John Douglas and Robert Ressler of the FBI's Behavioral Sciences Unit (BSU), aka the "Hannibal Lecter Squad." Between 1979 and 1983, Douglas and Ressler interviewed thirty-six convicted sexual killers (most of them serial killers), asking them about their backgrounds, crimes, and victims. The purpose of their research was to come up with a theoretical model to explain the behavior of sexually motivated killers through an analysis of various psychological and sociological factors. The data that Douglas and Ressler collected laid the foundation for a statistical analysis of the characteristics of serial killers in a general sense, and their results were published in 1995 under the title *Sexual Homicide: Patterns and Motives*.

The application of such analysis in actual criminal investigations is called criminal profiling or offender profiling. According to Ressler et al., "Criminal profiling and criminal personality assessment are ways in which law enforcement has sought to combine the results of studies in other disciplines with more traditional investigative techniques in an effort to combat violent criminal behavior."[6] In practice, this means that crime scenes are analyzed in the hopes of finding minute clues that will indicate likely characteristics of the offender and thus narrow the field of investigation.

Criminal profiling has come under attack lately, due in part to the romanticized portrayal of profilers on TV and in movies like *Manhunter* and *The Silence of the Lambs*. Critics argue that criminal profiling is more in the realm of fiction than scientific fact. In an article in the *New Yorker* magazine, journalist Malcolm Gladwell wrote that offender profiling was nothing more than a "parlour trick." There is probably some truth in this, and profiling has indeed been shown to be frequently inaccurate in predicting an offender's behavior and character traits, such as age, race, profession, and so on. Yet the basic concept of profiling is both valid and natural, and according to the FBI, profiling should be thought of as just another tool that is used to focus a criminal investigation. When specific aspects of a profile are used to eliminate suspects, however, an investigation might start to go off the tracks. In any case, it is not my intention to assess the viability of criminal profiling, but instead to look at the general characteristics of serial killers and see whether Aaron Kozminski has those traits.

One of the most fundamental findings of the BSU study was that the majority of sexual killers were preoccupied with active and deep-rooted fantasies "devoted to violent sexualized thoughts." As a result, Ressler and Douglas came up with the hypothesis that "fantasy drives behavior." The fantasies were typically established early on and came to play a central role in the killer's thought patterns. "One assumption regarding early traumatic events," the report stated, "is that the child's memories of frightening and upsetting life experiences shape his developing thought patterns. The type of thinking that emerges develops structured, patterned behaviors that in turn help generate fantasies and daydreams."[7] Such fantasies were usually violent and sexual in nature and often involved a role reversal, from being the victim to being the victimizer. The authors speculated that fantasies "used to cope with childhood abuse and unsatisfactory family life might turn a child away from reality and into a private world of violence where the child can exert control." Predictably, the fantasies would often revolve around themes of domination and control of others.

At some point, the fantasy would reach a point where its "inner stress" became overpowering, and a negative event in the person's life would act as a "trigger," causing him to move beyond fantasy to actually acting out his urges in real life. Often the trigger would be a negative personal event, such as the loss of a job, the death of a significant person, or the breakup of a relationship. Ressler and Douglas believed that aspects of a killer's fantasy represented an unconscious desire he was trying to fulfill, and that the killing itself was often secondary to this primary "need." This theory formed the basis of a differentiation between a killer's modus operandi and his "signature."

Modus Operandi and Signature

Modus operandi (MO) is the method used by a criminal to achieve his (or her) goals, without being captured. As pointed out by author Brent Turvey, this "is not the same thing as an offender's motive."[8] Signature, on the other hand, is more closely related to the underlying motivation behind the murders (that is, the fantasy) and is defined as what the killer is driven to do. Examples might include posing the body, taking souvenirs, or arranging objects at the crime scene. According to Turvey, "an offender signature is a pattern of distinctive behaviors that are characteristic of, and satisfy, emotional and psychological needs."[9] The concept is illustrated by the following, rather chilling, statement of serial killer Edmund Kemper. "I am sorry to sound so cold about this," he said, "but what I needed to have was a particular experience with a person, and to possess them in the way I wanted to: I had to evict them from their human bodies."[10] In other words, for Kemper, murder was merely an MO to achieve his goal of possessing a human body.

Some experts claim that a serial killer's MO can evolve over time as the killer learns from his mistakes and develops more efficient methods of killing. Predictably, this evolution is most evident in the earliest murders in a series. As noted in the Douglas and Ressler study, the killer's fantasies "prior to the first murder, focused on killing," as opposed to "fantasies that evolved after the first murder, which often focused on perfecting various phases of the murder."[11] In contrast, it is believed that the essence of a killer's signature will not fundamentally change. Jack the Ripper's signature, for example, was the mutilation of his victims' abdomens and reproductive organs. The Ripper's MO, on the other hand, involved killing his victims quickly and silently in dark and secluded locations, so that he could achieve this goal, ideally without being interrupted for some amount of time.

In his essay "The Importance of Fairy Fay, and Her Link to Emma Smith," Quentin L. Pittman suggested that the murders of Annie Millwood and Emma Smith and the attempted murder of Ada Wilson were examples of the Ripper "learning his craft." In the case of Wilson, it is possible that the Ripper made an attempt at slashing the throat, which failed when Wilson fought back and began to scream. Autopsies on the later victims suggest that the Ripper may have strangled his victims into unconsciousness before cutting their throats. This may have been a learned behavior. As Pittman suggested, "Perhaps the killer began not in August, but in February, with the awkward, unseen attack on Annie Millwood in White's Row. Then in March, he ventured to Mile End, where coincidentally Annie Millwood was recuperating at the South Grove Workhouse, and attacked Ada Wilson. After a narrow escape, he then returned west, to his epicentre, where in April he crudely attacked Smith."[12]

Indeed, many serial killers have acknowledged the confused nature of their first attempts at murder. The following quote from one of the subjects in the BSU study illustrates this: "It was almost like a black comedy of errors, the first killings, two people, it was terrible because I made three fatal errors in the first twenty-four hours. I should have been busted. I saw how loose I was and I tightened it up, and when it happened again and again I got tighter and tighter and there weren't any more slips."[13]

Likewise, Ted Bundy described his earliest failed attempt at abduction and murder as "sort of half-hearted, sort of confused. Several years later this process continued. The acting out, getting closer and closer . . . it wasn't a complete, total, focused kind of aggression when I knew what I was doing . . . in Ocean City I realized just how inept I was." He added, "I didn't do that again for a long time. It scared me." In a second failed attempt, Bundy said, "I ran in there and hopped on top of the bed and tried to put a pillow on top of the girl's face. She struggled and started to scream and I ran away. End of story."[14] Bundy was horrified after his early botched attempts at murder, which he described as taking a step you "couldn't ever return from." After each attack, he would desperately try to overcome his violent urges, but as time passed, the shame at what he'd done would diminish and the old urges would come back again.

In their first murders, some serial killers go out with only a vague idea that they might actually commit a murder. Bundy referred to this as taking his fantasy "out for a walk" or a "test drive." The first murder is nearly always the most difficult for serial killers, both emotionally

and psychologically and also in terms of technique. The killer might
not bring a weapon with him, or if he does, it might be an inappropriate one, such as a clasp knife, for example. Later, the technique would
improve, and the murders would be planned in advance. In one of
Peter Sutcliffe's first attempts at murder, he put some rocks and dirt
into a sock and swung it at the back of a woman's head. He later used
a hammer for a similar purpose, still striking his victims in the back
of the head. Such behavior illustrates an evolution of the same basic
impulse. A similar lack of planning is evident in the following quote by
Bundy (it was supposedly so emotionally difficult for Bundy to describe
his own murders that he referred to himself in the third person when
doing so):

> On one particular evening, when he had been drinking a
> great deal . . . and he was passing a bar, he saw a woman leav-
> ing the bar and walk up a fairly dark side street. And we'd say
> that for no . . . the urge to do something to that person seized
> him—in a way he'd never been affected before. . . . And it
> seized him strongly. And to the point where, uh, without
> giving a great deal of thought, he searched around for some
> instrumentality to uh, uh, attack this woman with. He found
> a piece of a two-by-four in a lot somewhere and proceeded
> to follow and track this girl. . . . And he reached the point
> where he was, uh, almost driven to do something—there was
> really no control at this point.[15]

The murders of Millwood and Smith and the attempted murder of
Wilson may fall into a similar category of early, bungled Ripper attacks.
The murder of Martha Tabram, which has already been discussed in
detail, would represent a further evolution in technique, along the
same lines.

Family History
Much of the BSU study focused on the quality of family relationships
and on formative events in an offender's childhood, such as sexual or
psychological abuse. A large percentage of the offenders who were
interviewed "revealed that multiple problems existed in family structures." As one said, "The breakup of the family started progressing into

something I just didn't understand. I always thought families should always be together. I think that was part of the downfall. I had no male supervision."[16] Other subjects reported a change in "sibling order" as a result of reconstituted families, with new stepbrothers and stepsisters.

In almost 50 percent of the cases in the FBI study, the killers reported the absence of the biological father before they reached the age of twelve. According to Douglas and Ressler, "The psychological and emotional disengagement" resulting from an absent father figure perhaps enhanced a sense of "negative human attachment or the disregarding of potential positive ones that might have been expected."[17] As one offender said, "I believe what caused the rapes on the street was when I was a kid I never had a dad around. He was gone."[18] This aspect of the generic profile of serial killers clearly fits Aaron Kozminski, whose father died in 1874, when Aaron was only nine years old. After this, Kozminski's household was presumably dominated by females—specifically, his three older sisters (ages twenty-six, twenty, and seventeen) and his mother, Golda, who was then about fifty-two years old. The only other male in the family was Kozminski's brother Woolf, who at the time of their father's death was only fourteen years old. (Kozminski's other brother, Isaac, had left Poland when Kozminski was five or six years old.) In 1881, Kozminski was separated from his mother when the family fled Russia. Arriving in London, he may have scarcely remembered or even recognized Isaac, who was fourteen years his senior. After the onset of Kozminski's insanity around 1885, Kozminski's older siblings seem to have assumed a role like parental figures in the reconstituted family structure, a fact that Kozminski may have resented.

Instability of Residence
The BSU report also showed that the majority of the interviewed killers grew up with instability of residence—half reported "occasional instability," while another 17 percent disclosed "chronic instability or frequent moving." The authors thought that "Frequent moving reduced the child's opportunities to develop positive, stable relationships outside the family."[19]

This is another characteristic that seems to fit Kozminski. After moving to London as part of a massive wave of refugees, the

Kozminskis found themselves in a strange and unwelcoming new city. The move itself must have been traumatic, and the family may have been fleeced by swindlers, as many Jewish immigrants were. They then probably stayed with Isaac or other relatives before finding more permanent residences. After this, Kozminski's siblings apparently shared the responsibility of taking care of him. And following the onset of his insanity around 1885, Kozminski was quite possibly very difficult to live with and may have been shuffled back and forth between residences.

Unsteady Employment

Data from the BSU interviews indicated that only 20 percent of the interviewed killers reported "steady employment." The vast majority (69 percent) said they had "unsteady employment," and the remainder (11 percent) revealed their "unemployment." Unsteady employment, according to Douglas and Ressler, led to a sense of failure in the real world, and to compensate for this, the offender would turn to fantasies, in which he was able to control the outcome of any situation. An offender might think that murder was an area in which he could rise above his failure, as a compensation or revenge for poor performance in other areas of life. The study also noted that 60 percent of interviewed offenders cited employment difficulties as a "precipitating stress factor" or trigger that caused them to start killing.

From what little information we have about Kozminski's employment, it seems that he was either unemployed or underemployed at the time of the Ripper murders. In 1891, Jacob Cohen stated that Kozminski had "not attempted any kind of work for years," but it is not clear how many years Cohen meant. It is likely that Kozminski's mental deterioration and his psychotic delusions made it increasingly difficult, if not impossible, for him to hold down a steady job.

Compulsive Masturbation

"Compulsive masturbation" was one of the most commonly reported traits of serial killers in the BSU study—more than 80 percent of the interviewed murderers said they engaged in compulsive masturbation in childhood, adolescence, and adulthood. The authors of the study theorized that the prevalence of compulsive masturbation among killers was the result of an ineffective social environment, which led to the development of negative personal traits, such as a mistrust of society at large and the inability to form close personal relationships. This, in turn, would cause a person to rely on fantasy "as a substitute for human encounter." According to the report, "The personal traits critical to the development of the murderers in our study include a sense of social isolation, preferences for autoerotic activities and fetishes, rebelliousness, aggression, chronic lying, and a sense of privilege and entitlement. The murderers' sense of social isolation is profound."[20]

The "cause of insanity" on Kozminski's Colney Hatch admission record is given as "self-abuse." This corresponds with Sir Robert Anderson's statement that Jack the Ripper was "a loathsome creature whose utterly unmentionable vices reduced him to a lower level than that of the brute," and Melville Macnaghten's statement that Kozminski "became insane owing to many years indulgence in solitary vices." The term "self-abuse," aka "the solitary vice" or "onanism," was a Victorian-era euphemism for masturbation, which in the nineteenth century was thought to be the cause of numerous mental and physical disorders, including insanity. In fact, at one time almost 60 percent of medical and mental illnesses were thought to have been caused by masturbation. As one nineteenth-century expert claimed, "That insanity arises from masturbation is now beyond a doubt." To combat the evils accruing from masturbation, various deterrents were prescribed, including mechanical restraints, male "chastity devices," and physical discipline. Between the years 1856 and 1932, the U.S. Patent Office awarded more than thirty patents to antimasturbation devices, and one doctor even went so far as to invent a contraption that administered electric shocks to a sleeping boy's penis on erection. Other forms of "punitive therapies," such as penile cauterization, were experimented with.

Although masturbation was certainly not the real cause of Kozminski's insanity, it is an important factor in comparing him to the generic profile of serial killers. The fact that both Anderson and Macnaghten mentioned Kozminski's self-abuse so prominently as the cause of his insanity suggests that Kozminski may have masturbated compulsively, and perhaps openly, for years. Indeed, it might have been difficult to hide such behavior from members of his family, given what were probably overcrowded living quarters, with little chance of privacy.

The FBI's Profile of Jack the Ripper

In 1988, the centenary of the Jack the Ripper murders, FBI agent and self-proclaimed "mind hunter" John Douglas was asked to prepare a profile of Jack the Ripper for a television program called *The Secret Identity of Jack the Ripper*. Douglas agreed to the task because he thought it might prove to be a useful tool for training agents and also because he found it "difficult to resist matching wits, even a century later, with the most famous murderer in history." Roy Hazelwood, also of the BSU, assisted. The FBI's profile was based on an analysis of the Ripper's crime scenes, police reports, autopsy reports, post-mortem photographs, victim histories, maps, and the demographics of the East End.

The FBI profile described Jack the Ripper as a white male of average intelligence, in his mid- to late twenties, who was single and had never been married. Hazelwood and Douglas claimed that the Ripper was the type of killer who killed "as opportunity presents itself," and thought that he "wasn't nearly as clever as he was lucky." He derived pleasure from postmortem mutilation of his victims. According to Hazelwood, "By displacing or removing his victims' sexual parts and organs, Jack was neutering or desexing them so that they were no longer women to be feared."[21] Among other things, the FBI profile noted that the Ripper lived near the crime scenes; had "poor personal hygiene, and a dishevelled appearance"; was a loner, who "had difficulty interacting appropriately with anyone, but particularly women"; "was mentally disturbed"; "was a sexually inadequate person, with a lot of generalized rage against women," who "simultaneously hated and feared women"; and "did not have any degree of medical knowledge."[22] These aspects of the FBI's profile clearly seem to fit Kozminski. Perhaps most important is the claim that the Ripper had "a lot of generalized rage against women," and "simultaneously hated and feared women." This fits

Macnaghten's albeit uncorroborated statement that Kozminski had a "great hatred of women, specially of the prostitute class, & had strong homicidal tendencies."[23]

The producers of the TV show presented Douglas and Hazelwood (and the other panelists) with five Ripper suspects and asked whether any of them fit the profile. Both Douglas and Hazelwood came to the conclusion that Kozminski was the strongest suspect on the list. "Our profile fit one of the suspects almost dead bang," Hazelwood said. "That doesn't mean he did it. It simply means he fit the characteristics and traits that we believe would have been possessed by the individual known as Jack the Ripper. And that was an individual by the name of Kozminski."[24]

One of the classifications used in the FBI's profiling model for serial killers is the differentiation between organized and disorganized killers. Generally speaking, an organized offender is intelligent and controlling, plans the crimes in advance, and is socially competent. This type of offender is responsible for the archetype of the "Hollywood" serial killer—a highly intelligent monster like Hannibal Lecter in *The Silence of the Lambs*, outwitting the police at every turn. Disorganized killers, on the other hand, are less socially competent and more impulsive, and their crimes are often opportunistic and random in nature. According to the FBI, a disorganized-type killer is usually a person of "low intelligence or low birth-status in the family," who often has an instable work history and is unmarried, either living alone or with parental figures. He is "preoccupied with obsessional and/or primitive thoughts" and "may have developed a well-defined delusional system."[25] He is fearful of people, is often sexually incompetent, and may have sexual aversions.

The FBI profile of Jack the Ripper shows that he fits the description of a disorganized-type serial killer. "We thought that," said Hazelwood, "because of the locations where he committed four of the five crimes. They were outdoors—they were on the streets or in a courtyard—a very high-risk crime. In other words, whoever this person was, was almost oblivious to the risk. All the bodies were very quickly discovered. So there's not a lot of planning that went into those crimes."[26] "I don't see how anyone who knows anything at all about violent crime can say that was an organized crime," Hazelwood later added.[27] The disorganized offender also generally uses a "blitz style attack" and kills suddenly, often from behind, as the Ripper probably did. The study noted that a disorganized offender often "depersonalizes the victim. Specific areas of the body may be targeted for extreme brutality. Overkill or excessive assault to the face is often an attempt to dehumanize the victim." In addition, with a disorganized killer, "Any sexually sadistic acts, often in the form of mutilation, are usually performed after death." The Ripper seems to fit all of the previous characteristics. Laura Richards, of Scotland Yard's Homicide Prevention Unit, stated that the Ripper is "certainly no Einstein. We know that he's a risk-taker, he's impulsive, irresponsible, but this is someone who hasn't been detected, and you can say 80 percent of that's probably due to chance and luck, and 20 percent may be down to his tactical planning around what he's done."[28]

Many of the characteristics of a disorganized killer also fit what we know of Kozminski. Kozminski was of "low birth-status," being the youngest child in the family, and had an instable work history, as noted in his asylum records. He was single and lived with parental figures (siblings) who took care of him. He was also obsessed with delusions, as is made clear in his Colney Hatch file.

A Motivational Model

One of the biggest questions in any serial killer case is why? How could a man have so much hatred and anger that he could unleash such fury on innocent women? The FBI's study in this regard focused on the effect of negative formative events and environmental factors in the development of a serial killer–type mentality. Specifically, the study theorized that an "ineffective" and hateful social environment (especially during childhood) might cause a potential killer to develop "cognitive distortions" and negative attitudes, which would later provide a justification for his violent acts toward others. As the study noted, "Many of the murderers felt they were not dealt with fairly by adults throughout their formative years." In addition, the BSU study theorized that because the offenders believed "that they live in an unjust world, fantasy emerges as an important escape and a place in which to express emotion and control regarding other human beings."[29]

Many modern criminologists theorize that Jack the Ripper must have experienced traumatic events in his life that left him with a sense of powerlessness and humiliation—plagued by feelings of inadequacy, crippled by resentment and anger, and desiring revenge against the society that had wronged him. According to Richards, there is often "something that's traumatic, something around physical, emotional, or sometimes psychological abuse which has led [violent serial offenders] to become the person they are. Powerless people would always seek to take the power back, and I put Jack the Ripper in that bracket. . . . The Ripper's cruelty had its roots in something he himself had suffered."[30]

In this context, the anti-Semitic persecution that Kozminski experienced, both in his youth in Russia and again in his teens and young adult life in London, may provide a plausible explanation for his general anger toward society. As we have seen, the Whitechapel murders did not cause the anti-Semitism in the East End of London—instead, they merely aggravated a festering hatred of Jews that had already risen to the surface. The East End Jews were blamed for various things prior to the murders—high unemployment, unfair competition, overcrowding, and so on—and as a result, anti-Semitism in the East End was on the rise during the decade that led up to the Ripper murders. It seems possible that the escalation of anti-Semitic tension and rhetoric in late 1887 and early 1888 may have been a trigger that caused the Ripper to go beyond fantasizing to actually committing murder.

Was it merely a coincidence that the Ripper murders started just as anti-Semitism in the East End reached a fevered peak? The murders began in the middle of the public outcry against sweating in the Jewish tailoring industry, while two government commissions loomed: one to investigate Jewish immigration, and the other to investigate the "social plague" of foreign-born sweaters and tailors, who were perceived as taking jobs away from native-born English citizens. Kozminski's family was at the receiving end of all of this blame and derision, which came not only from native-born English, but also from Jewish socialists, primarily those of the Berner Street club, who were among the most outspoken opponents of the oppressive masters in the tailoring industry. Both Jews and sweaters in the tailoring trade undoubtedly perceived the commissions as official government sanction and sympathy for anti-Jewish and antisweating sentiments in East London. The Kozminski family was targeted in both instances. The situation was tense, and by early 1888, the newspapers had suggested that pogroms might break out in the East End. The House of Lords Committee on Sweating met for the first time on March 16, 1888, just two weeks before the murder of Emma Smith, the first of the officially documented Whitechapel murders. On June 27, 1888, the London Tailors' Association met at a hall on Goulston Street to address a large audience about the evils of the sweating system. Only ten days later, Martha Tabram was brutally murdered in the George Yard Buildings. Goulston Street was, of course, the location of the chalked message, possibly left by the murderer, which read, "The Juwes are the men that will not be blamed for nothing."

Anti-Semitism in the East End ratcheted up another few notches in the weeks leading up to the murders of Liz Stride and Kate Eddowes. It was widely reported that the police were looking for a Jewish suspect, and the much-publicized apprehension of John Pizer added more fuel to the fire. The police were clearly worried about the possibility of riots against the Jews. And indeed, riots very nearly broke out on September 15, when the *East London Observer* reported, "It was repeatedly asserted that no Englishman could have perpetrated such a horrible crime as that of Hanbury-street and that it must have been done by a Jew—and forthwith the crowds proceeded to threaten and abuse such of the unfortunate Hebrews as they found in the streets."[31] The Goulston Street graffito must be considered in this context, because it expressed a theme that had widespread currency at the time—specifically, blaming the Jews.

As an immigrant Jew, Kozminski had essentially been blamed for his whole life. In Russia, the Jews were called leeches, despised as a mistrusted alien presence, and blamed for exploiting the Russian peasantry. Such views were unofficially endorsed by the Russian government, which itself unfairly blamed the Jews for various societal problems. In the 1870s, the decade of Kozminski's adolescence and early teenage years, there was a further increase in anti-Semitism in Russia. The decade began with violent anti-Jewish pogroms in Odessa in 1871. Ten years later, the Jews were wrongly blamed for the assassination of Czar Alexander II, which led to much more widespread and devastating pogroms across the southwestern regions of the Pale. The Jews were even blamed for the pogroms themselves, because the government declared that Jews had "innate views that nourished the hostility of their neighbors, especially among the lower classes." While the Jews were robbed and beaten, the Russian authorities stood by, in some cases powerless to stop what was happening, and in others completely disinterested in protecting the Jews from attack. The general sentiment was that the Jews deserved whatever happened to them. They were constantly reminded that the violence of the pogroms came about as a direct result of their own collective guilt.

The pogroms caused thousands of Jewish refugees to migrate to the East End of London. Once again, fifteen-year-old Kozminski would have found himself in a similarly hostile environment, plagued by a festering distrust of the foreign invaders and characterized, once again, by Judenhetze and scapegoating. By 1888, the Jews were routinely being blamed for unfair labor practices, strike breaking, and unemployment in the East End.

It is not a stretch to imagine that Kozminski may have begun to develop a general resentment of society and authority figures as a result of such factors. After noticing the inability of the Russian police to protect the Jews during the pogroms and later, amid the overwhelming criminality of the East End, Kozminski may have begun to perceive that the social system and the police were generally weak and ineffectual in stopping crime and violence. In addition, in both Russia and London, the police and other authority figures (for example, judges) often sympathized with the anti-Semitic sentiments of the mob. Likewise, at the highest levels of government authority, both Ignatiev's commissions investigating the 1881 Russian pogroms and the British parliamentary inquiries into sweating and the alien question seemed to validate the notion that the Jews were in fact to blame for the outpouring of hatred and aggression against them. Kozminski must have perceived that both he and the Jews in general were being treated unfairly. Such a realization, combined with the

volatile admixture of paranoid schizophrenia, might have caused him
to mistrust adults and authority figures and led to the development of
an antisocial (that is, psychopathic) personality.

Along the lines of such an interpretation, the message "The Juwes
are the men who will not be blamed for nothing" may be a key
to understanding Jack the Ripper's motivation to commit murder.
Kozminski's feelings of persecution may have developed into full-blown
paranoid delusions, supporting, for example, the belief that he was
being poisoned. If such factors worked their way into both Kozminski's
psychoses and his violent fantasies, then the murders might have been
a sort of psychological retaliation against an anti-Semitic society that
"blamed" the Jews for their own oppression. Indeed, the murders could
be seen as a sort of climax to a decade of rising anti-Semitism, representing a rupture in the fabric of the East End tensions between Jews
and gentiles.

24

Geographic Profiling

Geographic profiling is a technique in which a mathematical model, based on a spatial analysis of the location of crime scenes, is used to predict the approximate location of a criminal's residence. This technique, first proposed by D. Kim Rossmo, is now used in police jurisdictions in both the United States and Great Britain. Geographic profiling developed over time in association with a broad range of methodologies, including distance-to-crime research, demographic analysis, environmental psychology, landscape analysis, and psychological criminal profiling. In practice, geographic profiling relies on "certain known propensities of serial criminals," such as "a tendency to hunt in known areas" and "a desire to disguise the home location."[1] The general idea is that a criminal's behavior in a given environment is based not only on the external, physical, and geographical features of an area, but also on the criminal's psychological and emotional perception of that area. Geographic analysis is partly based on "rational choice theory" as well, which holds that "patterns of behavior in societies reflect the choices made by individuals as they try to maximize their benefits and minimize their costs."[2]

Most modern researchers believe that Jack the Ripper was a resident of the East End, whose familiarity with the district's mazelike streets, courtyards, and alleys helped him avoid detection by the police.

In addition to the location of the crime scenes, a few other bits of evidence may suggest hints about where the Ripper lived. Ideally, all of these geographic elements would point to the address of the killer. For this reason, it would be nice to know exactly where Kozminski was living when the murders took place in the summer and the fall of 1888. Various sources tell us that Aaron Kozminski lived in the very heart of the district in which the murders were committed. George Sims, moreover, wrote about a Polish Jew suspect (clearly, a reference to Macnaghten's "Kosminski") who "was the sole occupant of certain premises in Whitechapel after night-fall. This man was in the district during the whole period covered by the Whitechapel murders."[3] We do not actually know for certain where Kozminski resided in 1888, but we can infer where he was probably living to a good degree of certainty.

Kozminski's two admissions to Mile End are the only known occasions when his address was ever recorded. On July 12, 1890, he was living at 3 Sion Square, the home of his brother Woolf Abrahams, and on February 4, 1891, he resided at 16 Greenfield Street with his sister, Matilda, and her husband, Morris Lubnowski. This suggests that Kozminski lived with Woolf for some time prior to July 1890 and then with Matilda and Morris for a period of time before February 1891— but obviously it does not tell us Kozminski's home address in 1888. We can guess that Kozminski, as an unemployed schizophrenic, was unable to take care of himself, financially or otherwise. If Kozminski did not reside with family members, he may have been homeless at times, sleeping in poor shelters or on the streets. Yet it seems fairly safe to assume that he probably lived with his siblings during most, if not all, of the time he was in London, from 1881 to 1891. It is also possible that Kozminski's siblings shared the responsibility of housing him, and that he stayed with all three siblings at various times. This means that we can narrow down Kozminski's probable address during the Ripper murders to one of three likely locations: either 16 Greenfield Street (the home of Kozminski's sister, Matilda, and her husband, Morris), 74 Greenfield Street (where Isaac lived and had his workshop), or wherever Woolf was living in 1888.

One likely possibility is that Kozminski lived with Woolf. Woolf was closest to Kozminski in age, and he is listed as "nearest relative" on Kozminski's workhouse and asylum records. Unfortunately, Woolf's address during the time of the Jack the Ripper murders in the summer and the fall of 1888 is still a mystery. He lived at 62 Greenfield Street in July 1887, but by 1888 he had moved, and his address remains unknown until March 1889, by which time he had moved to 34 Yalford Street, a narrow street parallel to Greenfield Street. It is possible that Woolf lived on Yalford Street during the Ripper murders, but this is still not known for sure. Yalford Street was a narrow street of rundown slum houses inhabited by very poor Jews. The tenements were overcrowded and dilapidated. A sanitary inspector reported in 1884 that many houses on the street were "without water supply or dustbins, that the woodwork was rotten through filth, that the stones of the yard exuded when trodden upon damp filth, and that overpowering smells, from the condition of the houses, pervaded the interiors."[4] If nothing else, this sounds like a fitting description of the street where Jack the Ripper would have lived. In any case, it seems almost certain that Woolf resided in that immediate vicinity in 1888, because, although he moved several times in the 1880s, he never strayed far from Greenfield Street.

The other likely possibility, as previously discussed, is that Kozminski may have inhabited the workshop of his other brother, Isaac, at the time of the murders. This hypothesis is compelling because it provides a secluded location where Kozminski "could go and come and get rid of his blood-stains in secret," as Anderson wrote.[5] Several sources would seem to back up such a theory. Sims, for one, spoke of a Polish Jew suspect who was the "sole occupant of certain premises" in the East End.[6] And Henry Cox mentioned conducting surveillance on a suspect who occupied several shops. Either way, it seems almost certain that Kozminski lived on either Greenfield Street or Yalford Street in 1888, and we may use these addresses interchangeably in our geographic profiling model, because they are so close to each other.

One of the simplest applications of geographic profiling is circle theory, developed by David Canter, the director of the Centre for Investigative Psychology, which is based at the University of Liverpool. Circle theory proposes that if all of the crime scenes of a single offender are placed within a circle on a map, the offender's residence would probably lie within that circle, close to the center. Often, there is also a "buffer zone" in the immediate vicinity of the offender's home in which no crimes will be committed. Thus, for the most simple geographic analysis of the Jack the Ripper murders, one would draw the smallest circle that contains the murder sites of the five canonical Ripper victims: Polly Nichols, Annie Chapman, Elizabeth Stride, Kate Eddowes, and Mary Kelly. The center of this "smallest circle" is located 260 feet north of St. Mary Matfelon Church on Whitechapel High Street.

By all accounts, St. Mary Matfelon was the epicenter of the earliest Whitechapel murders. The murder of Martha Tabram occurred only eight hundred feet from St. Mary's. Emily Holland also claimed that she last spoke to Nichols, the first "canonic" Ripper victim, "nearly opposite the parish church" at the corner of Whitechapel High Street and Osborn Street. The man whom the *Star* reported had been seen wiping his hands shortly after the Stride murder was sitting on a door-step in Church Lane, adjacent to St. Mary's church. And Emma Smith (who admittedly is not thought by most researchers to have been a Ripper victim) claimed that she was accosted by two or three youths who began to follow her from St. Mary's. The distance from St. Mary's to Isaac Abrahams's workshop on Greenfield Street was a mere eight hundred feet. In short, Kozminski could have walked from his likely residence on Greenfield Street to any of the murder sites in only a few minutes. The distance from Isaac's shop to Dutfield's Yard, the site of the Stride murder, was only about nine hundred feet and can be walked in about three minutes. Moreover, the largest apparent buffer zone within the smallest circle containing all of the murder sites is centered around Whitechapel Road just north of Fieldgate Street, and slightly to the east of the circle's center. The center of this zone was just a one- or two-minute walk from Isaac's shop.

In reality, geographic profiling is more complex than this, and crime scenes are often distributed in complex spatial patterns. As Dr. Karen Shalev, of the Institute of Criminal Justice Studies, pointed out, one problem with circle theory is that "the use of the two furthest crimes as an indicator of the criminal range makes a judgement about the behaviours of an offender throughout a crime series by examining the information from only two crimes, and then further generalises these behaviours to the entire series. Second, all the remaining crimes are being ignored."[7] Another problem is that the offender may live in numerous different residences during a crime series.

Also contributing to the difficulties in this method, according to Joshua David Kent, are "the psychological and physical boundaries that, among other impedance factors, conspire to distort an already complex analytical investigation."[8] For example, a recent spatial analysis of the Ripper crimes by Colin Roberts used not a circle, but instead an oval tilted at a slight angle (approximately parallel to Whitechapel Road). According to Roberts, the oval shape was a better approximation of the spatial distribution of the crime scenes, on account of "the mobility provided by Aldgate High Street/Whitechapel High Street/ Whitechapel Road." Based on his model, Roberts claimed, "There was merely a 22 percent likelihood that Jack the Ripper resided in closer proximity to the murder-site epicenter than did Aaron Kosminski."[9]

It should be noted that all of the Whitechapel murders—with the exception of the murder of Stride at Berner Street—occurred north of Whitechapel High Street/Whitechapel Road/Aldgate High Street, and it is possible that this major thoroughfare was a sort of psychological boundary in the mind of the Ripper. Kozminski lived in the area south of Whitechapel High Street/Whitechapel Road and may have considered the area around his home a sort of buffer zone in which he did not commit any murders. Such behavior is addressed by Canter, who described two models of offender behavior, known as the "marauder" and the "commuter" models. The marauder model assumes that an offender will "strike out" from his home base in the commission of his crimes, whereas the commuter model assumes that an offender will travel some distance from his home base before engaging in criminal activity. According to Rossmo, "For any crime to occur, there must have been an intersection in both time and place between the victim and the offender."[10] In the case of Jack the Ripper, a sexual predator who targeted prostitutes, this means he had to go where the prostitutes were—which is to say, Spitalfields. In 1889, Arthur G. Morrison referred to "White's Row, or Dorset Street, with its hideous associations," and described Fashion Street, Flower and Dean Street, Thrawl Street, and Wentworth Street with "dark, silent, uneasy shadows passing and crossing—human vermin in this reeking sink."[11] This was the center of the high-crime area, the area with the greatest incidence of prostitutes, and, we may assume, as the police did in 1888, the Ripper's primary hunting ground.

By contrast, the area south of Whitechapel High Street and Whitechapel Road was at least somewhat more respectable. For example, Morrison described walking around in the Jewish residential neighborhoods south of Whitechapel High Street, in the vicinity of Mansell Street, Great Alie Street, and Leman Street, as follows: "The houses are old, large, of the very shabbiest-genteel aspect, and with a great appearance of being snobbishly ashamed of the odd trades to which many of their rooms are devoted." He added, "We are tired, perhaps, of all this respectability."[12] The areas in the vicinity of Greenfield Street were somewhat worse, according to Booth's 1889 Poverty Map, but still better than the "vicious, semi-criminal" areas around Flower and Dean Street and Dorset Street. For example, when speaking of Berner Street, P.C. Smith noted, "Very few prostitutes were to be seen there."[13] The location of the murder sites seems to suggest that the Ripper's preferred hunting area did not generally include the more respectable areas south of Whitechapel Road, including Greenfield Street and thereabouts. We can guess that the Ripper would not normally go searching for prostitutes in this area, especially if it was closer to his own residence.

In certain cases, however (especially with a disorganized or psychotic killer), if an opportunity arises when the killer feels comfortable enough to kill with minimum risk, he may choose to kill outside his normal activity space. "Routine Activity Theory," developed by Larry Cohen and Marcus Felson in 1979, explored this concept and found that sometimes serial killers would commit murders with little or no planning. Stride's murder may fall into this category, a fact that may explain the anomalies in that particular murder, such as the comparatively early hour of the event. If Kozminski was Jack the Ripper, he may have considered the Stride murder site to be riskier, because he was only about a fifth of a mile away from his residence, probably within what he considered his buffer zone, in a somewhat respectable area inhabited mostly by immigrant Poles and Germans.

Apart from the murder sites, the only geographic clue to the Ripper's residence was the bloody apron found in Goulston Street, along with the chalked message, "The Juwes are the men that will not be blamed for nothing." It is likely that this clue indicates the general direction of the killer's residence, because after the Eddowes murder, the Ripper would have wanted to return to the safety of his home as fast as he could. It is clear, simply by looking at a map, that the apron was dropped along a route in the general direction of Kozminski's residence. But let's go a step further. If we assume that Kozminski had just murdered Eddowes in Mitre Square and wanted to get back to Greenfield Street as safely and quickly as possible, which way would he have gone? On a map, the most direct route would have been to walk south on Duke Street and then northeast along Aldgate/Whitechapel High Street. The problem is that this would have required Kozminski to walk along a busy main thoroughfare, which was likely to be populated with people and police. In fact, if the killer had taken this route, he would have walked right past Detective Halse and two other City detective constables who were, at the time, standing at the corner of Houndsditch and Aldgate High Street, near St. Botolph's Church.

Clearly, the Ripper would have preferred to take an alternate route, which would allow him to skulk along, unseen, on the dark back streets. The most obvious alternative would have been to walk down Wentworth and Old Montague streets, a route that snakes along roughly parallel to, and to the north of, Whitechapel High Street. The most direct way to get to this street from Mitre Square was via St. James Place, then northeast along Stoney Lane and past Goulston Street, where the apron was ditched. Kozminski would have continued walking along Old Montague Street until he could slip down an alley and quickly cross over Whitechapel Road to Fieldgate Street to his home. Anyone who studies a map of the area will come to the same conclusion—simply, that the Ripper dropped the apron along what would have been the safest direct getaway route leading from Mitre Square back to Kozminski's likely residence. In fact, if this route is plotted on a map, it looks somewhat like an arrow pointing toward a bull's-eye, the center of which represents (generally speaking) both Kozminski's home and the center of the smallest circle containing all of the murder sites.

So it seems that every geographic analysis of the Ripper murders fits with a model that has the Ripper living at or near Kozminski's presumed residence on either Greenfield Street or Yalford Street.

25

Schizophrenia and Violence

Schizophrenia cannot be understood without understanding despair.

—*R. D. Laing*

I n the Victorian era, although detailed taxonomies of lunacy existed for upper- and middle-class patients, pauper lunatics were generally just lumped into one of three categories: those suffering from mania, melancholia, or dementia. Unfortunately, the use of these labels was inconsistent, and one modern study of British asylum entries between 1870 and 1875 found, "We could not discern exactly what differentiated the principal diagnoses, mania, dementia and melancholia."[1] "Dementia" was a blanket term that seems to have been applied to any patient with a cognitive deficit, including those suffering from brain damage or head trauma, and the insane. "Melancholia" was defined as depression characterized by underactivity, whereas "mania" was defined by overactivity. According to the study, "The term [dementia] applied to a huge variety of cases, including both patients with cognitive difficulties from any cause and psychotic patients who were not behaviourally overactive enough to be described as manic."[2]

In practice, it seems that if a patient was "overactive" or excitable, a diagnosis of mania would be applied, even if the patient had symptoms of insanity or schizophrenia. As noted in Dr. Henry Monro's treatise, On the Nomenclature of the Various Forms of Insanity (1856), "Dementia should always be applied to a passive rather than an active state."[3] By the 1870s, however, the terms mania, melancholia, and dementia began to evolve and eventually acquired meanings at least somewhat analogous to the modern definitions of mania, depression, and schizophrenia, respectively. Still, the difference between mania and dementia was not very clearly defined, and even as late as 1899, Emil Kraeplin's Lehrbuch der Psychiatrie (6th edition) noted that the primary differentiator between mania and dementia was that mania did not have a deteriorating course, whereas dementia was chronic and typically incurable. The fact that mania and dementia were not clearly differentiated or defined is not surprising, given the Victorians' limited understanding of mental disorders. In some measure, this confusion persists even today—as a recent study noted, "The boundaries between schizophrenia and mood disorders are obscure."[4]

The ambiguous use of such labels in the Victorian era adds some confusion to our assessment of Aaron Kozminski's mental condition, especially since in some cases patients were described with all three terms. Dr. Edmund Houchin, for example, described Kozminski as melancholic, but then on Kozminski's Colney Hatch admission record, the "Form of Disorder" was given as "mania" with the symptom of "incoherence." The diagnosis of mania probably means (at the very least) that Kozminski was excitable, overactive, and out of control when admitted. Such behavior would warrant a diagnosis of mania, and as such, it is relevant to remember that Donald Swanson claimed that Kozminski was brought to Mile End Workhouse "with his hands tied behind his back." None of this changes the fact that Kozminski was almost certainly schizophrenic, as we shall see. Strictly speaking, however, the official diagnosis of his disorder, at least when he was first admitted to Colney Hatch in 1891, was "mania."

When Kozminski was transferred to Leavesden, his diagnosis was changed to "dementia." This probably indicates that he had become more passive and manageable, perhaps as a result of sedation, and no longer required restraint. On the other hand, Kozminski may have been transferred to the custodial purgatory of Leavesden Asylum simply because the doctors determined that his mental disease was incurable and deteriorating.

The term *schizophrenia*, meaning "splitting of the mind," was coined in 1908 by Eugene Bleuler in reference to a mental disorder that had previously been referred to as dementia praecox, among other terms. The cause of the disease was then, and still remains, largely a mystery and the subject of much debate. Yet the weight of opinion now seems to support the theory that a person might be born with a predisposition for the disorder—either genetic or caused by complications in childbirth or brain damage—which is later "unmasked" by "stressors" in the form of difficult psychological, emotional, or social situations.[5] As noted on the Web site for England's National Schizophrenia Fellowship (Rethink.org), studies have shown that "possible causing factors include stress caused by institutional and individual racism, low employment levels, poor housing and lack of cultural identity."

People with schizophrenia typically begin to exhibit strange behavior many years before the disease actually manifests itself. In adolescence, they are often introverted and withdrawn, with few friends. As a study conducted at Emory University noted, "Subjects who go on to develop schizophrenia show a pattern of escalating adjustment problems. This gradual increase in problems includes feelings of depression, social withdrawal, irritability and noncompliance."[6] The onset of the disease is then preceded by a "prodromal phase," during which a person will exhibit "escalating signs of behavioral dysfunction and subclinical psychotic symptoms." This and other earlier pre-morbid symptoms are now considered stages in the evolution of schizophrenia. According to *Kaplan and Sadock's Synopsis of Psychiatry*,

> Family and friends may eventually notice that the person has changed and is no longer functioning well in occupational, social, and personal activities. During this stage, a patient may begin to develop an interest in abstract ideas, philosophy, and the occult or religious questions. Additional prodromal signs and symptoms can include markedly peculiar behavior, abnormal affect, unusual or bizarre speech, bizarre ideas, and strange perceptual experiences.[7]

The prodromal phase can last for a year or longer, after which time the onset of the mature form of the disease may either be sudden or gradually develop over time.

Today, schizophrenia is typically diagnosed based on criteria laid out in the *Diagnostic and Statistical Manual of Mental Disorders* (the *DSM-IV*), which identifies both positive symptoms (traits that are present in schizophrenics but lacking in normal people) and negative symptoms (traits that normal people have but schizophrenics lack). The primary positive symptoms of schizophrenia are bizarre delusional thinking, disorganized thoughts, and disorganized speech. A patient may speak in rambling sentences that seem to go nowhere, forming loose connections, getting sidetracked in midsentence, or jumbling words together incoherently in what is referred to as "word salad." Delusions are often bizarre. A patient may have delusions of grandiosity or omniscience or may be convinced he or she has special powers. Frequently, people suffering from schizophrenia will be obsessed with terrifying invisible forces or some external threatening presence that is plotting against them. Another common positive symptom of schizophrenia is auditory hallucination, in which a patient will hear voices that "are often threatening, obscene, accusatory or insulting." Negative symptoms can include a decline in motivation, movement, or speech. Some schizophrenics may experience an extreme fluctuation of emotional states, while others may have very limited and shallow emotional responses. It has also been shown that schizophrenics exhibit deficits in many aspects of cognitive functioning, including an impaired "ability to comprehend and solve social problems."[8]

One of the common subtypes of the disease is paranoid schizophrenia. In these cases, patients will commonly hear auditory hallucinations and be obsessed with paranoid delusions, typically of both grandeur and persecution. Yet disorganized thoughts, disorganized speech, and flat emotional responses are usually not as prominent in paranoid schizophrenics, and therefore people with this subtype of schizophrenia may be able to interact in society without immediately arousing suspicion that they are insane. Again, according to Sadock,

> Patients with paranoid schizophrenia are typically tense, suspicious, guarded, reserved, and sometimes hostile or

aggressive, but they can occasionally conduct themselves
adequately in social situations. Their intelligence in areas
not invaded by their psychosis tends to remain intact. . . .
Patients with the paranoid type of schizophrenia show less
regression of their mental facilities, emotional responses,
and behavior than do patients with other types of schizophrenia.[9]

Other modern theorists propose that schizophrenia is not one
disease but instead a cluster of symptoms along a spectrum. Such
theories tend to find that there is less differentiation between some
forms of schizophrenia and bipolar disorder, because both share many
symptoms. Some propose, for example, that paranoia is a separate disorder or "dimension," and that it should be considered at the milder
end of the spectrum of schizotypal symptoms than those symptoms
typically associated with more severe "disorganized" schizophrenia.
It even seems possible that the course of the disease might progress
from milder symptoms (paranoia and "mania") to more severe ones
(disorganization and depression or catatonia). As such, it is important
to point out that violent behavior is often associated with paranoid
delusional thinking.

It seems clear that Kozminski was suffering from some form of
schizophrenia. His belief that he was "ill, and his cure consists in
refusing food," and his belief that he was "under protection of [the]
Russian Consulate" are classic examples of delusional schizophrenic
thinking. He also claimed that "he knows the movements of all
mankind" and noted the presence of what he called an "instinct,"
which, as written on the Colney Hatch record, was "probably
aural hallucination."[10] For the three years that Kozminski was at
Colney Hatch, he was dominated by this instinct. For example, on
February 10, 1891, he was described as being "difficult to deal with
on account of the Dominant Character of his delusions. Refused to
be bathed the other day as his 'Instincts' forbade him."[11] Another
entry, on April 21, 1891, noted, "still the same 'instinctive' objection to weekly bath." Kozminski's instinct was probably what would
now be called a "command-type hallucination," a voice that told
him what to do and that commented on his actions. Kozminski

was still experiencing these hallucinations years later, as seen in an entry in his case file at Leavesden Asylum on February 2, 1916, that recorded, "He has hallucinations of sight and hearing and is at times very obstinate."[12]

The fact that Kozminski's instinct told him not to accept food from other people suggests that he believed his food was poisoned, and this, along with his grandiose delusions of omniscience, may indicate that he was a schizophrenic of the paranoid subtype. This is relevant to our assessment of Kozminski as a suspect in the Ripper case, because, as mentioned earlier, paranoid schizophrenics can appear outwardly more normal than disorganized schizophrenics do. According to Lauren Post, a licensed independent clinical social worker (LICSW) at the Boston Institute for Psychotherapy, "paranoid types tend to be more suspicious of other people and therefore are more guarded themselves, making them appear more distant. In that way, the less they reveal, the more likely they are to appear 'normal.'"[13] Still, as Post conceded, it would be impossible to give an accurate diagnosis based solely on Kozminski's surviving asylum documentation.

In any case, a purely clinical assessment of Kozminski's condition gives us no idea of what schizophrenia is actually like for the person who experiences it. For a more in-depth perspective, I turned to Elyn Saks's autobiography, *The Center Cannot Hold: My Journey through Madness*. Saks's story is an insightful and fascinating first-person account of her experience as a schizophrenic and of the ways the disorder was outwardly manifested and perceived by the people she interacted with. The book describes schizophrenia as a terrifying experience that Saks referred to as "disorganization," in which her brain essentially ceased to be able to organize thoughts coherently. "Consciousness gradually loses its coherence," she explained. "No core holds things together, providing the lens through which to see the world, to make judgements and comprehend risk." Her thought processes began to revolve increasingly around fantasies and delusions that were "extremely vivid and for me, not entirely distinguishable from reality."[14]

Saks was a highly intelligent woman who was admitted to a prestigious program in philosophy at Oxford University. Shortly after beginning her studies, however, she had a disastrous manic episode and quickly unraveled, to the extent that her doctors recorded that she seemed "physically and mentally retarded." According to Saks, this was because she had become unable to articulate the thoughts that were in her head. As she said, "I was finding it difficult to speak. Literally the words in my head would not come out of my mouth. . . . I'd start a sentence then be unable to remember where I was going with it. I began to stammer severely . . . disengaged from my surroundings, I sat in the dayroom for hours at a time, jiggling my legs, not noticing who came in or out, not speaking at all." She also began to hear voices. "In my fog of isolation and silence I began to feel I was receiving commands to do things. . . . The origin of the commands was unclear. In my mind, they were issued by some sort of powerful beings. Not real people with names and faces, but shapeless powerful beings that controlled me with thoughts."[15]

Saks was paranoid and thought people were trying to hurt her, but interestingly, this fear manifested itself in the delusion that she was in complete control of everything. "I am in control," she said. "I control the world. The world is at my whim. I control the world and everything in it."[16] She vacillated between these two seemingly opposite states: on the one hand, utterly dominated by outside forces, and on the other, being the controller—at times she was the victim, and at other times the victimizer. Yet occasionally, even while in a manic state, she was able to interact with people and could hide her delusional thinking from others by projecting a "normal" persona. As she wrote,

> Psychosis is like an insidious infection that nevertheless leaves some of your faculties intact. . . . Completely delusional, I still understood essential aspects of how the world worked. For example, I was getting my schoolwork done, and I vaguely understood the rule that in a social setting, even with the people I most trusted, I could not ramble on about my psychotic thoughts. To talk about killing children, or burning whole worlds, or being able to destroy cities with my mind was not part of polite conversation.[17]

Saks's insanity was degenerative and came in cycles. This is typical of the course of schizophrenia, which is characterized by "exacerbations and remissions." Acute psychotic episodes may come and go periodically for many years, and during remission the patient may function normally for long periods. According to the National Schizophrenia Fellowship, "Most people will be able to function normally for long periods at a time. . . . Approximately two-thirds of those who develop the condition experience fluctuating symptoms over many years."[18] Recovery is now typically achieved through the use of antipsychotic medications. Saks went through long periods where her psychosis was in recession, even without the use of antipsychotic drugs. Yet then she went through degenerative cycles, during which she became nearly catatonic, and even though she was high functioning and very intelligent, she was perceived as being "mentally retarded."

A realistic understanding of schizophrenia is crucial to our assessment of Kozminski as a suspect in the Whitechapel murders, especially since the symptoms noted in his asylum records are so often used as the basis of an argument that he could not have been Jack the Ripper. For this reason, Saks's account is very important, because in many ways it mirrors what we know about Kozminski's insanity. Like Saks, Kozminski had delusions that he was guided and controlled by "an instinct that informs his mind" and also had delusions of control, claiming that "he knows the movements of all mankind."[19] His psychosis was also apparently episodic, because he went through periods of "chronic mania," excitation, and incoherence and other periods when he was quiet, well behaved, and responsive to questioning.

Today, antipsychotic medication and psychotherapy are fairly effective in combating the symptoms of schizophrenia and halting the progress of the disease. But when Kozminski was in the asylum, there was basically no treatment for the disease at all, discounting sedation. When untreated, schizophrenia's course can be devastating. Kaplan and Sadock's *Synopsis of Psychiatry* notes that "deterioration in the patient's baseline functioning follows each relapse of the psychosis."[20] Patients would often eventually degenerate to the point where they became reduced to what is known as a catatonic stupor. This apparently happened with Kozminski, whose later case notes at Leavesden Asylum indicate that he had deteriorated to the point that he was mumbling to himself, largely mute and unresponsive to questioning. By 1910 (after sixteen years in the asylums), Kozminski was unable to answer simple questions and was, like Saks, described as "dull and stupid in manner and faulty in his habits."[21]

Because of the degenerative nature of schizophrenia, we must not make assumptions about Kozminski's mental state in 1888. In all likelihood, he got worse gradually, over a period of years. He may have started having delusional thoughts as early as 1885, followed by periods during which he was able to function normally. We do know that by the time he was brought to the workhouse in 1890, his family was aware that there was something wrong with him. Yet prior to this, the extent of his mental disease is not known, and it may have been less severe. Like Saks, Kozminski may have been able to hide the outward symptoms of his disorder, making him seem at least superficially normal. In 1888, the year of the murders, Kozminski may have still been able to speak with people without immediately arousing their suspicions, while at the same time, in his mind, he was highly delusional, living in a fantasy world and receiving auditory hallucinations and instructions from his "instinct."

The link between schizophrenia and violent behavior is a highly debated topic. Although past research suggested that there was no causal link between schizophrenia and violence, recent studies have shown that this may not be the case. "Most studies confirm the association between violence and schizophrenia," a 2002 study noted. "Recent good evidence supports a small but independent association. Comorbid substance abuse considerably increases this risk."[22] Another study cited data showing that "5 percent to 10 percent of those charged with murder in Western countries have a schizophrenia spectrum disorder."[23] Both studies concluded that alcohol abuse dramatically increased the likelihood of violence in schizophrenics. The largest study yet of the link between schizophrenia and violence found that 8.2 percent of the schizophrenic study group had been convicted of a violent offense—a rate 4.5 times the 1.8 percent of those without mental illness.

Another study, by Pamela Taylor, Bruce Link, et al., reported, "Strong predictors of violence in the mentally ill are the feeling that others are out to harm them and a feeling that their mind is dominated by forces beyond their control or that thoughts are being put into their head."[24] A further study revealed that the causal relationship between schizophrenia and violent behavior was largely due to "threat/control override" symptoms, defined as "experiences of patients feeling that people are trying to harm them and experiences of their minds being dominated by forces outside their control."[25] Such symptoms clearly fit Kozminski.

In yet another study, researchers determined that 19 percent of schizophrenic participants had had an incident of minor or severe violence within a six-month period. "Although most individuals with mental illnesses are not violent," the study director pointed out, "violence by a subgroup of individuals with schizophrenia is far from rare."[26] Violence was found to be associated with a cluster of positive psychotic symptoms, such as "hallucinations, paranoid delusions, delusions of persecution, and grandiosity." The odds of violence were also found to "vary with factors other than psychotic symptoms." The study found, for example, that "serious violence was associated with depressive symptoms" and "having been victimized." Because of such findings, both Kozminski's domination by an "instinct" and the anti-Semitism he experienced in Russia and London are relevant, because they have been shown to be predictors of violence in schizophrenics.

Another study found that there was a high rate of violence in schizophrenics who had comorbid (simultaneous) psychopathic characteristics—in other words, among insane patients who were also psychopathic. The concepts of psychosis and psychopathy are often confused. "Psychosis" is a generic psychiatric term that means an "abnormal condition of the mind," as characterized by a general break with reality (hallucinations, delusional thinking, and so on). For example, a person with a mental illness such as schizophrenia would be described as psychotic, meaning insane. On the other hand, psychopathy (also known as sociopathy or antisocial personality disorder) is not recognized as a form of insanity but instead is considered a personality disorder.

The concept of psychopathy was first recognized in the early eighteenth century, when Philippe Pinel used the term *la folie raisonnante* (insanity without delirium) to describe patients whose "reasoning abilities were unimpaired," that is, they were not insane but were at the same time "under the dominion of instinctive and abstract fury." In 1835, the British alienist J. C. Prichard coined the term "moral insanity" to describe a "form of mental derangement in which the intellectual functions appear to have sustained little or no injury," but "the moral or active principles of the mind are strangely perverted or depraved, the power of self-government is impaired, and the individual is found to be incapable, not of talking or reasoning upon any subject proposed to him, but of conducting himself with a decency and propriety in the business of life."[27] Prichard's definition, although archaic in tone, is actually quite similar to the modern meaning of the term. At the end of the nineteenth century, Emil Kraepelin began to use the term *psychopath* in a way that is similar to how we use the term today.

The modern meaning of the term was laid out in Hervey Cleckley's groundbreaking 1941 work *The Mask of Sanity*. Cleckley defined a psychopath as "an intelligent person characterised by poverty of emotions, who has no sense of shame, is superficially charming, is manipulative, who shows irresponsible behaviour, and is inadequately motivated."[28] According to Cleckley, with the psychopath, "We are dealing here not with a complete man at all but with something that suggests a subtly constructed reflex machine which can mimic the human personality perfectly."[29] Cleckley's book was the basis for Robert Hare's Psychopathy Checklist (PCL), which identified twenty traits that indicate a diagnosis of psychopathy. These included glibness/superficial charm, a grandiose sense of self-worth, pathological lying, cunning/manipulation, lack of remorse or guilt, shallow affect, a lack of empathy, the failure to accept responsibility, promiscuous sexual behavior, "socially deviant lifestyle," the need for stimulation/proneness to boredom, a parasitic lifestyle, poor behavioral control, the lack of realistic long-term goals, impulsivity, irresponsibility, juvenile delinquency, early behavior problems, numerous short-term marital relationships, revocation of conditional release, and criminal versatility.

The rate of psychopathy in the population is now estimated to be about 1 percent. The disorder is a common trait of serial killers and is tied to a general lack of socialization. A 1965 study of mass murderers and serial killers showed that they "gave preponderant evidence of never having experienced normal communication with a dependable, understanding part of the social world about them. They had no workable system of social or personal frames of reference."[30] As noted by

Robert Ressler, Ann Burgess, and John Douglas, "Seldom does the lust murderer come from an environment of love and understanding. It is more likely that he was an abused and neglected child who experienced a great deal of conflict in his early life and was unable to develop and use adequate coping devices."[31]

A 1999 study found that a significant percentage of violent patients with schizophrenia scored high on Hare's Psychopathy Checklist, suggesting that they may have had psychopathic traits that preceded the emergence of psychotic symptoms (that is, schizophrenia). The report found that "approximately two-thirds of the violent subjects in this sample were rated as possibly or definitely psychopathic" and concluded that "underlying personality features may be responsible for some of the violent behavior of patients with schizophrenia." The study also found that schizophrenic patients in the violent group had a lower socioeconomic status, a lower IQ, and an earlier age of onset of schizophrenic symptoms.[32]

A similar report noted, "Evidence suggests that the presence of psychopathic traits that do not meet the threshold diagnostic criteria for psychopathy also elevates the likelihood of violent behaviour in schizophrenia patients."[33] In other words, schizophrenic patients who possessed even some of the traits from Hare's PCL checklist were more likely to be violent, even if they did not score high enough to be diagnosed as psychopaths. The report concluded that "a proportion of violence in patients with schizophrenia is attributable to comorbidity with psychopathy and possibly other personality disorders." It also noted, "There are at least three aetiological subtypes of violence in schizophrenia (i) that related directly to positive psychotic symptoms, (ii) impulsive violence and (iii) violence stemming from comorbidity with personality disorders, particularly psychopathy." Interestingly, the study claimed that its findings were "consistent with the concept of 'pseudopsychopathic schizophrenia' that was used 50 years ago to describe cases that began as conduct-disorder type behavioural problems and then developed schizophrenia."

The results of these studies provide a good explanation for violent behavior in schizophrenics and suggest that much of the violent behavior attributed to schizophrenics is *not* motivated by command-type hallucinations, as some people have assumed. Instead, as noted in

"Psychopathy and Violent Behavior," "Psychotic symptoms do not fully account for violence in schizophrenia."[34] Of course, this does not mean that psychosis is not a factor in violent behavior, merely that it is probably not a sufficient explanation of the phenomenon. For example, one report found that "only about 20 percent of assaults committed by psychotic inpatients are directly attributable to positive symptoms [in other words, command hallucinations]."[35]

As noted by England's National Schizophrenia Fellowship, auditory hallucination "can describe activities taking place, carry on a conversation, warn of dangers, or even issue orders to a person."[36] There are several well-known examples of people who claimed that they were ordered to kill by command-type auditory hallucinations. One such case was the widely reported murder of Kendra Webdale in 1999 by a schizophrenic man named Andrew Goldstein of Queens, New York. In the decade following his first psychotic episode at age eighteen, Goldstein received various diagnoses from psychiatrists, including paranoid schizophrenia and schizoaffective disorder. Goldstein checked himself into numerous hospitals and desperately wanted help, but despite the fact that doctors considered him dangerous both to himself and to others, he was always released. Goldstein told doctors that he was controlled by someone called Larry, and that he was "concerned about his impulses to hurt women."[37] Goldstein acted on these impulses numerous times, and in one two-year period, he attacked thirteen people (mostly women) in various places—several were hospital nurses, but others were simply strangers in a bookstore or a fast-food restaurant. "Someone is inhabiting me and making me do things," Goldstein said. "You feel like something's entering you, like you're being inhabited. I don't know. And then, and then it's like an overwhelming urge to strike out or to push or punch. And then, I feel like it's not there, that sensation. Now I'm sane again. Then I'm normal. And then, it's there again and then, it's not."[38]

During Goldstein's final hospital admission in December 1998, it was reported that he was "disorganized, thought disordered, and delusional," and that he was unwashed and smelled bad (December 9); on December 10, the records showed that he "remains psychotic"; on December 11, he "remains paranoid."[39] Doctors attempted to have

Goldstein admitted to a long-term care facility, but finding no vacancy, they instead released him a few days later.

On Sunday, January 3, 1999, Goldstein spent much of the day listening to Madonna and claimed that he "drew pictures in his mind of a blimp on a green lawn in Germany during the 1930s." In the afternoon he went out to a record store, and at 5 p.m., he descended into the subway station at Broadway and 23rd Street. According to witnesses, in the subway station Goldstein was mumbling to himself, alternately standing on his tiptoes and pacing back and forth. He approached a young blond woman named Dawn Lorenzino and tried to talk to her, but Lorenzino turned around and said, "What are you looking at?" Goldstein then approached a second woman, Kendra Webdale, and asked her the time. After Webdale answered, Goldstein walked away and stood near the wall behind her.

As the train began to enter the station, according to Goldstein, "He felt a sensation, like a ghost or a spirit entering him and he got the urge to push, kick or punch the woman with blonde hair [that is, Lorenzino]." Then, inexplicably, he rushed forward and instead shoved Webdale so hard that she flew in front of the train "like a skydiver." When police arrived at the scene, Goldstein was sitting calmly on the floor, surrounded by a crowd of people. "I don't know the woman," he said. "I just pushed her."[40]

In a taped interview that was shown during his trial, Goldstein was asked why he did it. "Oh, I don't know," he responded. "I feel like people talk, uh, talk through me, you know."

"Who talks through you?" the interviewer asked.

"People. Like they say things, you know, like it's a plot or something."

"What's a plot?"

"Against, against, against me."[41]

Goldstein's case is interesting because he apparently had psychopathic characteristics in addition to hearing command-type hallucinations. At his trial, the prosecution argued that he had a relatively mild disorder "in the schizophrenic spectrum," but that he "had 'anti-social' features that were more relevant to his act than his schizophrenia."[42] Although the statement that Goldstein's mental disorder was "mild" is almost certainly inaccurate, given the overwhelming evidence of his psychosis, it is quite possible that a psychopathic antisocial tendency was an even greater factor in his numerous attacks on women. The prosecution, for example, presented evidence that Goldstein had a great anger due to rejection by women, and that a former roommate's stripper girlfriend had teased him. Goldstein's landlady testified that when the maid went downstairs to clean the apartment, she found Goldstein "lying on his bed exposed and he didn't cover himself." According to the prosecution, this was evidence that Goldstein "had been sexually inappropriate with women." Yet at the same time, Goldstein's roommate testified that he "was never disrespectful and never violent and very calm." This presents a complex picture, but in many respects, Goldstein may have been similar to Kozminski. Like Goldstein, Kozminski claimed to be controlled by an "instinct," was unwashed, and clearly exhibited disorganized, delusional thinking. And Melville Macnaghten's statement that Kozminski "had a great hatred of women, specially of the prostitute class, & had strong homicidal tendencies" may be evidence of comorbid psychopathic characteristics.

Several notorious serial killers have been diagnosed with schizophrenia, including Ed Gein, Ottis Toole, Andrei Chikatilo, Albert Fish, Issei Sagawa, and Robert Napper. Others, such as David Berkowitz (the Son of Sam) and Peter Sutcliffe (the Yorkshire Ripper), apparently faked insanity in the hope of getting a lighter sentence. Although Berkowitz and Sutcliffe claimed that they heard voices that told them to commit murder—for the Son of Sam, it was a neighbor's dog, whereas Sutcliffe claimed that God ordered him to rid the world of prostitutes—both were too organized and methodical to have been likely schizophrenics. True schizophrenic serial killers tend to be more disorganized, and their murders are frenzied, brutal affairs that often involve postmortem mutilation and cannibalism.

One such example was Marc Sappington, a young black man who became known as the Kansas City Vampire. The son of a schizophrenic mother, Sappington was raised as a regular churchgoer and was described as well spoken, intelligent, and funny. But the temptations of street life in the ghettos of Kansas City loomed as a constant threat, and in his teens Sappington began to drift into drug use, first smoking "danks," cigarettes dipped in embalming fluid, and then graduating to phencyclidine (PCP), a powerful dissociative drug with hallucinogenic effects similar to those experienced by schizophrenics. When Sappington reached the age of twenty, full-blown schizophrenia set in, and he began to receive orders to kill from voices inside his head. As he walked the ghetto streets, he would ask the voices, "How about her? What about him?"[43] Sappington ultimately killed three or four people. He tried to drink the blood of his victims and, in one case, ate part of a victim's leg.

An interesting example from the FBI's Behavioral Sciences Unit study was a man referred to only as Warren. After his incarceration for "assault with intent to commit murder," Warren underwent a series of psychological evaluations and was diagnosed a paranoid schizophrenic with a severe antisocial personality disorder. He was found to be "uncooperative, withdrawn, irritable, resentful and hostile," and although he had a tested IQ of 115, he was described as "pre-occupied, and at times he seemed to be listening to some inner voice (as though he were experiencing auditory hallucinations, which he denied)."[44] Warren sounds eerily similar to Kozminski as he was described in some of his psychiatric evaluations. Warren was eventually released and went on to commit several murders, some of which included postmortem mutilations. In one case, reminiscent of the Mary Kelly murder, Warren removed both of the victim's breasts and put them between her legs.

Another clear example of a very dangerous schizophrenic serial killer was Richard Chase, the so-called Vampire of Sacramento, who killed six people during a span of one month in the late 1970s. Chase believed that he had soap-dish poisoning, the result of which was that "his blood was turning to powder and that he thus needed blood from other creatures to replenish it." This became, in Chase's mind, a justification for several murders in which he cannibalized his victims and drank their blood. Like Kozminski, Chase was paranoid—he believed that Nazis were behind the soap-dish poisoning and later thought that prison officials were poisoning his food.[45]

Probably the most notable example of an extremely dangerous schizophrenic serial killer was Herbert Mullin. Mullin began to exhibit signs of insanity in his early twenties and then, at the age of twenty-five, started to receive telepathic messages from his father ordering him to kill. In a five-month period between October 1972 and February 1973, Mullin murdered thirteen people—in one instance, cutting open a woman's stomach and removing her intestines. He killed for a variety of reasons that made sense only in the context of his paranoid fantasies. Among other reasons, he claimed that he killed to prevent a catastrophic earthquake from happening in California, and because he thought the victims themselves sent him telepathic messages offering to be sacrificed. As Mullin explained to the jury at his trial, "One man consenting to be murdered protects the millions of other human beings living in the cataclysmic earthquake/tidal area. For this reason, the designated hero/leader and associates have the responsibilities of getting enough people to commit suicide and/or consent to being murdered every day."[46] Enough said.

In many respects, the Ripper seems to have been similar to these schizophrenic killers. In fact, according to former FBI agent Roy Hazelwood, Jack the Ripper was a classic example of a particular type of serial killer called a disorganized "lust murderer."[47] Defined as a killer whose focus is a "mutilating attack or displacement of the breasts, rectum, or genitals," the disorganized lust murderer is often mentally disturbed and "approaches his victim in much the same way as an inquisitive child with a new toy . . . in an exploratory examination of the sexually significant parts of the body in an attempt to determine how they function and appear below the surface." A lust murderer sometimes takes souvenirs from the body, eats body parts, or "inserts foreign objects into body orifices in a probing and curiosity-motivated, yet brutal, manner." Such behavior, according to Hazelwood, reflects a "desire to outrage society and call attention to his total disdain for societal acceptance." Hazelwood also suggested that "while there is no evidence to support anthropophagy [cannibalism], given the dissection and taking of body parts, it is my opinion that the Ripper likely consumed parts of his victim's bodies away from the murder scenes."[48] If this is true, this would perhaps support the notion that the "From Hell" letter, which referred to eating part of Eddowes's kidney, may have been from the real killer.

Hazelwood argued that societal rejection and a sense of "social inadequacy" would drive a potential lust murderer "away from the expression of normal or healthy sexuality" to "a world in which [he] imagined increasingly sadistic and violent erotic encounters." Such fantasies are reinforced through compulsive masturbation and typically revolve around paraphilias, or "sexual arousal to objects or situations that are not part of normative stimulation." As he noted,

> Lust murderers exhibit a progression of brutality, and each subsequent murder becomes more vicious and sadistic. Erotophonophiliacs establish a violently sexualized relationship in their minds that they have rehearsed repeatedly while masturbating. . . . They are impulsive and unable to escape their fantasy world. This is a sexualized imagined realm that is robust with themes of power, control, sex, violence and mutilation.

Moreover, Hazelwood added, for the lust murderer, "The onset of aberrant sexual proclivities was linked to a developmental change. This change included the transition from a normal sexualized fantasy life to that of a paraphilic masturbatory fantasy life." This is especially relevant to our assessment of Kozminski as a suspect in the Ripper murders, because the psychological trauma induced by the family's flight from Russia as part of a mass exodus of refugees fleeing anti-Semitism and oppression essentially coincided with the onset of puberty when Kozminski was fifteen years old.

Clearly, Jack the Ripper seems to fit this type of killer—a disorganized, primitive, and impulsive killer, whose murders were frenzied, involved postmortem mutilation, and exhibited a "progression of brutality," each one "more vicious and sadistic" than the last. In fact, Hazelwood told me that the FBI came to the conclusion that Jack the Ripper was probably schizophrenic, largely because he fit the profile of a disorganized-type lust murderer. When I asked why this detail was not included in the FBI's profile of Jack the Ripper, he responded,

> When providing a profile, our "clients" are typically law enforcement professionals. It has always been my belief that including mental health terminology (i.e., "schizophrenic" or "psychopath") would make the profile meaningful only to mental health professionals. However, providing the law

enforcement client with the characteristics and traits of a schizophrenic or psychopath gives them specific and more helpful information.

"Jack the Ripper wasn't good, he was lucky," Hazelwood told me. "I don't see how anyone who knows anything at all about violent crime can say that was an organized crime." I asked whether he thought Kozminski, as a schizophrenic, would have been able to hide his insanity enough to convince his victims to go off with him as a client. "Kozminski fit like a hand in a glove," he replied. "You have to remember that the victims were prostitutes, and all Kozminski would have had to say was, 'I'll give you a shilling for a blowjob,' and they would have gone with him."

26

Murder Will Out

Mordre wol out, that se we day by day;
Mordre is so wlatsom, and abhomynable
To God, that is so just and resonable,
That he ne wol nat suffre it heled be.
Though it abyde a yeer, or two, or thre,
Mordre wol out, this my conclusion.

—*Geoffrey Chaucer, "The Nun's Priest's Tale"*

In the summer of 2005, I stepped off a rickety train onto the railway platform of Kłodawa train station. All around me, fields stretched toward the horizon, punctuated by a few isolated farm buildings. In the road sprawled out next to the station, I found an old man standing in front of his house, and with the help of my Polish phrasebook, I asked him how to get to the village center. He looked at me, confused, and started speaking to me in Polish. Seeing that it was obvious I didn't understand, he held up five fingers and said something that sounded like "kilometers," pointing north. "Djenkuja," I replied. Then I turned around and started walking. "What the hell am I doing here?" I wondered, as I made my way toward Aaron Kozminski's old home town. Even by Polish standards, it seemed that I was in the middle of nowhere. I passed by some cows grazing in a field, and wondered how many tourists had visited the town recently. Along the road, I met two teenage girls and asked them (in English) if I was going the right way to Kłodawa. They replied yes and then broke out giggling, looking at me as though I were an alien from another planet.

When I finally got to the town center, I walked around looking at the old buildings and trying not to draw attention to myself. I had no idea where the old Jewish quarter had once been, and I realized there was no chance I would find Kozminski's house, which was listed only as "number 25" in the town's Book of Residents. Most of the buildings didn't look that old anyway. I didn't even bother trying to talk to anyone, because I realized that it would have been impossible to explain what I was doing there. So I just walked around, taking photos. "Could this nondescript place have been the birthplace of Jack the Ripper?" I wondered. The phrase "from hell" did not seem to fit. It would have been more accurate to have written "from nowhere." After a while, I started to feel as though the whole trip was a waste of time, so I bought a hamburger, and then started walking back to the train station. In truth, however, I did go to Kłodawa looking for something. But what was I looking for? What did I think I might find there? It was a fool's errand. I was trying to solve one of history's most notorious and confounding mysteries, and I was getting nowhere. I took a few photos of myself standing in front of the sign on the train platform, and then I left Kłodawa, feeling just as confused as I had been before I came.

Of course, I was not alone. Trying to solve the Jack the Ripper mystery has been a pastime for armchair detectives like myself for decades. "Murder will out," Chaucer once wrote. God would "not suffer its concealment," he argued, although "things may lie hidden for a year or two."[1] Yet it has now been 120 years, and the truth of the Ripper case has not been revealed. During this time, countless people have tried to find some scrap of evidence that will solve the case once and for all. Researchers have put forth hundreds of theories and hundreds of suspects, and numerous books have boasted, "case closed" or "the mystery is finally solved!" None have yet succeeded in presenting a case that is even remotely convincing.

The problems in trying to solve the case are legion. No physical evidence from the period has survived, so there is no possibility of a DNA match or anything of that sort. Nor is it likely that someone will find a document in an attic somewhere that reveals the Ripper's identity. Ripperologists, to their credit, tend to be skeptical of overly optimistic "solutions"—they do not like guesswork or speculation, and they detest blatant fantasy and overt fabrication. They like facts.

In the end, the real problem with Kozminski as a suspect in the Ripper case is simply how little we know about him. Of course, the police must have known a great deal about him. They must have had files on him, and it is possible that they had a stronger case against him than we will ever know. Yet even if we take Robert Anderson at his word, the police didn't have sufficient evidence to convict Kozminski in a court of law. The police may have had circumstantial evidence or the statements of suspicious relatives, for example, but this wouldn't have been good enough. If the police couldn't convict Kozminski then, how can we possibly expect to prove his guilt today, beyond a reasonable doubt? The answer is that we cannot.

I previously discussed the Ripper's escape route after the murder of Kate Eddowes and noted that on a map, it looks like an arrow pointing toward the center of a dartboard. The terminus of that arrow—the bull's-eye, so to speak—was, in all likelihood, Jack the Ripper's home. The arrow clearly points in the direction of Kozminski's residence on Greenfield Street, but, of course, it only goes partway. After Goulston Street, the Ripper may have taken a turn and continued in some other direction, to another destination. The missing part of that arrow represents an unknown. In a sense, we might think of this as a metaphor for all of the "evidence" that seems to point to Kozminski as a Ripper suspect. There are a lot of arrows, but each has a piece missing. None of them alone is sufficient to prove conclusively that Kozminski was the Ripper, but all of the arrows seem to be pointing in the same direction.

Ultimately, all that we have to work with is a complex jumble of fragmentary and often-contradictory statements, memoirs, and newspaper reports, from which we must try to imagine the whole picture. Some pieces fit, while others don't, confusing matters further. Yet if we take a step back and look at all of the fragments together, the general form of a solution seems to emerge, even if the details remain unclear.

Sir Arthur Conan Doyle's *A Study in Scarlet* was published in November 1887, just a few months before the beginning of the Whitechapel murders. This story marked the first appearance of Sherlock Holmes, the cocaine-using London detective who solved crimes using a combination of observation and intellectual analysis. Holmes would serve as the archetype for countless detectives in novels and movies, including Johnny Depp's portrayal of a highly fictionalized detective Frederick Abberline in the 2001 Ripper movie *From Hell*. In the movie, Abberline is depicted as an opium addict who solves crimes with the aid of drug-induced visions and dreams. Sherlock Holmes's crime-solving techniques were grounded in a somewhat more practical methodology—so much so, in fact, that Holmesian deduction is now taught to members of the UK's security services, MI5 and MI6. "The ideal reasoner," Holmes once said, "would, when he had once been shown a single fact in all its bearings, deduce from it not only all the chain of events which led up to it but also all the results which would follow from it."[2] Holmes was much like the modern criminal profiler, attempting to solve crimes given only the scantest, apparently most insignificant pieces of physical evidence. "You know my method," Holmes said. "It is founded upon the observation of trifles." In Conan Doyle's stories, Holmes often solved problems by making a series of inferences from known or observed facts and then deducing the most probable explanation of them.

In the absence of any single conclusive piece of evidence, we must use similar tactics in assessing Kozminski as a suspect in the Ripper case. Specifically, we must compare the known facts of the Ripper case with what is known (or may be inferred) about Kozminski and then draw the best (and, if possible, the simplest) conclusion that explains these facts.

The Macnaghten memorandum, for example, is one of the more damning bits of "evidence" against Aaron Kozminski as a suspect, because it states that he "had a great hatred of women, specially of the prostitute class, & had strong homicidal tendencies."[3] As we have seen, however, the memorandum contains several factual errors regarding the other two suspects mentioned, and therefore we must be cautious here. On the other hand, only one statement about Kozminski in the memorandum is demonstrably incorrect, and much of what

Macnaghten wrote about Kozminski was true. The real problem is simply that several of Macnaghten's statements about Kozminski are not backed up by other sources—there is no reason to assume these statements are incorrect, but we cannot know for sure. If the statements about Kozminski's hatred of women and about his "homicidal tendencies" are true, they would obviously have a great bearing on our understanding of Kozminski's psychological makeup. A delusional schizophrenic hearing command-type auditory hallucinations is one thing, but a schizophrenic psychopath who hates prostitutes is a different beast altogether.

Sometimes, where there is a gap in our knowledge, another source may provide some support, if not full corroboration. For example, City detective Harry Cox spoke of conducting surveillance on a suspect who he thought was "not unlikely to be connected with the crimes." The suspect, Cox said, "was a misogynist, who at some time or another had been wronged by a woman."[4] Generally, this statement seems to support Melville Macnaghten's statement about Kozminski's "great hatred of women." On the other hand, it is not much of a stretch to assume that the Ripper had a great hatred of women, and it is impossible to know whether Cox's statement was mere theory or a statement of known facts regarding the suspect in question.

It is difficult to combine all of the evidence against Kozminski and make sense out of it. As with circumstantial evidence, if enough is accumulated, one might reasonably infer guilt. While all of this seems suggestive of a possible solution, can we conclude that the police knew, without a doubt, that Aaron Kozminski was Jack the Ripper? Obviously, we cannot. Our knowledge remains too fractured, and there is too much room for reasonable doubt. Moreover, many of the ideas presented in this book are in the realm of speculation and theory. Despite many suggestions and plausible scenarios pointing to a guilty verdict, there is simply not enough here for us to draw any definite conclusions.

In the end, the most likely explanation is that several head officials at Scotland Yard considered Kozminski a very strong suspect in the case—probably the strongest suspect they had. The police obviously knew more about Kozminski than we know today, and there must have been something that convinced Anderson (and probably Donald

Swanson) that Kozminski was the Whitechapel fiend. It is possible that the "evidence" against him was entirely circumstantial or inculpatory. And Scotland Yard's one hope to secure a conviction, the identification by a witness, was probably not as conclusive as Anderson implied. No jury in its right mind would convict a suspect based on such evidence, as Anderson realized. Anderson's "definitely ascertained fact" should therefore probably be interpreted more along the lines of a strong hunch . . . strong enough, indeed, to convince the head of the CID that that the Ripper's identity was "a simple matter of fact" and not "a matter of theory."

In another famous serial murder case, the Green River Killer prostitute murders in Seattle in the 1980s, the police for many years had a similarly strong hunch about a man named Gary Ridgway. Their hunch was based almost entirely on circumstantial evidence, but there was a lot of it. Ridgway had been arrested for soliciting prostitutes, and several prostitutes on the Sea-Tac strip actually suggested that he was the killer. Over the years, the police questioned Ridgway on several occasions and also searched his house and his vehicles. Ridgway admitted that he fished on the Green River, near the sites where some of the victims' bodies were dumped, and even that he'd had "dates" with some of the girls who were murdered. On one of these dates, Ridgway began to strangle a prostitute, but when she begged for her life, he let go. The woman went to the police and picked Ridgway's photo out in a police album. When Ridgway was questioned about the incident, he cooperated with the police and even admitted to strangling the woman for ten or fifteen seconds, after she had bitten him during oral sex. The police had no option but to release him. They never found any hard evidence to convict him. Despite this, King County sheriff Dave Reichart, the man in charge of the Green River investigations, was pretty convinced that Ridgway was the killer.

Unfortunately, Gary Ridgway was only one of about a dozen suspects on the task force's A-list. There was no consensus among the detectives working the case—each had a different theory and a different favorite suspect. "You go to one detective's desk," said task force lieutenant Gary Nolan, "and he'll have half a dozen names and he'll swear one of them is the killer. Go to the next desk a couple of feet away, and that guy will have ten different names and he'll swear up and down that one of them has got to be the Green River Killer—and both of them can give you lots of good reasons why."[5] Finally, in 2001, the police made a conclusive DNA match to a suspect. When detective Tom Jensen received the DNA results, he went to Reichart (then retired from the case) and handed him an envelope. He said that it contained a photo of the Green River Killer. "I don't even have to open it," Reichart said. "It's Gary Ridgway." Of course, he was right.

But what if there had not been any conclusive DNA evidence? If Ridgway had never been caught, Reichart may well have said something very similar to what Anderson said about the Ripper—something like, "We knew who the Green River Killer was, but we didn't have the evidence to convict him." He may have even said it was "a definitely ascertained fact" that Ridgway was the killer. Such a statement would have been true, from Reichart's perspective. Still, it would have been only a strong suspicion—a "moral proof" perhaps, but ultimately just a theory. Apart from the DNA evidence, there was nothing conclusive to prove that Ridgway was the Green River Killer, despite a mountain of circumstantial evidence.

Most Ripperologists today believe that the Jack the Ripper case will never be solved. Given the nature of the field, it seems highly unlikely that the experts would ever come to any consensus on a solution to the case, even if a plausible solution were presented. It would ruin the mystique and glamour of an unsolved mystery. I think it is likely that Aaron Kozminski was Jack the Ripper, but I am unable to prove it. Ultimately, the reader must come to his or her own conclusions. According to what we now know about serial killers, there is certainly nothing that disqualifies Kozminski as a suspect, nor is there any reason to believe Anderson was lying. In the end, Kozminski is probably the only known suspect against whom a plausible case may be made. Yet despite this, our modern case against him cannot reach the level of Anderson's "definitely ascertained fact." Unless new documents come to light, perhaps this is as close as we will ever come to solving the mystery. Like Jack the Ripper, Aaron Kozminski seems destined to remain an enigma, a shadowy figure lurking in dark corners, obscured by the fog of history and the human imagination.

Notes

Introduction

1. Paraphrased from Paul Begg's talk at the Docklands Museum, London, May 17, 2008.
2. Sir Robert Anderson, "The Lighter Side of My Official Life," *Blackwood's Edinburgh*, March 1910.
3. Reference MEPO 3/140, ff. 177–183. Most of the quotes I have cited from official police documents related to the case are from Stewart Evans and Keith Skinner, *The Ultimate Jack the Ripper Companion: An Illustrated Encyclopedia* (New York: Carroll and Graf, 2000).
4. Donald Swanson, marginalia in his personal copy of Robert Anderson's book *The Lighter Side of My Official Life*. Property of Nevill Swanson, on permanent loan to New Scotland Yard's Crime Museum.

1. "Fear God and the King"

1. John Klier and Shlomo Lambroza, eds., *Pogroms: Anti-Jewish Violence in Modern Russian History* (Cambridge, UK: Cambridge University Press, 1992), 4.
2. Ibid., 5–6.
3. Simon M. Dubnow, *History of the Jews in Russia and Poland from the Earliest Times until the Present Day*, vol. 2 (Philadelphia: Jewish Publication Society of America, 1918).
4. William J. Fishman, *East End Jewish Radicals, 1875–1914* (London: Duckworth, 1975), 4–7.
5. *Jewish Chronicle*, March 25, 1881.
6. Dubnow, *History of the Jews in Russia and Poland from the Earliest Times until the Present Day*, 40.
7. Ibid., 96.
8. "The Assassination of the Czar," *Jewish Chronicle*, March 18, 1881.
9. Eugene C. Black, *The Social Politics of Anglo-Jewry 1880–1920* (Oxford, UK: B. Blackwell, 1988), 243.
10. Fishman, *East End Jewish Radicals*, 17.
11. Klier and Lambroza, *Pogroms*, 31.
12. Ronnie Po-chia Hsia, "The Real Blood of Passover," www.haaretz.com/print-edition/features/the-real-blood-of-passover-1.213323.
13. Ukase of January 17, 1835, quoted in Klier and Lambroza, *Pogroms*, 14.
14. I. Michael Aronson, "The Anti-Jewish Pogroms in Russia in 1881," in Klier and Lambroza, *Pogroms*, 47.
15. Nicholas Ignatiev, memorandum of March 12, 1881. Cited in Hans Rogger, *Jewish Policies and Right-Wing Politics in Imperial Russia* (Berkeley: University of California Press, 1986), 58.

2. 1881: The Storm Breaks

1. Edvard Radzinsky, *Alexander II: The Last Great Tsar*, trans. Antonina W. Boius (New York: Free Press, 2005), 414.
2. John Klier and Shlomo Lambroza, eds., *Pogroms: Anti-Jewish Violence in Modern Russian History* (Cambridge, UK: Cambridge University Press, 1992), 39.
3. "The Late Czar," *Jewish Chronicle*, March 25, 1881.
4. "The Late Emperor of Russia," *Jewish Chronicle*, April 1, 1881.
5. "The Assassination of the Czar," *Jewish Chronicle*, March 18, 1881.
6. Klier and Lambroza, *Pogroms*, 39.
7. Ibid.
8. I. Michael Aronson, "The Anti-Jewish Pogroms in Russia in 1881," in Klier and Lambroza, *Pogroms*, 45.
9. "Outrages upon Jews in Russia," *Jewish Chronicle*, May 6, 1881.
10. "Outrages upon Jews in Russia," *Jewish Chronicle*, May 13, 1881.
11. "Outrages upon Jews in Russia," *Jewish Chronicle*, May 6, 1881.
12. "Outrages upon Jews in Russia," *Jewish Chronicle*, May 13, 1881.
13. "Outrages upon Jews in Russia," *Jewish Chronicle*, May 6, 1881.
14. Ibid.
15. Ibid.
16. "The Jews in Russia," *Jewish Chronicle*, May 20, 1881.
17. Simon M. Dubnow, *History of the Jews in Russia and Poland from the Earliest Times Until the Present Day*, vol. 2 (Philadelphia: Jewish Publication Society of America, 1918), 254–255.
18. "The Jews in Russia," *Jewish Chronicle*, May 20, 1881; and Dubnow, *History of the Jews in Russia and Poland*, 254.
19. "The Jews in Russia," *Jewish Chronicle*, May 20, 1881.
20. "The Jews in Russia," *Jewish Chronicle*, June 24, 1881.
21. *Jewish Chronicle*, May 1881, www.vladimirets.org/pale_of_settlement.htm.
22. "The Jews in Russia," *Jewish Chronicle*, May 20, 1881.
23. Klier and Lambroza, *Pogroms*, 39.
24. Aronson, "The Anti-Jewish Pogroms in Russia in 1881," in Klier and Lambroza, *Pogroms*, 50.
25. Daniel Field, "Nationality Groups in Russia around 1900," www.choices.edu/resources/supplemental_russianrevolution_2.php.
26. Walter Moss, *A History of Russia* (London: Anthem Press, 2005), 84. Moss cites Robert F. Byrnes, *Pobedonostev: His Life and Thought* (Bloomington: Indiana University Press, 1968), 207.
27. William J. Fishman, *East End Jewish Radicals, 1875–1914* (London: Duckworth, 1975), 30.

3. The Victorian East End

1. "London: The Greatest City," Channel4.com, www.channel4.com/history/microsites/H/history/i-m/london4.html.
2. Arthur Morrison, *Tales of Mean Streets* (Boston: Roberts Bros., 1895), 15.
3. John Henry Mackay, *The Anarchists: A Picture of Civilization at the Close of the Nineteenth Century* (New York: Humboldt Publishing, 1894), 152.
4. "At Last," *Times* (London), September 19, 1888.
5. "The Whitechapel Tragedies. A Night Spent with Inspector Moore," *Pall Mall Gazette*, November 4, 1889.
6. William J. Fishman, "Tower Hamlets 1888." Originally published in the *East London Record*, no. 2, 1979.
7. "At Last," *Times* (London).

8. Alan Palmer, *The East End, Four Centuries of London Life* (London: J. Murray, 1989), 73.

9. Ibid., 90–92.

10. John Law (Margaret Harkness), *Captain Lobe: Or in Darkest London* (Cambridge, UK: Black Apollo Press, 1889), 103–104.

11. Helen Ware, "Prostitution and the State: The Recruitment, Regulation, and Role of Prostitution in the Nineteenth and Twentieth Century" (PhD thesis, University of London, 1969), 408.

12. William Acton, *Prostitution, Considered in Its Moral, Social and Sanitary Aspects*, 2nd edition (London: John Churchill and Sons, 1870).

13. Stephan Ridgway, "Sexuality and Modernity," A lecture for Sociology at Sydney University, 1996, www.isis.aust.com/stephan/writings/sexuality.

14. Charles Booth, Albert Fried, *Charles Booth's London: A Portrait of the Poor at the Turn of the Century, Drawn from His Life and Labour of the People in London*, ed. A Fried and R. Elman (Pantheon Books, 1968), 128.

15. Paula Bartley, *Prostitution: Prevention and Reform in England, 1860–1914* (New York: Routledge, 2000), 10.

16. Jack London, *People of the Abyss* (New York: Macmillan, 1903), 37.

17. Edward J. Bristow, *Prostitution and Prejudice: The Jewish Fight against White Slavery, 1870–1939* (Oxford: Clarendon Press, 1982), 21.

18. Ibid., footnote p. 55.

19. Rosemary O'Day and David Englander, *Mr Charles Booth's Inquiry: Life and Labour of the People in London Reconsidered* (London: Hambledon Press, 1993), 79, cites Passfield MS Diary, xii, 172.

20. Hermann Adler, "Report to Home Office on the Problem of Prostitution in the Jewish Community," in James Knowles, ed., *The Nineteenth Century*, vol. 23 (London: Kegan Paul, Trench 1888), 415.

21. Bristow, *Prostitution and Prejudice*, 237.

22. William J. Fishman, *East End Jewish Radicals, 1875–1914* (London: Duckworth, 1975), footnote p. 51.

23. Robert F. Haggard, "Jack the Ripper as the Threat of Outcast London," in *Essays in History*, published by the Corcoran Department of History at the University of Virginia, 1993.

24. Andrew Mearns, *Bitter Cry of Outcast London: An Inquiry into the Condition of the Abject Poor* (London: James Clarke, 1883).

25. London, *People of the Abyss*, 25.

26. Mearns, *Bitter Cry of Outcast London*, 6.

27. London, *People of the Abyss*, viii.

28. Queen Victoria to William Gladstone, October 30, 1883, in G. E. Buckle, ed., *Letters of Queen Victoria*, second series (London: John Murray, 1926), III, 452, quoted in Palmer, *The East End*, 83.

29. Palmer, *The East End*, 83.

30. MEPO, Supt. Arnold (H Division), report submitted to Commissioner Monro, August 3, 1889.

31. "Whitechapel Horrors," *Times* (London), July 23, 1889.

32. Jacqueline Banerjee, "How Safe Was Victorian London?" Victorian Web, www.victorianweb .org/history/crime/banerjee1.html.

33. MEPO, Supt. Arnold (H Division), report submitted to Commissioner Monro, August 3, 1889.

34. Home Office, August 6, 1889, A49301/173, cited in Stewart Evans and Keith Skinner, *The Ultimate Jack the Ripper Companion: An Illustrated Encyclopedia* (New York: Carroll and Graf, 2000), 473–474.

35. "The Whitechapel Tragedies. A Night Spent with Inspector Moore," *Pall Mall Gazette*, November 4, 1889.
36. Letter from James Monro to the Home Office, May 5, 1889.
37. "The Whitechapel Tragedies. A Night Spent with Inspector Moore," *Pall Mall Gazette*, November 4, 1889.

4. Jewish Tailors in the East End
1. E-mail correspondence with Adam Weglowski, of *Focus Historia* monthly (Poland), June 2008.
2. Marriage Certificate of Abram Jozef Koziminskiewicz and Golda Lubnowska, 1844, State Archives, Poznan, Poland. The exact year of Golda's birth is again unknown and is based on her age in later documents, which vary somewhat.
3. Birth certificates of Pessa Elka Kozminska, Hinde Kozminska, Iciek Szyme Kozminski, Malke Ruchel Kozminska, Blimbe Laje Kozminska, and Aron Mordke Kozminski, all from the State Archives, Poznan, Poland.
4. Michał Rawita-Witanowski, *Kłodawa i jej okolice: Pod względem historyczno-ludoznawczym*, http://books.google.com/books?id=woIBAAAAYAAJ&client=safari&source=gbs_navlinks_s.
5. Death certificate, Abram Kozminski, January 18/30, 1874. Register of Jewish deaths at Kłodawa, 1874, number 1, State Archives, Poznan, Poland.
6. Book of Permanent Residents (Index and Book 130, p. 104), Kłodawa, Polish State Archives, Konin, undated entries.
7. Mosiek and Malke's marriage certificate has not yet been found.
8. Birth certificate of Mosiek Lubnowski, January 6, 1857, State Archives, Poznan, Poland.
9. Correspondence with a descendant of Matilda and Morris Lubnowski, 2007.
10. The Lubnowskis' firstborn son, Joseph, was born in Germany circa 1878–1880 (as indicated on the 1891 London Census).
11. Marriage certificate of Wolek Lajb (later Woolf) Kozminski and Brucha (later Betsy) Kozminska (at Kolo), May 5/17, 1881.
12. William J. Fishman, *East End Jewish Radicals, 1875–1914* (Nottingham: Five Leaves Publications, 2004), 37.
13. Ibid., 33, quotes Lloyd Gartner, *The Jewish Immigrant in England (1870–1914)* (London: Allen and Unwin 1960), 27.
14. Charles Booth, ed, *Life and Labour of the People in London*, vol. 1 (London: Williams and Norgate, 1889), 582–583.
15. George R. Sims, "Sweated London," in George R. Sims, ed., *Living London* (London: Cassell, 1902), 52.
16. Ibid, 53.
17. Booth, *Life and Labour of the People in London*, 148.
18. Fishman, *East End Jewish Radicals*, 47.
19. "Our Foreign Poor," editorial in the *Jewish Chronicle*, August 12, 1881.
20. Fishman, *East End Jewish Radicals, 1875–1914*, 32–33.
21. Testimony of Ellis Franklin to House of Commons Select Committee on Alien Immigration, First Report, 1888.
22. Isaac Abrahams's son Mark was born on December 19, 1872, at which time Isaac's address was listed as 13 Fieldgate Street. Birth registration, January 18, 1873. General Register Office (GRO) reference: Whitechapel 1c 399.
23. Charles Booth online archive, http://booth.lse.ac.uk/. Survey notebooks concerning the tailoring trade, B109, p. 69.
24. Woolf Abrahams's naturalization application, December 1886–January 1887, HO 144/187/A45961.
25. *Illustrated Police News*, April 24, 1886.

26. Booth notebooks, B8, pp. 91, 93. In July 1887, Woolf was still registered at 62 Greenfield Street (1888 electoral register). By July 1888, his address was unknown.

27. Booth Poverty Map, 1889, Charles Booth Online Archive, http://booth.lse.ac.uk.

28. Morris Lubnowski Naturalization Application, June–August 1888.

29. Booth notebooks, B109, p. 69.

30. Booth, "The Inhabitants of Tower Hamlets (School [June 1887] Board Division), Their Condition and Occupations," *Journal of the Royal Statistical Society* (1887): 370.

31. Booth notebooks, A19, p. 38, and B109, p. 69. These workshops can be seen on an 1894 London Ordinance Survey map of the area.

32. Booth notebooks, A19, pp. 78–82.

33. Ibid., p. 79.

34. Lou Taylor, *The Study of Dress History* (New York: Palgrave, 2002), 94. Quoting Arthur A. Baumann, MP, "Possible Remedies for the Sweating System," *National Review* 12, no. 69 (November 1888): 289–307.

35. J. A. Dyche, "A Trade Created by Jewish Immigrants: The History of the Mantle Trade in England," *Jewish Chronicle*, April 22, 1898.

36. Ibid.

37. Booth, ed., *Life and Labour of the People in London*, 102.

38. Interview with Mr. Zeitlin, December 9, 1887, Booth notebooks, A19, pp. 53–57.

39. Myer Wilchinski, "History of a Sweater," *Commonweal*, May and June 1888, cited in Fishman, *East End Jewish Radicals, 1875–1914*, p. 45, and Bishop of Bedford to House of Lords' Committee, in William H. Wilkins, *The Alien Invasion* (London: Methuen, 1892), 43.

40. Wilkins, *The Alien Invasion*, 44.

41. "Busy and Slack in London," *Poilishe Yidl*, September 19, 1884, quoted in Fishman, *East End Jewish Radicals, 1875–1914*, 144.

42. Sims, *Living London*, 55.

43. Fishman, *East End Jewish Radicals, 1875–1914*, 136.

44. *Jewish Chronicle*, May 16, 1884, cited in Fishman, *East End Jewish Radicals*, 136.

45. "The Haunts of the East End Anarchist," *Evening Standard*, October 2, 1894.

46. Alan Palmer, *The East End, Four Centuries of London Life* (London: J. Murray, 1989), 105.

47. *Poilishe Yidl*, no. 11, October 3, 1884, cited in Fishman, *East End Jewish Radicals*, 90.

48. Letter to the *Pall Mall Gazette*, February 1886, quoted in Palmer, *The East End, Four Centuries of London Life*, 100.

49. Stephen Fox, "The Invasion of the Pauper Foreigners," *Contemporary Review* (June 1888): 861. Quoted in "Jack the Ripper as the Threat of Outcast London," by Robert F. Haggard, *Essays in History* (Corcoran Department of History at the University of Virginia, 1993).

50. *Pall Mall Gazette*, March 9, 1887.

51. "Memorial of Chinese Laborers, Resident at Rock Springs, Wyoming Territory, to the Chinese Consul at New York," 1885, U.S. House Report (1885–1886), 49th Congress, 1st Session, no. 2044, p. 28–32. Cited in Judy Yung, Gordon H. Chang, and H. Mark Lai, *Chinese American Voices: From the Gold Rush to the Present* (Berkeley and Los Angeles: University of California Press, 2006), 52.

52. *St. James's Gazette*, May 1887, cited in Fishman, *East End Jewish Radicals*, 70.

53. Arnold White, "The Modern Jew," letter to the editor, *London Times*, 1899.

54. Fishman, *East End Jewish Radicals, 1875–1914*, 71.

55. *East London Advertiser*, March 3, 1888, cited in Anne J. Kershen, *Strangers, Aliens, and Asians: Huguenots, Jews, and Bangladeshis in Spitalfields, 1660–2000* (New York: Routledge, 2005), 177.

56. Interviews with Mr. Goldstein, Mr. Rosen, and Mr. Solomon, conducted March 1, 1888, Booth notebooks, A19, pp. 78–82.

57. Dyche, "A Trade Created by Jewish Immigrants."
58. Beatrice Potter, "Pages from a Work-Girl's Diary," in *Nineteenth Century* (London: Kegan Paul, Trench 1888), 120.
59. *Diary of Beatrice Webb*, vol. 1 (Cambridge, MA: Belknap Press, Harvard University, 1982), 267.
60. Beatrice Webb, *My Apprenticeship* (Cambridge, UK: Press Syndicate of the University of Cambridge, 1979), 331.
61. Ibid.
62. Booth, *Life and Labour of the People in London*, 108.
63. Fishman, *East End Jewish Radicals*, 71.
64. Booth, *Life and Labour of the People in London*, 492.
65. Arnold White, *The Destitute Alien in Great Britain* (London: S. Sonnenschein, 1892), 87.
66. Fishman, *East End Jewish Radicals, 1875–1914*, 44.
67. Select Committee of the House of Lords, Report on the Sweating System, Parliamentary Papers, 1890, vol. XVII.
68. Ibid.
69. Ibid.
70. Ibid.
71. Ibid.
72. Ibid.
73. Wilchinski, "History of a Sweater," cited in Fishman, *East End Jewish Radicals, 1875–1914*, 46.
74. "The Pages from a Work Girl's Diary," *Nineteenth Century*, September 1888.
75. Select Committee of the House of Lords, "Report on the Sweating System."
76. "A Sweater's Meeting," *East London Observer*, Saturday, June 30, 1888.
77. "The Magistrate and the Pole," *Jewish Chronicle*, September 14, 1888.
78. *Arbeter Fraint*, March 15, 1889, cited in Fishman, *East End Jewish Radicals*, 165.
79. Fishman, *East End Jewish Radicals*, 167.
80. Ibid., 163–168.
81. Ibid., 173.
82. Ibid., 166.
83. "Interview with the Secretary," *East London Observer*, September 21, 1889.
84. *Jewish Chronicle*, September 6, 1889, cited in Fishman, *East End Jewish Radicals*, 174.
85. Fishman, *East End Jewish Radicals*, 73; and Fishman, "Tower Hamlets 1888."
86. Robert K. Ressler, Ann Wolbert Burgess, and John E. Douglas, *Sexual Homicide: Patterns and Motives* (New York: Simon and Schuster, 1995), 71.
87. Letter printed in the *Pall Mall Gazette*, February 1886.

5. The Murders Begin

1. "Alleged Fatal Stabbing Case in Whitechapel," *Eastern Post and City Chronicle*, April 7, 1888. (Most of the newspaper reports cited concerning the murders were from the very extensive "Press Reports" section of the Web site casebook.org. I am indebted to the Web site and to the many people who spent countless hours transcribing the reports.)
2. Ibid.
3. "Attempted Murder at Mile End," *East London Observer*, March 31, 1888.
4. "Money or Your Life," *East London Advertiser*, March 31, 1888.
5. "Extraordinary Outrage at Bow. Attack on a Dressmaker," *Eastern Post and City Chronicle*, March 31, 1888.
6. Ibid.
7. Quentin L. Pittman, "The Importance of Fairy Fay, and Her Link to Emma Smith," posted at www.casebook.org/dissertations/importance-fairy.html.

8. "Extraordinary Outrage at Bow. Attack on a Dressmaker," *Eastern Post and City Chronicle*, March 31, 1888. Two of the other Whitechapel murders also occurred on or near Jewish holidays. The attack on Annie Millwood took place on the first day of Purim, which was scheduled to begin after sundown on February 25. The murder of Annie Chapman took place on the second day of Rosh Hashanah, a holiday during which Jews believe that God passes judgment on all humanity and the wicked receive a judgment of death.

9. "Alleged Fatal Stabbing Case in Whitechapel," *Eastern Post and City Chronicle*, April 7, 1888.

10. Philip Sugden, *The Complete History of Jack the Ripper* (New York: Carroll and Graf, 2002), chap. 2, n. 25.

11. "Horrible Affair in Whitechapel," *People* (London), April 15, 1888.

12. Ibid.

13. "Horrible Murder in Whitechapel," *Lloyd's Weekly Newspaper*, April 8, 1888.

14. "A Brutal Murder," *Walthamstow and Leyton Guardian* (UK), April 14, 1888.

15. "Horrible Murder in Whitechapel," *Lloyd's Weekly Newspaper*, April 8, 1888.

16. MEPO, Report of Inspector Edmund Reid, in Stewart Evans and Keith Skinner, *The Ultimate Jack the Ripper Companion* (New York: Carroll and Graf, 2000), 4.

17. Ibid.

18. "Inquests," *Times* (London), April 9, 1888.

19. "The Horrible Murder in Whitechapel," *Morning Advertiser* (London), April 9, 1888.

20. "The Latest Whitechapel Mystery," *Eastern Post and City Chronicle*, April 14, 1888.

6. Martha Tabram

1. "The Theatre. Mr. Richard Mansfield at the Lyceum," *Daily News* (London), August 6, 1888.

2. "A Dull Bank Holiday," *Star* (London), August 7, 1888.

3. "The Whitechapel Murder," *Eastern Post and City Chronicle*, August 18, 1888.

4. "Supposed Murder in Whitechapel," *Daily News* (London) and other papers, August 8, 1888.

5. "A Whitechapel Mystery," *East London Observer*, August 11, 1888.

6. "Dreadful Murder in Whitechapel," *East London Advertiser*, August 11, 1888.

7. "Whitechapel Mystery," *Echo*, August 13, 1888.

8. "Brutal Murder of a Woman," *Morning Advertiser*, August 8, 1888.

9. Report of Inspector Reid, MEPO, August 24, 1888.

10. "The Whitechapel Tragedy. Verdict of the Coroner's Jury on the Revolting Murder," *Star*, August 24, 1888.

11. "The Whitechapel Mystery," *East London Observer*, August 25, 1888.

12. Report of Inspector Reid, MEPO, August 16, 1888.

13. Report of Inspector Reid, MEPO, September 24, 1888.

14. "The Whitechapel Mystery," *East London Observer*, August 25, 1888.

15. Ibid.

16. "Whitechapel Mystery. Soldiers Parade at the Tower," *Echo*, August 13, 1888.

17. Report of Inspector Reid, MEPO, September 24, 1888.

18. "The Murder Mystery. A Clue at Last," *Echo*, August 17, 1888; and Report of Inspector Reid, MEPO, September 24, 1888.

19. MEPO, summary report by Donald Sutherland Swanson, dated September 1888.

20. "A Whitechapel Mystery," *East London Observer*, August 11, 1888.

21. "Brutal Murder of a Woman," *Morning Advertiser*, August 8, 1888.

22. "Whitechapel Mystery," *Echo*, August 10, 1888.

23. "The Whitechapel Murder. Inquest," *Evening News* (London), August 10, 1888.

24. "A Whitechapel Mystery," *East London Observer*, August 11, 1888.
25. MEPO, summary report by Donald Sutherland Swanson, September 1888.
26. "A Whitechapel Mystery," *East London Observer*, August 11, 1888.
27. Ibid.
28. "Alleged Fatal Stabbing Case in Whitechapel," *Eastern Post and City Chronicle*, April 7, 1888.
29. "A Whitechapel Mystery," *East London Observer*, August 11, 1888.
30. "Dreadful Murder in Whitechapel," *East London Advertiser*, August 11, 1888.
31. *Illustrated Police News*, August 18, 1888, cited in Philip Sugden, *The Complete History of Jack the Ripper* (New York: Carroll and Graf, 2002), 18.
32. *Daily Telegraph*, August 23, 1888, found at www.casebook.org/official_documents/inquests/inquest_tabram.html.
33. "Whitechapel Mystery," *Echo*, August 10, 1888.
34. Ibid.
35. "A Whitechapel Mystery," *East London Observer*, August 11, 1888.

7. Polly Nichols

1. "The Whitechapel Murder," *Times* (London), September 4, 1888.
2. Philip Sugden, *The Complete History of Jack the Ripper* (New York: Carroll and Graf, 2002), 44.
3. Neal Shelden, *The Victims of Jack the Ripper* (Knoxville: Inklings Press, 2007), 9.
4. Sugden, *The Complete History of Jack the Ripper*, 45.
5. James Greenwood, *In Strange Company: Being the Experiences of a Roving Correspondent* (London: Vizetelly, 1883), 158–160.
6. "Amadeus" (correspondent), *Tower Hamlets Independent*, February 4, 1882, cited in William J. Fishman, *East End Jewish Radicals, 1875–1914* (London: Duckworth, 1975), 58.
7. Sugden, *The Complete History of Jack the Ripper*, 35.
8. "The Whitechapel Murders," *Times* (London), September 24, 1888.
9. Sugden, *The Complete History of Jack the Ripper*, 35.
10. Leonard Matters, *The Mystery of Jack the Ripper: The World's Greatest Crime Problem* (London: Hutchinson, 1929), 36.
11. "The Whitechapel Murder: Inquest Resumed," *Echo*, September 3, 1888.
12. Ibid.
13. "The Whitechapel Murder," *Daily Telegraph*, September 3, 1888.
14. "The Whitechapel Murders," *Times* (London), September 18, 1888.
15. "The Murder in Whitechapel," *Evening Standard* (London), September 3, 1888.
16. *Daily Telegraph*, Monday, September 3, 1888.
17. MEPO, Report of Inspector J. Spratling, August 31, 1888.
18. "Whitechapel-Road Murder: To the Editor of the *Echo*," *Echo*, September 5, 1888.
19. "The Whitechapel Murder," *Times* (London), September 3, 1888.
20. "The Whitechapel Murder: Funeral of the Victim," *Echo*, September 6, 1888.

8. The Police

1. CID Report, October 19, 1888. Cited in Stewart P. Evans and Keith Skinner, *The Ultimate Jack the Ripper Companion: An Illustrated Encyclopedia* (New York: Carroll and Graf, 2000), 29.
2. *Echo*, September 5, 1888, www.casebook.org/press_reports/echo/18880905.html.
3. "Leather Apron," *Star*, September 5, 1888.
4. "Leather Apron. Mysterious Murders in London Credited to a Strange, Half Crazy Character," *Atchison Daily Globe*, September 5, 1888.
5. Report by Inspector Joseph Henry Helson, Local Inspector, CID, J Division, September 7, 1888; Ref MEPO 3/140, ff. 235–238.
6. Stewart P. Evans and Donald Rumbelow, *Jack the Ripper: Scotland Yard Investigates* (Stroud: Sutton, 2006), 10.

7. Paul Begg and Keith Skinner, *The Scotland Yard Files: 150 Years of the C.I.D. 1842–1992* (London: Headline, 1992), 98.

8. A. P. Moore Anderson, *Sir Robert Anderson K.C.B, LL.D., and Lady Agnes Anderson* (London: Marshall, Morgan and Scott, 1947), 23.

9. Ibid, 34.

10. Evans and Rumbelow, *Jack the Ripper*, 18.

11. Anderson, *Sir Robert Anderson K.C.B, LL.D., and Lady Agnes Anderson*, 37.

12. Sir Robert Anderson, *The Lighter Side of My Official Life* (London: Hodder and Stoughton, 1910), 92.

13. Ibid, 91, and Evans and Rumbelow, *Jack the Ripper*, 21.

9. Annie Chapman

1. Neal Shelden, *The Victims of Jack the Ripper* (Knoxville: Inklings Press, 2007), 13.

2. Ibid., 16–17.

3. Stewart P. Evans and Keith Skinner, *The Ultimate Jack the Ripper Companion: An Illustrated Encyclopedia* (New York: Carroll and Graf, 2000), 7.

4. Ralph Finn, *No Tears in Aldgate* (London: Robert Hale, 1963), 124.

5. Philip Sugden, *The Complete History of Jack the Ripper* (New York: Carroll and Graf, 2002), 79.

6. Ibid., 80–81.

7. "The Whitechapel Murders: The Inquest," *Times* (London), September 11, 1888.

8. Ibid.

9. Sugden, *The Complete History of Jack the Ripper*, 82.

10. Robin F. Rowland, "The Killer Stalked a Foul and Stinking Neighborhood," *Globe and Mail* (Toronto), August 30, 1988.

11. "The Whitechapel Murder: The Adjourned Inquest," *Times* (London), September 13, 1888.

12. "Inquests," *Times* (London), September 20, 1888.

13. "The Whitechapel Murders," *Daily Telegraph*, September 20, 1988.

14. Ibid.; and "Inquests," *Times* (London), September 20, 1888.

15. "Another Whitechapel Murder," *Echo*, September 8, 1988.

16. "The Whitechapel Crimes: Killed by Emotion," *Star*, September 13, 1988.

17. "The Whitechapel Murder. (Inquest)," *Times* (London), September 14, 1988.

18. Ibid.

19. "Inquests," *Times* (London), September 20, 1988.

20. Ibid.

21. Ibid.

22. "The Whitechapel Murders," *Lancet*, September 29, 1988.

23. "News from Whitechapel," *Daily Telegraph*, September 10, 1888.

24. Walter Dew, *I Caught Crippen: Memoirs of Ex-Chief Inspector Walter Dew, C.I.D., of Scotland Yard* (London: Blackie and Son, 1938).

25. *Report to Home Office*, October 29, 1888, HO 144/221/A49301C, ff. 163–170.

26. "A Riot against the Jews," *East London Observer*, September 15, 1888. "On Saturday" refers to the previous Saturday, September 8.

27. "Yesterday's Whitechapel Tragedy," *Lloyd's Weekly Newspaper*, September 9, 1888.

28. "The Editor's Draw: Slaughtering the Jews," *Evening News*, September 11, 1888. Hutt's letter was dated September 10.

29. "The Whitechapel Murders. Inquest on Mrs. Chapman," *Evening Standard*, September 13, 1888.

30. "The Whitechapel Horrors: Scenes at the Inquest," *East London Advertiser*, September 15, 1888.

31. George Sims ("Dagonet"), *Sunday Referee*, September 16, 1888, www.casebook.org/press_reports/dagonet.html.

32. "Notes of the Week," *Jewish Chronicle*, September 14, 1888.
33. *Jewish Standard*, September 14, 1888, http://forum.casebook.org/showpost.php?p=124935&postcount=2.
34. Sugden, *The Complete History of Jack the Ripper*, 124.
35. "The Whitechapel Murders," *Daily Telegraph*, September 20, 1888.
36. Letter from Sir Charles Warren, dated September 15, 1888.
37. Sir Charles Warren, September 19, 1888, report to Ruggles-Brise, HO 144/221/A49301C/8.
38. Phillip Sugden cites Public Records Office MEPO 3/3153, ff. 1–4.

10. Elizabeth Stride
1. From a report by Chief Inspector Donald S. Swanson to the Home Office, dated October 19, 1888, and from "Whitechapel," *Star*, October 1, 1888.
2. Donald Rumbelow, *The Complete Jack the Ripper* (London: Penguin, 2004), 53.
3. "The Murders at the East End," *Times* (London), October 2, 1888.
4. Ibid.
5. "The East End Murders," *Times* (London), October 3, 1888.
6. Ibid.
7. "The East End Murders," *Times* (London), October 3, 1888.
8. Ibid.
9. Philip Sugden, *The Complete History of Jack the Ripper* (New York: Carroll and Graf, 2002), 196.
10. MEPO 3/140/221/A49301C, ff. 215–216.
11. HO 144/221/A49301C, ff. 148–159.
12. "London Tragedies. Berner Street Inquest," *Daily Telegraph*, October 6, 1888.
13. "The East End Murders," *Times* (London), October 6, 1888.
14. Ibid.
15. "The Inquest," *Daily Telegraph*, Tuesday, October 2, 1888.
16. "The Whitechapel Murders," *Morning Advertiser*, October 6, 1888.
17. "London Tragedies. Berner Street Inquest," *Daily Telegraph*, Sunday, October 6, 1888.
18. "The Whitechapel Horrors: Horrible Murder of a Woman Near Commercial Road," *Evening News*, October 1, 1888.
19. "Two More Murders at the East End: Statements by Residents," *Daily News*, October 1, 1888.
20. Ibid.
21. "Two More Murders at the East End: The Murder in Berner Street," *Daily News*, October 1, 1888.
22. Report of Frederick Abberline, November 1, 1888.
23. *Die Tsukunft*, August 12, 1887, quoted in Martin L. Friedland, *The Trials of Israel Lipski: A True Story of a Victorian Murder in the East End of London* (New York: Beaufort, 1984), 118.
24. "Two More Murders at the East End: Statements by Residents," *Daily News*, October 1, 1888.
25. Dave Yost, "Elizabeth Stride: Her Killer and Time of Death," in *Ripperologist*, no. 21, February 1999.
26. Donald Swanson's report to the Home Office on the Stride murder, October 19, 1888. Stewart Evans and Keith Skinner, *The Ultimate Jack the Ripper Companion: An Illustrated Encyclopedia* (New York: Carroll and Graf, 2000), cites Ref. HO 144/221/A49301C, ff. 148–159.
27. Inquest testimony of P.C. Smith, reported in "London Tragedies. Berner-Street Inquest," *Daily Telegraph*, October 6, 1888.

11. Kate Eddowes
1. Inquest testimony of Frederick William Williamson, ref. Coroner's Inquest (L), 1888, no. 135, Catherine Eddowes inquest, 1888 (Corporation of London Records Office),

cited in Stewart P. Evans and Keith Skinner, *The Ultimate Jack the Ripper Companion: An Illustrated Encyclopedia* (New York: Carroll and Graf, 2000), 200.

2. Inquest testimony of Louis Robinson, as printed in Evans and Skinner, *The Ultimate Jack the Ripper Companion*, 209–210, and "The London Tragedies. Mitre Square Inquest," *Daily Telegraph*, October 12, 1888.

3. From inquest testimony of George H. Hutt, printed in Evans and Skinner, *The Ultimate Jack the Ripper Companion*, 210, and "The London Tragedies. Mitre Square Inquest," *Daily Telegraph*, October 12, 1888.

4. Toni L. Kamins, *The Complete Jewish Guide to Britain and Ireland* (New York: St. Martin's Griffin, 2001), 60.

5. "The East End Atrocities: The Mitre Square Murder, Inquest and Verdict," *Daily News*, October 12, 1888.

6. Neil Bell, "Jack by Gaslight," *Ripperologist*, no. 58, March 2005.

7. Inquest testimony of P.C. Watkins.

8. "The London Tragedies: Mitre Square Inquest," *Daily Telegraph*, October 12, 1888.

9. "The East End Murders," *Times* (London), October 5, and "The East End Murders," *Times* (London), October 12, 1888.

10. *Times* (London), October 5, 1888, as printed in Evans and Skinner, *The Ultimate Jack the Ripper Companion*, 221.

11. Philip Sugden, *The Complete History of Jack the Ripper* (New York: Carroll and Graf, 2002), 176.

12. Dr. F. Brown, Inquest, in Evans and Skinner, *The Ultimate Jack the Ripper Companion*, 204–207, 221–224.

13. Derek F. Osborne, "A Curious Find in Goulston Street," Ripper Notes, www.casebook.org/dissertations/rn-curious.html.

14. Daniel Halse, Inquest testimony, *Times* (London), October 12, 1888; and report of Donald S. Swanson to the Home Office, November 6, 1888, ref. HO 144/221/A49301C, ff. 184–194, cited in Evans and Skinner, *The Ultimate Jack the Ripper Companion*, 185–188.

15. P.C. Long, inquest testimony, *Times* (London), October 12, 1888.

16. Daniel Halse, inquest testimony, *Times* (London), October 12, 1888.

17. Commissioner Charles Warren, Report to Home Office, written November 6, 1888, in Evans and Skinner, *The Ultimate Jack the Ripper Companion*, 183–184.

18. P.C. Long, inquest testimony, *Times* (London), October 12, 1888.

19. Commissioner Charles Warren, report to the Home Office, written November 6, 1888, in Evans and Skinner, *The Ultimate Jack the Ripper Companion*, 182–184, ref. HO 144/221/A49301C, ff. 173–181.

20. Report of Donald Swanson submitted to the Home Office, November 6, 1888, in Evans and Skinner, *The Ultimate Jack the Ripper Companion*, 185, ref. HO 144/221/A49301C, ff. 184–194.

21. Halse, inquest testimony, *Times* (London), October 12, 1888.

22. Sugden, *The Complete History of Jack the Ripper*, 254.

23. Charles Warren, letter to Godfrey Lushington, October 10, 1888, in Sugden, *The Complete History of Jack the Ripper*, 256.

24. Israel Zangwill, "Zangwill's Ghetto. Petticoat Lane on a Sunday Morning," *Star* (New Zealand), November 18, 1899.

12. Lonesome October

1. "The Whitechapel Horrors: East London in a Panic," *East London Observer*, October 6, 1888.

2. The letter is in Scotland Yard's Crime Museum. Philip Sugden cites Public Record Office, MEPO 3/3153, ff. 1–4.

3. Letter to Godfrey Lushington at Home Office, October 10, 1888, National Archives, Commissioner's letters file, MEPO 1/48.

4. Sir Robert Anderson, "The Lighter Side of My Official Life," *Blackwood's Edinburgh Magazine*, March 1910.

5. "The Littlechild Letter," discovered by, and property of, Stewart Evans.

6. Stewart P. Evans and Donald Rumbelow. *Jack the Ripper: Scotland Yard Investigates* (Stroud: Sutton, 2006), 113.

7. Report of James McWilliam, head of Detective Department, City of London Police, October 27, 1888, cited in Stewart P. Evans and Keith Skinner, *The Ultimate Jack the Ripper Companion: An Illustrated Encyclopedia* (New York: Carroll and Graf, 2000), 181.

8. Sir Robert Anderson, "The Lighter Side of My Official Life," *Blackwood's Edinburgh Magazine*, March 1910.

9. Philip Sugden, *The Complete History of Jack the Ripper* (New York: Carroll and Graf, 2002), 300.

10. "Apprehensions Sought," *Police Gazette*, October 5, 1888.

11. Report of James McWilliam to Home Office, October 27, 1888.

12. Report of Chief Inspector Donald S. Swanson, November 6, 1888, to Home Office.

13. Sugden, *The Complete History of Jack the Ripper*, 291.

14. Report of Chief Inspector Donald S. Swanson, October 19, 1888, to Home Office.

15. Vienna Correspondent, "The Whitechapel Murders," *Times* (London), October 2, 1888.

16. Letter from Dr. Hermann Adler, "The Murder Near Cracow. To the Editor of the Times," *Times* (London), October 3, 1888.

17. Letter from Moses Gaster, "The Murder Near Cracow. To the Editor of the Times," *Times* (London), October 3, 1888.

18. Letter from A Butcher, "Is the Whitechapel Murderer a Jew? Important Letter," *Evening News*, October 9, 1888.

19. Ibid.

20. "The City Murder," *Jewish Chronicle*, October 12, 1888.

21. Testimony of Joseph Lawende, *Daily Telegraph*, October 12, 1888.

22. "The Murders," *Evening News*, October 9, 1888.

23. "Apprehensions Sought. Murder. Metropolitan Police District," *Police Gazette*, October 19, 1888.

24. "The Handwriting on the Wall," *Pall Mall Gazette*, October 12, 1888.

25. "The Writing on the Wall," *Evening News*, October 12, 1888.

26. "Dangerous Errors," *Star*, October 12, 1888.

27. "Notes of the Week," *Jewish Chronicle*, October 12, 1888.

28. Letter from Dr. Hermann Adler to Commissioner Warren, October 13, 1888.

29. "The East End Murders," *Evening News*, October 15, 1888.

13. The Batty Street "Lodger"

1. "East End Tragedies," *Echo*, October 15, 1888.

2. Ibid.

3. "The Murders," *Evening News*, October 16, 1888.

4. "East-End Atrocities," *Echo*, October 17, 1888.

5. "Ludwig Released," *Star*, October 2, 1888.

6. "Ludwig Flourishes a Knife," *Star*, October 17, 1888.

7. "The Batty Street Clue," *Echo*, October 17, 1888.

8. "The East End Murders. A House to House Search," *Daily News*, October 18, 1888.

9. "A Letter from 22, Batty Street," *Evening News*, October 18, 1888.

10. "Interview with the Landlady in Berner Street," *Evening News*, October 18, 1888.

11. Home Office memo to Henry Matthews, September 19, 1888, HO 144/221/A49301E/4.

12. "East End Atrocities," *Echo*, October 20, 1888.

13. Ibid.
14. "East End Atrocities. Police Active—Still No Clue," *Echo*, October 29, 1888.
15. Donald Swanson, marginalia in his personal copy of Robert Anderson's book *The Lighter Side of My Official Life*, property of Nevill Swanson, on permanent loan to New Scotland Yard's Crime Museum.
16. Sir Robert Anderson, "The Lighter Side of My Official Life," *Blackwood's Edinburgh*, March 1910.
17. Report of Donald S. Swanson, October 19, 1888, cited in Stewart P. Evans and Keith Skinner, *The Ultimate Jack the Ripper Companion: An Illustrated Encyclopedia* (New York: Carroll and Graf, 2000), 125.
18. Report of Robert Anderson to Home Office, October 23, 1888, cited in Evans and Skinner, *The Ultimate Jack the Ripper Companion*, 133–134.
19. Chief Inspector Donald S. Swanson report to Home Office, October 19, 1888.
20. The "From Hell" letter disappeared from the Metropolitan Police Archives, and its present whereabouts are unknown. A facsimile is online at www.casebook.org/images/lusk_big.jpg.
21. "The Whitechapel Tragedies," *Sunday Times*, October 21, 1888.
22. Report of James McWilliam, October 27, 1888.
23. John Douglas, Ann Burgess, Allen Burgess, and Robert Ressler, eds., *Crime Classification Manual* (San Francisco: Jossey-Bass, 2006), 464.

14. Mary Kelly

1. "Royalty in the East End," *Daily Telegraph*, November 1, 1888.
2. "A Marylebone Tragedy," *Star*, November 2, 1888.
3. "News of All Sorts," *Star*, November 5, 1888.
4. "The Fifth of November," *Daily News*, November 6, 1888.
5. "The Guy of the Unemployed," *Star*, November 6, 1888.
6. "He was Only Guying," *Evening News*, November 6, 1888.
7. "Lord Mayor's Day," *Times* (London), November 7, 1888.
8. "Whitechapel: Important Evidence at the Inquest To-day," *Star*, November 12, 1888.
9. Ibid.
10. "Dorset-Street Murder. Inquest and Verdict," *Daily Telegraph*, November 13, 1888.
11. Neal Shelden, *The Victims of Jack the Ripper* (Knoxville: Inklings Press, 2007), 43.
12. "Dorset Street Murder. Inquest and Verdict," *Daily Telegraph*, November 13, 1888.
13. "A Timeline of Events in the Life and Death of Mary Jane Kelly," Casebook Productions, www.casebook.org/timeline.kelly.html.
14. "The East End Tragedies: A Seventh Murder," *Daily Telegraph*, November 10, 1888.
15. The exact nature of the partition is unclear. This is discussed extensively on the casebook .org forums thread "Room 13 Miller's Court."
16. "The Inquest," testimony of Joseph Barnett, *Morning Advertiser*, November 13, 1888.
17. Letter from Mahatma Gandhi to his brother Laxmidas, November 9, 1888, posted on casebook.org message board, www.casebook.org/forum/messages/4920/22806.html.
18. "The Murder of Mary Kelly in Whitechapel," *Penny Illustrated Paper*, November 17, 1888. There is still some confusion over whether the woman in Kelly's room that night was Lizzie Albrook or Maria Harvey, because statements that Harvey gave to the police and the press are somewhat contradictory on this point.
19. "Dorset Street Murder. Inquest and Verdict," *Daily Telegraph*, November 13, 1888, and "The Whitechapel Murder: The Inquest," *Morning Advertiser*, November 13, 1888.
20. "The Inquest," *Morning Advertiser*, November 13, 1888.
21. Ibid. There is some debate as to the exact location of Elizabeth Prater's room, because some reports state that Prater's room was directly above Kelly's, whereas others say that she lived at the front of the house.

22. Statement of George Hutchinson, November 12, 1888, ref. MEPO 3/140, ff. 227–229, in Stewart P. Evans and Keith Skinner, *The Ultimate Jack the Ripper Companion: An Illustrated Encyclopedia* (New York: Carroll and Graf, 2000), 376–377.

23. A similar story was reported in "Another Whitechapel Murder," *Times* (London), November 10, 1888.

24. "Dorset Street Murder. Inquest and Verdict," *Daily Telegraph*, November 13, 1888; "The Spitalfields Murder," *Daily News*, November 13, 1888; and "The Whitechapel Murder: The Inquest," *Morning Advertiser*, November 13, 1888.

25. "Dorset Street Murder. Inquest and Verdict," *Daily Telegraph*, November 13, 1888; and "The Whitechapel Murder: The Inquest," *Morning Advertiser*, November 13, 1888.

26. Sarah Lewis's inquest testimony as reported in the *Daily Telegraph*, the *Daily News*, and the *Morning Advertiser*, November 13, 1888.

27. Elwyn Jones and John Lloyd, *The Ripper File* (London: Arthur Baker, 1975), www.casebook .org/forum/messages/4926/19145.html.

28. "The Latest Horror," *Evening News*, November 12, 1888.

29. Dew's recollection of events has come under harsh skepticism by Ripperologists. The above was his recollection of events as printed in his memoir, *I Caught Crippen: Memoirs of Ex-Chief Inspector Walter Dew, C.I.D., of Scotland Yard* (London: Blackie and Son, 1938), 86, 143–155.

30. "The Whitechapel Murder: The Inquest," *Morning Advertiser*, November 13, 1888.

31. "Dorset Street Murder. Inquest and Verdict," *Daily Telegraph*, November 13, 1888.

32. Walter Dew, *I Caught Crippen: Memoirs of Ex-Chief Inspector Walter Dew, C.I.D., of Scotland Yard* (London: Blackie and Son, 1938), 86, 143–155.

33. "The East End Tragedies," *Daily Telegraph*, November 10, 1888.

34. Ibid.

35. "The Whitechapel Murder: The Inquest," *Morning Advertiser*, November 13, 1888.

36. Ibid.

37. "The Whitechapel Murder," *Barking and East Ham Advertiser*, Saturday, November 24, 1888.

38. "The Whitechapel Tragedies. A Night Spent with Inspector Moore," *Pall Mall Gazette*, November 4, 1889.

39. Statement of George Hutchinson, November 12, 1888, ref. MEPO 3/140, ff. 227–229, in Stewart P. Evans and Keith Skinner, *The Ultimate Jack the Ripper Companion: An Illustrated Encyclopedia* (New York: Carroll and Graf, 2000), 376–377.

15. The Curtain Falls

1. "The Whitechapel Murder," *Times* (London), November 12, 1888.

2. *Jewish Chronicle*, November 16, 1888.

3. "The Poplar Murder," *Daily Chronicle*, December 29, 1888.

4. Report of Monro to the Home Office, December 23, 1888.

5. Report of Robert Anderson, January 11, 1889, cited in Stewart P. Evans and Keith Skinner, *The Ultimate Jack the Ripper Companion: An Illustrated Encyclopedia* (New York: Carroll and Graf, 2000), 434.

6. "Is He a Thug?" *Star*, December 24, 1888.

7. Report of James Monro, January 26, 1889, cited in Evans and Skinner, *The Ultimate Jack the Ripper Companion*, 440–441.

8. Report of James Monro, March 15, 1889, cited in Evans and Skinner, *The Ultimate Jack the Ripper Companion*, 444.

9. Statement by Inspector Henry Moore, July 17, 1889, MEPO 3/140 ff. 294–297, and inquest testimony Elizabeth Ryder, *Times* (London), July 18, 1889, and of Margaret Franklin, *Times* (London), July 19, 1889.

10. "The Whitechapel Murder," *Times* (London), July 19, 1889, and HO 3/140, f. 275.
11. Statement of E. Badham, July 17, 1889, cited in Evans and Skinner, *The Ultimate Jack the Ripper Companion*, 448.
12. Report of Dr. Phillips, July 22, 1889, ref. MEPO 3/140, ff. 263–271.
13. Report of Dr. George Phillips, July 22, 1889, cited in Evans and Skinner, *The Ultimate Jack the Ripper Companion*, 455–460.
14. Report of Dr. Bond, ref. MEPO 3/140, ff. 259–262.
15. Ref. HO144 221/A49301I, ff. 5–6.
16. "Does He Know the Ripper?" *New York Herald* (London edition), September 11, 1889.
17. "Does This Man Know the Ripper?" *New York Herald* (London edition), September 11, 1889.
18. Report of Commissioner Monro, September 11, 1889.
19. Report cover from CID Central Office, ref. MEPO 3/140, f. 175.

16. An Encore? The Murder of Frances Coles
1. Report of Superintendent Arnold, February 13, 1891, ref. MEPO 3/140, ff. 112–114.
2. Statement of P.S. John Don, ref. MEPO 3/140, ff. 117–118.
3. Statement of James Thomas Sadler, February 14, 1891, taken by Donald S. Swanson, ref. MEPO 3/140, ff. 97–108.
4. "The Whitechapel Murder," *Times* (London), February 24 and 28, 1891.
5. Statement of Thomas Fowles, taken by Sergeant James Nearn, reference MEPO 3/140, ff. 83–85.
6. Report of Donald Swanson, December 11, 1891, ref. MEPO 3/140, ff. 89–90.

17. Downward Spiral
1. John K. Walton, "Mad Dogs and Englishmen: The Conflict of Rabies in Late Victorian London," *Journal of Social History* 13 (1979): 219–239.
2. Ibid.
3. Charles Dickens, *Dickens's Dictionary of London* (London: Charles Dickens, 1879), 48.
4. Leslie C. Staples, ed., *The Uncommercial Traveller and Reprinted Pieces* (Oxford: Oxford University Press, 1996), 495.
5. "Fined for Unmuzzled Dogs," *Lloyd's Weekly News*, December 15, 1889.
6. "The Rabies Order," *City Press*, December 18, 1889.
7. Commissioner James Monro, interview, *Cassel's Saturday Journal*, c. June 1890.
8. Sir Robert Anderson, "Sir Robert Anderson and Mr. Balfour: To the Editor of the Times," *Times* (London), April 30, 1910.
9. E. M. Leonard, *The Early History of the English Poor Law*, 1900, cited at Peter Higginbotham, Workhouse Web site, http://users.ox.ac.uk/~peter/workhouse/Abingdon/Abingdon .shtml?=.
10. Peter Higginbotham, Workhouse Web site, www.workhouses.org.uk.
11. Anonymous ("One of Them"), *Indoor Paupers* (London: Chatto and Windus, 1885), www .workhouses.org.uk/index.html?IndoorPaupers/IndoorPaupers.shtml.
12. Admissions and Discharge Book, Mile End Old Town Workhouse, StBG/ME/114/4; microfilm X111/145 and Mile End Old Town creed registers, StBG/ME/116/5; microfilm X111/166.
13. Admissions and Discharge Book, Mile End Old Town Workhouse, StBG/ME/114/4; microfilm X111/145 and Mile End Old Town creed register, StBG/ME/116/5; microfilm X111/166.
14. Orders for reception of lunatics into asylums, 1889–1891, LMA StBG/ME/107/8, no. 1558.
15. "Police Intelligence," *Daily Telegraph*, October 18, 1888.
16. Phil Fennell, *Treatment without Consent: Law, Psychiatry and the Treatment of Mentally Disordered People since 1845* (New York: Routledge, 1996), 2.

17. J. B. Sharpe, "Report, together with the Minutes of Evidence, and an Appendix of Papers, from the Committee appointed to consider of Provision being made for the Better Regulation of Madhouses in England" (London: Baldwin, 1815), in *British Review and London Critical Journal*, vol. 6 (London: Baldwin, Cradock and Joy, 1815), 533.

18. Andrew Scull, *Most Solitary of Afflictions: Madness and Society in Britain, 1700–1900* (New Haven, CT: Yale University Press, 2005), 61n.

19. John Thurnam, *Observations and Essays on the Statistics of Insanity* (London: Simpkin, Marshall, 1845), 123.

20. Charles Augustus Tulk, "The Sixty-Eighth Report of the Visiting Justices Appointed to Superintend the Management of the County Lunatic Asylum at Hanwell," October 26, 1843, 3.

21. William Ireland, *The Mental Affections of Children: Idiocy, Imbecility and Insanity* (Edinburgh: James Thin, 1898), 392.

22. E-mail correspondence with the author David Wright, April 2009.

23. Peter Higginbotham, "The Metropolitan Asylums Board," www.workhouses.org.uk.

24. Private correspondence with David Wright, April 2009.

25. Gwendoline M. Ayers, *England's First State Hospitals and the Metropolitan Asylums Board, 1867–1930* (Berkeley: University of California Press, 1971), 42.

26. Nick Connell, "Did Kosminsky Try to Return to Colney Hatch?" *Ripperana*, no. 16, April 1996.

27. Report of local government inspector and observation of medical superintendent, 1898, GLRO MAB 2403.

28. November 1899, GLRO MAB 368, vol. 18.

29. Nick Connell, "The Leavesden Escapee," *Ripperana*, no, 17, July 1996.

30. Fennell, *Treatment without Consent*, 41.

31. John Diarmid, cited in Fennell, *Treatment without Consent*, 37.

32. D. R. Brower, "Hyoscyamine in the Treatment of Insanity," *American Journal of Neurology and Psychiatry* (New York: B. Westermann, 1883).

33. Fennell, *Treatment without Consent*, 44; and D. Pierce, "Unsound in Body, Mind, and Institution: Against Interpretation of Insanity and Asylums," http://home.eol.ca/~glaurung/essays/insanity.htm.

34. John Crammer, *Asylum History: Buckinghamshire County Pauper Lunatic Asylum—St. John's* (London: RCPsych Publications, 1990), 133.

35. Colney Hatch, *Register of Admissions Males*, no 3. H12/CH/B2/2, and *Male Patients Day Book, New Series*, no. 20, Middlesex Asylum, Colney Hatch. Also, 1891 Census, Colney Hatch, RG 12/1058, f. 102.

36. *Colney Hatch Case Book Male Side, New Series*, no. 20, H12/CH/B13/39.

37. Colney Hatch Mental Hospital, *Deaths and Discharges*, M and F, H12/CH/B6/5, 1891–1896; Hamlet of Mile End Old Town, Leavesden Asylum ADMISSION ORDER No. 737, StBG/ME/112/4 no. 441.

38. 1901 Census (March 31, 1901), RG 13/1322, f. 154.

39. Leavesden Asylum *Male Patients Case Register* 12A.

40. H26/LEA/B/02/031 Modern Folder Labeled "Leavesden Hospital Deaths and Discharges March 1919."

18. Anderson's Suspect

1. Robert Anderson, *The Lighter Side of My Official Life* (London: Hodder and Stoughton, 1910), 138.

2. "The 'Jack the Ripper' Theory: Reply by Sir Robert Anderson. To the Editor of the Jewish Chronicle," *Globe*, March 7, 1910.

3. If the reader is interested, the issue is discussed extensively in Philip Sugden's *The Complete History of Jack the Ripper* (New York: Carroll and Graf, 2002) and in Stewart P. Evans and Donald Rumbelow's *Jack the Ripper: Scotland Yard Investigates* (Stroud: Sutton, 2006), although I do not agree with the authors' conclusions on the matter.

4. "Representative Men at Home: Dr. Anderson at New Scotland Yard," *Cassell's Saturday Journal*, June 11, 1892, 895–897.

5. "Dr. Anderson on Criminal 'Show Places,'" *Pall Mall Gazette*, November 4, 1889.

6. "Representative Men at Home: Dr. Anderson at New Scotland Yard," *Cassell's Saturday Journal*, June 11, 1892, 895–897.

7. "The Detective in Real Life," *Windsor* 1 (January to June 1895): 507.

8. Arthur Griffiths, *Mysteries of Police and Crime: A General Survey of Wrongdoing and Its Pursuit*, vol. 1 (London: Cassell, 1899), 28.

9. "Punishing Crime," *Nineteenth Century*, February 1901.

10. Robert Anderson, *Criminals and Crime: Some Facts and Suggestions* (London: J. Nisbet, 1907), 81.

11. Nicholas Bunnin and Jiyuan Yu, *The Blackwell Dictionary of Western Philosophy* (Malden, MA: Blackwell Publishing, 2004), 444.

12. Robert Anderson, preface, in Hargrave Lee Adam, *The Police Encyclopedia*, vol. 4 (London: Waverly, 1920), www.casebook.org/ripper_media/rps.adam1.html.

13. "Scotland Yard and Its Secrets," *People* (London), June 9, 1912.

14. Hargrave Lee Adam, *C.I.D.: Behind the Scenes at Scotland Yard* (London: S. Low, Marston, 1931), 12.

15. "The Ripper Crimes," *Daily Chronicle*, September 1, 1908.

16. Anderson, *The Lighter Side of My Official Life*.

17. Robert Anderson, "Criminals and Crime—a Rejoinder," in *The Nineteenth Century and After*, vols. 19–20 (London: Spottiswoode, 1908), 200n.

18. Anderson, "The Lighter Side of My Official Life (Part VI), *Blackwood's Edinburgh*, March 1910.

19. "The House of Commons," *Times* (London), April, 22, 1910.

20. Great Britain. Parliament, *House of Commons, Parliamentary Debates: Official Report*, vol. 16 (London: H.M. Stationery Office, 1910), mxc.

21. Statement of Monro, read in Commons Sitting by Winston Churchill, December 21, 1910, HC Deb, April 21, 1910, vol. 16, cc2322–2324.

22. Andrew Morrison, *A Very Discreet Man: James Monro and the Whitechapel Murders*, www.casebook.org/police_officials/po-monro.html.

23. Ibid.

24. Leopold Greenberg, "In the Communal Armchair," *Jewish Chronicle*, March 4, 1910.

25. Anderson, "The Lighter Side of My Official Life (Part VI)."

26. "The 'Jack the Ripper' Theory: Reply by Sir Robert Anderson. To the Editor of the Jewish Chronicle," *Globe*, March 7, 1910.

27. "The 'Jack the Ripper' Theory: Reply by Sir Robert Anderson," *Jewish Chronicle*, March 11, 1910.

28. Ibid.

29. Chaim Bermant, *Point of Arrival* (London: Macmillan, 1975), 118.

30. Anderson, *The Lighter Side of My Official Life*, 139.

19. Macnaghten and Swanson

1. Report of Melville Macnaghten, February 23, 1894, MEPO 3/141, ff. 179–180.

2. Philip Sugden, *The Complete History of Jack the Ripper* (New York: Carroll and Graf, 2002), 379, cites "'Memorandum on articles which appeared in the *Sun* re JACK THE RIPPER on 13 Feb. 1894 and subsequent dates' by 'my father Sir M. M.,' copied by Christabel Aberconway, pp. 5–6, 6A, 6B. Document in private ownership."

3. The "Aberconway draft" of the Macnaghten memorandum, cited in John Eddleston, *Jack the Ripper: An Encyclopedia* (Santa Barbara, CA: ABC-CLIO, 2001), 175.

4. Chris Scott, quoted on podcast "Killers on the Loose: Eliminating the Suspects," Rippercast, January 2009, www.casebook.org/podcast.

5. Letter of James Swanson, cited by Paul Begg at www.jtrforums.com/showthread .php?p=103121.

6. Property of Nevill Swanson, great-great-grandson of Donald Sutherland Swanson, on permanent loan to Scotland Yard's Crime Museum.

7. Charles Nevin, "Has This Man Revealed the Real Jack the Ripper?" *Daily Telegraph*, October 19, 1987.

8. Posted on casebook.org message boards thread "The Swanson Marginalia," January 23, 2006.

9. E-mail correspondence with Paul Begg. In 1900, the Borough of Stepney was formed by combining fourteen civil districts, including Mile End Old Town, Whitechapel, Spitalfields, St. George in the East, and several other areas.

10. Swanson apparently believed this as early as 1895, as noted in an article in the *Pall Mall Gazette* on May 7, 1895, cited online at "Donald Swanson," http://wiki.casebook.org/index .php/Donald_Swanson.

11. Stewart P. Evans, "Kosminski and the Seaside Home," 1999, www.casebook.org/ dissertations/dst-koz.html.

12. Charles Nevin, "Whitechapel Murders. Sensational New Evidence," *Daily Telegraph*, October 19, 1987.

13. Charles Nevin, "Has This Man Revealed the Real Jack the Ripper?" *Daily Telegraph*, October 19, 1987.

20. A Few Possible Leads

1. George R. Sims, "My Criminal Museum," *Lloyd's Weekly News* (London), September 22, 1907.

2. Ibid.

3. Ibid.

4. "A Sherlock Holmes in Real Life," *City Press* (London), December 6, 1924.

5. "A Notable Career," *Brighton Gazette*, December 6, 1924.

6. "A Famous City Detective. Some of His Experiences Retold," *City Press* (London), January 7, 1905.

7. Justin Atholl, "Who Was Jack the Ripper?" *Reynold's News*, Great Unsolved Mysteries series, September 15, 1946.

8. Ibid.

9. Donald Swanson, marginalia in his personal copy of Robert Anderson's book *The Lighter Side of My Official Life* (London: Hodder and Stoughton, 1910), property of Nevill Swanson, on permanent loan to New Scotland Yard's Crime Museum.

10. Scott Nelson, "The Butcher's Row Suspect. Was He Jack the Ripper?" *Ripperologist*, October 2007.

11. "Mr. Henry Cox, Ex-Detective-Inspector, London City," *Police Review and Parade Gossip*, December 7, 1906.

12. "The Truth about the Whitechapel Mysteries, Told by Harry Cox," *Thomson's Weekly News*, Saturday, December 1, 1906. This article was discovered by Stewart Evans and Nick Connell around 1999.

13. Henry J. Bowsher was conducting house-to-house surveys of "Jailor Street [sic Yalford Street] and Plumber's Row" on October 5, 1888.

14. "East-End Atrocities," *Echo*, October 17, 1888.

15. Swanson marginalia.

16. Anderson, *The Lighter Side of My Official Life*, 137.
17. Stewart P. Evans and Donald Rumbelow, *Jack the Ripper: Scotland Yard Investigates* (Stroud: Sutton, 2006), 231.
18. Orders for reception of lunatics into asylums, 1889–1891, LMA StBG/ME/107/8, no. 1558.
19. "East End Atrocities," *Echo*, October 20, 1888.
20. "The Truth about the Whitechapel Mysteries, Told by Harry Cox," *Thomson's Weekly News*, December 1, 1906. This article was discovered by Stewart Evans and Nick Connell around 1999.

21. The Identification, the Witness, and the Informant

1. Robert Anderson, *The Lighter Side of My Official Life* (London: Hodder and Stoughton, 1910), 138.
2. Inquest report of Joseph Levy, Corporation of London Records Office, coroner's inquest (L), 1888, no. 135, Catherine Eddowes inquest.
3. Macnaghten memorandum, Aberconway draft. Philip Sugden cites "Memorandum on articles which appeared in the *Sun* re JACK THE RIPPER on 13 Feb. 1894 and subsequent dates' by 'my father Sir M. M.,' copied by Christabel Aberconway, pp. 5–6, 6A, 6B. Document in private ownership." in *The Complete History of Jack the Ripper* (New York: Carroll and Graf, 2002).
4. Sugden, *Complete History of Jack the Ripper*, 406.
5. Posted on the casebook.org message boards thread "Ep. #28—Kosminski Was the Suspect," September 24, 2008.
6. Anderson, *The Lighter Side of My Official Life*, 138.
7. Donald Swanson, marginalia in his personal copy of Anderson's book *The Lighter Side of My Official Life*, property of Nevill Swanson, on permanent loan to New Scotland Yard's Crime Museum.
8. Macnaghten memorandum, Aberconway draft.
9. George R. Sims, "My Criminal Museum," *Lloyd's Weekly News* (London), September 22, 1907.
10. Testimony of Joseph Lawende, *Daily Telegraph*, October 12, 1888.
11. "The East End Atrocities, the Mitre Square Murder, Inquest and Verdict," *Daily News* (London), October 12, 1888.
12. "Supposed Clue," *Evening News*, October 9, 1888.
13. Swanson marginalia.
14. Elizabeth Loftus, *Eyewitness Testimony* (Cambridge, MA: Harvard University Press, 1996).
15. "Eyewitness misidentification," www.innocenceproject.org/understand/Eyewitness-Misidentification.php.
16. Swanson marginalia.
17. Hargrave Lee Adam, *C. I. D. Behind the Scenes at Scotland Yard* (London: S. Low, Marston, 1931), 13.
18. "The Littlechild Letter," discovered by, and property of, Stewart Evans.
19. Swanson marginalia.
20. Private correspondence, March 2009.
21. *Charities Register and Digest* (London: Longman's Green, 1890).
22. Posted by Chris Phillips on casebook.org message boards thread "Anderson—More Questions Than Answers," October 2008.
23. Justin Atholl, "Who Was Jack the Ripper?" *Reynold's News*, Great Unsolved Mysteries series, September 15, 1946.
24. "The Truth about the Whitechapel Mysteries, Told by Harry Cox," *Thomson's Weekly News*, December 1, 1906.

25. Ibid.
26. Swanson marginalia.
27. "The Truth about the Whitechapel Mysteries, Told by Harry Cox."
28. Ibid.
29. Phillips, "Anderson—More Questions Than Answers."
30. "Representative Men at Home: Dr. Anderson at New Scotland Yard," *Cassell's Saturday Journal*, June 11, 1892, 895–897.
31. "East-End Atrocities," *Echo*, October 17, 1888.
32. David Wright, *Mental Disability in Victorian England: The Earlswood Asylum, 1847–1901* (Oxford: Clarendon Press, 2001), 55–56.
33. "Jack the Ripper's Vacation," *Galveston (Texas) Daily News*, July 29, 1890.
34. Discovered by Stephen Ryder and published by him in his article "Emily and the Bibliophile: A Possible Source for Macnaghten's Private Information," www.casebook .org/dissertations/dst-emily.html.
35. The "Aberconway draft" of the Macnaghten memorandum, cited in John Eddleston, *Jack the Ripper: An Encyclopedia* (Santa Barbara, CA: ABC-CLIO, 2001), 175.

22. Not Guilty?
1. Charles Nevin, "Has This Man Revealed the Real Jack the Ripper?" *Daily Telegraph*, October 19, 1987.
2. Philip Sugden, *The Complete History of Jack the Ripper* (New York: Carroll and Graf, 2002), 423.
3. Report of Melville Macnaghten, February 23, 1894, MEPO 3/141, ff. 179–180.
4. Fido argued that "Kosminski" was in fact a man named Nathan Kaminsky who (Fido theorized) was later entered into an asylum under the name David Cohen. I do not agree with this theory.
5. Leavesden Asylum Male Patients Case Register 12A.
6. Colney Hatch, Register of Admissions Males, no 3. H12/CH/B2/2.
7. Kozminski is listed as a lunatic in the 1901 census of Leavesden patients, PRO, ref. RG 13/1322.
8. Private correspondence with David Wright, April 2009.
9. Orders for reception of lunatics into asylums, 1889–1891, LMA StBG/ME/107/8, no. 1558.
10. Posted by Chris Phillips on the casebook.org message boards thread "Did Anderson Know?" May 2009.
11. Posted by Martin Fido on the casebook.org message boards thread "The Only Patient Who Fits Anderson's Account?" August 2008.

23. A Modern Take on Serial Killers
1. Peter Vronsky, *Serial Killers: The Method and Madness of Monsters* (New York: Berkley, 2004), 45–49. Vronsky cites the manuscript of an ecclesiastical trial in Archives de la Loire-Atlantique, G. 189.
2. Joseph Richardson Parke, "Human Sexuality: A Medico-Literary Treatise on the Laws, Anomalies, and Relations of Sex, with Especial Reference to Contrary Sexual Desire," 1906. The account was first published in Paul Johann Anselm Fuerbach's *Aktenmassige Darstellung Merkwurdiger Verbrechen* (Giessen, 1828).
3. Vronsky, *Serial Killers*, 58–59.
4. Richard von Krafft-Ebing, *Psychopathia Sexualis, with Especial Reference to Contrary Sexual Instinct*, trans. by Charles Gilbert Chaddock, MD (Philadelphia: F. A. Davis, 1894), 303.
5. Cesar Lombroso, *Criminal Man*, trans. Mary Gibson and Nicole Hahn Rafter (Durham, NC: Duke University Press, 2006), 1.
6. Robert K. Ressler, Ann Wolbert Burgess, and John E. Douglas, *Sexual Homicide: Patterns and Motives* (New York: Free Press, 1992), 9.

7. Ibid., 71.
8. Brent E. Turvey, *Criminal Profiling: An Introduction to Behavioral Evidence Analysis* (San Diego: Academic Press, 2002), 313.
9. Ibid., 323.
10. Vronsky, *Serial Killers*, 164.
11. Ressler, Burgess, and Douglas, *Sexual Homicide*, 33.
12. Quentin L. Pittman, "The Importance of Fairy Fay, and Her Link to Emma Smith," posted on casebook.org, http://www.casebook.org/dissertations/importance-fairy.html.
13. Ressler, Burgess, and Douglas, *Sexual Homicide*, 42.
14. Polly Nelson, *Defending the Devil: My Story as Ted Bundy's Last Lawyer* (New York: William Morrow, 1994), 283–284.
15. Stephen G. Michaud and Hugh Aynesworth, *Ted Bundy: Conversations with a Killer* (Irving, TX: Authorlink Press, 2000), 77.
16. Ressler, Burgess, and Douglas, *Sexual Homicide*, 21.
17. Ibid.
18. Ibid., 23.
19. Ibid., 20.
20. Ibid., 73.
21. Roy Hazelwood and Stephen G. Michaud, *Dark Dreams: Sexual Violence, Homicide and the Criminal Mind* (New York: St. Martin's Press, 2001), 163.
22. John Douglas and Mark Olshaker, *Mind Hunter, Inside the FBI's Elite Serial Killer Crime Unit* (New York: Scribner, 1995), 373–375. See Hazelwood and Michaud, *Dark Dreams*, 162–163.
23. Report of Melville Macnaghten, February 23, 1894, MEPO 3/141, ff. 179–180.
24. "Jack the Ripper: An On-Going Mystery," Discovery Channel, directed by Brian Kelly and Virginia Williams, produced by Henninger Productions, 2000.
25. Ressler, Burgess, and Douglas, *Sexual Homicide*, 130.
26. "Jack the Ripper: An On-Going Mystery."
27. Phone conversation with Roy Hazelwood, February 2010.
28. "Jack the Ripper: the First Serial Killer," in *Revealed*, directed by Dan Oliver, 2006.
29. Ressler, Burgess, and Douglas, *Sexual Homicide*, 34.
30. "Jack the Ripper: The First Serial Killer."
31. "A Riot against the Jews," *East London Observer*, September 15, 1888.

24. Geographic Profiling
1. "How Does Geographic Profiling Work?" Environmental Criminology Research, Inc., www.ecricanada.com/geopro/howdoesitwork.html.
2. "Rational Choice Theory," Wikipedia.org, http://en.wikipedia.org/wiki/Rational_choice_theory.
3. George R. Sims, "My Criminal Museum," *Lloyd's Weekly News* (London), September 22, 1907.
4. "Dwellings of the Working Classes," *Times* (London), January 20, 1886.
5. Robert Anderson, "The Lighter Side of My Official Life (Part VI)," *Blackwood's Edinburgh*, March 1910.
6. Sims, "My Criminal Museum."
7. "The Circle Hypothesis Revisited: Modelling Property Offenders' Spatial Behaviour Using Sketch Maps," Dr. Karen Shalev, lecturer, University of Portsmouth, Institute of Criminal Justice Studies, from a presentation given at the 8th International Investigative Psychology Conference, December 2005, www.i-psy.co.uk/conferences/8/presentations/karen_shalev.ppt.
8. Joshua D. Kent, "Using Functional Distance Measures When Calibrating Journey-to-Crime Distance Decay Algorithms," Louisiana State University, 2003.

9. Colin Roberts, "Informal Preview of Geo-Spatial Analysis Project," casebook.org message board, February 2009.

10. D. Kim Rossmo's Environmental Criminology Research, Inc., Web site, company overview, http://mypage.uniserve.ca/~ecri/about/index.html.

11. Arthur G. Morrison, "Whitechapel," *Palace Journal*, April 24, 1889, www.casebook.org/victorian_london/whitechapel3.html.

12. Ibid.

13. Philip Sugden, *The Complete History of Jack the Ripper* (New York: Carroll and Graf, 2002), 214.

25. Schizophrenia and Violence

1. Simon A. Hill and Richard Laugharne, "Mania, Dementia and Melancholia in the 1870s: Admissions to a Cornwall Asylum," *Journal of the Royal Society of Medicine* 96 (July 1, 2003).

2. Ibid.

3. Henry Munro, "On the Nomenclature of the Various Forms of Insanity," *British Journal of Psychiatry* 2 (1856): 286–305, cited in Hill and Laugharne, "Mania, Dementia and Melancholia in the 1870s."

4. Elaine Walker, Lisa Kestler, Annie Bollini, and Karen M. Hochman, "Schizophrenia: Etiology and Course," Emory University, *Annual Review of Psychology* 55 (February 2004): 401–430.

5. *U.S. Surgeon General's Report on Schizophrenia* (2002), www.schizophrenia.com/research/surg.general.1.2002.htm.

6. Walker, Kestler, Bollini, and Hochman, "Schizophrenia: Etiology and Course."

7. Benjamin J. Sadock, Harold I. Kaplan, and Virginia A. Sadock, *Kaplan and Sadock's Concise Textbook of Clinical Psychiatry* (Philadelphia: Lippincott, Williams and Wilkins, 2008), 167.

8. Walker, Kestler, Bollini, and Hochman, "Schizophrenia: Etiology and Course."

9. Sadock, Kaplan, and Sadock, *Kaplan and Sadock's Concise Textbook of Clinical Psychiatry*, 476.

10. Orders for reception of lunatics into asylums, 1889–1891, LMA StBG/ME/107/8, no. 1558; Colney Hatch, Register of Admissions Males, no 3. H12/CH/B2/2; and Male Patients Day Book, New Series, no. 20, Middlesex Asylum, Colney Hatch. See also, 1891 Census, Colney Hatch, RG 12/1058, f. 102.

11. Colney Hatch Case Book Male Side, New Series, no. 20, H12/CH/B13/39.

12. Leavesden Asylum Male Patients Case Register 12A.

13. E-mail correspondence with Lauren Post, June 2009.

14. Elyn Saks, *The Center Cannot Hold: My Journey through Madness* (New York: Hyperion, 2007), 51.

15. Ibid., 84.

16. Ibid., 92.

17. Ibid., 98.

18. National Schizophrenia Fellowship Web site, Rethink.org, www.rethink.org/about_mental_illness/mental_illnesses_and_disorders/schizophrenia/index.html.

19. Orders for reception of lunatics into asylums, 1889–1891, LMA StBG/ME/107/8, no. 1558.

20. Sadock, Kaplan, and Sadock, *Kaplan and Sadock's Concise Textbook of Clinical Psychiatry*, 488.

21. Leavesden Asylum Male Patients Case Register 12A.

22. E. Walsh, A. Buchanan, and T. Fahy, "Violence and Schizophrenia: Examining the Evidence," *British Journal of Psychiatry* 180 (June 2002): 490–495.

23. Paul E. Mullen, "Schizophrenia and Violence: From Correlations to Preventive Strategies," Royal College of Psychiatrists, Monash University, Melbourne, 2006.

24. Edwin Fuller Torrey, *Out of the Shadows: Confronting America's Mental Illness Crisis* (New York: John Wiley and Sons, 1996), 52.

25. Elizabeth Walsh, "Violence and Schizophrenia: Examining the Evidence," *British Journal of Psychiatry* 180 (2002): 490–495.

26. Jeffrey W. Swanson et al., "A National Study of Violent Behavior in Persons with Schizophrenia," *Archives of General Psychiatry* 63 (May 2006): 490–499, www.treatmentadvocacycenter.org/index.php?option=com_content&task=view&id=127.

27. James Cowles Pritchard, *A Treatise on Insanity* (London: Sherwood, Gilbert and Piper, 1835), 4.

28. Ian Pitchford, "The Origins of Violence: Is Psychopathy an Adaptation?" *Human Nature Review* 1 (November 5, 2001): 28–36.

29. Hervey Milton Cleckley, *The Mask of Sanity: An Attempt to Reinterpret the So-Called Psychopathic Personality*, 3rd ed. (St. Louis: Mosby, 1955), 424.

30. Edward Mitchell, "The Aetiology of Serial Murder" (unpublished master's thesis, University of Cambridge, UK, 1996–1997).

31. Robert R. Hazelwood and John Douglas, "The Lust Murderer," *FBI Law Enforcement Bulletin*, April 1980.

32. Karen A. Nolan, Jan Volavka, Pavel Mohr, and Pal Czobor, "Psychopathy and Violent Behavior among Patients with Schizophrenia or Schizoaffective Disorder," Nathan S. Kline Institute for Psychiatric Research, *Psychiatric Services* 50 (June 1999): 787–792.

33. J. L. Volavka and L. Citrome, "Heterogeneity of Violence in Schizophrenia and Implications for Long-Term Treatment," *International Journal of Clinical Practice* 62, no. 8 (August 2008).

34. Nolan, Volavka, Mohr, and Czobor, "Psychopathy and Violent Behavior among Patients with Schizophrenia or Schizoaffective Disorder."

35. Jan Volavka and Leslie Citrome, "Heterogeneity of Violence in Schizophrenia and Implications for Long-Term Treatment," *International Journal of Clinical Practice* 62 (2008): 1237–1245.

36. "Mental Health," www.rethink.org/dualdiagnosis/pdfs/chapters/Section_4_-_Mental_health.pdf.

37. Edie Magnus, "A Deadly Encounter," *Dateline NBC*, January 20, 2007.

38. Michael Winerip, "Oddity and Normality Vie in Subway Killer's Confession," *New York Times*, October 18, 1999.

39. Magnus, "A Deadly Encounter."

40. Dan Ackman, "Goldstein Lawyers Put Mental Healthcare System on Trial," Graduate School of Journalism, Columbia University (1999), www.msnbc.msn.com/id/16713078.

41. Edie Magnus, "A Deadly Encounter," *Dateline NBC*, January 20, 2007.

42. *The People & c., Respondent, v. Andrew Goldstein, Appellant*, 1 N.Y. Ct. App. 155, 2005 N.Y. Int. 156 (December 20, 2005).

43. Daniel Diehl and Mark P. Donnelly, *Eat Thy Neighbor* (Stroud, UK: Sutton, 2008), 253–263.

44. Ressler, Burgess, and Douglas, *Sexual Homicide*, 84.

45. Katherine Ramsland, "Richard Trenton Chase," Tru TV Crime Library, www.trutv.com/library/crime/index.html.

46. Shirley Lynn Scott, "Herb Mullin," Tru TV Crime Library, www.trutv.com/library/crime/index.html.

47. The quotes are from Robert R. Hazelwood and John Douglas, "The Lust Murderer," *FBI Law Enforcement Bulletin*, April 1980. Additional quotes are from private correspondence and phone conversations with Roy Hazelwood.

48. Private e-mail correspondence, February 2010.

26. Murder Will Out

1. Alfred Pollard, ed., *Chaucer's Canterbury Tales: The Nun's Priest's Tale* (London: Macmillan, 1915), 11, lines 4242–4247.
2. Arthur Conan Doyle, "The Five Orange Pips," first published in the *Strand* magazine in November 1891.
3. Report of Melville Macnaghten, February 23, 1894, MEPO 3/141, ff. 179–180.
4. "The Truth about the Whitechapel Mysteries, Told by Harry Cox," *Thomson's Weekly News*, December 1, 1906.
5. "Gary Ridgway: The Green River Killer," *King County Journal*, 2003. This same lack of agreement was evident among the top officials at Scotland Yard concerning the Ripper murders. Macnaghten, for example, believed that Montague Druitt was the Ripper.

Photo Credits

Page 56 (top, middle), courtesy Tomek Wisniewski Collection, www.bagnowka.com; page 58, courtesy Julie Guernsey, www.1860-1960.com; pages 60 (bottom), 61 (top), 173 (top left), 174 (top), 249 (bottom), courtesy Rob Clack; pages 61 (bottom), 170 (middle), 171 (bottom), 172 (middle), 173 (top right, bottom left, bottom right), 175 (top, middle), 249 (middle), courtesy Stewart P. Evans; page 169 (top), courtesy Andrew Firth; page 170 (middle), from *Jack the Ripper: A New Theory* by William Stewart (1938); page 171 (top left), courtesy Neal Sheldon; pages 171 (top right), 248 (bottom), courtesy Paul Begg; page 174 (top), courtesy Richard Whittington Egan; page 248 (top right), courtesy Nevill Swanson; page 249 (top), courtesy the Christian Police Association.

Index

Page numbers in *italics* refer to illustrations.

CPSIA information can be obtained at www.ICGtesting.com
Printed in the USA
LVOW07*2315191114

414530LV00007B/206/P